D1190221

Nebraska Symposium on Motivation

Series Editor
Debra A. Hope
Lincoln, Nebraska, USA

For further volumes:
http://www.springer.com/series/7596

Robert F. Belli

Editor

True and False Recovered Memories

Toward a Reconciliation of the Debate

 Springer

Editor
Robert F. Belli
Department of Psychology
University of Nebraska-Lincoln
Nebraska, USA
bbelli2@unl.edu

ISSN 0146-7875
ISBN 978-1-4614-1194-9   e-ISBN 978-1-4614-1195-6
DOI 10.1007/978-1-4614-1195-6
Springer New York Dordrecht Heidelberg London

Library of Congress Control Number: 2011941015

Printed on acid-free paper

Springer is part of Springer Science+Business Media (www.springer.com)

Preface

The volume editor for this 58th volume of the Nebraska Symposium on Motivation is Robert Belli. The volume editor coordinated the symposium that led to this volume including selecting and inviting the contributors. This year he had the additional challenge of a volcanic eruption in Iceland that disrupted air travel from Europe, home to three presenters. Fortunately all three were able to participate, in person or via streaming video, opening a new era in technology for the Symposium. My thanks go to Bob and to our contributors for their perseverance over obstacles and for outstanding presentations and chapters. The debate on recovered memories has had significant implications for our understanding of memory, the law and, most importantly, the wellbeing of individuals whose lives have been changed by this controversy.

This Symposium series is supported by funds provided by the Chancellor of the University of Nebraska-Lincoln, Harvey Perlman, and by funds given in memory of Professor Harry K. Wolfe to the University of Nebraska Foundation by the late Professor Cora L. Friedline. We are extremely grateful for the Chancellor's generous support of the Symposium series and for the University of Nebraska Foundation's support via the Friedline bequest. This symposium volume, like those in the recent past, is dedicated to the memory of Professor Wolfe, who brought psychology to the University of Nebraska. After studying with Professor Wilhelm Wundt in Germany, Professor Wolfe returned to this, his native state, to establish the first undergraduate laboratory in psychology in the nation. As a student at Nebraska, Professor Friedline studied psychology under Professor Wolfe.

Debra A. Hope
Series Editor

Acknowledgments

I am grateful to the efforts of a number of individuals who helped with the symposium and this volume. The organizational skills of staff in the Department of Psychology, especially Claudia Price-Decker and Roxane Earnest, were critical toward the success of the symposium. Both were a pleasure to work with, and their attention to all of the logistical details facilitated the ability of the presenters and the audience to devote their attention to thoughtful discourse concerning complex issues. Justin Coleman, a PhD student in the cognitive psychology program, had made the visit of the presenters more pleasant by arranging and chauffeuring their ground travel.

Of course, I extend my gratitude to all of the speakers and authors in contributing their scholastic talents to the symposium and this volume, but special thanks are given to some of the presenters and authors who made an extra effort in difficult circumstances. Although Jennifer Freyd was unfortunately unable to present at the symposium because of an unexpected and serious illness that had afflicted her spouse, she nevertheless ensured that the perspective of betrayal trauma theory would be represented at the symposium and in the volume. With short notice, Steven Gold did an excellent job of providing an insightful presentation at the symposium that included aspects of betrayal trauma theory and related work; Anne DePrince assumed the responsibilities of lead author and orchestrated the excellent and provocative contribution contained within this volume. The symposium was also held on dates that shortly followed the Eyjafjallajökull volcanic eruptions in Iceland that had disrupted trans-Atlantic air travel. Both Chris Brewin and Elke Geraerts original flights were cancelled (fortunately, Mike Anderson was already in the US), and although the valuable time each had spent in attempts to reschedule their flights ended in failure, both Chris and Elke were able to secure teleconferencing facilities during a period when their demand was high. Hence, those attending the symposium were able to virtually witness their very compelling presentations; we did nevertheless miss their physical presence. I am also incredibly grateful to the

Collaboration Technologies unit, and especially John Gilliam and Donald Robertson, who were able to assemble and manage the portable teleconferencing equipment in the facility originally reserved for the symposium. Finally, a heartfelt thank you is extended to Deb Hope, Series Editor of the Nebraska Symposium on Motivation, who saw the project through from beginning to end, and whose good humor and encouragement sustained my efforts despite the unique challenges that we faced.

Contents

Contributors

Michael C. Anderson is a Senior Scientist and Program Leader at the MRC Cognition and Brain Sciences Unit in Cambridge, England. Anderson's research focuses on the cognitive and neural control mechanisms underlying people's ability to suppress unwanted memories.

Elizabeth Ankudowich is a Research Assistant in the Psychology Department at Yale University, New Haven, CT, USA. She is involved in behavioral and fMRI studies of episodic memory and self-referential processing.

Robert F. Belli is Professor of Psychology at the University of Nebraska, Lincoln, NE, USA. An applied experimental cognitive psychologist, Belli's research interests center on autobiographical memory, and the impact of suggestion on autobiographical memory quality.

Chris R. Brewin is Professor at University College London, England, and a practicing clinical psychologist treating traumatized persons with cognitive-behavior therapy. One of his major research interests concerns the effects of trauma in childhood and adulthood on memory and identity.

Laura S. Brown is a clinical and forensic psychologist in private practice in Seattle, WA, USA, and Director of the Fremont Community Therapy Project. She is interested in complex trauma and how it can be responded to in culturally competent manners.

Ross E. Cheit is Associate Professor of Political Science and Public Policy at Brown University, Providence, RI, USA. His current research on child sexual abuse is at the intersection of law, public policy and psychology.

Anne P. DePrince is Associate Professor of Psychology and Director of the Center for Community Engagement and Service Learning at the University of Denver, Denver, CO, USA. A clinical psychologist, DePrince's research focuses on the cognitive and emotional consequences of violence against women and children as well as interventions.

Jennifer J. Freyd is Professor of Psychology at the University of Oregon, Eugene, OR, USA. She is attempting to understand the causes and impact of betrayal trauma.

Elke Geraerts is an Associate Professor of Clinical Psychology at the Erasmus University Rotterdam, the Netherlands. Geraerts's research focuses on traumatic memory and the cognitive functioning of trauma survivors.

Steven N. Gold is Professor of Psychology and Director of the Trauma Resolution and Integration Program at Nova Southeastern University in Fort Lauderdale, FL, USA. His research focuses on the long term impact of child sexual abuse, particularly dissociative processes, memory impairment and sexual addiction.

Ean Huddleston is a Ph.D. candidate in Neuroscience at the University of Cambridge, England, working at the MRC Cognition and Brain Sciences unit. His research focuses on the influence of control mechanisms on neocortical memory representations during retrieval suppression.

Marcia K. Johnson is Sterling Professor of Psychology at Yale University, New Haven, CT, USA. A major research focus is the cognitive and neural mechanisms underlying the subjective experience of remembering.

Richard J. McNally is Professor and Director of Clinical Training in the Department of Psychology at Harvard University, Cambridge, MA, USA. His main research focus concerns the cognitive aspects of anxiety disorders.

Karen J. Mitchell is a Senior Research Scientist in the Psychology Department at Yale University, New Haven, CT, USA. Her research focuses on the component cognitive processes and neural substrates of episodic memory.

Kathy Pezdek is Professor of Psychology and directs the Ph.D. program in Applied Cognitive Psychology at Claremont Graduate University in Claremont, CA, USA. Pezdek's research focuses on eyewitness memory, autobiographical memory, and the role of suggestibility on autobiographical memory.

Kathryn Quina is Professor of Psychology and Women's Studies and Associate Dean of the Feinstein College of Continuing Education at the University of Rhode Island, Providence, RI, USA. Her research has examined the sequelae of childhood trauma in its various forms, including HIV risk and incarceration.

Carol L. Raye is a Senior Research Scientist in the Psychology Department at Yale University, New Haven, CT, USA. She is interested in component processes of cognition and memory, and their neural correlates.

Introduction: In the Aftermath of the So-Called Memory Wars

Robert F. Belli

Abstract The term "memory wars" has been used by some to characterize the intense debate that emerged in the 1990s regarding the veracity of recovered memories of child sexual abuse. Both sides in this debate have been motivated by scientific and ethical concerns. Recent years have witnessed a burgeoning of relevant behavioral and neuroimaging evidence that when taken together, points the way toward reconciliation. All of the contributors to this volume acknowledge that true recoveries characterize a substantive proportion of recovery experiences and that suggestive therapeutic techniques may promote false memories. Disagreements continue to exist on the cognitive and motivational processes that can lead to true recoveries and the extent to which false recovered memories occur.

Keywords False memories • Memory wars • Recovered memories • Scientific debate

Debate in science, including psychological science, is an inherent part of the scientific approach that considers the critical examination of data and theory to be the primary means on which empirical truth can become established. Although scientific debates can become intense, psychology in the 1990s, with the recovered memory debate, witnessed a "heated and polarized debate" (Sivers, Schooler, & Freyd, 2002, p. 170) so strong to be considered by some as consisting of "memory wars" (Crews, 1995; Hyman, 2000; Schacter, 1996, Chap. 9) that were "raging out of control" (Toglia, 1996, p. 313) with "divisive, fierce, and destructive" force (Lindsay & Briere, 1997, p. 632), and which were "as much about politics as [they] ever will be about science" (Brown, 1996, p. 351). In editing a special journal issue on the debate, Banks and

R.F. Belli (✉)
University of Nebraska, Lincoln, NE, USA
e-mail: bbelli2@unl.edu

R.F. Belli (ed.), *True and False Recovered Memories: Toward a Reconciliation of the Debate*, Nebraska Symposium on Motivation, DOI 10.1007/978-1-4614-1195-6_1, © Springer Science+Business Media, LLC 2012

Pezdek (1994) were to lament that "we wanted vital social interest, but we got something closer to a religious war" (p. 265).

To understand the level of emotionality that has framed this debate requires an examination of the professional perspectives that came into conflict during this period. Adherents to both of these perspectives were seeking to understand the processes that have led to some adults—without apparent prior awareness—remembering having been sexually abused while they were children. The key struggle was to determine whether these memories are true recoveries of forgotten events, false memories induced via suggestions, or whether some of these experiences are true whereas others are false. Adherents who placed the bulk of their attention on one side or the other, and some who sought to take a middle position, recognized the importance of the consequences of either a true recovery or a false memory of such a socially and personally tragic event as leading to an opportunity for either healing or harming, and all were motivated by doing the right thing.

One of these perspectives had been principally advocated by clinical and counseling psychologists/psychiatrists who had not so distantly learned of the surprising and disturbing high prevalence of child sexual abuse (CSA) as reported by individuals who had continually remembered being victimized (Alpert, Brown, & Courtois, 1998a; Courtois, 1996; Harvey & Herman, 1996). Although principally advocated by those in these clinical professions, those who advocated for this position also included experimental psychologists (e.g., Freyd, 1996; Pezdek, Finger, & Hodge, 1997; Schooler, Bendiksen, & Ambadar, 1997). Being rightfully concerned about the potential for psychological damage that results from victimization, the phenomenon of recovered memory experiences provided even more troubling evidence that the prevalence of abuse was being underestimated. To these scientist-practitioner professionals, it was understandable that as sexual abuse victimization was most often accompanied by confusion, secrecy, shame, and potentially trauma, that in some individuals the memory for these experiences could become repressed, inhibited, fragmented, or psychically numbed in some fashion, only to return in more complete form years later. The overriding ethical concern that governed these advocates was to protect children, one of the most vulnerable groups in society. As an important corollary concern, these professionals sought to help those who had already been victimized.

The second of these perspectives has been principally advocated by experimental psychologists who had become troubled by a body of evidence that pointed to the unreliability of eyewitness testimony (Lindsay, 1994; Lindsay & Read, 1994; Loftus, 1979); those who were to share similar views also were to include those with clinical backgrounds (e.g., Lynn & Nash, 1994; Yapko, 1994). For adherents to this perspective, memory is an imperfect construction of past experience in which what was remembered as having occurred in reality could have its actual source in suggestions, imaginations, visualizations, or combinations thereof (Johnson, Hashtroudi, & Lindsay, 1993; Johnson & Raye, 1981). False accusations and inaccurate reports of what one had witnessed in forensic settings were an outcome of ordinary imperfect memory processes. To these professionals, it was noteworthy that there were elements of recovered memory experiences that indicated the presence of false memories. Some recoveries were so outlandish as to almost certainly be false[1]; evidence appeared that some in the helping professions through self-help books and in therapy were unwittingly engaging in powerful suggestive techniques that were highly prone to induce false memories of childhood sexual abuse (Lindsay & Read, 1994; Belli & Loftus, 1994). The overriding ethical concern governing these professionals was to protect the falsely accused, primarily in legal contexts, as court cases based on recovered memories of abuse were emerging (Loftus, 1997; Loftus & Ketchum, 1994). As an important corollary concern, these professionals noted that false memories would be the source of unfortunate family estrangements that should otherwise have been avoided (Belli & Loftus, 1994).

In an attempt to deal with this controversy, the American Psychological Association in 1993 sanctioned the formation of a working group to investigate the recovered memory phenomenon with the hope that the chasm that had formed between these conflicting advocates could be narrowed, if not closed. The working group consisted of three scientist-practitioners in law and clinical psychology (Judith L. Alpert, Laura S. Brown, and Christine S. Courtois), and three experimental developmental or cognitive psychologists (Stephen C. Ceci, Elizabeth F. Loftus, and Peter A. Ornstein). Although a short report on final conclusions had been produced (APA Working Group, 1998), what had become most noteworthy was a series of published papers that merely formalized the chasm that had already become apparent (Alpert et al., 1998a, Alpert, Brown, & Courtois, 1998b, 1998c; Ornstein, Ceci, & Loftus, 1998a, 1998b). There were some points of agreement in (1) recognizing the seriousness of the existence of CSA and its lack of historical recognition, (2) observing that most victims of childhood sexual abuse remember all or part of their victimization, (3) that both true recovery and false memory are possible, and (4) that there are gaps in knowledge and hence, there is the need for more research. Despite the recognition on both sides of the possibility of true recoveries and false memories, in terms of disagreement, each side had downplayed the position of the other in terms of differentiating between possibility and probability. Also noteworthy in terms of disagreement was an epistemic divide on the respective value of clinical experience and observations versus experimental memory research, to the point that the same sets of data were provided with conflicting interpretations.

Of course, a number of years have passed since the height of the so-called memory wars in the 1990s and the presentations of the 58th Nebraska Symposium on Motivation in April 2010. As a topic for the symposium, the recovered memory debate is most apt; in psychological terms either a true or false recovery[2] reveals a complex interplay of cognitive, motivational, and emotional processes. Moreover, as illustrated above, the conflicting professional and scientific points of view that

---

[1] Examples include recovery of satanic ritual abuse (Ofshe & Watters, 1994) and of alien abductions (Persinger, 1992).

[2] My use of the terms true and false recoveries is not intended to convey the notion that there is a simple and clear dichotomy between veracity and its lacking. Almost all memories contain true and false elements. Rather, the terms are meant to convey a distinction between recovered memories that are fundamentally true, or fundamentally false, with regard to one having been a victim of CSA.

have framed this debate are fueled by motivational, emotional, and ethical concerns. Importantly, pertinent research and scientific interpretations of the recovered memory phenomena has continued since the height of the so-called memory wars to the current day, and the contributors to this volume have represented some of the most active scholars exploring issues of true recovery and false memory during these years. My aim in extending invitations to this select few[3] was to provide an updated and comprehensive set of perspectives that would shed new light in the search for a thorough understanding of recovered memory experiences.

A Burgeoning of Recent Research

A review of the contributions to this volume quickly reveals that an extensive body of research relevant to the recovered memory debate has accumulated since the height of the so-called memory wars in the 1990s. Electrophysiological and neuroimaging laboratory research have revealed neural activation correlates to basic cognitive processes relevant to the creation of false memories on one hand (Johnson, Raye, Mitchell, & Ankudowich, 2012, this volume), and on the other hand to the manifestation of motivated forgetting such as may occur with a victim of CSA (Anderson & Huddleston, 2012, this volume). New theories to account for the forgetting of traumatic events, including betrayal trauma theory have been developed and elaborated (DePrince et al., 2012, this volume), and an appreciation of the role of the self-concept in autobiographical memory has led to the perspective that the lacking of an integrated self which can accompany victimization will impact both the forgetting and later recovery of abuse experiences (Brewin, 2012, this volume). Cognitive processes relevant to the recovery experience such as the forget-it-all-along (FIA) effect—in which persons will forget prior instances of remembering—have been discovered (Schooler, 2001; Schooler et al., 1997; Shobe & Schooler, 2001), and laboratory-based cognitive research with persons who have continuous and recovered memories of abuse (Geraerts, 2012, this volume; McNally, 2012, this volume) have provided a firmer penetration on how individual differences in having FIA experiences and in susceptibility to suggestion may contribute respectively to the materialization of both true and false recoveries in the real world.

As noted by Johnson et al. (2012, this volume) and other volume contributors (Brewin, 2012, this volume; DePrince et al., 2012, this volume; Geraerts, 2012, this volume), the source monitoring framework (SMF) has often been implicated in the recovered memory debate as revealing processes that are relevant to the development of false or imperfect memories of CSA, as well as veridical ones. Specific to

---

[3] The tradition of the Nebraska Symposium on Motivation is to produce a symposium volume from those scholars who had been asked to speak (and to permit coauthorship at the discretion of the speakers). Because of budget constraints, I was limited in the number of invitees; those who participated in the symposium are a subset of scholars who have made substantive contributions to this debate.

issues regarding the recovered memory debate, the SMF provides a description of cognitive processes by which people come to believe that a mental experience consists of a memory for past events. According to the SMF, believing that one has remembered the past is an attributional process based on the characteristics contained in the mental experience. Most of the time, these attributional processes lead to correct inferences, and hence, when people believe that the source of a current mental experience is a memory of a past event, they are usually correct. However, attributions can be wrong, and one can misattribute a mental experience as being a memory, especially when suggestive techniques are used that encourage the visualizing or imagining of events, or combinations of events, that never occurred. In their contribution, Johnson et al. consider that the uncritical use of memory recovery practices among mental health professionals is all too common, raising concerns of induced false memories of CSA. Their detailed assessment of neuroimaging research reveals a complex interplay of hippocampal, amygdala, frontal and parietal regions that underlie both true and false memories, and also demonstrates that neural activation patterns correlate well with the experiential and attributional processes that are described in the SMF. Overall, then, Johnson et al. illustrate how fundamental neural and cognitive processes underlie remembering processes that can become implicated in veridical as well as false memories of complex events including those that are characterized as CSA.

Whereas Johnson et al. (2012, this volume) concentrate on the fundamental processes associated with remembering, Anderson and Huddleston (2012, this volume) devote their attention to describing fundamental neural and cognitive processes underlying forgetting, and especially the motivated forgetting of unwanted memories. Inspired by Freyd's (1996) betrayal trauma theory, which highlights the motivational aspects that would surround victims of incestuous CSA in desiring to not remember their abuse, Anderson and Huddleston detail a program of laboratory-based research that reveals how not thinking of an event when prompted by relevant cues will impair the ability to remember that event in the presence of cuing opportunities at later points in time. Two inhibitory mechanisms are revealed, thought substitution in which events that are different from the unwanted memory are thought about, and direct retrieval suppression in which all thoughts are suppressed in the presence of a relevant cue. Whereas the inhibition that follows from thought substitution does not generalize across different cues, the inhibition that follows from direct suppression does generalize across cues. Neuroimaging research reveals that inhibitory mechanisms are associated with increased activation in the prefrontal cortex and decreased activation in the hippocampal regions; with emotional stimuli, inhibition is also associated with decreased activation in the amygdala. Electrophysiological research has observed that direct suppression reduces the conscious recollection of an event having been previously experienced. By revealing the fundamental neural and cognitive processes that underlie motivated forgetting, Anderson and Huddleston are able to piece together a model regarding how victims of CSA may forget events associated with their victimization, especially when there are motives to do so. Further, the authors propose that shifts in the contexts that produce cuing opportunities may lead to the recovery of CSA events.

McNally (2012, this volume) challenges notions of motivated forgetting which assert that CSA events are so traumatic that a special forgetting mechanism, oftentimes termed as repression, is needed to keep CSA events out of awareness. By reviewing a number of claims for the presence of repression, McNally argues that different explanations, including everyday forgetfulness, failure to encode, psychogenic, organic, and childhood amnesias, and choosing not to disclose nor think about experiencing CSA, better fit the observations. In developing a laboratory based research program seeking to uncover the existence of repression, McNally and colleagues recruited participants who had continuous memories of CSA, who recovered CSA experiences, and who claimed to have repressed CSA events without explicitly remembering any abusive incidents. In examining these groups on depression, stress, dissociation, and in applying various cognitive laboratory paradigms that have induced either forgetting or false remembering, McNally observed patterns of results that did not support a repression interpretation. According to McNally, those who claim repression likely believe that their depressive symptomology is evidence of a traumatic CSA past that did not exist. As for recovered memory participants, they reveal induced forgetting patterns that are similar to control participants, even for trauma-related stimuli, and that their only differentiating characteristic is that they are more susceptible to false remembering. Although McNally rejects the notion that traumatic events can become repressed, he still believes that true recoveries happen. According to his model, CSA events—especially in the case of incestuous abuse—are likely confusing and anxiety provoking to those who are victimized, but they are usually not traumatic. Choosing not to think about these events gives victims a sense of their having been forgotten, especially when, years later, the events become spontaneously remembered. Hence, it is precisely because CSA events are not traumatic at the time of occurrence that they lose attentional force, and like other nontraumatic events that will not reach awareness for a period of time, may become open to spontaneous recovery. Ironically, however, with greater maturation and a fuller understanding of the nature of sexuality, the recovery experience is often accompanied by a sense of shock and betrayal, which can then lead to considerable psychological distress, including developing posttraumatic stress disorder (PTSD).

In direct contrast to the views of McNally (2012, this volume), Brewin (2012, this volume) asserts that traumatic events—including those that can be characterized as CSA—are sometimes forgotten. To fully understand the memory recovery process, one has to have an appreciation of the impact that emotional responses to trauma have on both forgetting and remembering. Recovery experiences provide insight into the role of trauma on memory; recoveries of CSA are sometimes similar to the intrusive memories of traumatic events that characterize PTSD in being fragmented, accompanied by emotional fear and shock, and provide a sense of reliving the past. Recent research into PTSD has uncovered that many sufferers do not experience symptoms immediately following exposure to traumatic events, but rather, their symptoms emerge over time. Such delayed onset PTSD results from an increased sensitization to general anxiety that eventually leads to a delayed full blown onset of symptoms. The course of development of delayed onset PTSD is consistent with notions of delayed recovered recall with victims of CSA in which one can experience vivid intrusive memories of abuse events during adulthood that were not present in childhood. One factor that is implicated with delayed recovered recall of trauma, in contrast to continuous trauma recall, is that those who experience delayed onset have had prior exposure to trauma or other severe stressors. Extending perspectives from research on autobiographical memory that emphasizes the role of self-identity in the structure of autobiographical knowledge (Conway, 2005), Brewin presents a model in which exposure to severe trauma leads to a fragmented self, which in turn, may lead to difficulties in remembering traumatic experiences. Those persons with fuller self-integration are more likely to have full recall, providing that the exposure to trauma challenges notions of the self; those persons with prior exposure to trauma may not have a well-integrated self and hence there may be no immediate challenge from a traumatic experience to one's conception of whom one is. For example, the trauma experienced as a result of CSA may lead to a fragmentation of self—or parallel selves—that will keep aspects of the traumatic exposure hidden from awareness on most occasions, but that will also permit aspects to become recovered without a full self-integration or awareness as shown by the FIA effect. Full recovery is characterized by the presence of unexpected cues that trigger not only the remembering of the traumatic CSA events, but also a fuller appreciation and integration of an alternate identity that recognizes oneself as being a victim of CSA.

Extending a research approach initialized by McNally and colleagues (McNally, 2012, this volume), Geraerts (2012, this volume) seeks to uncover the cognitive underpinnings of those who have CSA recovery experiences. In the research of Geraerts and colleagues, a variety of cognitive tasks are examined that assess either the propensity to develop false memories or to forget prior instances of remembering (the FIA effect; Arnold & Lindsay, 2002) among participants who claim never to be abused (control group), those with continuous memories of CSA, and participants who have recovered CSA experiences either spontaneously or within the context of suggestive therapy. This research also includes attempts to independently corroborate CSA events among continuous and both types of recovered memory groups. The findings clearly differentiate the cognitive abilities among groups. In an initial study that compared a recovered memory group with participants who had continuous memories, those with recovered memories showed a stronger FIA effect with autobiographical memories in comparison to those with continuous memories; in follow-up research (Geraerts et al., 2009), it was found that those who recover memories of CSA spontaneously show FIA effects in a word pairing test that are more pronounced in comparison to control participants, participants with continuous memories, and with participants who recovered memories in suggestive therapy. In contrast, participants with suggestive therapy recoveries demonstrated a heightened propensity to falsely recall words in the Deese-Roediger-McDermott (DRM; Roediger & McDermott, 1995) semantic word association test in comparison to the other three groups. Moreover, whereas participants in the continuous and spontaneous recovery groups showed equivalent levels of independent corroboration of the CSA, there was an inability to independently corroborate the presence of an abusive past among those whose recoveries occurred in suggestive therapy. Although the failure to independently corroborate abuse is not conclusive that abuse has not taken place, taken altogether, the results of this line of research indicates what Geraerts characterizes as a balanced picture that portrays individual differences in cognitive mechanisms that underlie the occurrences of both true and false recoveries. Geraerts's research also highlights the potential dangers of suggestive techniques in therapy among individuals who have a heightened propensity to falsely remember the past.

The contribution by DePrince et al. (2012, this volume) comprehensively evaluates betrayal trauma theory (BTT) and the implications that the theory provides to the recovered memory debate. Their views are wide ranging, and the most skeptical among all of the contributors with regard to the likeliness that false memories of CSA have readily occurred. According to BTT, the experience of CSA, and the impact that CSA has on forgetting and recovery, cannot be removed from the complex interpersonal dynamics that exist between perpetrators and victims. In the case of incestuous abuse, a child victim will be motivated to avoid awareness of the betrayal that CSA creates in order to maintain a sense of attachment to the abuser, as the victim is dependent on the perpetrator—at a minimum—for a sense of well-being. In addition, as awareness of the abuse would lead to traumatizing fear that one's well-being is in danger, BTT proposes two prongs for isolating the knowledge of CSA from awareness, both the betrayal and the trauma of abuse are to be avoided. Importantly, BTT does not argue that forgetting is always in the form of a complete lack of knowledge, as knowledge isolation for CSA includes both forgetting and misremembering. In terms of misremembering, a CSA victim may remember the relationship with the perpetrator as more positive, as more nurturing, than it actually was. A key prediction of BTT is that the extent of knowledge isolation will be a function of the closeness of the perpetrator-victim relationship, with closer relationships leading to greater levels of knowledge isolation. Although knowledge isolation occurs generally with the experiencing of traumatic events, a review of the evidence is supportive of their being increased knowledge isolation—in the form of heightened dissociation, reports of forgetting, and symptomology—among victims of incestuous abuse.

In terms of the implications of BTT, DePrince et al. note inherent difficulties in corroboration of CSA especially in terms of perpetrator confessions because perpetrators—like their victims—will also be motivated to isolate the knowledge of their abusive behavior from awareness, and hence, the importance of examining the accuracy of perpetrator memory in future research. Difficulties in corroboration challenge the conclusiveness of the evidence of Geraerts and colleagues (see Geraerts, 2012, this volume) regarding the notion that suggestive therapy will produce false memories of CSA; the evidence of Geraerts and colleagues is also considered to be ambiguous with regard to the extent that false recall in the DRM is generalizable to the notion that false memories of holistic events are readily produced in the real world. Although DePrince et al. are skeptical regarding the role of suggestive therapy in producing real world false memories of CSA, they nevertheless are disturbed that suggestive therapy occurs at all. In their view, the goal of the vast majority of trauma therapy is not to uncover incidents of CSA, and that only a minority of incompetent therapists would be using techniques that could be considered as suggestive. Importantly, DePrince et al assert that researchers who study forgetting and misremembering need to be cognizant of the wider sociopolitical context that seeks to preserve the dominance of certain groups, and to acknowledge the reality and tragedy of child abuse as one symptom of an unjust status quo.

Toward a Reconciliation of the Debate

In seeking the latest thinking and evidence pertaining to the recovered memory debate, the aim of the symposium was to provide a forum for contrasting views that would provide a comprehensive picture of the differing perspectives that characterize the current state of affairs. Indeed, as revealed in the contributions to this volume, this symposium has successfully met this goal! Although the contributions may point to higher levels of discord than consensus, and portray a picture that the debate remains nearly as contentious as ever, there has been movement toward reconciliation since the height of the so-called memory wars.

It is important to emphasize that despite differences in points of view, the face to face atmosphere at the symposium was genial. As one participant noted, "after years of contentious 'memory war' battles, it was a welcome relief to be able to discuss controversial issues in an open, collegial manner guided by empirical findings and soundly reasoned arguments" (Gold, email correspondence, 2010). Such collegiality, in and of itself, demonstrates a reconciliation in civility, but should not be taken as evidence of reconciliation in terms of developing a consensus regarding the nature of recovery experiences. In organizing a NATO Advanced Studies Institute sponsored conference of 95 expert participants in 1996 to explore differing perspectives on the recovered memory debate, Read and Lindsay (1997) observed a "convivial atmosphere…[that] created opportunities for in-depth and probing discussions of difficult and controversial issues…[, which] did not, of course, eliminate differences in perspective" (p. v). There are no doubts that this NATO conference did lead some participants to come closer in agreement on policy issues (e.g., Lindsay & Briere, 1997), and further, that some of the interactions at this conference promoted valuable research collaborations that shed further light on the controversial issues surrounding the debate. But it is also apparent that more recent years have produced an even greater narrowing of differences that had not existed at the time of this conference, or in the few years that followed it.

At the risk of oversimplification, there have been two contrasting views that have characterized the chasm among those involved in the debate. Although there has been recognition from all concerned that both true and false recoveries are possible, the debate has centered on one side arguing that true recoveries are the norm, and the other side arguing the opposite. A total reconciliation would consist of a consensus of opinion that either true memories constitute the substantive majority of recoveries and that false memories are rare, or that the substantive majority of false memories characterize the recovery experience with true memories being rare, or a consensus in which true and false memories are both seen to populate a substantive proportion of recoveries. Whereas the first two potential consensuses are asymmetric in that either true or false recoveries are found as characterizing the bulk of recovery experiences but not the other, the last potential consensus is symmetric in the sense that both true and false recoveries are found to have a nearly equivalent prevalence among recovery experiences.

Among the contributions to this volume, Geraerts (2012, this volume) provides the most explicitly symmetric perspective with evidence that points to true recoveries being the likely occurrence of spontaneous retrieval and false recoveries as a likely response to suggestive techniques used in therapy. All of the remaining contributions, with the exception of DePrince et al. (2012, this volume) whose examination of the available evidence leads to an explicit challenge of whether false recoveries populate a substantive proportion of recovered memories, reveal perspectives that do not take issue with a symmetric point of view. Hence, it can be seen that there is no clear consensus among the volume contributors with regard to whether a symmetric or asymmetric position best fits the available evidence, although, as noted below, there is movement toward reconciliation nevertheless.

While one must keep in mind that the volume contributors are a small subset of scholars who have been involved in the debate, each considers true recovery—to the extent to which any memory can be characterized as being veridical—as capturing a substantive proportion of recovery experiences. Although developers of the SMF (Johnson et al., 2012, this volume) characterize cognitive processes that may result in falsely believing mental experiences reflect past events, they also note that these same processes underlie veridical attributions of mental experiences to past events. In presenting evidence and arguments, Geraerts supports a symmetric position, and DePrince et endorse an asymmetric point of view in which the substantive majority of recovery experiences are seen as mostly faithful representations of abusive events. Although they differ in terms of the mechanisms that are responsible for the occurrence of true recoveries, McNally (2012, this volume), Brewin (2012, this volume), and Anderson and Huddleston (2012, this volume) each propose models to account for them.

As for false recoveries, Johnson et al. (2012, this volume) note that surveys of therapists indicate that suggestive techniques have been used in therapy and, according to the SMF, such techniques could lead to false memories. Both McNally (2012, this volume) and Geraerts (2012, this volume) present evidence that participants who reported having recovered memories of CSA are more susceptible to false remembering in the DRM task, which is a pattern of results consistent with the notion that there are recoveries that may be false. Both Anderson and Huddleston (2012, this volume) and Brewin (2012, this volume) point to the harm that suggestive procedures in therapeutic contexts may cause in leading to false memories. Although DePrince et al. (2012, this volume) express skepticism regarding the extent to which suggestive techniques in therapy have been used, they also express concern that suggestive techniques are used at all. In addition, they present evidence on what factors are most likely to lead to false recoveries, especially suggestions that increase a client's sense of plausibility of being a CSA victim. Hence, although there is not a clear consensus with regard to the prevalence of false recoveries, all of the contributors raise concerns about the dangers of suggestive therapeutic techniques.

Although the movement toward reconciliation should be recognized, as noted above, the volume contributions also reveal an ongoing debate that center on issues that are difficult to resolve. These continuing points of contention deserve attention, and I address those which I have judged as being most profound in an epilogue to this volume (Belli, 2012). I have decided not to address these issues at this juncture because I cannot do so without exposing my own leanings (despite my best attempts to be impartial). My preference is for readers of this volume to experience first-hand the complex and at times controversial issues that underlie the current debate as the authors had intended via their excellent contributions. Readers are then welcome to compare their independent assessment of the current status of the debate against my concluding comments.

References

Alpert, J. L., Brown, L. S., & Courtois, C. A. (1998a). Symptomatic clients and memories of childhood abuse: What the trauma and child sexual abuse literature tells us. *Psychology, Public Policy, and Law, 4*, 941–995.

Alpert, J. L., Brown, L. S., & Courtois, C. A. (1998b). Reply to Ornstein, Ceci, and Loftus (1998): The politics of memory. *Psychology, Public Policy, and Law, 4*, 1011–1024.

Alpert, J. L., Brown, L. S., & Courtois, C. A. (1998c). Comment on Ornstein, Ceci, and Loftus (1998): Adult recollections of childhood abuse. *Psychology, Public Policy, and Law, 4*, 1052–1067.

Anderson, M. C., & Huddleston, E. (2012, this volume). Towards a cognitive and neurobiological model of motivated forgetting. In Belli, R. F. (Ed.), *True and false recovered memories: Toward a reconciliation of the debate* (pp. 53–120). *Vol. 58: Nebraska Symposium on Motivation*. New York: Springer.

APA Working Group. (1998). Final conclusions of the American Psychological Association Working Group on investigation of memories of childhood abuse. *Psychology, Public Policy, and Law, 4*, 933–940.

Arnold, M. M., & Lindsay, D. S. (2002). Remembering remembering. *Journal of Experimental Psychology. Learning, Memory, and Cognition, 28*, 521–529.

Banks, W. P., & Pezdek, K. (1994). The recovered/false memory debate. *Consciousness and Cognition, 3*, 265–268.

Belli, R. F., & Loftus, E. F. (1994). Recovered memories of childhood abuse: A source monitoring perspective. In S. J. Lynn & J. Rhue (Eds.), *Dissociation: Theory, clinical, and research perspectives* (pp. 415–433). New York: Guilford Press.

Belli, R. F. (2012, this volume). Epilogue: Continuing points of contention in the recovered memory debate. In Belli, R. F. (Ed.), *True and false recovered memories: Toward a reconciliation of the debate* (pp. 243–255). *Vol. 58: Nebraska Symposium on Motivation*. New York: Springer.

Brewin, C. R. (2012, this volume). A theoretical framework for understanding recovered memory experiences. In Belli, R. F. (Ed.), *True and false recovered memories: Toward a reconciliation of the debate* (pp. 149–173). *Vol. 58: Nebraska Symposium on Motivation*. New York: Springer.

Brown, L. S. (1996). On the construction of truth and falsity: Whose memory, whose history. In K. Pezdek & W. P. Banks (Eds.), *The recovered/false memory debate* (pp. 341–353). San Diego: Academic.

Conway, M. A. (2005). Memory and the self. *Journal of Memory and Language, 53*(4), 594–628.

Courtois, C. A. (1996). Informed clinical practice and the delayed memory controversy. In K. Pezdek & W. P. Banks (Eds.), *The recovered/false memory debate* (pp. 355–370). San Diego: Academic.

Crews, F. (1995). *The memory wars: Freud's legacy in dispute.* New York: New York Review of Books.

DePrince, A., Brown, L., Cheit, R., Freyd, J., Gold, S. N., Pezdek, K., & Quina, K. (2012, this volume). Motivated forgetting and misremembering: Perspectives from Betrayal Trauma Theory. In Belli, R. F. (Ed.), *True and false recovered memories: Toward a reconciliation of the debate* (pp. 193–242). *Vol. 58: Nebraska Symposium on Motivation.* New York: Springer.

Freyd, J. J. (1996). *Betrayal trauma: The logic of forgetting childhood abuse.* Cambridge, MA: Harvard University Press.

Geraerts, E. (2012, this volume). Cognitive underpinnings of recovered memories of childhood abuse. In Belli, R. F. (Ed.), *True and false recovered memories: Toward a reconciliation of the debate* (pp.175–191). *Vol. 58: Nebraska Symposium on Motivation.* New York: Springer.

Geraerts, E., Lindsay, D. S., Merckelbach, H., Jelicic, M., Raymaekers, L., Arnold, M. M., et al. (2009). Cognitive mechanisms underlying recovered memory experiences of childhood sexual abuse. *Psychological Science, 20,* 92–98.

Harvey, M. R., & Herman, J. L. (1996). Amnesia, partial amnesia, and delayed recall among adult survivors of childhood trauma. In K. Pezdek & W. P. Banks (Eds.), *The recovered/false memory debate* (pp. 29–40). San Diego: Academic.

Hyman, I. E. (2000). The memory wars. In U. Neisser & I. E. Hyman (Eds.), *Memory observed: Remembering in natural contexts* (2nd ed., pp. 374–379). New York: Worth.

Johnson, M. K., Hashtroudi, S., & Lindsay, D. S. (1993). Source monitoring. *Psychological Bulletin, 114,* 3–28.

Johnson, M. K., & Raye, C. L. (1981). Reality monitoring. *Psychological Review, 88,* 67–85.

Johnson, M. K., Raye, C. L., Mitchell, K. J., & Ankudowich, E. (2012, this volume). The cognitive neuroscience of true and false memories. In Belli, R. F. (Ed.), *True and false recovered memories: Toward a reconciliation of the debate* (pp. 15–52). *Vol. 58: Nebraska Symposium on Motivation.* New York: Springer.

Lindsay, D. S. (1994). Memory source monitoring and eyewitness testimony. In D. F. Ross, J. D. Read, & M. P. Toglia (Eds.), *Adult eyewitness testimony: Current trends and developments* (pp. 27–55). New York: Cambridge University Press.

Lindsay, D. S., & Briere, J. (1997). The controversy regarding recovered memories of childhood sexual abuse: Pitfalls, bridges, and future directions. *Journal of Interpersonal Violence, 12,* 631–647.

Lindsay, D. S., & Read, J. D. (1994). Psychotherapy and memories of childhood sexual abuse: A cognitive perspective. *Applied Cognitive Psychology, 8,* 281–338.

Loftus, E. F. (1979). *Eyewitness testimony.* Cambridge, MA: Harvard University Press.

Loftus, E. F. (1997). Dispatch from the (un)civil memory wars. In J. D. Read & D. S. Lindsay (Eds.), *Recollections of trauma: Scientific evidence and clinical practice* (pp. 171–194). New York: Plenum.

Loftus, E. F., & Ketchum, K. (1994). *The myth of repressed memory.* New York: St. Martin's.

Lynn, S. J., & Nash, M. R. (1994). Truth in memory: Ramifications for psychotherapy and hypnotherapy. *The American Journal of Clinical Hypnosis, 36,* 194–208.

McNally, R. J. (2012, this volume). Searching for repressed memory. In Belli, R. F. (Ed.), *True and false recovered memories: Toward a reconciliation of the debate* (pp. 121–147). *Vol. 58: Nebraska Symposium on Motivation.* New York: Springer.

Ofshe, R., & Watters, E. (1994). *Making monsters: False memories, psychotherapy, and sexual hysteria.* New York: Scribner.

Ornstein, P. A., Ceci, S. J., & Loftus, E. F. (1998a). Comment of Alpert, Brown, and Courtois (1998): The science of memory and the practice of psychotherapy. *Psychology, Public Policy, and Law, 4,* 996–1010.

Ornstein, P. A., Ceci, S. J., & Loftus, E. F. (1998b). Adult recollections of childhood abuse: Cognitive and developmental perspectives. *Psychology, Public Policy, and Law, 4*, 1025–1051.

Persinger, M. A. (1992). Neuropsychological profiles of adults who report "sudden remembering" of early childhood memories: Implications for claims of sex abuse and alien visitation/abduction experiences. *Perceptual and Motor Skills, 75*, 259–266.

Pezdek, K., Finger, K., & Hodge, D. (1997). Planting false childhood memories: The role of event plausibility. *Psychological Science, 8*, 437–441.

Read, J. D., & Lindsay, D. S. (1997). Preface. In J. D. Read & D. S. Lindsay (Eds.), *Recollections of trauma: Scientific evidence and clinical practice* (pp. v–vii). New York: Plenum.

Roediger, H. L., III, & McDermott, K. B. (1995). Creating false memories: Remembering words not presented in lists. *Journal of Experimental Psychology. Learning, Memory, and Cognition, 21*, 803–814.

Schacter, D. L. (1996). *Searching for memory: The brain, the mind, and the past.* New York: Basic Books.

Schooler, J. W. (2001). Discovering memories of abuse in the light of meta-awareness. *Journal of Aggression, Maltreatment and Trauma, 4*, 105–136.

Schooler, J. W., Bendiksen, M. A., & Ambadar, Z. (1997). Taking the middle line: Can we accommodate both fabricated and recovered memories of sexual abuse? In M. Conway (Ed.), *False and recovered memories* (pp. 251–292). Oxford: Oxford University Press.

Shobe, K. K., & Schooler, J. W. (2001). Discovering fact and fiction: Case-based analyses of authentic and fabricated memories of abuse. In G. M. Davies & T. Dalgleish (Eds.), *Recovered memories: Seeking the middle ground* (pp. 95–151). Chichester: Wiley.

Sivers, H., Schooler, J., & Freyd, J. J. (2002). Recovered memories. *Encyclopedia of the Human Brain, 4*, 169–184.

Toglia, M. P. (1996). Recovered memories: Lost and found? In K. Pezdek & W. P. Banks (Eds.), *The recovered/false memory debate* (pp. 313–323). San Diego: Academic.

Yapko, M. D. (1994). *Suggestions of abuse: True and false memories of childhood sexual trauma.* New York: Simon & Schuster.

The Cognitive Neuroscience of True and False Memories*

Marcia K. Johnson, Carol L. Raye, Karen J. Mitchell, and Elizabeth Ankudowich

Abstract Of central relevance to the recovered/false memory debate is understanding the factors that cause us to *believe that a mental experience is a memory of an actual past experience*. According to the source monitoring framework (SMF), memories are attributions that we make about our mental experiences based on their subjective qualities, our prior knowledge and beliefs, our motives and goals, and the social context. From this perspective, we discuss cognitive behavioral studies using both objective (e.g., recognition, source memory) and subjective (e.g., ratings of memory characteristics) measures that provide much information about the encoding, revival and monitoring processes that yield both true and false memories. The chapter also considers how neuroimaging findings, especially from functional magnetic resonance imaging studies, are contributing to our understanding of the relation between memory and reality.

Keywords False memories • Functional magnetic resonance imaging (fMRI) • Neuroimaging and memory • Source monitoring framework (SMF)

The recovered/false memory debate has centered around two main issues: Can traumatic events be forgotten for many years and then remembered? Are memories of trauma, including recovered memories, susceptible to memory distortion? Our perspective on these issues does not require taking sides: (1) Important events (even events that are highly emotionally charged at the time) can be forgotten; and previously forgotten events (even those long forgotten) sometimes may be remembered

*Preparation of this chapter was supported by NIA grant AG009253.

M.K. Johnson (✉) • C.L. Raye • K.J. Mitchell • E. Ankudowich
Yale University, New Haven, CT, USA
e-mail: marcia.johnson@yale.edu

R.F. Belli (ed.), *True and False Recovered Memories: Toward a Reconciliation of the Debate*, Nebraska Symposium on Motivation, DOI 10.1007/978-1-4614-1195-6_2, © Springer Science+Business Media, LLC 2012

under appropriate cuing conditions. (2) Memories (even for highly emotional and significant events) can be inaccurate in consequential ways, but they sometimes can be quite accurate. The relative likelihood of each of these phenomena in everyday life, or their likelihood as sequelae to trauma, are methodologically challenging questions with important implications, for example, for legal and clinical practice. However, our lab has had a more specific focus relevant to the recovered/false memory debate: understanding the factors that cause us to *believe that a mental experience is a memory*.

With respect to this question, efforts from many labs have yielded much progress in the cognitive analysis of remembering. At a rapid pace, cognitive behavioral insights are being followed and extended by evidence from cognitive neuroscience. This chapter provides an overview of a theoretical framework that we believe is useful for thinking about memory, along with associated cognitive/behavioral findings, and an overview of some recent neuroimaging work related to issues of true and false memory.

Remembering

Remembering is a subjective mental experience. To provide context for the concept of remembering, it can be contrasted with forgetting and with forms of memory that do not involve the subjective sense of remembering.

Forgetting

Forgetting happens for many reasons: poor encoding; a failure to consolidate or to keep memories accessible through mechanisms like reactivation or rehearsal; absence of appropriate cues for remembering; interference when cues associated with the target information have become associated with other information (perhaps cuing memory for an entirely different event, or a reinterpretation of the original event). Furthermore, all of these factors are subject to motivational influences. For example, encoding of traumatic events may be poor because of avoidance (e.g., self-distraction, dissociation), or because reactivation or rehearsal of traumatic events is actively inhibited. Cues triggering memories of traumatic events may be deliberately avoided, or a less disturbing interpretation may be sought. Given the many reasons and ways (both incidental and deliberate) to forget, it is perhaps not surprising that we forget much of what we experience. Chapters in this volume discuss evidence concerning potential mechanisms of motivated forgetting, including inhibition (Anderson & Huddleston, 2012) and repression (McNally, 2012), as well as potential differences in the types of trauma that might induce motivated attempts to forget (DePrince et al., 2012) and individual differences in propensity to forget in populations reporting recovered memories (Geraerts, 2012).

Multiple Forms of Memory

Although there is relatively little of the totality of our experience that we can deliberately remember, this does not mean that all our "forgotten" experiences have no impact on us. As William James (1892) noted, "nothing we ever do is, in strict scientific literalness, wiped out" (see also Johnson, 1977, 1983). This general idea is reflected in many modern multiple memory system, or multiple representation, theories, which emphasize that there are manifestations of memory that do not necessarily involve or require conscious remembering (e.g., *habits, skills, procedures, implicit memories, priming, perceptual learning, semantic memory*, etc.). For example, Johnson and colleagues proposed a multiple-entry modular cognitive system (*MEM*) that supports different types of memory (Johnson, 1983; Johnson & Hirst, 1993), different aspects of consciousness (Johnson & Reeder, 1997), and different emotional experiences (Johnson & Multhaup, 1992). The idea that different aspects of experiences are processed by different mechanisms or subsystems can account for many observed phenomena, including acquisition of affective responses to stimuli even when the reasons for these affective responses are not consciously available, as in amnesia (Johnson, Kim, & Risse, 1985), or when vivid perceptual fragments are unexpectedly cued despite poorly integrated narrative accounts of events, such as occurs in individuals with PTSD (Brewin, 2012; Brewin, Gregory, Lipton, & Burgess, 2010; see also, e.g., Verwoerd, Wessel, de Jong, & Nieuwenhuis, 2009 for relevant evidence).

Forgetting and non-conscious forms of memory are clearly central to some of the main themes of the 58th Nebraska Symposium. However, we focus on another key and intriguing issue–the experience of remembering. The question under consideration in this chapter is what accounts for the phenomenal experience of having in mind a representation of a specific event that is believed to have actually taken place in our personal past. In particular, our lab has been interested for many years in the mechanisms of a cognitive system that yields both veridical and distorted memories. That is, how should we understand the formation, revival, and evaluation of true and false memories of specific autobiographical events? Theoretical ideas and empirical findings from laboratory studies of cognitive psychology and cognitive neuroscience are directly relevant to these questions. Of course, no single laboratory study embodies all the factors that occur in real life events. Laboratories are highly simplified contexts and we may as yet be missing some important factors, and undoubtedly we have an incomplete theoretical understanding about how some mechanisms work or interact. But there is no reason to believe that the relationships demonstrated in laboratory studies are not relevant to real life (Banaji & Crowder, 1989; Henkel & Coffman, 2004; Lindsay & Read, 1994; Wade et al., 2007).

What is a "Memory"?

Before attacking questions surrounding "memories" we could ask, what are "events" in the first place? An event is a collection of features (persons, objects, location,

Fig. 1 Possible interpretations of the ambiguous duck/rabbit figure. What one perceives and/or later remembers can vary both between people and within a person at different times (From Johnson, M.K. [1996]. Adapted from author's original.). For an interesting historical discussion of the duck/rabbit figure see http://socrates.berkeley.edu/~kihlstrm/JastrowDuck.htm

time, colors, tastes, semantics, actions, emotions, etc.) that are experienced as occurring in relation to each other (e.g., *the blue pen is on the table and George is reaching for it to sign the divorce papers*). Like the Duck/Rabbit in Fig. 1, the same person may see an event differently, depending on set or context and, of course, different people may see the same event differently, or even disagree on event boundaries. Encodings of events are not perfect representations of the "actual" event, but rather reflect an individual's prior knowledge, focus of attention, interests, motives, comprehension, and so on. Not only do we not expect memory of an event to be a perfect representation of the "actual" event, we do not even necessarily expect it to be a perfect representation of an individual's initial encoding of it. For example, at any point in time, set or context can change and appropriate cues may or may not be available, or new information may be incorporated into our interpretation of what happened. In short, encoding and remembering are the outcome of constructive and reconstructive processes—the processes that create both true and false memories (e.g., Barlett, 1932; Bransford & Johnson, 1972, 1973).

What is a "False" Memory?

As generally understood, errors of commission are *false memories* and errors of omission are *memory failures* or *forgetting*. Commission errors (distortions) have long been of interest (Barlett, 1932; Carmichael, Hogan, & Walter, 1932), including the mechanisms of "false recognition" of words (Anisfeld & Knapp, 1968; Cramer, 1970; Deese, 1959; Underwood, 1965) and of tacit implications of prose (e.g., Bransford &

Franks, 1971; Johnson, Bransford, & Solomon, 1973) and, more generally, constructive processes of memory (e.g., Bransford & Johnson, 1973; Loftus & Palmer, 1974). The similarities and differences among false perceptions, false memories, and false beliefs have also been of interest (e.g., in discussions of delusions, Johnson, 1988; see Wade et al., 2007, for a review of other early uses of the term "false memory"). As the term "false memory" became more widely used, and as issues of recovered memories of traumatic events increasingly raised clinical and legal issues that received a great deal of attention in the press, the term itself became a source of controversy. Some questioned the appropriateness of using the same term for relatively benign intrusions and false recognitions in tests of lists learned in the laboratory as for more consequential errors in memory for actual autobiographical events, especially for traumatic events (e.g., DePrince, Allard, Oh, & Freyd, 2004; Pezdek & Lam, 2007). Of course it is important to consider whether theoretical explanations or interpretations are being over-generalized and to be appropriately cautious in our claims of understanding. However, the term "false memory" is not a theoretical construct or an explanation. Rather, it refers to the fact of (or the presumption of) a commission error. If it is appropriate to use the terms "memory" and "forgetting" in both laboratory and real world contexts, then it is appropriate to use the term "false memory" in both contexts. Furthermore, there are a number of commonly used terms that are conceptually equivalent to "false memory" (*false recognition, intrusion, source memory error*) that refer to observed behavior in a variety of experimental paradigms (source memory tasks, misinformation paradigms, the Deese-Roediger-McDermott [DRM] semantic associates paradigm, exclusion paradigms, associative recognition paradigms, induced autobiographical memory paradigms, imagination inflation paradigms, unconscious plagiarism paradigms, etc.). It seems unlikely that we need completely different theoretical concepts to explain findings from each experimental paradigm or, as noted above, to explain laboratory vs. naturalistic phenomena.

Terms such as *reality monitoring failure, source confusion*, or *source misattribution*, on the other hand, tend to be used in a more theoretical (explanatory) way to connote the operation of specific factors in creating memory distortions, as outlined in the next section.

A Source Monitoring Framework

Within a general constructive/reconstructive view of cognition and memory, the Source Monitoring Framework (SMF, Johnson & Raye, 1981, 2000; Johnson, Hashtroudi, & Lindsay, 1993; Johnson, 2006; Mitchell & Johnson, 2000, 2009) has served as a guide for investigating memory for events (including imagined events), interpreting empirical findings, and highlighting similarities among different theoretical ideas. The constructs outlined in the SMF are probably among the most frequently invoked in discussions of the potential mechanisms of false memories (Belli & Loftus, 1994; Lindsay, 2008; Lindsay & Read, 1994; Loftus & Davis, 2006; Thomas, Hannula, & Loftus, 2007; Zaragoza, Belli, & Payment, 2006).

Briefly, the SMF posits that the sense that one is remembering is an attribution about a current mental experience which is based on features that seem to have been (and often, in fact, were) bound together during a specific event. The qualities of these mental experiences include perceptual information (e.g., color, sound), contextual information (e.g., spatial and temporal features), semantic concepts, emotion (either our own affective reaction or as a feature of an event, item, or other person), and information about cognitive operations (i.e., cognitive activities engaged such as imaging, noting relations, retrieving additional information), as well as less specific qualities such as familiarity and recency. These qualities guide judgments about the origin of a mental experience because, on average, different sources differ on these dimensions. For example, the content of dreams is often more bizarre than real life; events experienced perceptually may be associated with more egocentric spatial detail while imagined events may be more likely to contain allocentric spatial information. But, because the distributions of qualities from different sources often overlap, misattributions occur (e.g., when a particularly vivid previous imagination is claimed to have been a previous perception).

Memory attributions are the result of a source monitoring process that cumulates "evidence" across different features of mental experiences, but how each type of information or feature is weighted varies depending on past experience, task context, motives, etc. In addition to a relatively heuristic assessment of qualities of mental experiences, the cognitive system can engage in additional, more systematic processes such as retrieving additional information, examining internal consistency of a memory narrative, evaluating plausibility given prior knowledge, etc. Such heuristic and systematic processes are mutually correcting, helping to create doubt about vivid but implausible "memories" or about plausible but sketchy "memories." Doubt is extremely functional in that it may be the cue for further efforts at remembering, seeking corroboration, reserving judgment, or deciding to live with ambiguity. Both heuristic and systematic source monitoring processes are affected by prior knowledge and beliefs (e.g., What qualities should a memory from this source have?) and the social and cultural context in which memories are evaluated and consulted. Social/cultural context affects what kinds of things we remember, how often we do so, and what we take to be appropriate evidence of remembering an event. For example, someone giving testimony in court about what *did happen* might be expected to have an accuracy-driven agenda during remembering. They may therefore focus on specific details of the defendant's appearance, where and when they saw the defendant, and they may consult other information such as plausibility to corroborate their memory. On the other hand, someone encouraged in therapy to consider *possible* scenarios in which they *could* have encountered a person, might focus less on specific perceptual and temporal details and more on familiarity and emotional details. Even if the details initially encoded were the same in both cases, the extent to which different features (e.g., perceptual details vs. feelings) are weighted, and the extent to which heuristic vs. more systematic processing are brought to bear, would likely be different depending on the currently activated agenda and the social context (e.g., being cross-examined vs. being supported).

Many laboratory studies, using many paradigms (source identification, eyewitness testimony, unconscious plagiarism, etc.) have yielded evidence consistent with the SMF (see, Johnson, 2006; Lindsay, 2008; Mitchell & Johnson, 2009 for reviews). Imagined words (Foley, Johnson, & Raye, 1983), pictures (Durso & Johnson, 1980), actions (Anderson, 1984; Foley & Johnson, 1985; McDaniel, Lyle, Butler, & Dornburg, 2008), and complex events (Hashtroudi, Johnson, & Chrosniak, 1990; Loftus & Pickrell, 1995; Loftus, 2005; Zaragoza & Koshmider, 1989) can be misattributed to perception or action. Furthermore, perceptual and semantic similarity can increase source errors (Johnson, Raye, Wang, & Taylor, 1979; Johnson, Foley, & Leach, 1988; Lindsay, Johnson, & Kwon, 1991; Mitchell & Zaragoza, 2001; Roediger & McDermott, 1995; Mather, Henkel, & Johnson, 1997). Repeatedly imaging events increases their vividness (Suengas & Johnson, 1988), increases the likelihood they will be judged to have actually happened (Goff & Roediger, 1998; Henkel, 2004), and increases people's confidence that they did happen (Garry, Manning, Loftus, & Sherman, 1996). Of course, thinking about an actual event in ways that reactivate accurate details of the event can help consolidate and sustain an accurate memory (Hashtroudi et al.; Henkel, 2004). And thinking and talking about an event helps construct a narrative (Nelson, 1993; Nelson & Fivush, 2004) that itself may be less subject to distortion/suggestion (Henkel, 2008).

Thoughts and images that are created deliberately (compared to those that occur spontaneously or simply more easily), are less likely later to be misattributed to a perceptual (external) source, consistent with the idea that cognitive operations are encoded and can later be cues to source (Durso & Johnson, 1980; Finke, Johnson, & Shyi, 1988). In fact, it is perhaps the absence of cognitive operations information in certain mental experiences, for example, dreams (Johnson, Kahan, & Raye, 1984) or PTSD "flashbacks" (Brewin, 2012), that makes them feel like an external reality. Even when cognitive operations information is quite salient at encoding, it may not be available or considered later. For example, if people are forced to generate information that they know to be false in response to forced-recall questions, they sometimes later come to misremember their own deliberate confabulations as part of the witnessed event (Ackil & Zaragoza, 1998; see Chrobak & Zaragoza, 2009, for a review).

Information from an irrelevant modality (e.g., auditory) can influence judgments about whether we experienced an event in another, relevant, modality (e.g., visual). For example, participants may be more likely to claim to have seen an item (e.g., a dog) they imagined visually if they heard a sound associated with that item (e.g., barking, Henkel, Franklin, & Johnson, 2000; see Fig. 2). In addition, once an irrelevant memory is activated based on some feature-similarity with a target memory, other features from the irrelevant memory can be incorporated into the target memory (Lyle & Johnson, 2006). For example, people sometimes misattribute an imagined item (e.g., *ice cream cone, bowling pin*) to perception based on physical similarity (e.g., shape) with an actually seen item (e.g., *funnel, wine bottle*, respectively), and then also claim to have seen the imagined item in the location or color of the similar item that they did see. That is, similarity in one feature causes other features to be imported, or "borrowed" (Lampinen, Neuschatz, & Payne, 1999). Feature importing is an especially potent source of vivid false memories that can generate high confidence because memories constructed from bits and pieces of actual events are more compelling (seem more vivid and detailed, i.e., "real") than those constructed from

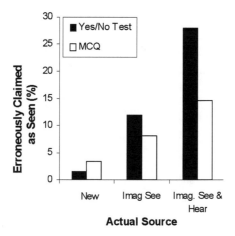

Fig. 2 Hearing the sound of an item that was only imagined (e.g., imagining seeing a basketball and actually hearing a bouncing ball) increases the rate of saying the item was seen. Note that the rate of false memories was reduced when participants rated memories on a memory characteristics questionnaire (MCQ) compared to when they simply indicated whether an item had been seen (Yes/No) (Adapted with permission from Henkel, et al., 2000)

imagination alone (Lyle &, Johnson). It should be noted that importing features from similar memories can also enhance accurate memories by increasing their vividness and detail (Lyle & Johnson, 2007).

Another important aspect of source monitoring is that the criteria used to make source attributions are flexible (Henkel et al., 2000; Lindsay & Johnson, 1989; Marsh & Hicks, 1998; Mather et al., 1997; Parker, Garry, Engle, Harper, & Clifasefi, 2008). Source misattributions are less likely if people are induced to examine their memories more carefully, for example, by asking specific questions about perceptual and affective detail (Henkel et al.; see Fig. 2). Interestingly, giving participants a placebo "drug" before a memory test and suggesting it will improve their memory also reduces source misattributions (Parker et al), presumably because the suggestion encourages a stricter criterion and/or more systematic processing.

The impact of emotion on source memory is, of course, especially important in the context of the recovered/false memory debate. Here we highlight just a few central issues. In general, if only item memory is considered, emotional items (e.g., words, stories, pictures) are recalled and recognized better than neutral items. The effect of emotion on source memory is more complex, depending on its role. Emotion can be a compelling feature in making source attributions, fostering a greater sense of recollection or confidence, even when it is not associated with greater accuracy (Dougal & Rotello, 2007; Ochsner, 2000; Sharot & Yonelinas, 2008; Talarico & Rubin, 2003). Emotional focus on oneself (e.g., how one feels about what two speakers are saying, in contrast to focusing on how the speakers are feeling), increases old/new recognition but decreases source memory (e.g., for who made which statement; Johnson, Nolde, & De Leonardis, 1996). Also, in a short-term memory task, people better remembered the location of neutral than emotional pictures (Mather et al., 2006). At the same time, some studies find better long-term source memory for emotional than neutral information (Doerksen & Shimamura, 2001; Kensinger & Corkin, 2003). Mather (2007) has suggested that arousal enhances within-object binding of features but it also impairs (or does not affect) associations between an object and other objects or between an object and its broader context (see also Kensinger, 2007). Differences in the impact of emotion on within-object and between-object binding could explain some inconsistencies in the literature.

Motivation can affect all of the aspects of source memory discussed above— influencing, for example, the kinds of events or features of events that are attended to initially, are thought or talked about after an event, and are accessed or given the most weight later during remembering. For example, people may selectively attend to or remember positive rather than negative information to regulate mood (e.g., Carstensen & Mikels, 2005; Mather & Carstensen, 2005), or misattribute information to sources based on desired outcomes (e.g., Barber, Gordon, & Franklin, 2009; Gordon, Franklin, & Beck, 2005).

Do the laboratory findings we have been discussing generalize to real life? Several lines of evidence suggest that they do. First, memories for highly emotional or traumatic public events like the Challenger explosion or the 9/11 terrorist attacks show source misattributions on delayed tests and confidence that may be out of line with accuracy (e.g., Greenberg, 2004; Hirst et al., 2009; Neisser & Harsch, 1992; Schmolck, Buffalo, & Squire, 2000; Talarico & Rubin, 2003). Also, investigators are able to induce participants to construct false autobiographical memories of reasonably complex, emotionally significant events (e.g., being taken to the hospital or being lost in a shopping mall; Ceci, Huffman, Smith, & Loftus, 1994; Hyman & Billings, 1998; Lindsay, Hagen, Read, Wade, & Garry, 2004; Loftus, 2005; Loftus & Pickrell, 1995; Porter, Yuille, & Lehman, 1999; see also Thomas et al., 2007). Researchers are able to induce false memories for complex autobiographical events using combinations of the same factors that work for words, lists, and stories—namely, encouraging imagination, repeated questioning (rehearsal), encouraging participants to relate a false target event to real events in their lives, and so on. For example, Lindsay et al. were able to greatly increase false memories of a childhood event that supposedly occurred at school by showing participants a class photo from the general period of the alleged event (see Fig. 3). Compared to those not seeing a photo, participants who saw the photo later presumably mistook the primed and readily available perceptual information about themselves, their friends, and their teacher as evidence that they had experienced the event. Moreover, studies of induced autobiographical memories further support previous suggestions (e.g., Dobson & Markham, 1993; Johnson et al., 1979) that individual differences in imagery, hypnotizability, and suggestibility, or high scores on a dissociative experiences scale, are associated with increased rates of false memories (Hyman & Pentland, 1996; Porter, Birt, Yuille, & Lechman, 2000).

These are the types of findings that fuel concerns about the uncritical use of memory-recovery practices that involve repeated suggestive questions, guided imagery, photos, hypnosis or sodium amytal, exposing individuals to accounts of sexual abuse in support

Fig. 3 Viewing a class picture increased adults' false memories of a childhood classroom event that never happened, both at session 1 and, especially, at session 2 (1 week later) (Adapted with permission of SAGE Publications from Lindsay et al., 2004, copyright © 2004 Association for Psychological Science)

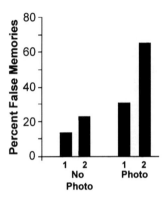

groups, or popular self-help books that encourage lax criteria for attributing a mental experience to memory (Kihlstrom, 2004; Lindsay & Read, 1994, 1995; Loftus, 2004; Loftus & Davis, 2006; McNally, 2003). Such practices are surprisingly common. A survey of therapists in the US and UK conducted by Poole, Lindsay, Memon, and Bull (1995) found that 25% of the therapists responding thought recovering memories is important, believed that they could indentify clients with hidden memories in the first therapy session, and reported using two or more memory recovery techniques that could be suggestive (see also, Polusny & Follette, 1996). A more recent survey of Canadian social workers, psychologists, and psychiatrists (Legault & Laurence, 2007), found that although 94% of respondents agreed that post-event information can interfere with a person's recall of an event, 53% also endorsed the idea that hypnosis can be used to recover memories of actual events from as far back as birth. In addition, respondents indicated that they use in their practice, on average, 2–3 "memory recovery techniques" to help their clients remember childhood events; hypnosis, age-regression, guided imagery, and imagination work were all endorsed at >20%; and 55% of those who responded to a question about childhood sexual abuse said that at least one of their clients had recovered such memories. These findings suggest that in spite of increased attention to research related to mechanisms of memory distortion, a substantial proportion of surveyed therapists still support the use of risky memory recovery practices.[1]

Of course, we are not the first to note that because some recovered memories may be false does not mean that all recovered memories are false. Corroborative evidence has been found for some reports of recovered memories (e.g., Schooler, Ambadar, & Bendiksen, 1997, Schooler, Bendiksen, & Ambadar, 1997; Shobe &

---

[1] Note that there were differences among professional groups in the level of endorsement of memory recovery work. In general, the psychiatrists were most likely to endorse the idea of memory fallibility and social workers the least likely. The reverse was true for endorsing the validity of recovered memories, with social workers being most likely to believe in the validity of such memories and psychiatrist the most skeptical. Respondents were also asked to indicate which, of a list of 13 memory recovery techniques, they either use or suggest clients use to "help them remember childhood events". Social workers and psychologists endorsed more of these techniques (M's = 3) than did psychiatrists (M = 2), and they also rejected fewer as totally inappropriate (M's: social workers = 1, psychologists = 2) than did psychiatrists (M = 4).

Schooler, 2001). Geraerts et al. (2007) found that memories of childhood sexual abuse that were recovered spontaneously outside of therapy were more likely to be corroborated than those recovered as a consequence of therapy (see also Clancy, McNally, Schacter, Lenzenweger, & Pitman, 2002 and Loftus & Davis, 2006 for discussions of the "recovery" of highly implausible "memories"). Furthermore, compared to individuals who report spontaneous recovery of memories of childhood sexual abuse, individuals who report that they recovered memories of childhood sexual abuse during therapy make more intrusions of semantically related items in laboratory tests of word list memory (Geraerts et al., 2009; Geraerts, 2012). Such findings further highlight the interaction of individual difference variables (imagery ability, suggestibility, prior beliefs) with potentially suggestive therapy practices. It should be noted that recovery of childhood memories is by no means thought by all therapists to be central to the success of therapy (DePrince et al., 2012; Polusny & Follette, 1996), providing an additional reason to be cautious about suggestive practices.

Interestingly, Geraerts et al. (2009, 2012) tested the same participants using a forgot-it-all-along paradigm (FIA, Arnold & Lindsay, 2002). In this procedure, participants learn items in one context (e.g., hand-*palm*) and then are later tested with cues reinstating the same (hand-p**m) or a different (tree-p**m) context. On a final test using only original first context cues, participants are asked if they previously recalled the item. Geraerts et al. found that participants who had recovered memories of childhood sexual abuse spontaneously were less likely than those who recovered memories in therapy to remember that they had previously remembered an item on the first test when the test context had changed but not when it remained the same. These findings suggest that those who forget (or believe they have forgotten) traumatic events may be particularly dominated by current context. If so, shifts in context may provide them greater "protection" against the cuing of previous events, and hence poorer memory for prior recall of those events. These findings highlight that forgetting, just like remembering, is an attribution based on the qualities of current mental experiences. Consistent with the idea that forgetting is an attribution, Belli, Winkielman, Read, Schwarz, and Lynn (1998) found that asking people to recall more events from childhood can lead them to judge their memory to be poorer than people asked to recall less.

Cognitive Neuroscience of Memory

Attempts to link the cognitive processes involved in memory to brain mechanisms have increased substantially in recent years as a result of developments in neuroimaging, especially functional magnetic resonance imaging (fMRI; for reviews see Davachi, 2006; Davachi & Dobbins, 2008; Mitchell & Johnson, 2009; Ranganath, 2010; Skinner & Fernandez, 2007). What follows is a brief overview of some relevant findings from a cognitive neuroscience approach to understanding memory.

MTL and memory. The importance of the medial temporal lobes (MTL) for memory, especially the hippocampus, has long been recognized because of the profound amnesia that results from bilateral hippocampal damage (e.g., Eichenbaum & Cohen, 2001;

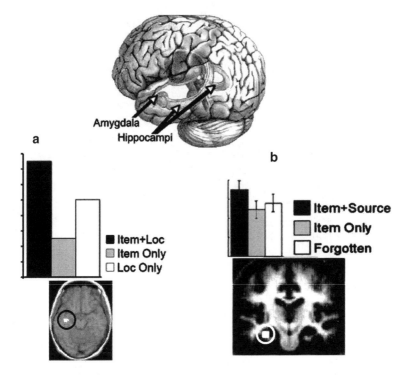

Fig. 4 Anterior hippocampus is associated with memory binding: (**a**) Greater activity during encoding when people were asked to remember items and locations, compared to just items or locations (Adapted with permission from Mitchell et al., 2000, copyright © 2000 Elsevier Science B.V.). (**b**) Greater activity at encoding associated with subsequent accurate source memory, compared to item memory or items that were forgotten (Adapted with permission from Davachi et al., 2003, copyright © 2003 National Academy of Sciences, U.S.A.). The schematic at the *top* shows the relationship of the hippocampus and amygdala within the MTL (Adapted with permission from Mitchell et al., 2009)

Milner et al., 1998; Squire & Knowlton, 2000). Although measures of hippocampal volume have been associated with measures of memory, findings are mixed, with some indication that the direction of the association depends on the specific populations studied (e.g., Bremner, Randall, Scott, et al., 1995, Bremner, Randall, Vermetten, et al., 1997; Duarte et al., 2006; Nestor et al., 2007; see Van Petten, 2004, for a review).

Our understanding of the role of MTL in memory is being expanded by functional neuroimaging studies. For example, as shown in Fig. 4, there is greater hippocampal activity when participants try to bind items together (e.g., a person and house, Henke, Buck, Weber, & Wieser, 1997; an object and location, Mitchell, Johnson, Raye, & D'Esposito, 2000) than when they simply try to encode individual items. Furthermore, greater hippocampal activity during encoding is associated with better source (but not necessarily better item) memory (Davachi, Mitchell, & Wagner,

2003; Kensinger & Schacter, 2006a; Ranganath et al., 2004). Darsaud et al. (2011) found greater hippocampal activity at encoding for those lists that later were less likely to produce false recognition of semantically related lures than lists which were more likely to produce semantically-related false positives. Presumably this activity was associated with the encoding/binding of source-specifying features that contributed to more accurate memory. With respect to brain activity during remembering, hippocampal activity is greater on test trials where participants remember the correct source than for trials on which they remember only the item (Cansino, Maquet, Dolan, & Rugg, 2002; Weis et al., 2004), for trials where they remember which two items went together compared to item recognition (Giovanello, Schnyer, & Verfaellie, 2004), and for items given "remember" vs. "know" responses (Eldridge, Knowlton, Furmanski, Bookheimer, & Engel, 2000). Furthermore, hippocampal activity while remembering autobiographical events is positively correlated with rated memory for details (Addis, Moscovitch, Crawley, & McAndrews, 2004).

Although it is generally agreed that the hippocampus is critical for binding features together (i.e., relational memory), the relative roles of other MTL regions (e.g., the entorhinal cortex, perirhinal cortex, and parahippocampal cortex) are less clear. A number of findings point to the importance of the perirhinal cortex for item or object memory (Brown & Aggleton, 2001; Davachi et al., 2003), or situations where information seems familiar but specific source information is not available (Eichenbaum, Yonelinas, & Ranganath, 2007), and to the importance of the parahippocampal cortex for memory for spatial context. Whether regions of MTL have been adequately dissociated is the topic of ongoing debate (e.g., Squire, Stark, & Clark, 2004).

Cortical representational areas. Evidence is also accumulating about the brain regions/networks that are involved in the representation of different qualitative features of memories. For example, brain regions have been identified that play a critical role in the representation of faces (fusiform face area, FFA, Kanwisher, McDermott, & Chun, 1997; Puce, Allison, Gore, & McCarthy, 1995), places/scenes (parahippocampal place area, PPA, Aguirre, Detre, Alsop, & D'Esposito, 1996; Epstein & Kanwisher, 1998), bodies (right lateral occipitotemporal cortex [extrastriate body area], Downing, Jiang, Shuman, & Kanwisher, 2001), words (visual word form area, left posterior occipitotemporal sulcus, Cohen & Dehaene, 2004), semantic information (anterior temporal cortex, Martin & Chao, 2001; Rogers et al., 2006), colors (posterior inferior temporal cortex, Chao & Martin, 1999; Kellenbach, Brett, & Patterson, 2001), sounds (left superior temporal sulcus [STS], Goldberg, Perfetti, & Schneider, 2006), objects (lateral occipital complex [LOC], Grill-Spector, Kourtzi, & Kanwisher, 2001; Malach et al., 1995), and even the "self" (medial prefrontal cortex [mPFC], Kelley et al., 2002). Furthermore, different aspects of a given type of information (e.g., place) may be differentially represented in different parts of a network. For example, the PPA appears to represent relatively specific place information whereas the retrosplenial cortex (RSC) appears to be involved in placing that information in a broader spatial context (Aminoff, Schacter, & Bar, 2008; Epstein & Higgins, 2007; Park, Chun, & Johnson, 2010).

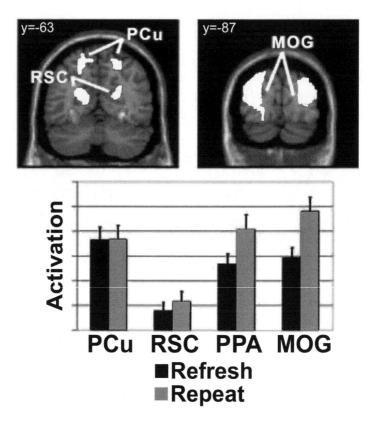

Fig. 5 Perceiving a scene (seeing it again, *Repeat*) and refreshing a scene (thinking of it again when it is no longer present but is still active, *Refresh*) resulted in activity in the same network of posterior scene-selective areas, but there was a gradient such that activity was more similar for perceiving and thinking in PCu than in MOG. See text for details. *MOG* medial occipital gyrus, *PCu* precuneus, *RSC* restrosplenial cortex (Adapted with permission from Johnson et al., 2007, copyright © 2007 Elsevier)

Importantly, the same regions that are involved in the perception of a particular type of information are also involved in thinking about such information (e.g., Ganis, Thompson, & Kosslyn, 2004; M. R. Johnson, Mitchell, Raye, D'Esposito, & Johnson, 2007; O'Craven & Kanwisher, 2000; Wheeler, Petersen, & Buckner, 2000). For example, Fig. 5 shows data from a study where, on each trial, participants saw a face and a scene and then either were shown one of the stimuli again or were cued with a location cue (a dot) to think back to (refresh) one of the items (M.R. Johnson et al.). Both seeing a scene again and refreshing a scene by thinking of it again resulted in activity in the same network of areas: middle occipital gyrus (MOG), PPA, RSC, and precuneus (PCu). In addition, there was a gradient such that activity was relatively greater in MOG for seeing compared to thinking and in PCu there was little difference. The fact that the relative similarity in levels of activation during perception and reflection differs across brain regions may provide important clues about potential differences in the contributions of different brain regions to true and false memories (see, e.g., Slotnick & Schacter, 2004).

Using a procedure similar to one used in behavioral studies investigating reality monitoring (e.g., Durso & Johnson, 1980) combined with fMRI, Gonsalves et al. (2004) assessed brain activity while participants saw and imagined pictures. They found that the activity was greater in PCu for imagined items that participants subsequently incorrectly called "seen" than for those subsequently correctly called "imagined" (see also Kensinger & Schacter, 2006b). This finding provides neural evidence that, as posited by the SMF, source attributions are made, in part, on the basis of the amount of activated perceptual information in mental representations.

The PCu is an area that frequently shows activity during episodic memory (Cavanna & Trimble, 2006; Lundstrom et al., 2003). The similarity in activity in PCu during perceiving and refreshing in the M.R. Johnson et al. (2007) study (see Fig. 5), along with the association of PCu activity with false memories in the Gonsalves et al. (2004) study, suggests that activity in this area is associated with a phenomenal experience of "perceptual" qualities that may contribute to the subjective experience of remembering, but alone may provide relatively poor evidence about the actual origin of mental experiences.

Consistent with behavioral findings that false memories tend to have less detail than true memories (e.g., Mather et al., 1997; Norman & Schacter, 1997; Schooler, Gerhard, & Loftus, 1986), several neuroimaging studies have found less activity for false than true memories in areas presumed to be involved in the encoding and/or retrieval of perceptual detail. Okado and Stark (2003) scanned participants during test trials for items that during encoding had been accompanied by an actual picture, or for which participants had imagined a picture. True memories for seen pictures showed greater activation in occipital cortex (primary visual cortex) than false memories (imagined items called seen). In a DRM study, Schacter et al. (1996) presented words auditorily, and found that later correct "yes" responses showed greater activity in an area associated with auditory processing (left temporoparietal cortex) than incorrect "yes" responses to semantically related distractors. Some differences between true and false memories in neural activity presumably correspond to differences in subjective experience that are detected in participants' ratings of their memories (e.g., Mather et al., 1997; Norman & Schacter; Henkel et al., 2000). However, it should be noted that presenting the same item again can produce priming even when participants do not recognize the item as old (e.g., Spencer, Montaldi, Gong, Roberts, & Mayes, 2009), and sometimes there is no difference in activity in early perceptual regions between old items that are correctly recognized and old items that are missed (Schacter & Slotnick, 2004). Thus, some differences between true and false memories in neural activity may reflect sensory/perceptual records (e.g., Johnson, 1983; Tulving & Schacter, 1990) that do not necessarily affect conscious introspection and thus would not be reflected in participants' ratings of their memories.

Also, when strong cues of one type are available, people may ignore other types of cues. For example, when participants are attempting to remember lists of related items (e.g., *night, dream*, etc.), they may be more likely to assess semantic than perceptual information, leading to high rates of false recognition of semantically related lures (e.g., *sleep*, Deese, 1959; Roediger & McDermott, 1995). Interestingly, when repetitive transcranial magnetic stimulation (rTMS)[2] was administered to left anterior temporal cortex (an area associated with semantic memory) after such lists were learned but before a recognition test, the false alarms to semantically related distractors were reduced, with no reduction in correct recognition of words that had been presented (Gallate, Chi, Ellwood, & Snyder, 2009; see also Boggio et al., 2009). At least two possibilities, not mutually exclusive, would be consistent with the SMF and behavioral findings (e.g., Mather et al., 1997; Norman & Schacter, 1997). First, the activation of related lures during list presentation may result in relatively weak semantic representations which are more likely to be disrupted by TMS than stronger semantic representations for perceived items. Second, perceived items are more likely to be associated with features in addition to semantic information (e.g., more vivid perceptual information), and when semantic representations are disrupted via TMS this other information is more influential in source judgments.

Misinformation paradigms have been used extensively in behavioral studies investigating false memories (e.g., Loftus, Miller, & Burns, 1978; see also Loftus, 2005; Mitchell & Johnson, 2000; Zaragoza et al., 2006, for reviews). Generally, misinformation paradigms present an original event (movie, slides) and then follow it with a second phase which includes the suggestion that some information was present in the original event that was, in fact, not present. Source errors occur when participants subsequently falsely claim the misinformation was present in the original event. At least two studies have attempted to adapt a misinformation procedure to the scanner (Baym & Gonsalves, 2010; Okado & Stark, 2005). Okado and Stark assessed neural activity during both the original event and misinformation phases of the procedure and found that activity in the left hippocampus and left perirhinal cortex predicted whether the original or suggested information would be selected on a subsequent forced-choice test: Activity was greater in these regions during the original event for items participants would later be accurate about than items participants would later be misled about, but greater during the misinformation phase for items associated with subsequent false than true memories. Furthermore, Baym and Gonsalves found that activity in visual processing areas (occipital and temporal [fusiform gyrus] cortex) during an original event was greater for items for which participants subsequently chose the true response rather than the false alternative. These findings are consistent with behavioral evidence that information encoded during a misinformation phase has a better chance of being misattributed to the original event when the corresponding information from the original phase has been weakly encoded (Pezdek & Roe, 1995; Sutherland & Hayne, 2001). Baym and Gonsalves did not observe any differences in right hippocampus or bilateral parahippocampus during the original event between items that subsequently resulted in

---

[2] rTMS is a non-invasive method for stimulating specific clusters of neurons; it can serve as a temporary virtual "knockout" to investigate the causal role of particular brain areas, as described here.

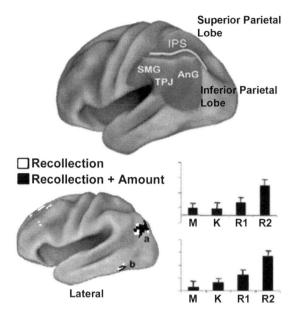

Fig. 6 Lateral parietal cortex, especially regions below the inferior parietal sulcus (IPS), is sensitive to the amount of information remembered (Adapted with permission from Uncapher and Wagner, 2009, copyright © 2009 Elsevier B.V.). The *lower figure* shows "recollection" responsive areas with greater activity for trials on which a "remember" response was given (i.e., R1 [a test picture was remembered but not the picture paired with it at study] or R2 [both test picture and paired picture remembered]) than a "know" response (K) (masked with K > Miss [M]). The subregions of these recollection areas labeled "Recollection + Amount" showed greater activity when more information was remembered (R2 > R1) (Adapted with permission from Vilberg & Rugg, 2007, copyright © 2007 Elsevier B.V.). *IPS* inferior parietal sulcus, *SMG* supramarginal gyrus, *TPJ* transparietal junction, *AnG* angular gyrus

true and false memories, but did observe more activity for these items than for subsequently forgotten items. They suggested that activity in these areas may reflect encoding of general contextual information and proposed that susceptibility to misleading information is most likely when general contextual information has been encoded but specific object details have not.

Parietal cortex and memory. Above we discussed precuneus, a medial part of the parietal cortex that is often activated during episodic remembering and imagery. But, there has been increasing interest in recent years about the role of various areas of lateral parietal cortex in episodic memory. Several studies have found activity in lateral parietal cortex (especially regions just below the inferior parietal sulcus [IPS], Brodmann Area [BA] 39; see Fig. 6) related to the number of features remembered, vividness, or for memories reported as a "recollection" (Uncapher, Otten, & Rugg, 2006; Vilberg & Rugg, 2007, 2008; Wagner, Shannon, Kahn, & Buckner, 2005; Wheeler & Buckner, 2004). Interestingly, when patients with bilateral parietal lesions are given source memory tests, they do not show a deficit in source accuracy, but they do show reduced confidence in their source judgments (Simons, Peers, Mazuz, Berryhill, & Olson, 2010). Furthermore, if asked to remember autobiographical experiences, their reports include less detail than do autobiographical memories of controls (Berryhill, Phuong, Picasso, Cabeza, & Olson, 2007). Simons et al. describe their patients as having "impaired subjective experience of rich episodic recollection" (p. 479). There are at least two ways such impairment in subjective experience might come about while not disrupting source memory for any particular individual feature when it is appropriately cued. Lateral parietal cortex may participate in the *integration* of multiple features, and such integration may contribute to a subjective sense of remembering. Alternatively, lateral parietal cortex may participate in iterative *attention* to different features. Thus, the parietal lobes may be where, as proposed in the SMF, evidence cumulates across different features of experience during source monitoring (Johnson & Raye, 1981; Johnson et al., 1993). A similar "accumulator" model was recently proposed by Donaldson, Wheeler, and Petersen (2010), who suggested that parietal cortex accumulates evidence for decision processes in memory (see also Cabeza, 2008; Ciaramelli, Grady, & Moscovitch, 2008 for related discussions of the functions of lateral parietal cortex).

Whether lateral parietal cortex subserves integration of or attention to multiple features during encoding and recollection of complex events, evidence indicates that for such functions, parietal cortex is part of a larger network involving frontal cortex.

Frontal cortex and memory. Key evidence of the importance of frontal cortex for memory comes from studies of patients with frontal damage (e.g., D'Esposito & Postle, 1999; Shallice & Burgess, 1991; Shimamura, 2000; Ranganath & Knight, 2003; Stuss & Levine, 2002). Frontal damage disrupts strategic search of memory. For example, it produces greater deficits in recall or source memory than old/new recognition memory (Mangels, Gershberg, Shimamura, & Knight, 1996; Shimamura, 1995). Furthermore, damage to frontal areas, especially ventromedial prefrontal cortex (VMPFC), can result in profound source misattributions that are clinically classified as *confabulations* (Damasio, Graff-Radford, Eslinger, Damasio, & Kassell, 1985; Johnson, 1991; Johnson, Hayes, D'Esposito, & Raye, 2000; Moscovitch, 1995; Schnider, 2008). Confabulations can range from the relatively trivial "filling in" of missing but highly likely information to quite bizarre "memories" of impossible events (e.g., having been a space pirate, Damasio et al.). Given that hallucinations and delusions—profound reality monitoring failures— are core cognitive problems in schizophrenia, it is not surprising that frontal dysfunction (Goldman-Rakic & Selemon, 1997; Weinberger, 1988) and disrupted source memory (Vinogradov, Luks, Schulman, & Simpson, 2008) are associated with the disorder. Frontal areas develop relatively slowly in children (Diamond, 2002; Fuster, 2002; Gogtay et al., 2004) and frontal areas also show evidence of neuropathology disproportionate to other brain regions in older adults (e.g., Raz & Rodrigue, 2006). Both children (e.g., Foley et al., 1983; Lindsay et al., 1991; see, Newcombe, Lloyd, & Ratliff, 2007, for a review) and older adults (Chalfonte & Johnson, 1996; Dehon & Bredart, 2004; Glisky & Kong, 2008; Hashtroudi, Johnson, & Chrosniak, 1989;

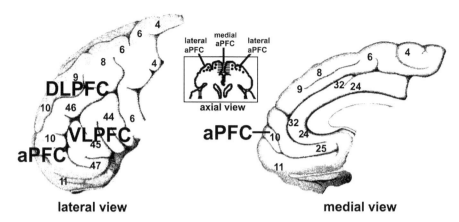

Fig. 7 Subregions of prefrontal cortex. *aPFC* anterior prefrontal cortex, *DLPFC* dorsolateral prefrontal cortex, *VLPFC* ventrolateral prefrontal cortex, the numbers are approximate Brodmann Areas (BA) (Adapted with permission from Mitchell and Johnson 2009)

Mitchell et al., 2000; see Mitchell & Johnson, 2009 for a review) show source memory deficits relative to young adults. (It should be noted that MTL may develop more slowly across childhood than has been assumed [Gogtay et al., 2006] and that normal aging is associated with some hippocampal dysfunction [e.g., Mitchell et al., 2000], thus some developmental effects may reflect MTL changes with age or a combination of MTL/PFC effects [see, e.g., Newcombe et al., 2007 for a discussion of consistent evidence in studies with children, Mitchell & Johnson, 2009 for evidence from aging studies]).

Along with other regions of the brain, frontal cortex is involved in both encoding and remembering. Frontally-mediated working memory/executive functions maintain agendas, refresh and rehearse relevant information, resist distraction, and direct attention to features, providing an opportunity for hippocampally-mediated feature binding. During remembering, frontal cortex is important for such functions as self-initiated cuing during effortful/strategic retrieval, assessing plausibility, and generating and comparing alternatives.

Differentiating among functions of various subregions of PFC is a major goal of cognitive neuroscience (see Fig. 7). Many studies have demonstrated that activity in ventrolateral PFC (VLPFC) during encoding is associated with subsequent memory (Blumenfeld & Ranganath, 2007; Ranganath & Blumenfeld, 2008; Staresina & Davachi, 2006; Wagner et al., 1998). In addition, encoding activity in VLPFC correlates with an index of later source memory (Staresina, Gray, & Davachi, 2008). Furthermore, different areas within VLPFC appear to play different roles. For example, anterior VLPFC (BA 47) is more active during semantic than nonsemantic encoding (Wagner et al.) and appears to be involved in a network with anterior temporal cortex in controlled semantic retrieval. Consistent with a role in semantic processing, Paz-Alonso, Ghetti, Donohue, Goodman, and Bunge (2008) found that, for healthy young adults, activity in left VLPFC (BA 47) was similar for hits and false alarms to semantically related lures. Other areas of VLPFC are involved in selection and/or interference resolution (BA 45 [mid VLPFC] Badre, Poldrack, Pare-Blagoev, Insler, & Wagner, 2005; Jonides & Nee, 2006; Thompson-Schill et al., 1997) and rehearsal (BA 44 [posterior VLPFC], Awh et al., 1996; Smith & Jonides, 1999; Jonides & Nee, 2006).

There is greater activity in dorsolateral PFC (DLPFC) for relational encoding than for item encoding (Murray & Ranganath, 2007) or for sequences that can be "chunked" compared to those with less structure (Bor, Duncan, Wiseman, & Owen, 2003). Also, DLPFC activity during encoding is associated with subsequent memory for bound features (e.g., face-house pairs, Summerfield et al., 2006). Activity in both VLPFC and DLPFC (Ranganath, Cohen, & Brozinsky, 2005; see also Ranganath & D'Esposito, 2001) appears to modulate hippocampal activity, affecting which information will and will not (Anderson & Huddleston 2012) be remembered later.

During testing, there is greater activity in lateral PFC (often including both VLPFC and DLPFC regions) during source memory than item memory tests (Mitchell, Johnson, Raye, & Greene, 2004; Nolde, Johnson, & D'Esposito, 1998; Ranganath, Johnson, & D'Esposito, 2000; Raye, Johnson, Mitchell, Nolde, & D'Esposito, 2000). An age-related deficit in source memory, which is associated with reduced activity in lateral PFC (Mitchell, Raye, Johnson, & Greene, 2006), may reflect deficits in evaluation/monitoring processes, and/or strategic retrieval processes. PFC activity, especially in anterior PFC, appears to be involved in setting the agenda for the type of source information that is being looked for (Dobbins & Han, 2006; Lepage, Ghaffar, Nyberg, & Tulving, 2000). There is some evidence that left PFC may be more involved in monitoring more specific (differentiated) information or engaging more strategic processes (e.g., retrieval) whereas right PFC may be more involved in source memory judgments that are made more heuristically (Dobbins, Rice, Wagner, & Schacter, 2003; Dobbins & Han; Kensinger, Clarke, & Corkin, 2003; Mitchell et al. 2004; Raye et al.), although this distinction may be too general to fully account for the findings (see Mitchell & Johnson, 2009 for further discussion and references).

Recently, investigators have focused attention on potential roles of anterior and medial PFC regions in source memory. These regions are found to be more active during self-referential tasks such as thinking about one's traits (Macrae, Moran, Heatherton, Banfield, & Kelley, 2004) or one's hopes and aspirations (Johnson et al., 2006) (see Amodio & Frith, 2006 and Van Overwalle, 2009 for reviews). They are also active during source decisions involving the self, for example, whether an item had been self- or other-generated (Simons, Henson, Gilbert, & Fletcher, 2008; Turner, Simons, Gilbert, Frith, & Burgess, 2008; Vinogradov et al., 2006). Interestingly, schizophrenia patients show deficits in this area during source monitoring of self-generated information (Vinogradov et al.).

Amygdala and memory. The amygdala is a region of the limbic system that is located in the MTL, near the anterior hippocampus (see Fig. 4). Various lines of evidence indicate that the amygdala is involved in the processing of emotion (e.g., LeDoux, 2000; McGaugh, 2004; Phelps, 2006). For example, bilateral amygdala damage eliminates the memory advantage for emotional over neutral items (Cahill, Babinsky, Markowitsch, & McGaugh, 1995; LaBar & Phelps, 1998). In healthy participants, during encoding, there is greater amygdala activity for emotional than neutral items (Cahill et al., 1996; Canli, Zhao, Brewer, Gabrieli, & Cahill, 2000; Hamann, Ely, Grafton, & Kilts, 1999), and greater amygdala activity at encoding for subsequently remembered than subsequently forgotten emotional items (Dolcos, LaBar, & Cabeza, 2004). There is also evidence that the amygdala may modulate activity in other MTL regions and the PFC (e.g., Dolcos & McCarthy, 2006; Kilpatrick & Cahill, 2003; Sharot, Verfaellie, & Yonelinas, 2007). For example, there is a larger correlation between activity in amygdala and other MTL regions for subsequently remembered emotional than neutral items (Dolcos et al.). The memory advantage for emotional items over neutral items is found for both positive and negative emotional items (e.g., Kensinger & Schacter, 2006a, 2008b). This is consistent with findings suggesting that the amygdala is more responsive to emotional intensity than valence (e.g., Anderson et al., 2003; Cunningham, Raye, & Johnson, 2004), but there is some controversy about the generality of this conclusion (Kensinger, 2009; Mather, 2007, 2009).

With respect to source memory, both behavioral and neuroimaging findings are mixed regarding the impact of emotion (see, e.g., Kensinger & Schacter, 2008a; Mather, 2007; Phelps & Sharot, 2008, for reviews). One under-investigated aspect proposed by the SMF that we would like to focus on here is that emotion can itself be a feature of a memory that contributes to the subjective sense of remembering (e.g., Johnson & Multhaup, 1992). For example, as in the behavioral studies discussed above, there is evidence that the subjective experience (sense of vividness or confidence) and amygdala activity are greater for emotional than neutral items even when memory for the emotional items is not more accurate (Phelps & Sharot; Sharot, Delgado, & Phelps, 2004). Interestingly, Qin et al. (2003) found that, compared to trauma-matched non-PTSD controls, participants who had PTSD prior to the 9/11 terrorists attacks had a tendency at 10 months after the attacks to remember their emotional response to the attacks as having been greater than they reported it to be 9 months earlier. One possibility is that individuals with PTSD may selectively rehearse or spontaneously experience reactivation of the most intense aspects of emotional experiences and thus memory for the "average" of the emotional experience may be inflated.

Rather than only an acute response to individual stimuli, emotion can also be a more sustained state (e.g., stress, depression, etc.). There is evidence that stress may enhance encoding of emotional but not neutral stimuli, but that it also may disrupt retrieval (Payne et al., 2007; see van Stegeren, 2009 for a review). In a situation where it is possible to induce very high levels of stress (i.e., military training), stress is associated with poorer memory (Morgan et al., 2004). Salivary cortisol level provides one index of stress and cortisol is associated with increased intrusions in memory for stories (Payne et al., 2007, see Fig. 8). Chronic stress (chronically increased cortisol levels) is associated with impaired PFC and hippocampal function (van

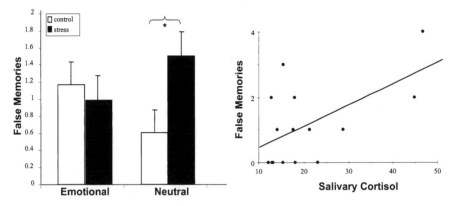

Fig. 8 Inducing stress increased false memories only for a neutral story (*left*); salivary cortisol levels and false memories were positively correlated (*right*) (Adapted with permission of author and copyright holder from Payne et al., 2007, copyright © 2007 Cold Spring Harbor Laboratory Press)

Stegeren). In one study (Grossman et al., 2006), PTSD and control participants were given hydrocortisone or a placebo before various cognitive tasks. Hydrocortisone did not affect the performance of either group on digit span forward and digit span backward tasks but the PTSD patients showed greater disruption than controls on working memory and long-term memory tasks that required more executive control. This pattern could suggest that individuals with PTSD show glucocorticoid-mediated impairments in memory (especially for more reflectively demanding tasks) at lower glucocorticoid levels than controls. Alternatively, additional cortisol may be added to an already elevated cortisol level, raising it to levels that impair performance.

Such individual differences in responsiveness to emotional stimuli are potentially important for understanding the etiology and/or maintenance of depression, anxiety, or other clinically significant symptoms (Etkin et al., 2004; Manuck, Brown, Forbes, & Hariri, 2007) associated with memory deficits (Hertel, 2000; Williams et al., 2007). In addition, recent studies suggest that some individual differences may be related to genetic variants (Canli & Lesch, 2007; Canli, 2004; Hariri et al., 2002; de Quervain et al., 2007; Rasch et al., 2009; see commentary by Todd & Anderson, 2009).

Administration of propranolol (a beta-adrenergic blocker) reduces the amygdala response to emotional expressions (Hurlemann et al., 2010), and reduces the startle response to items previously paired with a loud noise, without disrupting explicit memory for the item-noise contingency (Kindt, Soeter, & Vervliet, 2009; see also Kroes, Strange, & Dolan, 2010). Such findings have raised the possibility that dysfunctional emotional responses might be modified by drugs (e.g., in PTSD populations). However, the effects of propranolol may depend both on how arousing the emotional stimuli are (van Stegeren et al., 2005), and the current level of cortisol (van Stegeren, Wolf, Everaerd, & Rombouts, 2008). A new bioethics controversy has arisen from the possibility that drugs could be used to "change" memories by reducing the emotional response to an experienced event or by later reducing the emotional response associated with the memory of an emotional event (e.g., see Henry, Fishman, & Youngner, 2007, and associated commentaries). This possibility may create new "memory wars" arising again from the fact that memories are not fixed, but reflect a dynamic origami of past, present, and future (Johnson & Sherman, 1990).

Summary

Together, behavioral and neuroscience findings provide a perspective on issues of central relevance to the recovered/false memory debate. Like visual illusions help clarify the mechanisms of perception, the fact that memory distortions occur and that we can manipulate them in the laboratory helps us understand the mechanisms of memory. The fact that memory generally functions as well as it does and that it is not a hopeless quagmire in which all information is "equal" (or all source information is lost) points to the operation of critical reality/source monitoring mechanisms that differentiate experiences. The empirical findings discussed here, as well as many others, highlight that these mechanisms give rise to both true and false memories. Although our understanding is far from complete, various aspects of a cognitive model such as the SMF can be associated with different brain regions or networks.

Information (whether derived from perception or reflection) is encoded in various representational areas (such as faces in the fusiform gyrus), and different features are bound together as a consequence of MTL activity, especially in the hippocampus. Hippocampal activity is also modulated (e.g., disrupted or sustained, depending on the situation) by signals from the amygdala and PFC. For example, amygdala activity drives attention (e.g., orienting to and lingering on a stimulus), and PFC activity underlies the kind of strategic, organizational activity that creates associations crucial for voluntary recall. Emotion has both positive and negative effects on memory, depending on whether it sustains or disrupts processing relevant to later memory contexts. During both reflectively guided (voluntary) and spontaneous (involuntary) remembering, cues activate representational areas; activated information from different representational areas converges in the parietal cortex, potentially yielding an integrated, complex mental experience. The more cumulative and cohesive (i.e., differentiated) the resulting mental experience, the more it seems like a coherent and specific episode.

As in encoding, the prefrontal cortex is also involved in a number of aspects of remembering—setting and holding the agenda for what one is looking for, generating cues for retrieval, and evaluating activated information with respect to agendas and criteria. Emotion is a feature, much like any other, that is taken as evidence about the source of a mental experience. At the same time, emotion can facilitate or disrupt the PFC-mediated executive processes necessary for effective revival and evaluation of information. Although there can be top-down modulation at many levels of representation, it appears that remembering typically involves PFC-mediated evaluation processes targeted at parietal representations.

Hence, in fMRI studies of both encoding and remembering, activations of frontal, parietal, and MTL regions are frequently observed. Consistent with this picture, brain damage in any of these areas disrupts remembering. The most profound disruptions occur from MTL damage, especially hippocampal damage, because feature binding is crucial for any episodic memory experience. PFC damage disrupts strategically driven feature binding, and monitoring (retrieval and evaluation) processes. Parietal damage disrupts the subjective confidence in memories that is otherwise associated with cohesive and integrated representations (perhaps by disrupting the ability to shift to different features of mental experiences). An experience of familiarity can, of course, occur in response to features that may be fragments of actual events (or fragments of past imaginations). Such mental experiences can arise involuntarily, via cues of which a person may be unaware, and may arise from any level of representation in the cognitive system (including levels that may ordinarily be difficult to access deliberately). Whether these fragments are judged to be memories depends on the same kinds of factors relevant to more complex mental experiences. Hence, a very vivid, highly emotional, or apparently meaningful mental experience, even if quite incomplete, can seem real.

There are individual differences in the kinds of mental experiences individuals typically have, which may be related to differences in resolution of representational systems (e.g., FFA, PPA, LOC, etc.), or that may be related to differences in the levels of representation accessed or attended to during remembering. There are individual differences in the functioning of structures that support feature binding and executive function. And there are individual differences in the kinds and levels of emotion that energize or disrupt encoding and retrieval. In short, individuals differ in how vivid (perceptually, emotionally, semantically, etc.) their mental experiences are, which cues they weight most heavily in making memory attributions, how often they attempt to explicitly access the past, how often they deflect or attempt to inhibit memories, the availability of cues to past events in their environment, how much particular experiences are reflectively integrated with other autobiographical events, their likelihood of having engaged in similar events (real or imagined) that may be confused with a target event, the evidence they need to attribute a mental experience to memory, and their response to doubt about the origins of mental experiences. These myriad factors make memory a sometimes comforting and sometimes disturbing individual experience, but an always fascinating scientific pursuit.

References

Ackil, J. K., & Zaragoza, M. S. (1998). Memorial consequences of forced confabulation: Age differences in susceptibility to false memories. *Developmental Psychology, 34*, 1358–1372.

Addis, D. R., Moscovitch, M., Crawley, A. P., & McAndrews, M. P. (2004). Recollective qualities modulate hippocampal activation during autobiographical memory retrieval. *Hippocampus, 14*, 752–762.

Aguirre, G. K., Detre, J. A., Alsop, D. C., & D'Esposito, M. (1996). The parahippocampus subserves topographical learning in man. *Cerebral Cortex, 6*, 823–829.

Aminoff, E., Schacter, D. L., & Bar, M. (2008). The cortical underpinnings of context-based memory distortion. *Journal of Cognitive Neuroscience, 20*, 2226–2237.

Amodio, D. M., & Frith, C. D. (2006). Meeting of minds: The medial frontal cortex and social cognition. *Nature Reviews. Neuroscience, 7*, 268–277.

Anderson, A. K., Christoff, K., Stappen, I., Panitz, D., Ghahremani, D. G., Glover, G., et al. (2003). Dissociated neural representations of intensity and valence in human olfaction. *Nature Neuroscience, 6*, 196–202.

Anderson, M. C., & Huddleston, E. (2012). Towards a cognitive and neurobiological model of motivated forgetting. In R. F. Belli (Ed.), *True and false recovered memories: Toward a reconciliation of the debate* (pp. 53–120). *Vol. 58: Nebraska Symposium on Motivation*. New York: Springer.

Anderson, R. E. (1984). Did I do it or did I only imagine doing it? *Journal of Experimental Psychology: General, 113*, 594–613.

Anisfeld, M., & Knapp, M. (1968). Association, synonymity, and directionality in false recognition. *Journal of Experimental Psychology, 77*, 171–179.

Arnold, M. M., & Lindsay, D. S. (2002). Remembering remembering. *Journal of Experimental Psychology. Learning, Memory, and Cognition, 28*, 521–529.

Awh, E., Jonides, J., Smith, E. E., Schumacher, E. H., Koeppe, R. A., & Katz, S. (1996). Dissociation of storage and rehearsal in verbal working memory: Evidence from positron emission tomography. *Psychological Science, 7*, 25–31.

Badre, D., Poldrack, R. A., Pare-Blagoev, E. J., Insler, R. Z., & Wagner, A. D. (2005). Dissociable controlled retrieval and generalized selection mechanisms in ventrolateral prefrontal cortex. *Neuron, 47*, 907–918.

Banaji, M. R., & Crowder, R. G. (1989). The bankruptcy of everyday memory. *The American Psychologist, 44*, 1185–1193.

Barber, S. J., Gordon, R., & Franklin, N. (2009). Self-relevance and wishful thinking: Facilitation and distortion in source monitoring. *Memory & Cognition, 37*, 434–446.

Barlett, F. C. (1932). *Remembering: A study in experimental and social psychology*. Cambridge, England: Cambridge University Press.

Baym, C. L., & Gonsalves, B. D. (2010). Comparison of neural activity that leads to true memories, false memories, and forgetting: An fMRI study of the misinformation effect. *Cognitive, Affective, & Behavioral Neuroscience, 10*, 339–348.

Belli, R. F., & Loftus, E. F. (1994). Recovered memories of childhood abuse: A source monitoring perspective. In S. J. Lynn & J. W. Rhue (Eds.), *Dissociations: Clinical and theoretical perspectives* (pp. 415–433). New York: Guilford Press.

Belli, R. F., Winkielman, P., Read, J. D., Schwarz, N., & Lynn, S. J. (1998). Recalling more childhood events leads to judgments of poorer memory: Implications for the recovered/false memory debate. *Psychonomic Bulletin & Review, 5*, 318–323.

Berryhill, M. E., Phuong, L., Picasso, L., Cabeza, R., & Olson, I. R. (2007). Parietal lobe and episodic memory: Bilateral damage causes impaired free recall of autobiographical memory. *The Journal of Neuroscience, 27*, 14415–14423.

Blumenfeld, R. S., & Ranganath, C. (2007). Prefrontal cortex and long-term memory encoding: An integrative review of findings from neuropsychology and neuroimaging. *The Neuroscientist, 13*, 280–291.

Boggio, P. S., Fregni, F., Valasek, C., Ellwood, S., Chi, R., Gallate, J., et al. (2009). Temporal lobe cortical electrical stimulation during the encoding and retrieval phase reduces false memories. *PloS One, 4*, e4959. doi:10.1371/journal.pone.0004959.

Bor, D., Duncan, J., Wiseman, R. J., & Owen, A. M. (2003). Encoding strategies dissociate prefrontal activity from working memory demand. *Neuron, 37*, 361–367.

Bransford, J. D., & Franks, J. J. (1971). The abstraction of linguistic ideas. *Cognitive Psychology, 2*, 331–350.

Bransford, J. D., & Johnson, M. K. (1972). Contextual prerequisites for understanding: Some investigations of comprehension and recall. *Journal of Verbal Learning and Verbal Behavior, 11*, 717–726.

Bransford, J. D., & Johnson, M. K. (1973). Considerations of some problems of comprehension. In W. Chase (Ed.), *Visual information processing* (pp. 383–438). New York: Academic.

Bremner, J. D., Randall, P., Scott, T. M., Bronen, R. A., Seibyl, J. P., Southwick, S. M., et al. (1995). MRI-based measurement of hippocampal volume in patients with combat-related posttraumatic stress disorder. *The American Journal of Psychiatry, 152*, 973–981.

Bremner, J. D., Randall, P., Vermetten, E., Staib, L., Bronen, R. A., Mazure, C., et al. (1997). Magnetic resonance imaging-based measurement of hippocampal volume in posttraumatic stress disorder related to childhood physical and sexual abuse: A preliminary report. *Biological Psychiatry, 41*, 23–32.

Brewin, C. R. (2012). A theoretical framework for understanding recovered memory experiences. In R. F. Belli (Ed.), *True and false recovered memories: Toward a reconciliation of the debate* (pp. 149–173). *Vol. 58: Nebraska Symposium on Motivation*. New York: Springer.

Brewin, C. R., Gregory, J. D., Lipton, M., & Burgess, N. (2010). Intrusive images in psychological disorders: Characteristics, neural mechanisms, and treatment implications. *Psychological Review, 117*, 210–232.

Brown, M. W., & Aggleton, J. P. (2001). Recognition memory: What are the roles of the perirhinal cortex and hippocampus? *Nature Reviews. Neuroscience, 2*, 51–61.

Cabeza, R. (2008). Role of parietal regions in episodic memory retrieval: The dual attentional processes hypothesis. *Neuropsychologia, 46*, 1813–1827.

Cahill, L., Babinsky, R., Markowitsch, H. J., & McGaugh, J. L. (1995). The amygdala and emotional memory. *Nature, 377*, 295–296.

Cahill, L., Haier, R. J., Fallon, J., Alkire, M. T., Tang, C., Keator, D., et al. (1996). Amygdala activity at encoding correlated with long-term, free recall of emotional information. *Proceedings for the National Academy of Sciences of the United States of America, 93*, 8016–8021.

Canli, T. (2004). Functional brain mapping of extraversion and neuroticism: Learning from individual differences in emotion processing. *Journal of Personality, 72*, 1105–1132.

Canli, T., & Lesch, K. P. (2007). Long story short: The serotonin transporter in emotion regulation and social cognition. *Nature Neuroscience, 10*, 1103–1109.

Canli, T., Zhao, Z., Brewer, J., Gabrieli, J. D., & Cahill, L. (2000). Event-related activation in the human amygdala associates with later memory for individual emotional experience. *The Journal of Neuroscience, 20*, RC99.

Cansino, S., Maquet, P., Dolan, R. J., & Rugg, M. D. (2002). Brain activity underlying encoding and retrieval of source memory. *Cerebral Cortex, 12*, 1049–1056.

Carmichael, L., Hogan, H. P., & Walter, A. A. (1932). An experimental study of the effect of language on the reproduction of visually perceived form. *Journal of Experimental Psychology, 15*, 73–86.

Carstensen, L. L., & Mikels, J. A. (2005). At the intersection of emotion and cognition: Aging and the positivity effect. *Current Directions in Psychological Science, 14*, 117–121.

Cavanna, A. E., & Trimble, M. R. (2006). The precuneus: A review of its functional anatomy and behavioural correlates. *Brain, 129*, 564–583.

Ceci, S. J., Huffman, M., Smith, E., & Loftus, E. F. (1994). Repeatedly thinking about a non-event: Source misattributions among preschoolers. *Consciousness and Cognition, 3*, 388–407.

Chalfonte, B. L., & Johnson, M. K. (1996). Feature memory and binding in young and older adults. *Memory & Cognition, 24*, 403–416.

Chao, L. L., & Martin, A. (1999). Cortical regions associated with perceiving, naming, and knowing about colors. *Journal of Cognitive Neuroscience, 11*, 25–35.

Chrobak, Q., & Zaragoza, M. S. (2009). The cognitive consequences of forced fabrication: Evidence from studies of eyewitness suggestibility. In W. Hirstein (Ed.), *Confabulation: Views from neuroscience, psychiatry, psychology and philosophy* (pp. 67–90). Cambridge, MA: MIT Press.

Ciaramelli, E., Grady, C. L., & Moscovitch, M. (2008). Top-down and bottom-up attention to memory: A hypothesis (AtoM) on the role of the posterior parietal cortex in memory retrieval. *Neuropsychologia, 46*, 1828–1851.

Clancy, S. A., McNally, R. J., Schacter, D. L., Lenzenweger, M. F., & Pitman, R. K. (2002). Memory distortion in people reporting abduction by aliens. *Journal of Abnormal Psychology, 111*, 455–461.

Cohen, L., & Dehaene, S. (2004). Specialization within the ventral stream: The case for the visual word form area. *NeuroImage, 22*, 466–476.

Cramer, P. (1970). Semantic generalization: Demonstration of an associative gradient. *Journal of Experimental Psychology, 83*, 164–172.

Cunningham, W. A., Raye, C. L., & Johnson, M. K. (2004). Implicit and explicit evaluation: FMRI correlates of valence, emotional intensity, and control in the processing of attitudes. *Journal of Cognitive Neuroscience, 16*, 1717–1729.

D'Esposito, M., & Postle, B. R. (1999). The dependence of span and delayed-response performance on prefrontal cortex. *Neuropsychologia, 37*, 1303–1315.

Damasio, A. R., Graff-Radford, N. R., Eslinger, P. J., Damasio, H., & Kassell, N. (1985). Amnesia following basal forebrain lesions. *Archives of Neurology, 42*, 263–271.

Darsaud, A., Dehon, H., Lahl, O., Sterpenich, V., Boly, M., Dang-Vu, T., et al. (2011). Does sleep promote false memories? *Journal of Cognitive Neuroscience, 23*, 26–40.

Davachi, L. (2006). Item, context and relational episodic encoding in humans. *Current Opinion in Neurobiology, 16*, 693–700.

Davachi, L., & Dobbins, I. G. (2008). Declarative memory. *Current Directions in Psychological Science, 17*, 112–118.

Davachi, L., Mitchell, J. P., & Wagner, A. D. (2003). Multiple routes to memory: Distinct medial temporal lobe processes build item and source memories. *Proceedings of the National Academy of Sciences of the United States of America, 100*, 2157–2162.

de Quervain, D. J., Kolassa, I. T., Ertl, V., Onyut, P. L., Neuner, F., Elbert, T., et al. (2007). A deletion variant of the alpha2b-adrenoceptor is related to emotional memory in Europeans and Africans. *Nature Neuroscience, 10*, 1137–1139.

Deese, J. (1959). On the prediction of occurrence of particular verbal intrusions in immediate recall. *Journal of Experimental Psychology, 58*, 17–22.

Dehon, H., & Bredart, S. (2004). False memories: Young and older adults think of semantic associates at the same rate, but young adults are more successful at source monitoring. *Psychology and Aging, 19*, 191–197.

DePrince, A. P., Allard, C. B., Oh, H., & Freyd, J. J. (2004). What's in a name for memory errors? Implications and ethical issues arising from the use of the term "false memory" for errors in memory for details. *Ethics & Behavior, 14*, 201–233.

DePrince, A., Brown, L., Cheit, R., Freyd, J., Gold, S. N., Pezdek, K., & Quina, K. (2012). Motivated forgetting and misremembering: Perspectives from Betrayal Trauma Theory. In R. F. Belli (Ed.), *True and false recovered memories: Toward a reconciliation of the debate* (pp. 193–242). *Vol. 58: Nebraska Symposium on Motivation*. New York: Springer.

Diamond, A. (2002). Normal development of prefrontal cortex from birth to young adulthood: Cognitive functions, anatomy, and biochemistry. In D. T. Stuss & R. T. Knight (Eds.), *Principles of frontal lobe function* (pp. 466–503). London: Oxford University Press.

Dobbins, I. G., & Han, S. (2006). Cue-versus probe-dependent prefrontal cortex activity during contextual remembering. *Journal of Cognitive Neuroscience, 18*, 1439–1452.

Dobbins, I. G., Rice, H. J., Wagner, A. D., & Schacter, D. L. (2003). Memory orientation and success: Separate neurocognitive components underlying episodic recognition. *Neuropsychologia, 41*, 318–333.

Dobson, M., & Markham, R. (1993). Imagery ability and source monitoring: Implications for eyewitness memory. *British Journal of Psychology, -84*, 111–118.

Doerksen, S., & Shimamura, A. P. (2001). Source memory enhancement for emotional words. *Emotion, 1*, 5–11.

Dolcos, F., LaBar, K. S., & Cabeza, R. (2004). Interaction between the amygdala and the medial temporal lobe memory system predicts better memory for emotional events. *Neuron, 42*, 855–863.

Dolcos, F., & McCarthy, G. (2006). Brain systems mediating cognitive interference by emotional distraction. *Journal of Neuroscience, 26*, 2072–2079.

Donaldson, D. I., Wheeler, M. E., & Petersen, S. E. (2010). Remember the source: Dissociating frontal and parietal contributions to episodic memory. *Journal of Cognitive Neuroscience, 22*, 377–391.

Dougal, S., & Rotello, C. M. (2007). "Remembering" emotional words is based on response bias, not recollection. *Psychonomic Bulletin & Review, 14*, 423–429.

Downing, P. E., Jiang, Y., Shuman, M., & Kanwisher, N. (2001). A cortical area selective for visual processing of the human body. *Science, 293*, 2470–2473.

Duarte, A., Hayasaka, S., Du, A., Schuff, N., Jahng, G. H., Kramer, J., et al. (2006). Volumetric correlates of memory and executive function in normal elderly, mild cognitive impairment and Alzheimer's disease. *Neuroscience Letters, 406*, 60–65.

Durso, F. T., & Johnson, M. K. (1980). The effects of orienting tasks on recognition, recall, and modality confusion of pictures and words. *Journal of Verbal Learning and Verbal Behavior, 19*, 416–429.

Eichenbaum, H., & Cohen, N. J. (2001). *From conditioning to conscious recollection: Memory systems of the brain.* Oxford: Oxford University Press.

Eichenbaum, H., Yonelinas, A. P., & Ranganath, C. (2007). The medial temporal lobe and recognition memory. *Annual Review of Neuroscience, 30*, 123–152.

Eldridge, L. L., Knowlton, B. J., Furmanski, C. S., Bookheimer, S. Y., & Engel, S. A. (2000). Remembering episodes: A selective role for the hippocampus during retrieval. *Nature Neuroscience, 3*, 1149–1152.

Epstein, R. A., & Higgins, J. S. (2007). Differential parahippocampal and retrosplenial involvement in three types of visual scene recognition. *Cerebral Cortex, 17*, 1680–1693.

Epstein, R., & Kanwisher, N. (1998). A cortical representation of the local visual environment. *Nature, 392*, 598–601.

Etkin, A., Klemenhagen, K. C., Dudman, J. T., Rogan, M. T., Hen, R., Kandel, E. R., et al. (2004). Individual differences in trait anxiety predict the response of the basolateral amygdala to unconsciously processed fearful faces. *Neuron, 44*, 1043–1055.

Finke, R. A., Johnson, M. K., & Shyi, G. C.-W. (1988). Memory confusions for real and imagined completions of symmetrical visual patterns. *Memory & Cognition, 16*, 133–137.

Foley, M. A., & Johnson, M. K. (1985). Confusions between memories for performed and imagined actions: A developmental comparison. *Child Development, 56*, 1145–1155.

Foley, M. A., Johnson, M. K., & Raye, C. L. (1983). Age-related changes in confusion between memories for thoughts and memories for speech. *Child Development, 54*, 51–60.

Fuster, J. M. (2002). Frontal lobe and cognitive development. *Journal of Neurocytology, 31*, 373–385.

Gallate, J., Chi, R., Ellwood, S., & Snyder, A. (2009). Reducing false memories by magnetic pulse stimulation. *Neuroscience Letters, 449*, 151–154.

Ganis, G., Thompson, W. L., & Kosslyn, S. M. (2004). Brain areas underlying visual mental imagery and visual perception: An fMRI study. *Brain Research. Cognitive Brain Research, 20*, 226–241.

Garry, M., Manning, C., Loftus, E. F., & Sherman, S. J. (1996). Imagination inflation: Imagining a childhood event inflates confidence that it occurred. *Psychonomic Bulletin and Review, 3*, 208–214.

Geraerts, E. (2012). Cognitive underpinnings of recovered memories of childhood abuse. In R. F. Belli (Ed.), *True and false recovered memories: Toward a reconciliation of the debate* (pp. 175–191). *Vol. 58: Nebraska Symposium on Motivation.* New York: Springer.

Geraerts, E., Lindsay, D. S., Merckelbach, H., Jelicic, M., Raymaekers, L., Arnold, M. M., et al. (2009). Cognitive mechanisms underlying recovered-memory experiences of childhood sexual abuse. *Psychological Science, 20*, 92–98.

Geraerts, E., Schooler, J. W., Merckelbach, H., Jelicic, M., Hauer, B. J., & Ambadar, Z. (2007). The reality of recovered memories: Corroborating continuous and discontinuous memories of childhood sexual abuse. *Psychological Science, 18*, 564–568.

Giovanello, K. S., Schnyer, D. M., & Verfaellie, M. (2004). A critical role for the anterior hippocampus in relational memory: Evidence from an fMRI study comparing associative and item recognition. *Hippocampus, 14*, 5–8.

Glisky, E. L., & Kong, L. L. III. (2008). Do young and older adults rely on different processes in source memory tasks? A neuropsychological study. *Journal of Experimental Psychology. Learning, Memory, and Cognition, 34*, 809–822.

Goff, L. M., & Roediger, H. L. III (1998). Imagination inflation for action events: Repeated imaginings lead to illusory recollections. *Memory & Cognition, 26*, 20–33.

Gogtay, N., Giedd, J. N., Lusk, L., Hayashi, K. M., Greenstein, D., Vaituzis, A. C., et al. (2004). Dynamic mapping of human cortical development during childhood through early adulthood. *Proceedings of the National Academy of Sciences of the United States of America, 101*, 8174–8179.

Gogtay, N., Nugent, T. F., 3rd, Herman, D. H., Ordonez, A., Greenstein, D., Hayashi, K. M., et al. (2006). Dynamic mapping of normal human hippocampal development. *Hippocampus, 16*, 664–672.

Goldberg, R. F., Perfetti, C. A., & Schneider, W. (2006). Perceptual knowledge retrieval activates sensory brain regions. *Journal of Neuroscience, 26*, 4917–4921.

Goldman-Rakic, P. S., & Selemon, L. D. (1997). Functional and anatomical aspects of prefrontal pathology in schizophrenia. *Schizophrenia Bulletin, 23*, 437–458.

Gonsalves, B., Reber, P. J., Gitelman, D. R., Parrish, T. B., Mesulam, M. M., & Paller, K. A. (2004). Neural evidence that vivid imagining can lead to false remembering. *Psychological Science, 15*, 655–660.

Gordon, R., Franklin, N., & Beck, J. (2005). Wishful thinking and source monitoring. *Memory & Cognition, 33*, 418–429.

Greenberg, D. L. (2004). President Bush's false 'flashbulb' memory of 9/11/01. *Applied Cognitive Psychology, 18*, 363–370.

Grill-Spector, K., Kourtzi, Z., & Kanwisher, N. (2001). The lateral occipital complex and its role in object recognition. *Vision Research, 41*, 1409–1422.

Grossman, R., Yehuda, R., Golier, J., McEwen, B., Harvey, P., & Maria, N. S. (2006). Cognitive effects of intravenous hydrocortisone in subjects with PTSD and healthy control subjects. *Annals of the New York Academy of Sciences, 1071*, 410–421.

Hamann, S. B., Ely, T. D., Grafton, S. T., & Kilts, C. D. (1999). Amygdala activity related to enhanced memory for pleasant and aversive stimuli. *Nature Neuroscience, 2*, 289–293.

Hariri, A. R., Mattay, V. S., Tessitore, A., Kolachana, B., Fera, F., Goldman, D., et al. (2002). Serotonin transporter genetic variation and the response of the human amygdala. *Science, 297*, 400–403.

Hashtroudi, S., Johnson, M. K., & Chrosniak, L. D. (1989). Aging and source monitoring. *Psychology and Aging, 4*, 106–112.

Hashtroudi, S., Johnson, M. K., & Chrosniak, L. D. (1990). Aging and qualitative characteristics of memories for perceived and imagined complex events. *Psychology and Aging, 5*, 119–126.

Henke, K., Buck, A., Weber, B., & Wieser, H. G. (1997). Human hippocampus establishes associations in memory. *Hippocampus, 7*, 249–256.

Henkel, L. A. (2004). Erroneous memories arising from repeated attempts to remember. *Journal of Memory and Language, 50*, 26–46.

Henkel, L. A. (2008). Maximizing the benefits and minimizing the costs of repeated memory tests for older adults. *Psychology and Aging, 23*, 250–262.

Henkel, L. A., & Coffman, K. J. (2004). Memory distortions in coerced false confessions: A source monitoring framework analysis. *Applied Cognitive Psychology, 18*, 567–588.

Henkel, L. A., Franklin, N., & Johnson, M. K. (2000). Cross-modal source monitoring confusions between perceived and imagined events. *Journal of Experimental Psychology. Learning, Memory, and Cognition, 26*, 321–335.

Henry, M., Fishman, J. R., & Youngner, S. J. (2007). Propranolol and the prevention of posttraumatic stress disorder: Is it wrong to erase the 'sting' of bad memories? *The American Journal of Bioethics, 7*, 12–20.

Hertel, P. T. (2000). The cognitive-initiative account of depression-related impairments in memory. In D. Medin (Ed.), *The psychology of learning and motivation: Advances in research theory* (Vol. 39, pp. 47–71). San Diego, CA: Academic.

Hirst, W., Phelps, E. A., Buckner, R. L., Budson, A. E., Cuc, A., Gabrieli, J. D. E. et al. (2009). Long-term memory for the terrorist attack of September 11: Flashbulb memories, event memories, and the factors that influence their retention. *Journal of Experimental Psychology. General, 138*, 161–176.

Hurlemann, R., Walter, H., Rehme, A. K., Kukolja, J., Santoro, S. C., Schmidt, C., et al. (2010). Human amygdala reactivity is diminished by the beta-noradrenergic antagonist propranolol. *Psychological Medicine, 40*, 1839–1848.

Hyman, I. E., Jr., & Billings, F. .J. (1998). Individual differences and the creation of false childhood memories. *Memory, 6*, 1–20.

Hyman, I. E., Jr., & Pentland, J. (1996). The role of mental imagery in the creation of false childhood memories. *Journal of Memory and Language, 35*, 101–117.

James, W. (1892). *Psychology: Briefer course.* New York: Henry Holt.

Johnson, M. K. (1977). What is being counted none the less? In I. M. Birnbaum & E. S. Parker (Eds.), *Alcohol and human memory* (pp. 43–50). Hillsdale, NJ: Erlbaum.

Johnson, M. K. (1983). A multiple-entry, modular memory system. In G. H. Bower (Ed.), *The psychology of learning and motivation: Advances in research and theory* (Vol. 17, pp. 81–123). New York: Academic.

Johnson, M. K. (1991). Reflection, reality monitoring, and the self. In R. Kunzendorf (Ed.), *Mental imagery* (pp. 3–16). New York: Plenum.

Johnson, M. K. (1996). Fact, fantasy, and public policy. In D. Hermann, C. McEvoy, P. Hertzog, P. Hertel, & M. K. Johnson (Eds.), *Basic and applied memory research: Theory in context* (Vol. 1, pp. 83–103). Mahwah, NJ: Erlbaum.

Johnson, M. K. (2006). Memory and reality. *The American Psychologist, 61*, 760–771.

Johnson, M. K. (1988). Discriminating the origin of information. In T. F. Oltmanns & B. A. Maher (Eds.), *Delusional beliefs* (pp. 34–65). New York: Wiley.

Johnson, M. K., Bransford, J. D., & Solomon, S. K. (1973). Memory for tacit implications of sentences. *Journal of Experimental Psychology, 98*, 203–205.

Johnson, M. K., Foley, M. A., & Leach, K. (1988). The consequences for memory of imagining in another person's voice. *Memory & Cognition, 16*, 337–342.

Johnson, M. K., Hashtroudi, S., & Lindsay, D. S. (1993). Source monitoring. *Psychological Bulletin, 114*, 3–28.

Johnson, M. K., Hayes, S. M., D'Esposito, M., & Raye, C. L. (2000). Confabulation. In F. Boller, J. Grafman (Series Eds.), & L. S. Cermak (Vol. Ed.), *Handbook of neuropsychology: Vol. 2. Memory and its disorders* (2nd ed., pp. 383–407). Amsterdam: Elsevier Science.

Johnson, M. K., & Hirst, W. (1993). MEM: Memory subsystems as processes. In A. F. Collins, S. E. Gathercole, M. A. Conway, & P. E. Morris (Eds.), *Theories of memory* (pp. 241–286). East Sussex, England: Erlbaum.

Johnson, M. K., Kahan, T. L., & Raye, C. L. (1984). Dreams and reality monitoring. *Journal of Experimental Psychology. General, 113*, 329–344.

Johnson, M. K., Kim, J. K., & Risse, G. (1985). Do alcoholic Korsakoff's syndrome patients acquire affective reactions? *Journal of Experimental Psychology: Learning, Memory, and Cognition, 11*, 22–36.

Johnson, M. R., Mitchell, K. J., Raye, C. L., D'Esposito, M., & Johnson, M. K. (2007). A brief thought can modulate activity in extrastriate visual areas: Top-down effects of refreshing just-seen visual stimuli. *NeuroImage, 37*, 290–299.

Johnson, M. K., & Multhaup, K. S. (1992). Emotion and MEM. In S.-A. Christianson (Ed.), *The handbook of emotion and memory: Current research and theory* (pp. 33–66). Hillsdale, NJ: Erlbaum Associates.

Johnson, M. K., Nolde, S. F., & De Leonardis, D. M. (1996). Emotional focus and source monitoring. *Journal of Memory and Language, 35*, 135–156.

Johnson, M. K., & Raye, C. L. (1981). Reality monitoring. *Psychological Review, 88*, 67–85.

Johnson, M. K., & Raye, C. L. (2000). Cognitive and brain mechanisms of false memories and beliefs. In D. L. Schacter & E. Scarry (Eds.), *Memory, brain, and belief* (pp. 35–86). Cambridge, MA: Harvard University Press.

Johnson, M. K., Raye, C. L., Mitchell, K. J., Touryan, S. R., Greene, E. J., & Nolen-Hoeksema, S. (2006). Dissociating medial frontal and posterior cingulate activity during self-reflection. *Social Cognitive and Affective Neuroscience, 1*, 56–64.

Johnson, M. K., Raye, C. L., Wang, A. Y., & Taylor, T. H. (1979). Fact and fantasy: The roles of accuracy and variability in confusing imaginations with perceptual experiences. *Journal of Experimental Psychology. Human Learning and Memory, 5*, 229–240.

Johnson, M. K., & Reeder, J. A. (1997). Consciousness as meta-processing. In J. D. Cohen & J. W. Schooler (Eds.), *Scientific approaches to consciousness* (pp. 261–293). Mahwah, NJ: Erlbaum.

Johnson, M. K., & Sherman, S. J. (1990). Constructing and reconstructing the past and the future in the present. In E. T. Higgins & R. M. Sorrentino (Eds.), *Handbook of motivation and social cognition: Foundations of social behavior* (pp. 482–526). New York: Guilford Press.

Jonides, J., & Nee, D. E. (2006). Brain mechanisms of proactive interference in working memory. *Neuroscience, 139*, 181–193.

Kanwisher, N., McDermott, J., & Chun, M. M. (1997). The fusiform face area: A module in human extrastriate cortex specialized for the perception of faces. *Journal of Neuroscience, 17*, 4302–4311.

Kellenbach, M. L., Brett, M., & Patterson, K. (2001). Large, colorful, or noisy? Attribute- and modality-specific activations during retrieval of perceptual attribute knowledge. *Cognitive, Affective, & Behavioral Neuroscience, 1*, 207–221.

Kelley, W. M., Macrae, C. N., Wyland, C. L., Caglar, S., Inati, S., & Heatherton, T. F. (2002). Finding the self? an event-related fMRI study. *Journal of Cognitive Neuroscience, 14*, 785–794.

Kensinger, E. A. (2007). Negative emotion enhances memory accuracy: Behavioral and neuroimaging evidence. *Current Directions in Psychological Science, 16*, 213–218.

Kensinger, E. A. (2009). Remembering the details: Effects of emotion. *Emotion Review, 1*, 99–113.

Kensinger, E. A., Clarke, R. J., & Corkin, S. (2003). What neural correlates underlie successful encoding and retrieval? A functional magnetic resonance imaging study using a divided attention paradigm. *Journal of Neuroscience, 23*, 2407–2415.

Kensinger, E. A., & Corkin, S. (2003). Memory enhancement for emotional words: Are emotional words more vividly remembered than neutral words? *Memory and Cognition, 31*, 1169–1180.

Kensinger, E. A., & Schacter, D. L. (2006a). Amygdala activity is associated with the successful encoding of item, but not source, information for positive and negative stimuli. *Journal of Neuroscience, 26*, 2564–2570.

Kensinger, E. A., & Schacter, D. L. (2006b). Neural processes underlying memory attribution on a reality-monitoring task. *Cerebral Cortex, 16*, 1126–1133.

Kensinger, E. A., & Schacter, D. L. (2008a). Memory and emotion. In M. Lewis, J. M. Haviland-Jones, & L. F. Barrett (Eds.), *The handbook of emotions* (3rd ed., pp. 601–617). New York: Guilford.

Kensinger, E. A., & Schacter, D. L. (2008b). Neural processes supporting young and older adults' emotional memories. *Journal of Cognitive Neuroscience, 20*, 1–13.

Kihlstrom, J. F. (2004). An unbalanced balancing act: Blocked, recovered, and false memories in the laboratory and clinic. *Clinical Psychology: Science & Practice, 11*, 34–41.

Kilpatrick, L., & Cahill, L. (2003). Amygdala modulation of parahippocampal and frontal regions during emotionally influenced memory storage. *NeuroImage, 20*, 2091–2099.

Kindt, M., Soeter, M., & Vervliet, B. (2009). Beyond extinction: erasing human fear responses and preventing the return of fear. *Nature Neuroscience, 12*, 256–258.

Kroes, M. C. W., Strange, B. A., & Dolan, R. J. (2010). B-Adrenergic blockade during memory retrieval in humans evokes a sustained reduction of declarative emotional memory enhancement. *Journal of Neuroscience, 30*, 3959–3963.

LaBar, K. S., & Phelps, E. A. (1998). Arousal-mediated memory consolidation: Role of the medial temporal lobe in humans. *Psychological Science, 9*, 490–493.

Lampinen, J. M., Neuschatz, J. S., & Payne, D. G. (1999). Source attributions and false memories: A test of the demand characteristics account. *Psychonomic Bulletin & Review, 6*, 130–135.

LeDoux, J. E. (2000). Emotion circuits in the brain. *Annual Review of Neuroscience, 23*, 155–184.

Legault, E., & Laurence, J.-R. (2007). Recovered memories of childhood sexual abuse: Social worker, psychologist, and psychiatrist reports of beliefs, practices and cases. *Australian Journal of Clinical and Experimental Hypnosis, 35*, 111–133.

Lepage, M., Ghaffar, O., Nyberg, L., & Tulving, E. (2000). Prefrontal cortex and episodic memory retrieval mode. *Proceedings of the National Academy of Sciences of the United States of America, 97*, 506–511.

Lindsay, D. S. (2008). Source Monitoring. In J. Byrne (Series Ed.) & H. L. Roediger, III (Vol. Ed.), *Cognitive psychology of memory. Learning and memory: A comprehensive reference* (Vol. 2, pp. 325–348). Oxford: Elsevier.

Lindsay, D. S., Hagen, L., Read, J. D., Wade, K. A., & Garry, M. (2004). True photographs and false memories. *Psychological Science, 15*, 149–154.

Lindsay, D. S., & Johnson, M. K. (1989). The eyewitness suggestibility effect and memory for source. *Memory & Cognition, 17*, 349–358.

Lindsay, D. S., Johnson, M. K., & Kwon, P. (1991). Developmental changes in memory source monitoring. *Journal of Experimental Child Psychology, 52*, 297–318.

Lindsay, D. S., & Read, J. D. (1994). Psychotherapy and memories of childhood sexual abuse: A cognitive perspective. *Applied Cognitive Psychology, 8*, 281–338.

Lindsay, D. S., & Read, J. D. (1995). "Memory work" and recovered memories of CSA: scientific evidence and pubic, professional, and personal issues. *Psychology, Public Policy and the Law, 1*, 846–908.

Loftus, E. F. (2004). Dispatch from the (un)civil memory wars. *The Lancet, 364*, 20–21.

Loftus, E. F. (2005). Planting misinformation in the human mind: A 30-year investigation of the malleability of memory. *Learning and Memory, 12*, 361–366.

Loftus, E. F., & Davis, D. (2006). Recovered memories. *Annual Review of Clinical Psychology, 2*, 469–498.

Loftus, E. F., Miller, D. G., & Burns, H. J. (1978). Semantic integration of verbal information into a visual memory. *Journal of Experimental Psychology. Human Learning and Memory, 4*, 19–31.

Loftus, E. F., & Palmer, J. C. (1974). Reconstruction of automobile destruction: An example of the interaction between language and memory. *Journal of Verbal Learning and Verbal Behavior, 13*, 585–589.

Loftus, E. F., & Pickrell, J. E. (1995). The formation of false memories. *Psychiatric Annals, 25*, 720–725.

Lundstrom, B. N., Petersson, K. M., Andersson, J., Johansson, M., Fransson, P., & Ingvar, M. (2003). Isolating the retrieval of imagined pictures during episodic memory: Activation of the left precuneus and left prefrontal cortex. *NeuroImage, 20*, 1934–1943.

Lyle, K. B., & Johnson, M. K. (2006). Importing perceived features into false memories. *Memory, 14*, 197–213.

Lyle, K. B., & Johnson, M. K. (2007). Source misattributions may increase the accuracy of source judgments. *Memory & Cognition, 35*, 1024–1033.

Macrae, C. N., Moran, J. M., Heatherton, T. F., Banfield, J. F., & Kelley, W. M. (2004). Medial prefrontal activity predicts memory for self. *Cerebral Cortex, 14*, 647–654.

Malach, R., Reppas, J. B., Benson, R. R., Kwong, K. K., Jiang, H., Kennedy, W. A., et al. (1995). Object-related activity revealed by functional magnetic resonance imaging in human occipital cortex. *Proceedings of the Natural Academy of Science USA, 92*, 8135–8139.

Mangels, J. A., Gershberg, F. B., Shimamura, A. P., & Knight, R. T. (1996). Impaired retrieval from remote memory in patients with frontal lobe damage. *Neuropsychology, 10*, 32–41.

Manuck, S. B., Brown, S. M., Forbes, E. E., & Hariri, A. R. (2007). Temporal stability of individual differences in amygdala reactivity. *The American Journal of Psychiatry, 164*, 1613–1614.

Marsh, R. L., & Hicks, J. L. (1998). Test formats change source-monitoring decision processes. *Journal of Experimental Psychology. Learning, Memory, and Cognition, 24*, 1137–1151.

Martin, A., & Chao, L. L. (2001). Semantic memory and the brain: Structure and processes. *Current Opinion in Neurobiology, 11*, 194–201.

Mather, M. (2007). Emotional arousal and memory binding: An object-based framework. *Perspectives on Psychological Science, 2*, 33–52.

Mather, M. (2009). When emotion intensifies memory interference. *Psychology of Learning and Motivation, 51*, 101–120.

Mather, M., & Carstensen, L. L. (2005). Aging and motivated cognition: The positivity effect in attention and memory. *Trends in Cognitive Science, 9,* 496–502.

Mather, M., Henkel, L. A., & Johnson, M. K. (1997). Evaluating characteristics of false memories: Remember/Know judgments and memory characteristics questionnaire compared. *Memory & Cognition, 25,* 826–837.

Mather, M., Mitchell, K. J., Raye, C. L., Novak, D. L., Greene, E. J., & Johnson, M. K. (2006). Emotional arousal can impair feature binding in working memory. *Journal of Cognitive Neuroscience, 18,* 614–625.

McDaniel, M. A., Lyle, K. B., Butler, K. M., & Dornburg, C. C. (2008). Age-related deficits in reality monitoring of action memories. *Psychology and Aging, 23,* 646–656.

McGaugh, J. L. (2004). The amygdala modulates the consolidation of memories of emotionally arousing experiences. *Annual Review of Neuroscience, 27,* 1–28.

McNally, R. J. (2003). Progress and controversy in the study of posttraumatic stress disorder. *Annual Review of Psychology, 54,* 229–252.

McNally, R. J. (2012). Searching for repressed memory. In R. F. Belli (Ed.), *True and false recovered memories: Toward a reconciliation of the debate* (pp. 121–147). *Vol. 58: Nebraska Symposium on Motivation.* New York: Springer.

Milner, B., Squire, L. R., & Kandel, E. R. (1998). Cognitive neuroscience and the study of memory. *Neuron, 20,* 445–468.

Mitchell, K. J., & Johnson, M. K. (2000). Source monitoring: Attributing mental experiences. In E. Tulving & F. I. M. Craik (Eds.), *The Oxford handbook of memory* (pp. 179–195). New York: Oxford University Press.

Mitchell, K. J., & Johnson, M. K. (2009). Source monitoring 15 years later: What have we learned from fMRI about the neural mechanisms of source memory? *Psychological Bulletin, 135,* 638–677.

Mitchell, K. J., Johnson, M. K., Raye, C. L., & D'Esposito, M. (2000). fMRI evidence of age-related hippocampal dysfunction in feature binding in working memory. *Cognitive Brain Research, 10,* 197–206.

Mitchell, K. J., Johnson, M. K., Raye, C. L., & Greene, E. J. (2004). Prefrontal cortex activity associated with source monitoring in a working memory task. *Journal of Cognitive Neuroscience, 16,* 921–934.

Mitchell, K. J., Raye, C. L., Johnson, M. K., & Greene, E. J. (2006). An fMRI investigation of short-term source memory in young and older adults. *NeuroImage, 30,* 627–633.

Mitchell, K. J., & Zaragoza, M. S. (2001). Contextual overlap and eyewitness suggestibility. *Memory & Cognition, 29,* 616–626.

Morgan, C. A., III, Hazlett, G., Doran, A., Garrett, S., Hoyt, G., Thomas, P., et al. (2004). Accuracy of eyewitness memory for persons encountered during exposure to highly intense stress. *International Journal of Law and Psychiatry, 27,* 265–279.

Moscovitch, M. (1995). Recovered consciousness: A hypothesis concerning modularity and episodic memory. *Journal of Clinical and Experimental Neuropsychology, 17,* 276–290.

Murray, L. J., & Ranganath, C. (2007). The dorsolateral prefrontal cortex contributes to successful relational memory encoding. *Journal of Neuroscience, 27,* 5515–5522.

Neisser, U., & Harsch, N. (1992). Phantom flashbulbs: False recollections of hearing the news about Challenger. In E. Winograd & U. Neisser (Eds.), *Affect and accuracy in recall: Studies of "flashbulb" memories* (Vol. 4, pp. 9–31). New York: Cambridge University Press.

Nelson, K. (1993). The psychological and social origins of autobiographical memory. *Psychological Science, 4,* 7–14.

Nelson, K., & Fivush, R. (2004). The emergence of autobiographical memory: A social cultural developmental theory. *Psychological Review, 111,* 486–511.

Nestor, P. G., Kubicki, M., Kuroki, N., Gurrera, R. J., Niznikiewicz, M., Shenton, M. E., et al. (2007). Episodic memory and neuroimaging of hippocampus and fornix in chronic schizophrenia. *Psychiatry Research: Neuroimaging, 155,* 21–28.

Newcombe, N. S., Lloyd, M. E., & Ratliff, K. R. (2007). Development of episodic and autobiographical memory: A cognitive neuroscience perspective. In R. V. Kail (Ed.), *Advances in child development and behavior* (Vol. 35, pp. 37–85). San Diego, CA: Elsevier.

Nolde, S. F., Johnson, M. K., & D'Esposito, M. (1998). Left prefrontal activation during episodic remembering: An event-related fMRI study. *NeuroReport, 9*, 3509–3514.

Norman, K. A., & Schacter, D. L. (1997). False recognition in younger and older adults: Exploring the characteristics of illusory memories. *Memory & Cognition, 25*, 838–848.

O'Craven, K. M., & Kanwisher, N. (2000). Mental imagery of faces and places activates corresponding stimulus-specific brain regions. *Journal of Cognitive Neuroscience, 12*, 1013–1023.

Ochsner, K. N. (2000). Are affective events richly recollected or simply familiar? The experience and process of recognizing feelings past. *Journal of Experimental Psychology. General, 129*, 242–261.

Okado, Y., & Stark, C. (2003). Neural processing associated with true and false memory retrieval. *Cognitive, Affective, & Behavioral Neuroscience, 3*, 323–334.

Okado, Y., & Stark, C. E. L. (2005). Neural activity during encoding predicts false memories created by misinformation. *Learning & Memory, 12*, 3–11.

Park, S., Chun, M. M., & Johnson, M. K. (2010). Refreshing and integrating visual scenes in scene-selective cortex. *Journal of Cognitive Neuroscience, 22*, 2813–2822.

Parker, S., Garry, M., Engle, R. W., Harper, D. N., & Clifasefi, S. L. (2008). Psychotropic placebos reduce the misinformation effect by increasing monitoring at test. *Memory, 16*, 410–419.

Payne, J. D., Jackson, E. D., Hoscheidt, S., Ryan, L., Jacobs, W. J., & Nadel, L. (2007). Stress administered prior to encoding impairs neutral but enhances emotional long-term episodic memories. *Learning & Memory, 14*, 861–868.

Paz-Alonso, P. M., Ghetti, S., Donohue, S. E., Goodman, G. S., & Bunge, S. A. (2008). Neurodevelopmental correlates of true and false recognition. *Cerebral Cortex, 18*, 2208–2216.

Pezdek, K., & Lam, S. (2007). What research paradigms have cognitive psychologists used to study "false memory," and what are the implications of these choices? *Consciousness and Cognition, 16*, 2–17.

Pezdek, K., & Roe, C. (1995). The effect of memory trace strength on suggestibility. *Journal of Experimental Child Psychology, 60*, 116–128.

Phelps, E. A. (2006). Emotion and cognition: Insights from studies of the human amygdala. *Annual Review of Psychology, 57*, 27–53.

Phelps, E. A., & Sharot, T. (2008). How (and why) emotion enhances the subjective sense of recollection. *Current Directions in Psychological Science, 17*, 147–152.

Polusny, M. A., & Follette, V. M. (1996). Remembering childhood sexual abuse: A national survey of psychologists' clinical practices, beliefs, and personal experiences. *Professional Psychology: Research & Practice, 27*, 41–52.

Poole, D. A., Lindsay, D. S., Memon, A., & Bull, R. (1995). Psychotherapy and the recovery of memories of childhood sexual abuse: U.S. and British practitioners' opinions, practices, and experiences. *Journal of Consulting and Clinical Psychology, 63*, 426–437.

Porter, S., Birt, A. R., Yuille, J. C., & Lehman, D. R. (2000). Negotiating false memories: Interviewer and remember characteristics relate to memory distortion. *Psychological Science, 11*, 507–510.

Porter, S., Yuille, J. C., & Lehman, D. R. (1999). The nature of real, implanted, and fabricated memories for emotional childhood events: Implications for the recovered memory debate. *Law and Human Behavior, 23*, 517–537.

Puce, A., Allison, T., Gore, J. G., & McCarthy, G. (1995). Face-sensitive regions in human extrastriate cortex studied by functional MRI. *Journal of Neurophysiology, 74*, 1192–1199.

Qin, J., Mitchell, K. J., Johnson, M. K., Krystal, J. H., Southwick, S. M., Rasmusson, A. M., et al. (2003). Reactions to and memories for the September 11, 2001 terrorist attacks in adults with posttraumatic stress disorder. *Applied Cognitive Psychology, 17*, 1081–1097.

Ranganath, C. (2010). Binding items and contexts: The cognitive neuroscience of episodic memory. *Current Directions In Psychological Science, 19*, 131–137.

Ranganath, C., & Blumenfeld, R. S. (2008). Prefrontal cortex and memory. In J. Byrne (Series Ed.), & H. Eichenbaum (Vol. Ed.), *Learning and memory: A comprehensive reference: Vol. 3. Memory systems* (pp. 261–280). Oxford: Elsevier.

Ranganath, C., Cohen, M. X., & Brozinsky, C. J. (2005). Working memory maintenance contributes to long-term memory formation: Neural and behavioral evidence. *Journal of Cognitive Neuroscience, 17*, 994–1010.

Ranganath, C., & D'Esposito, M. (2001). Medial temporal lobe activity associated with active maintenance of novel information. *Neuron, 31*, 865–873.

Ranganath, C., Johnson, M. K., & D'Esposito, M. (2000). Left anterior prefrontal activation increases with demands to recall specific perceptual information. *The Journal of Neuroscience, 20*, RC108.

Ranganath, C., & Knight, R. T. (2003). Prefrontal cortex and episodic memory: Integrating findings from neuropsychology and event-related functional neuroimaging. In A. Parker, E. Wilding, & T. Bussey (Eds.), *The cognitive neuroscience of memory encoding and retrieval* (pp. 83–99). Philadelphia: Psychology Press.

Ranganath, C., Yonelinas, A. P., Cohen, M. X., Dy, C. J., Tom, S. M., & D'Esposito, M. (2004). Dissociable correlates of recollection and familiarity within the medial temporal lobes. *Neuropsychologia, 42*, 2–13.

Rasch, B., Spalek, K., Buholzer, S., Luechinger, R., Boesiger, P., Papassotiropoulos, A., et al. (2009). A genetic variation of the noradrenergic system is related to differential amygdala activation during encoding of emotional memories. *Proceedings of the National Academy of Sciences of the United States of America, 106*, 19191–19196.

Raye, C. L., Johnson, M. K., Mitchell, K. J., Nolde, S. F., & D'Esposito, M. (2000). fMRI investigations of left and right PFC contributions to episodic remembering. *Psychobiology, 28*, 197–206.

Raz, N., & Rodrigue, K. M. (2006). Differential aging of the brain: Patterns, cognitive correlates and modifiers. *Neuroscience and Biobehavioral Reviews, 30*, 730–748.

Roediger, H. L. III, & McDermott, K. B. (1995). Creating false memories: Remembering words that were not presented in lists. *Journal of Experimental Psychology. Learning, Memory, and Cognition, 21*, 803–814.

Rogers, T. T., Hocking, J., Noppeney, U., Mechelli, A., Gorno-Tempini, M. L., Patterson, K., et al. (2006). Anterior temporal cortex and semantic memory: Reconciling findings from neuropsychology and functional imaging. *Cognitive, Affective, & Behavioral Neuroscience, 6*, 201–213.

Schacter, D. L., Reiman, E., Curran, T., Yun, L. S., Bandy, D., McDermott, K. B., et al. (1996). Neuroanatomical correlates of veridical and illusory recognition memory: Evidence from positron emission tomography. *Neuron, 17*, 267–274.

Schacter, D. L., & Slotnick, S. D. (2004). The cognitive neuroscience of memory distortion. *Neuron, 44*, 149–160.

Schmolck, H., Buffalo, E. A., & Squire, L. R. (2000). Memory distortions develop over time: Recollections of the O.J. Simpson trial verdict after 15 and 32 months. *Psychological Science, 11*, 39–45.

Schnider, A. (2008). *The confabulating mind: How the brain creates reality*. New York: OxfordUniversity Press.

Schooler, J. W., Ambadar, Z., & Bendiksen, M. (1997). A cognitive corroborative case study approach for investigating discovered memories of sexual abuse. In D. S. Lindsay (Ed.), *Recollections of trauma: Scientific evidence and clinical practice* (pp. 379–387). New York: Plenum Press.

Schooler, J. W., Bendiksen, M., & Ambadar, Z. (1997). Taking the middle line: Can we accommodate both fabricated and recovered memories of sexual abuse? In M. A. Conway (Ed.), *Recovered memories and false memories* (pp. 251–292). New York: Oxford University Press.

Schooler, J. W., Gerhard, D., & Loftus, E. F. (1986). Qualities of the unreal. *Journal of Experimental Psychology. Learning, Memory, and Cognition, 12*, 171–181.

Shallice, T., & Burgess, P. W. (1991). Higher-order cognitive impairments and frontal lobe lesions in man. In H. S. Levin, H. M. Eisenberg, & A. L. Benton (Eds.), *Frontal lobe function and dysfunction* (pp. 125–138). New York: Oxford University Press.

Sharot, T., Delgado, M. R., & Phelps, E. A. (2004). How emotion enhances the feeling of remembering. *Nature Neuroscience, 7*, 1376–1380.

Sharot, T., Verfaellie, M., & Yonelinas, A. P. (2007). How emotion strengthens the recollective experience: A time-dependent hippocampal process. *PloS One, 2*, e1068. doi:10.1371/journal. pone.0001068.

Sharot, T., & Yonelinas, A. P. (2008). Differential time-dependent effects of emotion on recollective experience and memory for contextual information. *Cognition, 106*, 538–547.

Shimamura, A. P. (1995). Memory and the prefrontal cortex. In J. Grafman, K. J. Holyoak, & F. Boller (Eds.), Structure and function of the human prefrontal cortex. *Annals of the New York Academy of Sciences, 769*, 151–159.

Shimamura, A. P. (2000). Toward a cognitive neuroscience of metacognition. *Consciousness and Cognition, 9*, 313–323.

Shobe, K. K., & Schooler, J. W. (2001). Discovering fact and fiction: Case-based analyses of authentic and fabricated memories of abuse. In G. M. Davies & T. Dalgleish (Eds.), *Recovered memories: Seeking the middle ground* (pp. 95–151). Chichester, England: Wiley.

Simons, J. S., Henson, R. N. A., Gilbert, S. J., & Fletcher, P. C. (2008). Separable forms of reality monitoring supported by the anterior prefrontal cortex. *Journal of Cognitive Neuroscience, 20*, 447–457.

Simons, J. S., Peers, P. V., Mazuz, Y. S., Berryhill, M. E., & Olson, I. R. (2010). Dissociation between memory accuracy and memory confidence following bilateral parietal lesions. *Cerebral Cortex, 20*, 479–485.

Skinner, E. I., & Fernandes, M. A. (2007). Neural correlates of recollection and familiarity: A review of neuroimaging and patient data. *Neuropsychologia, 45*, 2163–2179.

Slotnick, S. D., & Schacter, D. L. (2004). A sensory signature that distinguishes true from false memories. *Nature Neuroscience, 7*, 664–672.

Smith, E. E., & Jonides, J. (1999). Storage and executive processes in the frontal lobes. *Science, 283*, 1657–1661.

Spencer, T. J., Montaldi, D., Gong, Q.-Y., Roberts, N., & Mayes, A. R. (2009). Object priming and recognition memory: Dissociable effects in left frontal cortex at encoding. *Neuropsychologia, 47*, 2942–2947.

Squire, L. R., & Knowlton, B. J. (2000). The medial temporal lobe, the hippocampus, and the memory systems of the brain. In M. Gazzaniga (Ed.), *The new cognitive neurosciences* (2nd ed., pp. 765–779). Cambridge, MA: MIT Press.

Squire, L. R., Stark, C. E. L., & Clark, R. E. (2004). The medial temporal lobe. *Annual Review of Neuroscience, 27*, 279–306.

Staresina, B. P., & Davachi, L. (2006). Differential encoding mechanisms for subsequent associative recognition and free recall. *The Journal of Neuroscience, 26*, 9162–9172.

Staresina, B. P., Gray, J. C., & Davachi, L. (2009). Event congruency enhances episodic memory encoding through semantic elaboration and relational binding. *Cerebral Cortex, 19*, 1198–1207.

Stuss, D. T., & Levine, B. (2002). Adult clinical neuropsychology: Lessons from studies of the frontal lobes. *Annual Review of Psychology, 53*, 401–433.

Suengas, A. G., & Johnson, M. K. (1988). Qualitative effects of rehearsal on memories for perceived and imagined complex events. *Journal of Experimental Psychology. General, 117*, 377–389.

Summerfield, C., Greene, M., Wager, T., Egner, T., Hirsch, J., & Mangels, J. (2006). Neocortical connectivity during episodic memory formation. *PLoS Biology, 4*, e128. doi:10.1371/journal. pbio.0040128.

Sutherland, R., & Hayne, H. (2001). The effect of postevent information on adults' eyewitness reports. *Applied Cognitive Psychology, 15*, 249–263.

Talarico, J. M., & Rubin, D. C. (2003). Confidence, not consistency, characterizes flashbulb memories. *Psychological Science, 14*, 455–461.

Thomas, A. K., Hannula, D. E., & Loftus, E. F. (2007). How self-relevant imagination affects memory for behavior. *Applied Cognitive Psychology, 21*, 69–86.

Thompson-Schill, S. L., D'Esposito, M., Aguirre, G. K., & Farah, M. J. (1997). Role of left inferior prefrontal cortex in retrieval of semantic knowledge: A reevaluation. *Proceedings of the National Academy of Sciences, USA, 94*, 14792–14797.

Todd, R. M., & Anderson, A. K. (2009). The neurogenetics of remembering emotions past. *Proceedings of the National Academy of Sciences of the United States of America, 106*, 18881–18882.

Tulving, E., & Schacter, D. L. (1990). Priming and human memory systems. *Science, 247*, 301–306.

Turner, M. S., Simons, J. S., Gilbert, S. J., Frith, C. D., & Burgess, P. W. (2008). Distinct roles for lateral and medial rostral prefrontal cortex in source monitoring of perceived and imagined events. *Neuropsychologia, 46*, 1442–1453.

Uncapher, M. R., Otten, L. J., & Rugg, M. D. (2006). Episodic encoding is more than the sum of its parts: An fMRI investigation of multifeatural contextual encoding. *Neuron, 52*, 547–556.

Uncapher, M. R., & Wagner, A. D. (2009). Posterior parietal cortex and episodic encoding: Insights from fMRI subsequent memory effects and dual attention theory. *Neurobiology of Learning & Memory, 91*, 139–154.

Underwood, B. J. (1965). False recognition produced by implicit verbal responses. *Journal of Experimental Psychology, 70*, 122–129.

Van Overwalle, F. (2009). Social cognition and the brain: A meta-analysis. *Human Brain Mapping, 30*, 829–858.

Van Petten, C. (2004). Relationship between hippocampal volume and memory ability in healthy individuals across the lifespan: Review and meta-analysis. *Neuropsychologia, 42*, 1394–1413.

van Stegeren, A. H. (2009). Imaging stress effects on memory: A review of neuroimaging studies. *Canadian Journal of Psychiatry, 54*, 16–27.

van Stegeren, A. H., Goekoop, R., Everaerd, W., Scheltens, P., Barkhof, F., Kuijer, J. P. A., et al. (2005). Noradrenaline mediates amygdala activation in men and women during encoding of emotional material. *NeuroImage, 24*, 898–909.

van Stegeren, A. H., Wolf, O. T., Everaerd, W., & Rombouts, S. A. R. B. (2008). Interaction of endogenous cortisol and noradrenaline in the human amygdala. In E. R. de Kloet, M. S. Oitzl, & E. Vermetten (Eds.), *Progress in Brain Research. Stress, hormones, and posttraumatic stress disorder: Basic studies and clinical perspectives. Vol. 167* (pp. 263–268). Oxford: Elsevier.

Verwoerd, J. R. L., Wessel, I., de Jong, P. J., & Nieuwenhuis, M. M. W. (2009). Preferential processing of visual trauma-film reminders predicts subsequent intrusive memories. *Cognition and Emotion, 23*, 1537–1551.

Vilberg, K. L., & Rugg, M. D. (2007). Dissociation of the neural correlates of recognition memory according to familiarity, recollection, and amount of recollected information. *Neuropsychologia, 45*, 2216–2225.

Vilberg, K. L., & Rugg, M. D. (2008). Memory retrieval and the parietal cortex: A review of evidence from a dual-process perspective. *Neuropsychologia, 46*, 1787–1799.

Vinogradov, S., Luks, T. L., Schulman, B. J., & Simpson, G. V. (2008). Deficit in a neural correlate of reality monitoring in schizophrenia patients. *Cerebral Cortex, 18*, 2532–2539.

Vinogradov, S., Luks, T. L., Simpson, G. V., Schulman, B. J., Glenn, S., & Wong, A. E. (2006). Brain activation patterns during memory of cognitive agency. *NeuroImage, 31*, 896–905.

Wade, K. A., Sharman, S. J., Garry, M., Memon, A., Mazzoni, G., Merckelbach, H., et al. (2007). False claims about false memory research. *Consciousness and Cognition, 16*, 18–28.

Wagner, A. D., Schacter, D. L., Rotte, M., Koutstaal, W., Maril, A., Dale, A. M., et al. (1998). Building memories: Remembering and forgetting of verbal experiences as predicted by brain activity. *Science, 281*, 1188–1191.

Wagner, A. D., Shannon, B. J., Kahn, I., & Buckner, R. L. (2005). Parietal lobe contributions to episodic memory retrieval. *Trends in Cognitive Sciences, 9*, 445–453.

Weinberger, D. R. (1988). Schizophrenia and the frontal lobe. *Trends in Neurosciences, 11*, 367–370.

Weis, S., Specht, K., Klaver, P., Tendolkar, I., Willmes, K., Ruhlmann, J., et al. (2004). Process dissociation between contextual retrieval and item recognition. *NeuroReport, 15*, 2729–2733.

Wheeler, M. E., & Buckner, R. L. (2004). Functional-anatomic correlates of remembering and knowing. *NeuroImage, 21*, 1337–1349.

Wheeler, M. E., Petersen, S. E., & Buckner, R. L. (2000). Memory's echo: Vivid remembering reactivates sensory-specific cortex. *Proceedings of the National Academy of Sciences of the United States of America, 97*, 11125–11129.

Williams, J. M. G., Barnhofer, T., Crane, C., Hermans, D., Raes, F., Watkins, E., et al. (2007). Autobiographical memory specificity and emotional disorder. *Psychological Bulletin, 133*, 122–148.

Zaragoza, M. S., Belli, R. S., & Payment, K. E. (2006). Misinformation effects and the suggestibility of eyewitness memory. In M. Garry & H. Hayne (Eds.), *Do justice and let the sky fall: Elizabeth F. Loftus and her contributions to science, law, and academic freedom* (pp. 35–63). Hillsdale, NJ: Lawrence Erlbaum Associates.

Zaragoza, M. S., & Koshmider, J. W., III. (1989). Misled subjects may know more that their performance implies. *Journal of Experimental Psychology. Learning, Memory, and Cognition, 15*, 246–255.

Towards a Cognitive and Neurobiological Model of Motivated Forgetting

Michael C. Anderson and Ean Huddleston

Abstract Historically, research on forgetting has been dominated by the assumption that forgetting is passive, reflecting decay, interference, and changes in context. This emphasis arises from the pervasive assumption that forgetting is a negative outcome. Here, we present a functional view of forgetting in which the fate of experience in memory is determined as much by motivational forces that dictate the focus of attention as it is by passive factors. A central tool of motivated forgetting is retrieval suppression, a process whereby people shut down episodic retrieval to control awareness. We review behavioral, neurobiological, and clinical research and show that retrieval suppression leads us to forget suppressed experiences. We discuss key questions necessary to address to develop this model, relationships to other forgetting phenomena, and the implications of this research for understanding recovered memories. This work provides a foundation for understanding how motivational forces influence what we remember of life experience.

Keywords Recovered memories • Retrieval-suppression • Motivated forgetting • Neuroimaging and memory control

Over the last century, experimental research on memory has focused on passive factors that make us forget. Emphasis has been given to hypotheses about simple changes that happen to people such as the passive decay of memory traces, the accumulation of similar interfering experiences in memory, and changes in environmental context. This emphasis fits most people's view forgetting as undesirable, and that anything that increases the chances of it occurring surely must not be purposeful. In contrast, one fundamental issue of this volume is whether some of the forgetting that human beings experience may not be accidental, but rather may be produced by the

M.C. Anderson (✉) • E. Huddleston
MRC Cognition and Brain Sciences Unit, University of Cambridge, England, UK
e-mail: michael.anderson@mrc-cbu.cam.ac.uk

R.F. Belli (ed.), *True and False Recovered Memories: Toward a Reconciliation of the Debate*, Nebraska Symposium on Motivation, DOI 10.1007/978-1-4614-1195-6_3, © Springer Science+Business Media, LLC 2012

desire to forget unpleasant events in life. More specifically, this volume is concerned with the forgetting and later recovery of memories of childhood abuse, and with explaining the nature of these experiences. Do such experiences reflect motivated forgetting? If so, how might this have been accomplished? These are some of the key questions that drive the *recovered memory debate*. In considering these questions, and the broader issue of motivation and memory, we present data relevant to a functional view of forgetting that diverges with the historical emphasis on passivity.

There can, of course, be little doubt that a motive to forget exists in all of us. People usually do not reminisce about unpleasant events, such as embarrassing incidents, quarrels, or physical discomfort. Some memories we would simply prefer to forget. Indeed, dwelling on major setbacks such as the death of a loved one, accidents, or significant personal failures can precipitate depression or anxiety. Such experiences are uninvited tenants in our memories, intruding into awareness when least expected, awakening our need to self-regulate. We are all are familiar with this process; an unwelcome reminder evokes a brief flash of experience and feeling, abruptly followed by efforts to evict the intruding memory from awareness and redirect our attention towards more pleasant thoughts. We do this to preserve our emotional state, to enhance our well-being, and to protect our sense of self; and sometimes, we do this simply to concentrate on what needs to be done in the present moment. These observations are so basic and universal as to be beyond dispute.

What people can disagree about, however, is whether limiting awareness of unwanted memories makes us forget them. On the one hand, people would be unhappy if they didn't have a way of forgetting the day-to-day unpleasantness of life. On this level motivated forgetting is obvious and adaptive. On the other hand, intuitions diverge about whether unusual and disturbing experiences can be forgotten. It is difficult for the average person to imagine how something like childhood sexual abuse could be forgotten; our instinct is *"if that happened to me, I'd remember it."* One is tempted to dismiss such reports as false, or perhaps not so much forgetting as denial of what one has always remembered. Yet, therapists claim to routinely observe forgetting on this scale. To many of them, motivated forgetting is an obvious fact of mental life. It is easier for them to believe that such forgetting is possible, because their experiences with patients are vivid and close to real circumstances; but the value of such cases has been challenged as scientific evidence, and this lies at the heart of the recovered memory debate. Are memories recovered in therapy genuine, or do they reflect suggestions by therapists, inclined to explain symptoms in terms of abuse? Clearly, progress on assessing the reality of recovered memories cannot rest solely on intuition or clinical observation.

In this article, we will consider how such experiences may emerge from motivational forces that shape retention, via mechanisms of cognitive control. In particular, we consider whether people's tendency to limit awareness of unwanted memories might cause forgetting, and whether laboratory science on this question can address the status of recovered memories. The ability to study motivated forgetting in the laboratory might seem limited by the assumption that it engages processes uniquely tied to trauma, and the consequent ethical difficulties of inducing trauma in controlled studies. In our research, we reject this tethering; instead, we assume that the processes underlying motivated forgetting are manifestations of broad cognitive control processes widely acknowledged to be crucial in the direction of action and thought. This assumption permits the decoupling of cognitive processes involved in motivated forgetting from trauma, enabling controlled study. We review the laboratory evidence on memory control via retrieval suppression, with an eye towards considering the mechanisms that might underlie some cases of recovered memories. We argue that although no linkage between retrieval suppression and recovered memories has been established (or sought), the mechanisms described here could potentially produce such experiences, under the right circumstances. We encourage further careful investigation of this issue.

An Observation and a Hypothesis

The current work originated from an invitation to discuss research on memory inhibition in relation to cases in which people reported recovering, often through therapy, long-forgotten memories of childhood sexual abuse. In the 1990s, such cases generated controversy, and a debate ensued in psychology about their origins and legitimacy. Early in this recovered memory debate, experimental psychologists primarily raised reasons to doubt the reality of the supposed memories underlying these recovered memory reports. This emphasis stemmed from a vivid appreciation of how fallible memory can be, and a reasonable suspicion about the dangers of overly suggestive therapeutic practices that might lead people to believe they had experienced something when they hadn't. Building on a strong body of research on suggestibility, experimental psychologists supported a skeptical stance to reports of recovered memories.

Though skepticism was clearly warranted, experimental psychology's response to this debate was initially one sided. The harm that suggestive therapy may cause to patients and their families needed to be mitigated, but neglecting the possibility that recovered memories might, in some cases, be real seems to go too far. If some fraction of cases is real, there is a hazard to past and future victims that must also be addressed. To consider this alternative, a conference was held entitled Trauma and Cognitive Science, one of the aims of which was to encourage cognitive psychologists to consider mechanisms that could produce authentic recovery experiences. The first author was invited to discuss his work on inhibitory control in memory in support of that aim. Might there be a motivated forgetting process underlying recovered memories that builds on general inhibition mechanisms that are of broad use in cognitive control?

The idea behind this possibility is straightforward. In our mental lives, we often need to suppress activity of responses or thoughts that interfere with our goals. For example, we often need to select one particular response from amongst a set of competitors vying for control over behavior. One solution to the problem of response selection is an inhibitory control process that de-activates the interfering response, rendering it non-interfering (see Anderson & Weaver, 2009 for a review). A similar inhibitory control process may be engaged during memory retrieval. Parallel issues of selection arise when we are recollecting personal experiences, and so selectively retrieving a desired memory may require inhibition of similar competing ones. For instance, recollecting where we parked today may require inhibition of similar parking events (where you parked yesterday) that interfere with retrieval. Consistent with this, the first author's earlier work on retrieval induced forgetting had shown that retrieving some items from memory impaired retention of related items (Anderson, Bjork, & Bjork, 1994). The impaired recall of competing memories appears to be produced, in part, by inhibitory control mechanisms that suppress distracting traces. The persisting effect of inhibition on competing memories renders them less accessible on later memory tests. Retrieval induced forgetting, initially observed with simple verbal materials (Anderson et al., 1994) has been generalized to a range of verbal and non-verbal materials (see Anderson, 2003; Levy & Anderson, 2002, for reviews), suggesting that inhibitory control may be an important general factor in producing unintended forgetting.

Although the inhibitory control hypothesis of forgetting was developed independently of the recovered memory debate, it is striking how much resemblance there is between the processes required to explain the laboratory data and the ones that could explain motivated forgetting. The inhibitory control hypothesis proposes a controllable process for suppressing distracting memories that renders them less accessible for a functional purpose. Although the initial framing of this functional purpose had focused on resolving interference during retrieval, inhibitory control might also be useful in suppressing memories that are unwanted because they are uncomfortable. Thus, simply broadening the scope of situations in which inhibitory control might be engaged led to a plausible mechanism for controlling unwanted memories. Indeed, this extension of inhibitory control naturally follows from the broader conceptualization of retrieval inhibition as an adaptive process (Bjork, 1989; see Benjamin, 2010 for reviews), and, in particular, from work on directed forgetting (Bjork, 1972; Bjork, Bjork, & Anderson, 1998; Geiselman, Bjork, & Fishman, 1983, Johnson, 1994; see Golding & MacLeod, 1998, for a historical review; see also later section entitled "Integration with Research on Directed Forgetting"). Could a person motivated to forget capitalize on retrieval-induced forgetting, and does any pattern of data in the clinical literature fit such a mechanism?

In considering this question, we came across an intriguing and counter-intuitive finding reported in Jennifer Freyd's (1996) book, *Betrayal Trauma Theory: The Logic of Forgetting Childhood Abuse*. Freyd argues that amnesia for sexual abuse may often reflect adaptive responses of a child who has been abused by a trusted caregiver. A child abused by a relative often has few options about how to respond. It thus may be in the child's best interests to forget the abuse if remembering it disrupts their ability to maintain attachment relationships with the caregiver. If so, one might expect to see more amnesia for abuse perpetrated by family members than for abuse by strangers, for whom no attachment relationships exist. This pattern has been observed. In a re-analysis of several data sets (Cameron, 1993; Feldman-Summers, & Pope, 1994; Williams, 1994), Freyd (1996) found greater rates of self-reported forgetting of childhood sexual abuse when the perpetrator was a family member. For instance, in Cameron's (1993) study, 72% of people abused by a parent reported a period of forgetting followed by recovery, whereas only 19% of those abused by a non-parent reported any period of forgetting. Similar patterns were observed in Feldman-Summers and Pope's data (53% versus 30% forgetting for those abused by a parent or stranger respectively). Increased subjective reports of forgetting for caregiver-related abuse has been subsequently reported in other studies (e.g., Freyd, DePrince, & Zurbriggen, 2006; Schultz, Passmore, & Yodor, 2003; see Freyd, DePrince, & Gleaves, 2007; DePrince et al., 2012, this volume, for reviews), although it has not been in observed samples in which abuse was likely to have been publicly disclosed in childhood (Goodman et al., 2003).

Taken at face value, these data are nothing less than astonishing. To appreciate why, one only needs to consider asking the average person who would be more likely to forget a particular past experience: someone who lived with reminders to that experience on a daily basis, or someone who was able to escape reminders for many years. Nearly everyone would say that the person who lived with reminders would have exceptional memory for the event, unavoidably so, because of the constant reminding. Yet, people abused by a family member are in precisely this situation – they must live with the abuser for years. Despite being in the presence of constant reminders of abuse, people abused by a family member are far more likely to report having had a period of forgetting, followed by recovery. Of course, people's retrospective claims about whether they forgot these memories might be doubted, and it is prudent to take these self-reports with a measure of skepticism (see, e.g., McNally, 2007 for arguments). Nevertheless, if this pattern truly reflects people's memory, it cries out for explanation, because it would seem to defy common sense and the established benefits of reminders. How could this be?

Upon reflection, we realized that understanding this counter-intuitive finding may lie in motivation. It seems uncontroversial to assume that the victim would be motivated to keep the abuse out of mind, regardless of who the perpetrator is. Importantly, however, the person abused at the hands of a family member faces a far greater and more consistent challenge in achieving this goal precisely because reminders to it would be inescapable, perhaps for many years. Keeping the abuse out of mind despite constantly confronting reminders requires a way to stop the reminder from eliciting the trace, and a way to retrain memory to elicit other thoughts upon seeing the abuser. Basically, if one cannot escape reminders, one must adapt one's internal landscape. We proposed that this was accomplished by retrieving diversionary thoughts unrelated to the abuse when the abuser is present, which we called the *selective retrieval hypothesis* (Anderson, 2001; see also, Bjork et al., 1998). If Freyd is correct, this motivated selective retrieval of non-abuse information would be especially likely in the case of parental abuse. The child would have powerful motives for not thinking of the abuse: if they are to sustain a necessary attachment relationship with the parent, the abuse cannot be on their minds, as it would undermine the ability to behave and feel appropriately. Thus, when motives to control awareness are present, constant reminders actually set the occasion for the engagement of processes that limit awareness of the memory, impairing retention.

Identifying inescapable reminders as a key trigger for inhibition raised the more general issue of how and whether people can stop the retrieval process at all. Perhaps retrieving alternative memories was only one way of engaging an inhibition process whose primary function was to shut down retrieval. By this view, one might be able, when confronted with a reminder, to stop or suppress retrieval directly without retrieving diversionary thoughts. Virtually no research had been done on this issue. So, motivated by this intriguing pattern we decided to study retrieval stopping as the elemental process that may underlie memory control, and that may be the foundational response to confronting inescapable retrieval cues. This led us to focus on developing a functional model of motivated forgetting based on controlled experiments on retrieval stopping.

A Functional Model of Motivated Forgetting

After an unpleasant experience, unwanted memories of the event tend to intrude into awareness. Indeed intrusive memories seem to leap to mind in response to reminders, despite attempts to avoid those memories. This reminding has a reflexive quality similar to habitual actions, and like habitual actions, we often try to stop them. Consider an example of motor stopping. One evening, the first author accidentally knocked a potted plant off his window sill. As his hand darted to catch it, he realized that the plant was a cactus. Mere centimeters from it, he stopped himself from catching the cactus. The plant fell and was ruined, but he was relieved to not be pierced with little needles. This example illustrates the clear need to have the ability to override a strong reflexive response, which is a basic function of cognitive control. Without the capacity to override prepotent responses, we could not adapt behavior to changes in our goals or circumstances. We would be slaves to habit and reflex.

Like automatic actions, people often attempt to stop the retrieval process. In the framework that guides the current work, we have proposed that this functional similarity between memory and motor stopping is important and provides a theoretical basis for understanding memory control. Under this view, retrieval and motor stopping constitute special cases of the broader ability to override prepotent responses, and the mechanisms underlying the two are similar, if not the same (Fig. 1). Because retrieval stopping is an elemental process underlying motivated forgetting, this view

-->

Fig. 1 (continued) instead be made (e.g., S–R compatibility and antisaccade tasks). As shown in (**d**), if no alternative response is warranted, the movement can simply be canceled (e.g., go/no-go, stop-signal, and countermanding saccade tasks). As shown in (**e**), sometimes inhibition must be initiated to selectively retrieve a memory with a weaker association to a cue that is shared by another trace (e.g., retrieving today's parking spot and suffering interference from the memory of yesterday's; RIF). In other circumstances (**f**), confronting a cue may activate an unwanted memory, leading the person to stop retrieval. For instance, when the sight of a picture of a person initiates retrieval of an unpleasant memory, retrieval might be stopped. This process can be assayed by TNT tasks. RIF, retrieval-induced forgetting; S–R, stimulus– response; TNT, think/no-think (Reprinted with permission from Anderson & Weaver, 2009, copyright © 2009 Elsevier Ltd.)

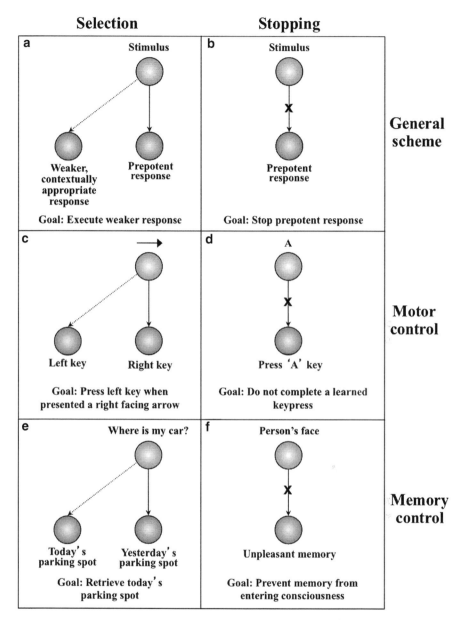

Fig. 1 Two situations that require response override in human action and thought (selection and stopping) and commonly used paradigms. The top row represents a schematization of these two situations. In each instance, a stimulus is associated with one or more responses, such that when the stimulus appears, the responses become active in proportion to their associative connection to the cue (represented by thickness of the line). In selection (**a**), the weaker response must be made, despite the existence of a strong competitor that becomes more active and threatens to capture control of behavior. In stopping (**b**), there is only one response, but it must be prevented. As shown in (**c**), sometimes the prepotent action is not the correct response, and a nondominant movement must

situates theorizing about this phenomenon squarely in the realm of cognitive control, one of the most widely studied areas in cognitive neuroscience. Indeed, one of most broadly accepted functions of cognitive control is to override automatic responses to stimuli when they are inappropriate (Luria, 1966; MacDonald, Cohen, Stenger, & Carter, 2000; Norman & Shallice, 1986). Within this framework then, research on retrieval stopping can be informed by cognitive and neurobiological research on how humans and non-human primates override reflexive, prepotent actions.

But how do humans and other organisms keep from being controlled by habitual actions? One widely discussed possibility is that we inhibit undesired actions to stop them. The function of this hypothetical inhibition process is much like the role of inhibition in response selection discussed previously, serving to limit activation of an undesired response. By this view, when we encounter a stimulus, "activation" spreads from that cue to possible responses. Activation can be thought of as the amount of "energy" a response has, influencing its accessibility; a response will be emitted once it is sufficiently activated. If one wishes to override the response, one may engage inhibitory control, a subtractive mechanism that reduces the response's activation. If motor actions are stopped in this manner, perhaps we control unwanted memories in a similar way. Like actions, memories can be triggered by activation spreading from reminders that we encounter. Might inhibition be recruited to stop retrieval, allowing us to avoid catching our "mental cacti"? If so, how would we study this question?

Stopping Retrieval: Basic Behavioral Findings

To study how people stop retrieval, Anderson and Green (2001) developed a procedure modeled after the widely used go/no-go task, a paradigm designed to investigate motor stopping. In a typical go/no-go task, people press a button as quickly as possible whenever they see a letter appear on a computer screen, *except* when the letter is an X, for which they are to withhold their response. Their ability to withhold the response measures inhibitory control over action (e.g., how well a person avoids catching the cactus). To see whether stopping retrieval also engages inhibitory control, Anderson and Green (2001) adapted this task to create an analogous procedure for studying memory control called the *think/no-think paradigm*.

The situation faced by participants in the think/no-think paradigm mimics situations in which we stumble upon a reminder to a memory that we prefer not to think about, and try to keep it out of mind. Participants study cue-target pairs (e.g., ordeal – roach), and are trained to recall the second word (roach) whenever they encounter the first word as a reminder (ordeal). Participants are then asked to exert control over retrieval during the think/no-think phase (Fig. 2). Most trials require them to recall the response whenever they see the reminder (hereinafter referred to as "Respond Trials" or sometimes "Think Trials"), but for certain reminders, participants are admonished to avoid retrieving the response (hereinafter referred to as "Suppress Trials" or sometimes, "No-Think Trials"). It is emphasized that it is

Think/No-Think Paradigm

| | Study/Training | Think/No-Think Phase | Test Phase | |
			Same Probe	Independent Probe
Suppression	Ordeal-Roach	Ordeal	Ordeal	Insect r___
Respond	Steam-Train	Steam	Steam	Vehicle t___
Baseline	Jaw-Gum	▲⋯⋯⋯⋯⋯▲ *Scanning*	Jaw	Candy g___

Fig. 2 Depiction of the think/no-think procedure. In the training phase participants study numerous word pairs, so that when they are presented with the left hand word they are able to recall the right hand word. Next, in the Think/No-Think (TNT) phase, for some left hand words (Ordeal), participants' task is to recall and think about the right hand word. However, for other left hand words (Steam), participants' task is to prevent the right hand word from coming to mind at all. A final group of word pairs act as baseline pairs, with no reminders being presented during the TNT phase. During the final test phase, participants' memory for the right hand words is tested in two ways. In the Same Probe test, the original left hand word is presented, and participants must recall the associated right hand word. In the Independent Probe test, a novel category cue is presented along with a letter stem, and participants must recall the studied word that is a member of that category that begins with the designated letter. (From Anderson et al., 2004, reprinted with permission from AAAS)

insufficient to avoid *saying* the response – they must prevent the memory from entering awareness altogether. Thus, to achieve this task, participants have to stop the cognitive act of retrieval. Can people recruit inhibitory control to prevent the memory from intruding into consciousness?

Since awareness cannot be observed, it is difficult to know whether a person truly prevents a memory from entering consciousness. Instead, the think/no-think procedure measures the aftereffects of stopping retrieval, based on the idea that inhibition of the unwanted memory might linger, making these memories harder to recall. To assess this behavioral footprint of suppression, a final test is given in which participants again see each reminder and are asked to recall every response they learned earlier. The percentage of originally studied items that are correctly recalled on this final test is computed separately for each condition. If stopping retrieval engages inhibitory control processes, we should find poorer recall of Suppress items on a later test. If so, it would suggest that people's common tendency to suppress awareness of unwanted memories in response to reminders may in fact have measurable aftereffects on the later retention of the suppressed trace, consistent with the existence of a motivated forgetting process.

Research using the Think/No-Think procedure documents a number of central facts about the effects of suppressing retrieval. Figure 3 illustrates these keys facts. Figure 3 (left) reports the results of a combined analysis of studies conducted in our own laboratory, irrespective of whether they were published or unpublished, and was first reported in Anderson and Levy (2006). Figure 3 (right) illustrates all data published to date, irrespective of laboratory, aggregating over 47 experiments from 32 articles (see Appendix A for listing), with 1669 participants measured in on the Same Probe test and 800 participants measured on the Independent Probe test (to be described in next section). These analyses are restricted to neurologically

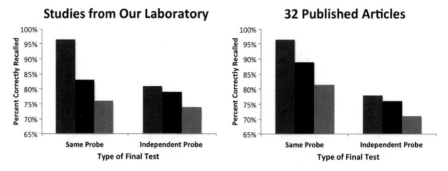

Fig. 3 Left panel: a meta-analysis of published and unpublished TNT studies run in our laboratory over multiple years. Right panel: data from 32 published articles for which full TNT data was reported on recall tests. For both panels, data are shown for the respond, baseline, and suppress conditions (in that order) for both the same probe and independent probe tests, when available. Only 180 participants overlap between the two analyses, with a total of 2,174 participants given the Same Probe test, and 1,305 participants given the Independent Probe test across the panels. Both data sets are restricted to neurologically and psychiatrically normal young adults. Data from the "Respond" and "Suppress" conditions were taken from the highest level of repetition used in a given study (most studies used 12 and 16 as maximum repetition values for Respond or Suppress trials). Four additional studies were not included in the right panel because (**a**) they lacked any behavioral data and focused only on imaging (Butler & James, 2010), (**b**) used an indirect memory test (Kim & Yi, 2008), or (**c**) did not report data from all relevant conditions (Depue et al., 2006; Marx et al., 2009). For the 32 included studies, a weighted average across experiments was constructed for each condition, depending on sample size. Appendix A contains a full listing of all studies, with sample size, and all populations studied, including other specialized samples (e.g., depressed patients, ADHD) not included in the figure

and psychiatrically normal young adult participants and represent (combined over left and right panels) the data from 2,174 participants from one dozen countries (only 180 participants overlap between the two panels). This extremely large sample conveys several broad generalizations about the aftereffects of suppressing retrieval on unwanted memories. First, after retrieval suppression, "Suppress" items are recalled significantly less often than are "Respond" items (Fig. 3). This large difference (22% vs 15% in the two panels), known as the *total control effect*, demonstrates vividly how one's disposition towards reminders of an experience may modulate its later retention. When one is favorably disposed towards a memory, a reminder may trigger retrieval that enhances later retention. In contrast, when one is motivated to exclude a memory from awareness, the normal benefits of retrieval are dramatically reduced, indicating a high level of control over the effects of reminders on memory.

Although the total control effect demonstrates the intentional control of memory, it does not address how it is produced. For example, one cannot tell whether the total control effect reflects the benefits of positive attention to the retrieved trace, the detrimental effects of suppressing the unwanted memory, or both. It is possible, for example, that stopping retrieval does no harm to a memory, but merely stops the retrieval process from unfolding, thereby preventing the benefits of reminders on memory.

Such a dynamic would still constitute an interesting an important determinant of which traces ultimately survive in memory because rehearsal and reactivation are key factors thought to enhance longevity of our experiences (Allen, Mahler, & Estes, 1969; Bjork, 1975; Carrier & Pashler, 1992; Karpicke & Roediger, 2008; Landauer & Bjork, 1978). Indeed, some have built the case that selective prevention of retrieval, by itself, is a key process of motivated forgetting (Erdelyi, 1996). Nevertheless, it is of interest to determine the separate positive and negative components to the effect, and, particularly, whether retrieval suppression has detrimental effects on the retention of unwanted memories.

To address these issues, the Think/No-Think paradigm includes a third set of pairs that are also studied initially, but that do not appear during the think/no-think phase. These pairs provide an estimate of how well participants would recall pairs given that they have neither retrieved nor suppressed memory for them in the intervening Think/No-Think phase and because they are studied and tested at the same time as Respond and Suppress pairs, they control for forgetting due to the passage of time. They thus provide a baseline condition (hereinafter referred to as "Baseline Items") for measuring both potential *positive control effects,* and *negative control effects.* A positive control effect would reflect enhanced memory for "Respond" items above that of Baseline items, and would confirm the expectation that reminders enhance later retention when people are inclined to remember. A negative control effect would reflect impaired memory for "Suppress" items below that of Baseline items arising from people's effort to stop retrieval. As Fig. 3 illustrates, both positive and negative control effects contribute to the total control effect. When considering the Same Probe data (i.e., when participants are cued on the final test with the same cue used to study the item), the average negative control effect is around 8% (range from 7% facilitation to 26% impairment across experiments), and the average positive control effect of 9–14%. These two analyses make an extremely clear and consistent point: when people are motivated to avoid being reminded of an unwanted memory, reminders do not merely fail to enhance memory, they actually trigger processes that impair retention of the suppressed memory.

The *negative control effect* is striking and counterintuitive, particularly when one considers that reminders to the suppressed items are directly confronted by subjects up to 16 times per item during the Think/No-Think phase (compared to Baseline items, which receive no reminders). Thus, the negative control effect turns our expectation about the effect of reminders on its head and powerfully illustrates the effects of motivation on memory. Importantly, the *negative control effect* occurs even when people are paid a reward for each item they remember, making it extremely unlikely that people are simply withholding responses on the final test. The negative control effect is even observed when people are led falsely to believe (just prior to the final memory test) that we, as experimenters, hope to see improved memory for suppressed items, showing that the effect does not reflect subjects withholding items simply to conform to perceived expectations (Anderson & Green, 2001). In contrast, asking people to merely avoid *saying* the response, instead of avoiding thinking about it, eliminates the *negative control effect,* isolating control over consciousness as the critical factor causing forgetting (Anderson & Green, 2001).

These findings establish a clear laboratory model through which one can study retrieval suppression. Understanding the mechanisms underlying retrieval suppression through this model task allows us to develop a theory of a core process involved in motivated forgetting, integrating this otherwise controversial process with fundamental and widely accepted mechanisms for controlling behavior. This theoretical framework may help us to understand when this type of forgetting will occur in clinical settings. Next we consider how this model task has been used to document core characteristics of the negative control effect that speak to the mechanisms that underlie it.

Characteristics of the Negative Control Effect

Although the negative control effect reveals a surprising level of control over memory retrieval, it could be produced in a number of ways. Since originally reported, however, a great deal has been learned about the characteristics of negative control effects, and what causes them, and also population differences in memory control. Here we discuss those characteristics and individual differences. Collectively, these findings support the view that the memory deficit is produced in part by an inhibitory control process acting on the unwanted memory, degrading its later retention. However, other processes are also likely to contribute, depending on how people approach the task of controlling awareness.

Cue-Independence

One characteristic that favors a role of inhibitory control in producing the negative control effect is the tendency for the forgetting to generalize to novel test cues. So, for example, if a participant had studied a pair such as "Ordeal-Roach," and then had suppressed "Roach" whenever they were cued with "Ordeal," later recall of "Roach" is impaired both when it is tested with Ordeal (i.e., Same Probe test), and a novel test cue such as Insect R – (i.e., Independent Probe test). This property, known as cue-independence, previously demonstrated in the context of retrieval-induced forgetting (Anderson & Spellman, 1995, see Anderson, 2003 for a review), has been observed in a number of studies of retrieval suppression (Anderson & Green, 2001; Anderson et al., 2004; Anderson, Reinholz, Kuhl, & Mayr, 2011; Bergström, de Fockert, & Richardson-Klavehn, 2009; Lambert, Good, & Kirk, 2010; Murray, Muscatel, & Kensinger, 2011; Paz-Alonso, Ghetti, Matlen, Anderson, & Bunge, 2009; Tomlinson, Huber, Rieth, & Davelaar, 2009; Tramoni et al., 2009). Figure 3a, b document the general pattern observed on independent probe tests within our lab (N = 687), and averaged across 800 participants in all published studies. The negative control effect for independent probes occurs in both these data sets, despite the fact that the cues provided are unrelated to those used to suppress the response initially. The median independent probe effect across these 1,305

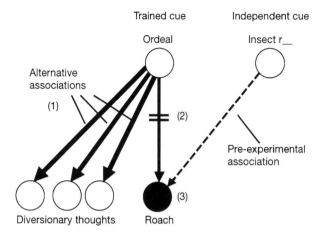

Fig. 4 Three mechanisms that can explain impaired recall in the same-probe condition, illustrated with a stimulus pair. Associative interference posits that suppression training leads subjects to generate diversionary thoughts (1) to the trained cue that interfere during later attempts to recall the target. Unlearning assumes that suppression training weakens the cue-target connection (2). The suppression hypothesis states that suppression training inhibits the target (3). Note that testing the target with an independent cue circumvents interference (1) and unlearning (2). Any impairment found with this test is likely to be localized to the target, consistent with inhibition (Reprinted with permission from Anderson & Green, 2001, copyright © 2001 Macmillan Publishers Ltd.)

participants (across both panels) is about 6%, slightly smaller than the typical effect observed for the Same Probe test (8%). The total control effect, by contrast is noticeably smaller on independent probe tests, primarily due to the fact that positive control effects largely disappear on such tests, suggesting that facilitation of retrieved items is largely cue-dependent.

Cue-independence is a theoretically important feature of the negative control effect because it suggests that retrieval suppression alters the accessibility of the unwanted memory in a general way, consistent with inhibition. If an inhibitory control mechanism had truly suppressed the unwanted memory, reduced activation of the excluded trace may produce aftereffects irrespective of whether that trace was tested with the same cue used to induce suppression or a different one, as we observed. This pattern suggests that other accounts of the negative control effect in terms of associative interference are not sufficient. For example, one might have imagined that participants, in response to the reminder "Ordeal," might have generated alternative, diversionary thoughts in response to it to distract themselves (Fig. 4). If so, perhaps they have difficulty recalling "Roach" because "Ordeal" now instead reminds them of their distracting thoughts – a form of interference. Although this process may contribute to the effect when measured with the original cue (Ordeal), it seems unlikely to contribute on tests using a novel cue like Insect R___. The fact that impairment generalizes to such cues suggests that inhibition contributes to the negative control effect (see, however, Tomlinson et al., 2009, for alternative view).

Although the cue-independence property has been replicated many times, there have also been clear cut cases in which this effect has not be found, even when the negative control effect is found with the original cue (Ordeal). This suggests that the negative control effect on the Same Probe test may be driven by several mechanisms, some of which are non-inhibitory in nature. Although it is not yet clear what factors dictate when the effect will be inhibitory, one likely contributor appears to be the strategy that people adopt to control their memories, a topic to which we will return shortly. But the clear existence of cue independence in the general case over an exceptionally large sample (Fig. 3) suggests that a control mechanism exists that renders an unwanted memory less accessible through its inhibition.

Thought Substitutes Increase the Effect

In most studies using the Think/No-Think paradigm, participants receive no instructions as to how they should prevent retrieval of the unwanted memory. When we developed the procedure, we did not wish to presuppose that one strategy might be better than others, and wanted to allow participants to develop their own natural solutions to memory control. When no instructions are given, however the approach to the task can vary. Indeed, in a recent article (Levy & Anderson, 2008), we documented many solutions (and their frequency in a large sample) that people use to avoid the unwanted memory, including perceptual analysis or phonological rehearsal of the cue, "mind blanking" and, of course, the generation of distracting words, thoughts, and memories related to the cue. In general, we have not observed correlations of these strategies with the negative control effect.

Other investigators, however, have argued that thought substitution is a superior method for forgetting unwanted memories, and have experimentally manipulated this behavior. In an early study, Hertel and Calcaterra (2005) gave participants alternative words to associate to the Suppress cues, and asked them to retrieve these "thought substitutes" as a way of preventing the unwanted memory from coming to mind whenever it's respective Suppress cue word appeared. They found a significantly larger negative control effect with thought substitutes (15%) compared to an Unaided group, who received conventional Suppress instructions without substitutes (0%), though the latter group was contaminated with non-compliant subjects who didn't obey the Suppress instructions (Hertel & Calcaterra, 2005). Moreover, in the Unaided group, the negative control effect was significantly larger for participants who reported distracting themselves with alternative thoughts (12%) compared to participants who reported not doing this (12% facilitation) (see also Hotta & Kawaguchi, 2009). Hertel and colleagues have reported robust negative control effects with thought substitutes (Hertel & McDaniel, 2010; Joormann, Hertel, Lemoult, & Gotlib, 2009; LeMoult, Hertel, & Joorman, 2010). Although thought substitutes do not always produce larger negative control effects than in the unaided group (Hertel & McDaniel, 2010), the tendency, in our combined analysis (Fig. 3, right) was for thought substitutes to produce larger effects on average (13%, N=262) than are produced in an uninstructed condition (7%, N=1407) on Same Probe tests. Indeed, thought substitution has, on some occasions produced impressively large effects (e.g., 30%; Joormann et al., 2009).

Research on thought substitution demonstrates that learning to retrieve alternative diversionary thoughts in response to a reminder can be an effective way to hasten the forgetting of an unwanted memory. This finding fits well with the selective retrieval hypothesis (Anderson, 2001) of the enhanced forgetting of parental abuse described at the outset. According to that hypothesis, victims of abuse who are faced with inescapable reminders to an unwanted memory are forced into a situation of retraining their memory's response to the reminder, by selectively retrieving alternative thoughts and memories about the abuser. Hertel's work clearly models these conditions, inasmuch as the instruction to not think of the unwanted memory provides the motive, and the thought substitute, the target for selective retrieval. It remains to be seen whether thought substitution could be used to enhance forgetting of complex, realistic experiences.

One might take research on thought substitution as evidence that the negative control effect is caused exclusively by thought substitution, and, moreover, that this process may simply reflect associative interference. This possibility might seem to be supported by Hertel and Calcaterra's finding that only those Unaided subjects who reported using self-distraction as a strategy showed negative control effects. Although it is clear that thought substitutes can cause a negative control effect, a number of considerations indicate that these conclusions are premature. First, Hertel and colleagues' never studied the effects of strategies other than thought substitution, but rather focused on comparisons with an Unaided group. As such, we cannot tell whether the advantage of thought substitution in their studies and in our meta-analysis reflects something special about this strategy that enhances forgetting, or, instead, whether encouraging the consistent use of any strategy improves the effect. It seems likely that participants in the Unaided group took some time to refine their strategy over blocks in the TNT phase, and this variability may contribute to smaller effects. Second, the larger negative control effects for Hertel's Unaided subjects who used self-distraction are substantially driven by the non-compliant subjects in their study (i.e., subjects who deliberately did not follow Suppress instructions; see later section entitled *The Negative Control Effect Sometimes Does Not Occur* for a discussion), who obviously would not have used self-distraction. Finally, even if thought substitution induces a negative control effect, this by no means implies that the effect is driven by associative interference, but rather could reflect inhibitory processes associated with retrieval-induced forgetting. Indeed, prior work on retrieval-induced forgetting has established that the mere effort to retrieve a target, even if not successful, can induce inhibition of competing items, suggesting that one should not presume that thought substitution effects are driven by interference (Storm, Bjork, Bjork, & Nestojko, 2006; see Storm, 2010 for a review). Evaluation of these possibilities would require the examination of strategies other than thought substitution.

Direct Suppression can Induce Negative Control Effects

Although thought substitution instructions appear sufficient to induce negative control effects, it is unclear from Hertel's research whether they are necessary. In a particularly informative example of this point, Bergstrom et al. (2009) contrasted the effects of thought substitution and direct suppression on the negative control effect. In their thought substitution condition participants were asked to prevent retrieval of the Suppress items by generating their own thought substitutes in response to the cue words during the think/no-think phase. In the direct suppression condition, by contrast, participants were instructed NOT to distract themselves with thought substitutes, but rather to focus on the cue and actively block out the unwanted associate if it happened to come to mind. If thought substitution is necessary to produce negative control effects, one should find memory impairment only in the thought substitution group. If an inhibitory control process contributes to the suppression of unwanted memories, however, negative control effects might be observed in both groups.

The results of this study, illustrated in Fig. 5, are striking and informative. Participants who generated thought substitutes in response to the cue words showed significant negative control effects, as one might expect from prior research. More interestingly, however, the direct suppression group showed these effects as well, and to no less an extent than subjects using thought substitution. Moreover, unlike participants who were instructed to generate thought substitutes, subjects who engaged in direct suppression showed negative control effects that generalized to independent probe test cues. Thus, direct suppression yielded cue-independent forgetting, whereas thought substitution did not. To the extent that cue-independence can be taken as a marker for the inhibitory control, these data suggest that instructions to directly expel a memory from awareness are implemented by an inhibitory process that suppresses the unwanted trace.

One might wonder whether Bergstrom et al.'s findings are truly caused by a direct suppression process or, instead, might reflect the generation of thought substitutes that went unmonitored by the experimenters. Two aspects of their data argue against this interpretation. First, the direct suppression group showed a qualitatively distinct pattern of forgetting, with generalization to independent cues, not experienced by subjects who were directly instructed to generate thought substitutes. If uncontrolled thought substitution underpinned this effect, one would not expect this functional dissociation. Second, Bergstrom et al. showed that direct suppression and thought substitution were dissociable electrophysiologically. As will be discussed in more detail later, direct suppression, but not thought substitution modulated the parietal Episodic Memory effect, which a large body of research has established as a reliable marker of recollection (Friedman & Johnson, 2000). Thus, direct suppression yielded little evidence of retrieval-related activity, whereas thought substitution did. Similar electrophysiological and behavioral effects of direct suppression have been found by others (Hanslmayr, Leipold, Pastötter, & Bäuml, 2009; Hanslmayr, Leipold, & Bauml, 2010).

Taken together, these findings indicate that direct suppression is sufficient to induce negative control effects, and may be accomplished in a qualitatively different

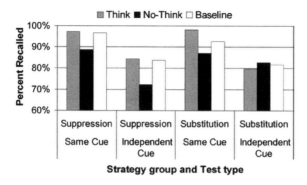

Fig. 5 Final recall data for the same-probe ("same-cue") and independent-probe ("independent-cue") tests, from Bergstrom et al., 2009. Both groups showed a significant Suppress impairment compared to baseline on the same-cue test, but only direct memory suppression impaired Suppress recall compared to baseline on the independent-cue test (Reprinted with permission, copyright © 2009 Elsevier)

way than thought substitution. Across the 96 participants (3 papers) in which this procedure has been used, the negative control effect averages around 9% slightly less than the effect observed for thought substitution, but an improvement over providing no specific instructions. Given the clear evidence that direct suppression induces cue-independent forgetting, these data provide strong indication that inhibitory control processes are involved in helping to expel unwanted memories from awareness. Importantly, these processes do not require retrieval of thought substitutes to be engaged.

Advance Warning Enlarges the Effect

Several studies by Hanslmayr and colleagues have shown that negative control effects increase when participants are given advance warning that an upcoming trial will require them to suppress retrieval, at least with direct suppression instructions. For example, Hanslmayr et al. (2010) asked participants to learn face-word associations and then perform the Think/No-Think task. In the preparation group, each Respond and Suppress trial was preceded by a 1-second task cross that was either colored red (Suppress) or green (Respond) to warn participants of the nature of the upcoming trial. The no-preparation group received no advance warnings. Hanslmayr et. al. found a 17% negative control effect in the prepared group, compared to a 3% effect in the unprepared group. In a related study that will be discussed more later, Hanslmayr et al. (2009) found that when participants receive a warning cue about an upcoming Suppress trial, electrophysiological markers of episodic retrieval mode in right prefrontal cortex (Duzel et al., 1999) are significantly reduced in preparation for the upcoming trial, and that the extent of this reduction predicts later negative control effects on the final test.

Effects of advance warning on memory suppression suggest that people can pre-engage the neural machinery necessary to directly suppress the retrieval process, thereby enhancing the efficacy of memory control. One can imagine how knowing in advance that one is likely to confront unwelcome reminders might help one to "steel" oneself against the unpleasant effects of those reminders. Thus, environments in which the appearance of these reminders is predictable and unavoidable might be expected to lead to larger negative control effects than environments where reminders are less predictable.

Negative Control Effects Build with Repetition

Many studies have found that the size of the negative control effect increases with the number of times people attempt to suppress retrieval. For instance, averaged over the three studies (n = 96) in Anderson and Green (2001), participants recalled 87%, 85%, 83% and 80% of the items after 0, 1, 8, and 16 suppression attempts. More recently, Anderson, Reinholz, Kuhl, and Mayr (2011) found 84%, 81%, 79%, and 76% across the same levels of repetition for younger adults. Similar parametric functions have been found by others (Joormann et al., 2009; Kim, Yi, Yang, & Lee, 2007; Hanslmayr, Leipold, & Bauml, 2010 ; Joormann, Hertel, Brozovich, & Gotlib, 2005; Lambert et al., 2010; Lee, Lee, & Tsai, 2007). Similar patterns are found on the Same and the Independent Probe tests (Fig. 6), and improvements with practice have been observed with thought substitution, direct suppression and without any particular suppression instructions.

Although negative control effects generally build with repetition, the functions that relate repetitions to the size of the effect are not well characterized, and there also appears to be variability in the patterns. For example, some studies have observed very gradual build-ups of impairment with repetition such as the ones mentioned above; others have found sizeable negative control effects after just a few repetitions, with very modest increases in the effect after a much larger number (e.g., 21% after 2 repetitions, 22% after 12 for Depressed subjects in Joormann et al., 2009). And sometimes, even when there is a gradual build-up, there is noise in the function, with unexpected increases in recall with larger numbers of repetitions, followed by decreases (e.g., 83%, 78%, 84%, and 74% after 0, 1, 8, and 16 repetitions respectively, in Anderson et al. 2011). In general, however, when one considers a larger sample, the function increases monotonically with repetition for young healthy adults, suggesting increasing efficacy with repetition.

The reasons for these variations have not yet been established, but two possibilities seem likely. First, many of the studies that show large early effects followed by minimal increases in the effect appear to be ones in which thought substitutes are provided by experimenters before the TNT phase has begun. Perhaps the large effect after a few repetitions represents the contributions of having just studied the thought substitutes, and the tendency for them to be mistakenly provided on the final test when the original cue is given. This explanation fits with the fact that such unusual functions are usually observed on Same Probe tests and not Independent Probe tests,

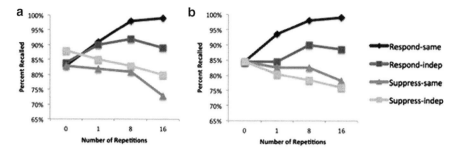

Fig. 6 Final recall for respond and suppression items as a function of the number of repetitions for the Same-probe and Independent-probe tests. (**a**), Anderson & Green, 2001 (Adapted by permission, copyright © 2001 Macmillan Publishers Ltd.); (**b**), Anderson et al., 2011. Note that negative control effects increases monotonically with repetitions on both the Same Probe and Independent Probe tests

which are highly constrained in the answers they allow. A second source of variability may be the overall duration of the Think/No-Think phase itself, and the contributions of fatigue. Because suppressing retrieval requires cognitive control, and because the Think/No-Think phase itself can last 25–40 min, subjects' efforts at retrieval suppression surely wane as blocks progress. If participants lapse at suppression in later blocks, they may allow yet-to-be inhibited Suppress items to intrude, causing facilitation on those items. Conditions with larger number of repetitions may include more of these failures, yielding a noisier function.

These observations suggest that experimenters would be wise to keep subjects consistently motivated during the Think/No-Think task, and to provide short rest breaks throughout. This would seem especially important when comparing populations on their inhibitory control abilities, if these populations vary in motivation or vigilance. Clinically, it is interesting that memory control may be vulnerable to conditions that lead to distraction or fatigue, such as depression, circadian arousal, or sleep loss.

Generalizes to Non-Verbal Materials

Although the majority of published studies have used verbal pairs, many studies have demonstrated negative control effects with other materials. Studies have used face-word pairs (Depue, Banich, & Curran, 2006; Hanslmayr et al., 2010; Hanslmayr et al., 2009), word-face and word-place pairs (Detre, Natarajan, & Norman 2010; Huddleston & Anderson, in preparation), word-line-drawing pairs (Kim & Yi, 2008), and face-scene pairs (Depue et al., 2006; Depue, Curran, & Banich, 2007; Depue, Banich, Burgess, Willcut, & Ruzic, 2010). For example, in a study by Depue et al. (2007), participants studied pairs composed of faces and complex scenes varying widely in content, and were trained on these pairs until they could recognize the scene that went with each face. During the Think/No-Think phase, participants were

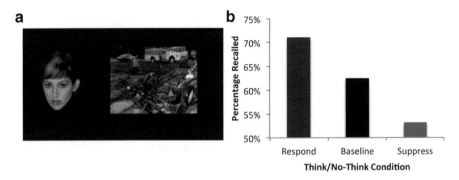

Fig. 7 (**a**), Depue et al., 2007 used faces for cues and both negative and neutrally valenced complex scenes as targets (reprinted with permission from AAAS); (**b**), final recall performance (scored from brief verbal descriptions in response to each face) for Respond, Baseline, and Suppress pictures in Depue et al.'s task

presented with the Faces as cues, and asked to either retrieve the associated scene or to suppress it. On the final test, participants were given each of the faces, and asked to provide a brief one sentence description of the associated scene, enough to allow independent judges to assess whether it had been retrieved. Independent raters then scored these verbal descriptions as to whether they signaled the appropriate scene. Depue et al. found that subjects showed a negative control effect (9%) for suppressed scenes, and a positive control effect for retrieved scenes (9%) for a total control effect of 18% (see also Depue et al., 2006). The demonstration of negative control effects across this range of stimuli indicates that the effect is not specific to verbal items, but affects episodic traces more generally.

Generalizes to Emotional Memories

It retrieval suppression is to provide a model of motivated forgetting, negative control effects should occur for traces with emotional content, particularly memories about negative experiences. A number of studies have found negative control effects in which the trace to be suppressed was negative, including negative words (Depue et al., 2006; Hertel & McDaniel, 2010; Joormann et al., 2005; Joormann et al.,2009; LeMoult et al., 2010; Kim et al., 2007; Lambert et al., 2010. Murray, Muscatel, & Kensinger, 2011) and negative pictures (Depue et al., 2007).

A particularly nice illustration comes from the study by Depue et al. (2007) discussed earlier, in which participants showed a 9% negative control effect in their ability to recall scenes in response to faces (Fig. 7). Importantly, all of the scenes used in this study were drawn from the International Affective Picture system (IAPS), and were highly unpleasant in character. Photographs included images of car accidents, people with injuries, and other unpleasant subject matter. These studies demonstrate that emotionally charged and unpleasant experiences are not immune to the effects of retrieval suppression, as one would expect if the process helps to control unwanted memories.

Although it is clear that emotional materials can be suppressed, it is less clear whether negative memories are more, less, or equivalently suppressible, compared to emotionally neutral or positive experiences. On the one hand, people may be motivated to suppress unpleasant items, resulting in larger negative control effects than would be observed for neutral materials. On the other hand, emotional experiences may be intrinsically more intrusive, and so might be difficult to suppress. Studies comparing the ability to suppress negative and neutral materials have yielded inconsistent results. Some have found that negative traces show larger negative control effects than do neutral or positive traces (Depue et al., 2006; Joormann et al., 2005; Lambert et al., 2010). Other authors have found that negative memories show smaller negative control effects than do neutral ones (Hertel & Gerstle, 2003; Marx, Marshall, & Castro, 2008; Nørby, Lange, & Larsen, 2010). Other authors have reported similar impairment on neutral, negative, and positive items (Hulbert, Anderson, & Kuhl, in preparation; Murray, Muscatell, & Kensinger, 2011).

It is unclear what underlies these variations. One explanation lies in the manner in which emotional stimulus sets are designed, and, in particular, whether neutral and negative stimuli are matched on variables other than valence and arousal that might vary across negative and neutral materials. Negative materials, for example, tend to come from a small set of categories that evoke strongly negative responses, including stimuli that concern death, disgust, anger, fear, and violence. Moreover, negative emotion words are generally more abstract, on average, than neutral words. In contrast, neutral words derive from a greater diversity of categories, and so may, on average, have greatly reduced inter-stimulus similarity. If negative items have higher inter-relatedness, one can no longer assume that performance on Respond and Suppress items is independent, as actively thinking about some pairs (e.g., Hill-Death) may make it harder to suppress highly related pairs (Lake-Kill) (see, e.g., Goodmon & Anderson, 2011 for demonstrations of how semantic relatedness insulates items from inhibition in retrieval-induced forgetting). Because neutral pairs will be less related, they would not suffer from this difficulty. Some of the variability across studies in the relative ease of suppressing neutral and negative materials surely arises from variations in the control of these factors. Supporting this view, Hulbert et al. (in preparation) demonstrated that when negative and neutral words are matched on inter-item similarity, concreteness, frequency, length and other variables, the negative control effects are similar for emotional and nonemotional stimuli.

Nevertheless, it would be desirable to experimentally manipulate inter-pair relatedness to verify that this factor modulates the negative control effect.

Effects of Retention Interval on the Effect are Unclear

Only two studies have examined whether the negative control effect changes over time, and these studies have yielded somewhat inconsistent findings. Norby et al. (2010) found a significant negative control effect for neutral materials on an immediate test (13%), but no negative control effect when those same participants were brought back to the laboratory and retested on the same items one week later (+1% facilitation). In contrast, Hotta and Kawaguchi (2009) found significant negative control effects on an immediate test (20%) and a re-test on those same items conducted after 24 h (10%).

The reliable effect observed by Hotta and Kawaguchi after 24 h indicates that the negative control effect is not merely a momentary deficit that dissipates shortly after retrieval suppression has ended. Nevertheless, there is some indication that this effect may dissipate. Both studies both show the negative control effect to be reduced after an extended delay, even though it remained significant in one. Perhaps the full release observed by Norby et al. arose simply because they waited a week to retest the items, whereas Hotta and Kawaguchi only waited one day. Unfortunately, one cannot be confident that the reductions in the negative control effect reflect its dissipation with time. Both studies used a test-retest method that complicates interpretation. For example, successful retrieval practice improves an item's later retention, and, moreover, retards the rate of forgetting over longer retention intervals (e.g., Karpicke & Roediger, 2008), particularly when the retrieval is difficult. Perhaps the initial test strengthened items that were retrieved, and differentially so, depending on whether retrieval was difficult (Suppress items) or easy (Baseline items). If so, one might expect this initial retrieval to create items with differing forgetting rates, with initially retrieved baseline items being forgotten more quickly than initially retrieved Suppress items. Moreover, the first test may have released inhibition for some items, creating an underestimate of the inhibition that might have occurred on a delayed test had no initial test happened. A purer test of the effects of delay on the negative control effect is clearly warranted.

It is worth noting that the effects of delay on other inhibitory phenomena are similarly inconsistent. For instance, in research on retrieval-induced forgetting, some authors have reported full recovery from inhibition after a day or more (Chan, 2009; MacLeod & Macrae, 2001; Saunders & MacLeod, 2002), concluding that the effect is transient, whereas other authors have reported inhibition after 24 h (Ford, Keating, & Patel, 2004; Conroy & Salmon, 2005; Conroy & Salmon, 2006; Garcia-Bajos, Migueles, & Anderson, 2009; Storm et al., 2006; Racsmány, Conway, & Demeter, 2010; Tandoh & Naka, 2007). Indeed, Garcia-Bajos, Migueles, and Anderson found, using an eyewitness memory video, retrieval-induced forgetting after a week that was significant and undiminished (Garcia-Bajos et al., 2009). Notably many of these demonstrations do not suffer from the repeated testing problem described above. Here again, what determines whether inhibition dissipates or persists remains unclear. One possibility is that persisting effects are more likely when the later retrieval of the suppressed representation cannot easily be supported by pre-existing semantic knowledge, and is thus more strictly episodic in character. This might arise for example, if episodic representations are more disrupted by inhibition (Anderson & Spellman, 1995; Anderson, 2003). A parallel possibility may also exist with the negative control effect.

Although evidence for dissipation of the negative control effect is theoretically interesting, one must be cautious about generalizing conclusions about durability in these studies to real life cases of memory control. For instance, even if the negative control effect dissipates after a week in the conventional Think/No-Think paradigm, one must bear in mind that the effects induced by this procedure reflect the efforts of participants in a single brief session, with the total duration of suppression lasting only about 1 min (12 repetitions, 4 s each). In contrast, real cases that require memory control are likely to entail more instances of suppression, distributed over longer time intervals (in some cases, perhaps years), and implemented by a highly motivated person. One cannot be sure how the impact of distributed efforts to suppress accumulates over time, and whether effects of greater duration are possible. Nevertheless, evidence from the few studies that have been conducted suggests that memories, once suppressed, can later be recovered. This suggests that it may be possible to forget, and later recover a suppressed experience, under the right conditions.

The Negative Control Effect Sometimes Does Not Occur

Although, the negative control effect has been replicated many times, sometimes no reliable effect is observed even though it would be expected (e.g., Bulevich et al., 2006; Bergström, Velmans, de Fockert, & Richardson-Klavehn, 2007; Mecklinger, Parra, & Waldhauser, 2009; Hertel & Mahan, 2008; Hertel & Calcaterra, 2005). For instance, Bulevich et al. conducted three experiments with variants of the Think/No-Think paradigm that closely paralleled earlier studies and observed 3%, 4%, and 1% negative control effects on the Same probe test, and similarly small effects on the Independent Probe test. Mecklinger, Parra and Waldhauser found a 1% Same Probe effect and a 5% Independent Probe effect. Hertel & Mahan observed 4% negative control effects in two samples, and Hertel & Calcaterra found no negative control effects in their uninstructed group. A question arises as to why negative control effects failed to emerge in cases like these.

There are likely to be several reasons why null effects sometimes occur. First, some are explained by subjects' noncompliance with the Suppress instructions. Unless one takes care to disguise mention of "memory" and "testing," some participants willfully disregard the instructions and use the cue presentation as an opportunity to intentionally retrieve and rehearse the suppression item. Moreover, even when participants think they are complying with Suppress instructions, they occasionally "just check their memory to still see if they know the answer" either during or after the Suppress trial has ended. When subjects are non-compliant, one cannot reasonably expect to see memory deficits for Suppress items, as subjects are not faithfully suppressing retrieval. We address this issue by eliminating all mention of memory (in the procedure, consent forms, sign up sheets, etc.), and emphasizing that the experiment is a study of attention. We also administer a post-experimental rating scale to quantify noncompliance. Other authors may not take these precautions, and so may have elevated rates of non-compliance.

To illustrate the effects of compliance on the negative control effect, consider the study by Hertel and Calcaterra (2005) that manipulated whether participants were given thought substitutes. Hertel and Calcaterra administered the non-compliance

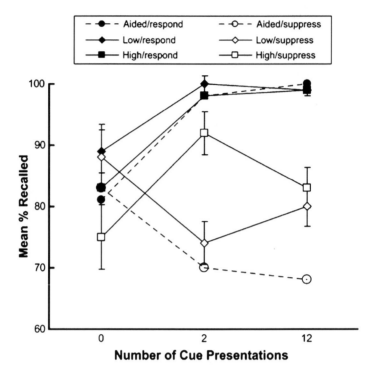

Fig. 8 Final recall for Respond and Suppression items as a function of the number of repetitions, from Hertel & Calcaterra, 2005 (Reprinted with permission, copyright © 2005 Springer Science + Business Media). Scores for noncompliance with suppression instructions (low vs. high) were derived based on the summed ratings of a strategy questionnaire administered after the final test phase. These scores were used to conduct a median split of subjects into low and high non-compliance, matching for counterbalancing. Of importance here is the difference between the low/suppress group and the high/suppress groups. The low/suppress (low noncompliance) group showed a significantly larger negative control effect than did the high/suppress (high noncompliance) group, who actually showed marginally significant facilitation

questionnaire we devised, and divided their uninstructed group into high and low compliance groups, matching on all counterbalancing dimensions. The results of this analysis are reported in Fig. 8. The pattern is what one would expect: non-compliant subjects who reported intentionally thinking of Suppress items showed progressive facilitation above baseline (+7%) with increasing repetitions for Suppress items; by contrast, compliant subjects who honestly attempted to suppress showed a negative control effect (−8%). Thus, the overall lack of a negative control effect in the uninstructed group reflects the prevalence of non-compliance, and the consequent canceling of negative control effects with retrieval practice benefits.

We do not think that compliance is the sole issue, however. Some null effects may arise because subjects do not remain vigilant for the full 30 min they are required to do so. Because controlling retrieval is effortful, fatigue is a substantial factor that undermines vigilance, and we know, from post-experimental measures, that subjects' efforts wane over blocks. Indeed, a drop in retrieval suppression performance with sustained effort would be predicted based on research on ego depletion, which consistently finds self-control deficiencies after a sustained period of control (Baumeister, Bratslavsky, Muraven, & Tice, 1998; see Hagger, Wood, Stiff, & Chatzisarantis, 2010 for a meta-analysis). If subjects lose vigilance in later blocks, some Suppress items may intrude, and, in effect, be given retrieval practice, countering impairment that may have arisen for other successfully suppressed items. As such, variations in whether researchers give rest breaks, the procedure is run in early morning, or experimenters keep participants motivated over blocks may account for some null negative control effects. This would make sense because forgetting should not arise if participants don't make an effort to suppress retrieval. However, although the negative control effect is sometimes not observed, it is clear from the combined analyses presented in Fig. 3 that the negative control effect is the typical pattern. Moreover, the total control effect, as far as we know, has always been found in published studies, showing that retrieval suppression generally terminates the benefits of seeing reminders. This suggests that effective intentional retrieval control is the rule.

Trial Duration

Several other variables have been proposed to affect the magnitude of the negative control effect, though these effects require further replication. For instance, Lee et al. (2007) hypothesized that longer duration trials result in weaker negative control effects than shorter ones. By this hypothesis, longer duration trials provide more opportunity for control to fail, and for the item to intrude, facilitating retention. Consistent with this, they observed that a group of participants given 3 s trials showed a 10% negative control effect, whereas a group given 5 s trials showed a 0% negative control effect. This result is consistent with the possibility that having to sustain cognitive control for longer durations may pose a substantial challenge.

Although this finding is intriguing, we unfortunately cannot disentangle whether the effect reflects the duration of individual trials or to the total duration of the think/no-think phase, which is necessarily confounded in their between subjects design. In the latter case, the smaller effect may reflect fatigue affecting later trials, as discussed in the preceding section. Nevertheless, if this finding reflects trial duration, it would indicate that inescapable cues provide especially strong challenges to cognitive control, requiring sustained efforts over time to achieve full control over unwanted memories.

Effects of Test Type

Although most studies have used cued recall, several have examined whether negative control effects occur on tests that provide the item intact for recognition or on other indirect tasks. In a study by Kim and Yi (2008), participants studied word-drawing pairs and then performed the Think/No-Think task with words as cues.

Kim and Yi tested retention on indirect tests, including perceptual identification of the picture under conditions of extremely rapid (35 ms) presentation (Experiment 1), and identification of pictures in perceptual noise (Experiments 2 and 3). In all cases, twelve suppression attempts impaired performance on these tasks compared to baseline. For instance, participants identified only 33% of the pictures after 12 suppression attempts, compared to 44% in the baseline condition. Experiments 2 and 3 showed that when the test introduced visual noise, participants needed to have more noise eliminated from the picture before they could identify it if it had been suppressed. Interestingly, these suppression effects only occurred for intact, but not mirror-reversed stimuli, indicating that suppression had affected perceptual representations of the pictures.

Similar effects can also be observed on explicit tests of recognition, although there are inconsistencies. For instance, Waldhauser, Johanssen, & Lindgren (submitted) observed a negative control effect on item recognition (6%) with words. Recently, in unpublished work, we have observed a reliable 9% negative control effect on item recognition with verbal items that is qualitatively similar in magnitude to the cued recall effect. However, Tomlinson et al. (2009) reported a small but non-reliable negative control effect on item recognition (2%), even when negative control effects were observed in cued recall. It must be noted, however, that their recognition test was administered after their recall test, and overall recognition performance was close to ceiling, either of which potentially complicates interpretation. Nevertheless, further study would be helpful to clarify the conditions under which this memory deficit occurs.

Correlations with Stop Signal Inhibition

Suppressing retrieval may be related to the capacity to override prepotent motor responses. One widely used tool that quantifies the ability to stop motor actions is the Stop-Signal paradigm, which measures the speed with which one can terminate an initiated motor action when a (typically) auditory signal is given (Logan, Cowan, & Davis, 1994). Using this measure of motor inhibition, Depue et al. (2010) observed a negative correlation between stop signal reaction time on a motor response task (−.58) and the proportion of emotionally negative pictures items successfully forgotten after retrieval suppression. Thus, the faster people were able to stop an initiated motor action, the more memory inhibition they showed, indicating that motor stopping speed is related to retrieval suppression ability. Moreover, performance on both retrieval suppression and stopping tasks correlated with engagement of right lateral prefrontal cortex during retrieval suppression, suggesting that the mechanisms underlying performance on these tasks may be related. In addition, as will be discussed later, Mecklinger et al. (2009) found that the N2, an electrophysiological component related to cognitive control was elevated for Suppress items and also for motor stopping trials on a stop signal task done with the same subjects one year later. Interestingly, despite that interval, the N2 increase in each stopping task was correlated. Although more work needs to be done to firmly establish the relationship between these capacities, the behavioral and neural similarities of these tasks suggests that the response override model of retrieval suppression may be correct (Anderson & Weaver, 2009).

Population Differences in the Negative Control Effect

When one conducts research on retrieval suppression, one cannot help but be impressed at the variability in the negative control effect across participants. Whereas the average effect may be 7–10%, it is not uncommon to find subjects who are exceedingly good at it (showing 50–60% negative control effects), and also to find subjects who are exceedingly bad (showing substantial reversals of the effect). Correspondingly, the variability in the *perceived difficulty* of the task is striking, with some participants proclaiming the task to be trivial, and others, with equal insistence, stating that it was impossible for them to ever exclude memories from consciousness. This variability hints at important individual differences in the ability to control unwanted memories that are obscured when we average over large numbers of subjects with varying characteristics. This variability may be important in predicting which people may be vulnerable to intrusive memories in the aftermath of traumatic experience. The question naturally arises as to what causes this variability.

One key hypothesis about the variability in memory control ability is that it originates from broader deficits in the inhibitory control of action and thought. A growing body of research has examined this *executive deficit hypothesis* (|Levy & Anderson, 2008) in populations hypothesized to have deficits in inhibition. The motivation for studying these populations is often twofold. First, to the extent that prior research indicates that the population has diminished control, a deficit in retrieval suppression would suggest that it engages more general mechanisms, as hypothesized in our response override framework. Second, documenting a deficiency in memory control indicates vulnerability to intrusive memories that may be of clinical significance. Research on memory control has focused on effects of age, attention deficits, depression, and traumatic experience as sources of individual differences.

Aging Effects

A number of investigators have proposed that cognitive control declines with age, and that inhibitory control declines in particular (e.g., Hasher & Zacks, 1988; see Lustig, Hasher, & Tonev, 2001, 2010b, for a review). If negative control effects reflect the action of a general inhibitory control mechanism, one should find that older adults are less able to suppress unwanted memories, and show reduced negative control effects. To date, there are have been two studies, and the data provide mixed support for this hypothesis. For instance, Anderson, Reinholz, Kuhl, and

Mayr (2011) conducted two experiments in which they manipulated the number of suppression trials for younger and older adults. Anderson et al. predicted that older adult should show reduced negative control effects, particularly on the independent probe test, which eliminates the interference component of the effect. Consistent with this prediction, younger adults showed reliable negative control effects on the independent probe test (8% and 7% in Experiments 1 and 2, respectively), whereas older adults did not (4% facilitation above baseline in both Experiments). In contrast, on the Same Probe test, older and younger adults showed negative control effects that did not differ, consistent with a role of interference on that test.

A different finding was observed by Murray, Muscatel, & Kensinger (2011), who also manipulated the emotional valence of to-be-suppressed items. These authors found reliable negative control effects on the Same Probe test that did not differ by age in several experiments, consistent with Anderson et al.'s findings. Moreover, in the one experiment with older adults they conducted using independent probes, older adults did not show negative control effects on neutral items, consistent with Anderson et al. (2011). However, for memories with positive or negative emotional valence, older adults showed reliable negative control effects on an independent probe test. On the face of it, these results indicate that, at least for emotionally valenced materials, inhibitory control may be sufficiently preserved to support reliable negative control effects, at least in this sample. However, when all of the independent probe data is considered in the aggregate across all published studies (weighted average), young adults (N = 104) show a 9% negative control effect, whereas older adults (N = 81) show a 2% effect. Thus, the overall tendency is for there to be an inhibitory deficit in older adults. Nevertheless, it is clearly desirable to identify why in some cases older adults show negative control effects.

Developmental Effects

Cognitive control improves across late childhood and early adolescence, and a number of investigators have argued that this development reflects increasingly effective inhibitory control (e.g., Harnishfeger & Pope, 1996; Wilson & Kipp, 1998). If so, one should observe a developmental progression in the ability to suppress unwanted memories with negative control effects emerging in middle childhood (10–12 year of age). This was tested by Paz-Alonso et al. (2009) who compared negative control effects across 8–9 year olds, 10–12 year olds, and young adults. Strikingly, the negative control effect increased with age, being absent for the youngest group, but present in middle childhood and in adulthood on both the Same Probe and Independent Probe tests. There was a continuous improvement with age, within childhood in the size of the negative control effect. Of interest, this negative control effect during middle childhood years occurred against a backdrop of overall improvements in declarative memory over this age range. Recently, Ogle and Paz-Alonso's (in preparation) have replicated this developmental trend of negative control effect improvement during middle childhood years with neutral non-arousing materials as well as with negative arousing word stimuli. These findings are consistent with recent evidence suggesting developmental progressions in inhibitory control as reflected in retrieval-induced forgetting (Aslan & Bäuml, 2010) (see also, our later section on neural mechanisms, for a developmental fMRI study of retrieval suppression).

Attention Deficit Disorder

One prominent theory attributes symptoms of attention deficit disorder to impaired attentional control, and in particular, diminished inhibitory control (Adams, Derefinko, Milich, & Fillmore, 2008; Barkley, 1997; Nigg, 2000, 2001; Quay, 1997). People with ADHD are less able to suppress prepotent motor responses in tasks such as the Go/No-Go and the Stop-Signal task (Oosterlaan, Logan, & Sergeant, 1998), and, moreover, do not effectively engage right lateral prefrontal cortex in support of motor response inhibition in those same tasks (Booth et al., 2005; Tamm et al., 2004; Casey et al., 1997; Rubia et al., 2005). If retrieval suppression engages response override mechanisms, people with attention deficit disorder may show smaller negative control effects, and have difficulty controlling unwanted memories. Consistent with this possibility, Depue et al. (2010) observed reliably larger negative control effects for age matched controls (9%) than for adults with ADHD (0%) when people tried to suppress aversive photographs. Similarly, participants with ADHD show diminished retrieval-induced forgetting when tests control the influence of associative blocking (Storm & White, 2010). These findings support the hypothesis that common functional systems may underlie memory and motor response suppression.

Depression

Depression is accompanied impaired memory and attention, and also a tendency towards ruminations about sadness. Several authors have proposed that depression diminishes cognitive control, making control over negative thoughts and feelings difficult (e.g., Hertel, 1994, 1998; Joormann, Yoon, & Zetsche, 2007). Four studies have examined whether diminished memory control accompanies mild or clinical depression (Hertel & Gerstle, 2003; Joormann et al., 2005, 2009; Hertel & Mahan, 2008). All four report that participants with either mild (Hertel & Gerstle, 2003) or major depressive disorder (Joormann et al., 2005, 2009; Hertel & Mahan, 2008) show no negative control effect or a reversal of it, with recall of Suppress items improving as a function of repetition. These effects have been observed for positive and negative materials. The exception to this finding is a report of a substantial negative control effect for negative words in major depressive disorder, even though suppression of positive words was impaired (Joormann et al., 2005).

Although these findings are consistent with a deficit in memory control, additional work should be done to establish that this reflects an inhibition deficit. For example, no study has yet examined whether negative control effects can be observed on independent probe tests, which provides a cleaner assessment of whether inhibitory function is intact. Nevertheless, these findings are highly suggestive and are also consistent with a clinically relevant deficit. Consistent with this, the total control effect is correlated with scores on the Rumination on Sadness Scale (Hertel & Gerstle, 2003), suggesting that a clinically relevant capacity is being measured. Moreover, this work has established extremely useful findings indicating that thought substitution can be used to improve control over unwanted memories (20–30% negative control effects) even in major depressive disorder (Joormann et al., 2009).

Effects of Trauma Frequency

The more one practices cognitive or motor skills, the better one's performance. Perhaps this principle extends to retrieval suppression. According to this plasticity hypothesis, people with more experience at memory control might be better at suppressing unwanted memories and show larger negative control effects.

To get at this issue, Hulbert, Kuhl, & Anderson (2011) examined the negative control effect in people who, prior to college, had few or many traumatic experiences. The frequency of such experiences was assessed with the Traumatic Experience Scale (Goldberg & Freyd, 2006), which measures a broad spectrum of traumas, including accidents, disasters, violence, sexual assault or abuse, emotional abuse, and death of important people. In one experiment, participants were divided into groups based on their responses to this scale, administered after the Think/No-Think task. In a second one, participants were prescreened as part of a course requirement, and we selected people with higher and lower scores. In both studies, we found larger negative control effects in people with more traumatic experiences, particularly when measured with an independent probe test. This advantage occurred for both negative and neutral words, and occurred even when (a) participants were offered money for right answers on the final test, and (b) experimenters and their supervisors were blind to the trauma status of subjects during the administration of the experiment and coding of the data.

The foregoing findings support the view that retrieval suppression ability is not fixed, but rather exhibits important plasticity. This plasticity raises the prospect that people suffering deficits in memory control may be able to improve mastery over intrusive experiences with proper training. The improvements may derive from strengthening an existing ability for retrieval suppression, or, instead, the development of adaptive strategies that improve forgetting, as illustrated by Joormann et al. (2009). It must be noted however, that a better demonstration of plasticity would involve randomly assigning participants to conditions and establishing a training effect, which remains to be done. Nevertheless, the fact that traumatic life experience predicts the negative control effect in the laboratory suggests that it measures mechanisms that may be engaged in everyday life. This suggests that the negative control effect provides a good model of motivated forgetting outside the laboratory.

Psychogenic Amnesia

One intriguing study reported the memory control abilities of a psychogenic amnesic patient P.P., who suffered profound loss of his personal history at the age of 32, despite no evidence of brain damage or dysfunction (Tramoni et al., 2009). P.P. had a complete loss of autobiographical memory, but nevertheless had intact new learning ability, normal executive control function, and a higher than average IQ. P.P.'s memory control ability was examined with the version of the Think/No-Think task used by Anderson et al. (2004) to see whether he might have particularly large negative control effects, compared to control subjects. P.P. had no difficulty learning the pairs to the 60% criterion, and showed baseline and Respond item performance that was nearly identical, if not slightly higher than that exhibited by the group of 12 control subjects.

Strikingly, however, P.P. exhibited a 40% negative control effect on the same probe test, and a 60% effect on the independent probe test. Whereas he showed very high baseline performance (90% ad 80% on the Same and Independent Probe tests), he showed extremely low recall of Suppression items (50% and 20% on the same and independent probe tests). This was appreciably larger than the control subjects who showed a 7% negative control effect on the Same Probe test and a 10% effect on the independent probe test, typical of most studies. The authors concluded that P.P. appears to exhibit "hyper-suppression," which they speculate was triggered in response to the trauma that led to his psychogenic amnesia, and which may partially contribute to it.

Although it is difficult to know what to conclude from a single case study such as this one, and it is unclear how the putative hyper-suppression process might lead to involuntary forgetting of personal life experiences, this study is intriguing in its linkage of the negative control effect to a real life case of psychogenic amnesia. Nevertheless, further work needs to be done to establish whether other cases of psychogenic amnesia might be accompanied by hyper-suppression (see a related case in our later discussion of neural mechanisms), and to clearly articulate the mechanisms by which this might occur.

Summary of Evidence for Retrieval Suppression

As the foregoing review illustrates, people clearly can control retrieval, as indexed both by the total control effect and the negative control effect. Nearly every study conducted on retrieval suppression shows a total control effect, indicating that reminders do not intrinsically improve accessibility to related memories; rather, whether one benefits from reminders depends upon ones intentions and motivations, and whether those lead to the engagement of processes that shut down retrieval and terminate the normal benefits that would be expected by reminders.

The negative control effect indicates that retrieval stopping is accomplished by one or more processes that disrupt retention of the suppressed trace. The negative control effect has been replicated widely and, in the aggregate, yields clear evidence that retrieval suppression causes memory disruption, even after as little as 30–60s of suppression (12–16 repetitions of 3 s each). The negative control effect is likely to be multiply determined, with inhibition and associative interference contributing, depending on strategy and test type. Both thought substitution and direct suppression without thought substitutes induce negative control effects. Inhibition is most evident on the independent probe test, which is related to individual differences in inhibitory control and this effect may be larger in people with more traumatic experiences. The negative control effect generalizes to non-verbal and emotional stimuli, and can be found on recall and recognition tests. Importantly, the negative control effect is related more generally to the ability to override prepotent responses, including motor actions. Collectively, these findings provide a promising model for understanding the specific cognitive mechanisms that may underlie people's ability to control unwanted memories.

A Neurobiological Model of Motivated Forgetting

Response override provides a useful model of how motivated forgetting may occur. When people override retrieval, it impairs memory and does so, in part, by inhibiting the unwanted trace. Thus, motivated forgetting in real life circumstances may arise when people control unwanted memories by engaging systems that suppress overt action. However, although our functional analysis is a useful beginning, a more complete model of motivated forgetting would entail an understanding of its neural substrates. In this section, we discuss our efforts to build a neurocognitive model of memory suppression.

In our model, stopping retrieval is similar to stopping a motor action, except for the nature of the thing being stopped. If so, a common underlying network may be involved in implementing both types of stopping. Fortunately, a lot is known about the neural mechanisms of motor stopping, providing hypotheses about how memory stopping might be done. For example, in humans, imaging studies of motor suppression have shown that response override is associated with a network of control-related regions, including both ventrolateral and dorsolateral prefrontal cortex (e.g., Garavan et al., 2002; Menon et al., 2001; see Levy & Wagner, 2011, for a meta-analysis). Correspondingly, animal research with the "go/no-go" task indicates that lesions to the lateral prefrontal cortex in monkeys impair their ability to stop a response (Iversen & Mishkin, 1970). Even more striking, electrical stimulation of this same prefrontal region during a "go" response actually leads monkeys to terminate their motor response (Sasaki, Gemba, & Tsujimoto, 1989). Thus the lateral PFC plays a critical role in stopping motor responses. Indeed, humans with lesions to the lateral prefrontal cortex show impaired stop-signal reaction time, indicating a substantial problem with stopping motor behavior (Aron et al., 2003). If retrieval suppression builds on mechanisms of response override, suppressing unwanted memories might also engage lateral prefrontal cortex.

Although the stopping process may be similar, the nature of the representation that gets suppressed must vary between memory and motor stopping. Given that the goal of retrieval suppression is to suppress conscious recollection of a past experience, a process ascribed to the hippocampus (e.g., Squire, 1992; Eldridge et al., 2000), the hippocampus seems a likely candidate target to be affected. Thus, control-related regions in lateral prefrontal cortex may disengage hippocampal processes to prevent conscious recollection. This hippocampal modulation may be how we avoid catching our "mental cacti" and disrupt retention of unwanted memories. A number of studies have examined these neural hypotheses using functional magnetic resonance imaging.

Neural Mechanisms of Retrieval Suppression: Basic Findings

Anderson et al. (2004) addressed the foregoing hypotheses by using fMRI to identify brain regions that support retrieval suppression. Using a task similar to that described earlier, they scanned participants during the Think/No-Think phase. On a final test, they replicated the negative control effects on the Same and Independent Probe tests; they found that subjects recalled fewer suppression words than baseline words, indicating that participants had successfully suppressed their memories. To determine which brain regions were involved in retrieval suppression, they contrasted activation on "Suppress" trials and "Respond" trials. As predicted by the response override hypothesis, "Suppress" trials engaged control-related regions that overlapped strongly with those typically involved in stopping motor action, including lateral prefrontal cortex (both dorsolateral and ventrolateral regions), lateral premotor cortex, and anterior cingulate cortex (see Fig. 9). The strong engagement of control regions during suppression indicates that this goal is accomplished not by a passive failure to engage retrieval, but by engaging processes to prevent unwanted memories from coming to mind. Importantly, these findings support the idea that common brain regions may control stopping both unwanted memories and unwanted actions.

But what representation or system did retrieval suppression target to prevent retrieval? To examine this, Anderson et al. (2004) identified brain regions that were less active during Suppress trials compared to Respond trials. Importantly, there was a reduction in hippocampal activity bilaterally. This difference suggests that subjects are able to phasically regulate the activity of the hippocampus to engage or disengage the recollective process, as necessitated by the current goals of the rememberer. While this difference could be explained by increased hippocampal activity during "Respond" trials, it is also consistent with the hippocampus being down-regulated during suppression. Supporting the latter explanation, the degree of hippocampal activity during retrieval suppression was related to the size of the negative control effect observed on the later memory test (see Anderson et al., 2004, for a description of this relationship). The fact that hippocampal activity during suppression is correlated with below-baseline behavioral suppression suggests that subjects can strategically down-regulate mnemonic activity in the hippocampus to prevent conscious recollection and disrupt later memory.

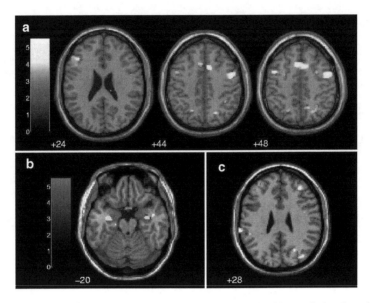

Fig. 9 TNT imaging data from Anderson et al., 2004 (Reprinted with permission from AAAS), showing that attentional control regions are recruited to control declarative memory retrieval. (**a**), lighter shaded areas are more active during retrieval suppression than during retrieval, and include areas generally associated with attentional control, including lateral prefrontal cortex (far *left* slice), anterior cingulate cortex (*central* area in several slices), lateral premotor cortex (rightmost 2 slices) and intraparietal sulcus (rightmost 2 slices, posterior left and right side). (**b**), lighter shaded areas are less active during suppression trials than respond trials, showing the hippocampus (*middle*, *left* and *right* side of image), a structure important for memory retrieval. (**c**), suppression-related areas in the DLPFC (anterior, *right* side) that predicted memory inhibition. It is hypothesized that the DLPFC exerts control over the hippocampus, reducing activation in the hippocampus, preventing memory retrieval from taking place and impairing retention

Neural Mechanisms of Emotional Memory Suppression

Although the study by Anderson et al. (2004) confirms the viability of response override as a model of motivated forgetting, the study used simple pairs of words without emotional content. Would the brain systems identified in that study be engaged by non-verbal materials that are aversive in character? Depue et al. (2007) studied this issue using the face-scene associations described earlier. Importantly, during the Think/No-Think task, when participants viewed a face and tried to suppress retrieval of the associated aversive image, they showed significantly more activation in right dorsolateral prefrontal cortex than during the Respond condition. As in the Anderson et al. study, activation in this region predicted individual differences in the negative control effect, with more activation associated with greater memory impairment. These findings converge with the view that the lateral prefrontal cortex is instrumental in disrupting retention via response override mechanisms.

Depue et al. observed several additional findings that may prove important to understanding retrieval suppression more broadly. First, suppressing retrieval of the aversive image reduced activation in right hippocampus below that observed on trials in which participants passively viewed a fixation cross on the screen, and were thus neither retrieving nor suppressing anything. This reduction is consistent with the view that retrieval suppression reduces hippocampal activity to disrupt conscious recollection, and broadly replicates earlier findings by Anderson et al. (2004) despite considerably more complex, naturalistic stimuli. Second, retrieval suppression significantly reduced amygdala activity, which fits with the broadly established role of this structure in emotion processing. Thus, whereas thinking of aversive pictures generated an emotional response reflected in elevated amygdala activity, suppressing retrieval reduced amygdala activity below passive fixation, suggesting that suppressing awareness of the unwanted memory pre-empted or attenuated unpleasant emotions that would have arisen had the participant recalled the unpleasant memory. Consistent with this view, other studies that have made suppressing unpleasant words difficult by extensive overtraining and by limiting suppression time (2 s instead of 4), actually show elevated hippocampal and amygdala activity during retrieval suppression, possibly reflecting the unpleasant character of intrusions (Butler & James, 2010). Taken together, these finding suggest an important role of retrieval suppression in regulating emotions after trauma: the more effectively memories can be inhibited, the less likely unpleasant retrievals will occur.

Finally, Depue et al. observed a progressive improvement in the intentional modulation of mnemonic activity in the hippocampus over blocks in the Think/No-Think phase. Whereas initial blocks showed suppression-related hippocampal activation elevated above a fixation baseline, increasing practice progressively reduced hippocampal activity below this baseline. In fact, the reduction in hippocampal activation during retrieval suppression in the final block predicted the negative control effect on the final test. Interestingly, Depue et al. suggested that practice may induce a qualitative shift in the networks that underlie retrieval suppression. In support of this, in early blocks, people did not show hippocampal modulation, but did show reductions in activity in visual cortex, together with engagement of ventrolateral prefrontal cortex. In later blocks, however, activation in dorsolateral prefrontal cortex became more prominent, as hippocampal reductions grew more effective. Depue suggested that this change with practice may reflect a shift in the mechanisms of control from ones that primarily prevent reinstatement of imagery associated with unpleasant scenes, to a DLPFC-hippocampal network that suppresses retrieval itself. This two-phase process needs further replication and formal testing. Nevertheless, these findings suggest that practice may make people more effective in engaging the neural systems that suppress retrieval, hinting at the viability of training interventions for people deficient in memory control.

Electrophsyiological Indices of Retrieval Suppression

A growing subfield in research on retrieval suppression seeks to develop electrophysiological indices of effective retrieval control using EEG. This research builds on a large body of evidence revealing a distinct signature of the subjective experience of recollecting a past event. ERP studies of recognition memory reveal a larger late positive component (LPC) over parietal scalp sites for older words compared to new distractor words. This component, which is sometimes referred to as the Parietal Episodic Memory (EM) effect (Friedman & Johnson, 2000), appears 400–800 milliseconds after a target has been presented on a recognition test. Its amplitude increases with study-test repetitions when an item is consciously recollected (Johnson et al., 1998), is larger in association with those items rated as consciously remembered (Smith, 1993; Smith & Guster, 1993), and is larger for words whose study context is correctly retrieved (Trott et al., 1999; Wilding et al., 1995; Wilding & Rugg, 1996). If the parietal EM effect reflects conscious recollection, and if retrieval suppression terminates conscious recollection, one should find reduced effects during Suppress trials compared to Respond trials.

This prediction has been confirmed in numerous studies. For instance, using an adaptation of the standard Think/No-Think task, Bergstrom et al. (2007) examined whether retrieval suppression would modulate the parietal EM effect. They focused on two questions: (a) when examining only those items that were successfully learned initially and that could be successfully recalled on the final memory test (and thus were fully encoded and retained in memory), would suppressing retrieval modulate the parietal EM effect, and (b) how complete would the suppression of this effect be, in comparison to Suppress items that subjects never learned or recollected on the final test? Strikingly, Bergstrom et al. (2007) found that suppressing retrieval significantly reduced the parietal EM effect, though not quite to the level of never-learned Suppress items. This modulation of the parietal EM effect has been replicated repeatedly (Bergstrom, de Fockert, & Richardson-Klavehn, 2009; Bergström et al., 2009; Hanslymar, Leipold, & Bauml, 2010; Mecklinger et al., 2009). In a related finding, Bergstrom, Anderson, Buda, Simons, & Richardson-Klavehn (submitted) found significant reductions of late parietal positivity with cues to richly encoded visual scenes, in response to retrieval suppression instructions. Interestingly, Bergstrom et al. (2007) also demonstrated that participants could, for the very same items, make the parietal EM effect come and go when instructions changed from retrieval to suppression.

Importantly, however, retrieval suppression does not always modulate the parietal EM effect, because it depends on the mechanism one uses to control retrieval. Bergstrom et al. (2009) compared the modulation of the parietal EM effect in people who controlled unwanted memories by thought substitution, with another group who used the direct suppression process discussed earlier. Importantly, subjects using direct suppression significantly modulated this component, as in prior studies, whereas subjects using thought substitution showed no modulation. If the LPC component truly indexes conscious recollection, as numerous studies have shown, this finding indicates that direct suppression is not accomplished by occupying awareness with alternative memories. Thought substitution presumably did not modulate this effect because recollecting thought substitutes itself would generate a parietal EM effect, making the two conditions indistinguishable. These data thus support the existence of qualitatively different approaches to memory control.

Despite the evidence for control over conscious recollection manifest in the modulation of the parietal EM effect, the modulation of this component does not predict negative control effects (Bergstrom et al., 2007; Hanslmayr et al., 2010). Other electrophysiological effects have been successfully related to inhibition, however, at least in the context of direct suppression. Hanslmayr et al. found that asking people to suppress retrieval using direct suppression instructions significantly reduced positivity compared to Respond trials across right prefrontal and left parietal cortex late in the Suppress trial (from 1.6 s onwards). Importantly, the extent of this positivity reduction increased with the number of Suppress repetitions, but not the number of Respond repetitions, and its magnitude predicted the negative control effect (Fig. 10). Intriguingly, Hanslmayr also found a similar effect occurred in advance of Suppress trials during preparatory cues signalling the nature of the upcoming trial, suggesting that people can pre-engage control processes while preparing to shut down retrieval. These findings provide an electrophysiological window into the benefits of advanced preparation in enhancing negative control effects.

Finally, the evidence indicates that electrophysiological markers of cognitive control, such as the N2, are larger during retrieval suppression. This finding is significant because ERP studies examining motor stopping consistently report enhanced N2 components for stopping, such as the no-go N2 (Bekker et al., 2005; Bokura et al., 2001; Donkers & van Boxtel, 2004; Eimer, 1993; Falkenstein et al., 1999; Garavan et al., 2002) and the stop signal N2 (Band & van Boxtel, 1999; Logan et al., 1994; Schmajuk et al., 2006; van Boxtel et al., 2001; Ramautar et al., 2004). For example, Mecklinger et al. (2009) found significantly larger N2 for Suppress items in comparison to Respond items, and, importantly found this effect to be especially pronounced for Suppress items that were later forgotten on an independent probe test. Prior work on the motor No-Go N2 suggest that it may reflect either inhibition of the motor act itself (Kopp et al., 1996), detection of response conflict (Falkenstein, 2006) or both. The source of the effect is thought to be the anterior cingulate cortex, but the lateral prefrontal cortex has also been suggested (Lavric et al., 2004), consistent with brain areas involved in retrieval suppression. Bergstrom et al. (2009) also observed a similar, though earlier ERP negativity that predicted individual differences in later independent probe forgetting, and a later ERP negativity that predicted forgetting of individual Suppress items. Finally, Mecklinger et al. (2009) found that the magnitude of the N2 enhancement during stop-signal trials in a motor response suppression task was correlated with the enhanced N2 for Suppress trials. These findings provide converging evidence for the view that motor and memory stopping share underlying mechanisms.

Taken together, the foregoing findings build a compelling body of evidence that retrieval suppression can be indexed by electrophysiological markers that indicate whether people are successful at controlling mnemonic awareness. Moreover, these markers provide useful insights into the mechanisms that underlie retrieval stopping that converge with data from functional magnetic resonance imaging.

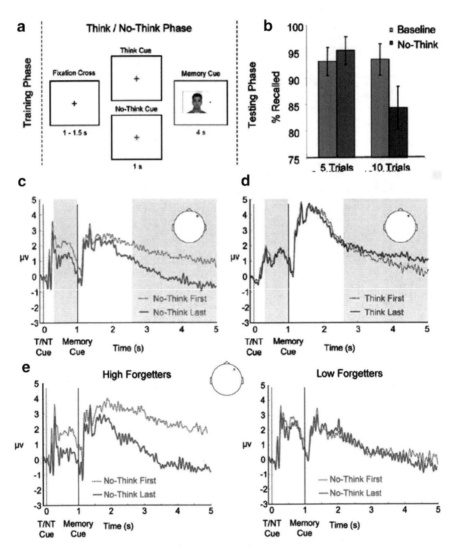

Fig. 10 Adapted from Hanslmayr et al., 2009. (**a**), Faces served as cues and words as responses. During the TNT phase, advance warning was given as to whether the trial would be a Suppress/No-Think (*red*) or Think (*green*) trial. (**b**), Behavioral results. In the final cued recall test, forgetting (Baseline > Suppress) was absent after five Suppress trial repetitions, but was present after 10 Suppress trial repetitions. Error bars represent SE. (**c**), ERP waveforms for the first five (*dotted line*) and the last five (*solid lines*) Suppress trial repetitions for one representative electrode. Gray bars indicate the time windows during which significant differences emerged. (**d**), ERP waveforms for the first five (*dotted line*) and the last five (*solid lines*) Think trial repetitions for one representative electrode. (**e**), ERP waveforms for the first five (*dotted line*) and the last five (*solid line*) Suppress trial repetitions plotted for high and low forgetters, as deduced from a balanced median split on the forgetting scores (Adapted with permission, copyright © 2009 by the Society of Neuroscience)

Population Differences in Neural Mechanisms of Memory Suppression

Several studies have compared the neural systems underlying retrieval suppression in neurologically normal adults to those engaged in other populations thought to have diminished or enhanced inhibitory control. In general, populations thought to be deficient in inhibitory control show diminished engagement of lateral prefrontal cortex in service of retrieval suppression.

Attention Deficit Disorder

Neuroimaging studies of attention deficit disorder have shown that individuals with ADHD do not engage right lateral prefrontal cortex as effectively as controls during motor response suppression (Booth et al., 2005; Casey et al., 1997; Depue et al. 2010; Rubia et al., 1999; Rubia, Brammer, Tonne, & Taylor, 2005; Tamm, Menon, Ringel, & Reiss, 2004). Based on the possibility that retrieval suppression may engage related response override mechanisms, Depue et al. (2010) used his face-scene think/no-think procedure to compare retrieval suppression in adults with and without attention deficit disorder to determine whether the former suffers deficits in retrieval suppression. As noted earlier, adults with ADHD showed smaller negative control effects than matched controls. Would these behavioural differences in retrieval suppression be reflected in the ability to modulate hippocampal activity? The imaging data revealed that matched controls engaged dorsolateral and ventrolateral prefrontal cortex during retrieval suppression, and significantly reduced activation in the hippocampus, replicating prior work by Anderson et al. (2004). Importantly, they showed a significant negative correlation between dorsolateral prefrontal cortex and hippocampus, and the size of this negative correlation predicted individual differences in forgetting of suppression items. In contrast to matched controls, ADHD participants failed to engage right dorsolateral prefrontal cortex during retrieval suppression and correspondingly failed to reduce mnemonic activity in the hippocampus. None of these interregional or behavioural correlations were observed for participants with ADHD. Interestingly, behavioural severity of ADHD symptomatology was related to the strength of the correlations between frontal and posterior cortical areas, with inattentive symptomatology predicting the magnitude of DLPFC-hippocampal negative correlations. These findings are consistent with the hypothesis that fronto-hippocampal modulation is a crucial neural mechanism underlying the suppression of unwanted memories and with the view that ADHD in part, reflects a deficit in inhibitory control. They further suggest that adults with attention deficit disorder should have difficulty with controlling intrusive memories.

Development of Retrieval Suppression

The majority of research on retrieval suppression has focused on adults. A unique window on the systems essential to this ability, however, is provided by studying its development. As mentioned earlier, behavioural work has established an increasing efficacy at suppressing unwanted memories in middle childhood (Ogle & Paz-Alonso, in prep; Paz-Alonso et al., 2009). Recently, Paz-alonso et al. (2011) have studied the neural basis of this shift. Forty-three participants from three age groups (fifteen 8–9 year olds, fourteen 11–12 year olds, and 14 young adults) were scanned as they performed the Think/No-Think task. Aggregating across all 43 participants showed robust engagement of right DLPFC and VLPFC during retrieval suppression, and a clear reduction in hippocampal activity during Suppress trials, consistent with the foregoing imaging studies by Anderson et al. (2004) and Depue et al. (2007). Moreover, activity in DLPFC was functionally related to activity in the hippocampus during retrieval suppression, indicating an interaction between these regions that helps to implement the process of retrieval suppression.

Comparing across age groups reveals several neural changes that characterize the development of memory control. First, whereas younger adults engaged lateral pre-frontal cortex and posterior parietal cortex while effectively suppressing memory retrieval, 8–9 year olds did not effectively engage these regions. Second, in contrast to adults, children did not effectively modulate hippocampus activation during retrieval suppression. The 11–12 year olds showed an intermediate pattern of control and modulation. Finally, during retrieval suppression, the data revealed increased engagement of right posterior parietal cortex (BA 40/7) in adults compared to 8–9 year olds, together with a broad increase in functional connectivity between lateral prefrontal, cingulate, lateral posterior parietal, precuneus, and hippocampal regions, reflecting increasingly effective inter-regional communication with age. Thus, the emergence of the capacity to suppress unwanted memories reflects increasingly effective engagement of prefrontal cortex to control hippocampal activity, and, importantly, tighter coupling of the fronto-parietal-hippocampal network of regions involved in this process.

These data suggest that future work examining individual differences in memory control as well as the effects of practice on retrieval suppression would profit from looking at changes in inter-regional connectivity that might support superior control over unwanted memories. More generally, however, they suggest that retrieval suppression relies upon the emergence of cognitive control, supporting the view that this ability builds upon mechanisms of response override that are of broad importance in mental life. These findings also raise the question of how and whether the typical development of memory control might constrain the ability to suppress unwanted memories of abuse. Are the developmental time courses observed in these studies determined strictly by maturation, constraining when children can be expected to be effective at motivated forgetting? Or might early life challenges to memory control alter the pace of development of neural systems underlying memory control?

Psychogenic Amnesia

The foregoing studies indicate that retrieval suppression engages lateral prefrontal cortex to reduce activation in the hippocampus as a means of controlling awareness of unwanted memories. Although the mechanisms observed in these studies could underlie real cases of intentional suppression, cases arise that do not, on their face, seem well characterized as being intentional. For instance, intensely stressful periods can sometimes induce psychogenic amnesia, in which the person may fail to remember large chunks of their personal experiences, forgetting who they are, even though their general knowledge and learning ability may remain intact. Could psychogenic amnesia sometimes be the result of spontaneous, involuntary application of the mechanisms identified here, as suggested by the earlier reviewed work of Tramoni et al. (2009)?

There is intriguing preliminary evidence that this involuntary control may happen. In a recent study, Kikuchi et al. (2010) studied two patients with dissociative amnesia. Both patients were well educated, and neurologically normal, and of normal intelligence, but both had undergone a recent stressful event or period of time that lead to extensive retrograde amnesia. For instance, Patient 1, a 27 year-old businessman exhibited focal retrograde amnesia for all events, people, and activities that took place in the 4.5 year period prior to the onset of his amnesia, even though he could recall experiences and people from before that period. Patient 2 presented a similar, but more extensive retrograde amnesia. No neurological abnormalities could be detected, and they appeared to remember all new experiences that happened to them after the onset of the amnesia, showing normal new learning.

Kikuchi et al. scanned these two patients as they viewed photographs of individuals taken from various periods of their lives. Specifically some photographs were of individuals they knew from the periods of their lives that they could still remember (recognizable photos), whereas others were from the window of retrograde amnesia (unrecognizable photos). Novel photographs of people unknown to the patients were also included. Participants simply judged whether or not they recognized each photograph as it was presented. The authors found that unrecognizable faces showed greater activation in dorsolateral and ventrolateral prefrontal cortex, compared to both recognizable and novel control faces, indicating the engagement of a network similar to that involved in with retrieval suppression. Moreover, these patients showed reduced hippocampal activation in response to the unrecognizable faces, compared to novel faces and recognizable faces consistent with the possibility that retrieval was being suppressed. Kikuchi et al. raised the intriguing possibility that extreme psychological distress may lead retrieval suppression processes to be engaged involuntarily in reaction to certain stimuli, over long periods of time, creating a pattern resembling that observed in laboratory studies of retrieval suppression. They acknowledge, however, reduced hippocampal activation for unrecognizable faces may reflect participants' lack of recollection of those faces, compared to recognizable items and that further work is required to establish their active down-regulation interpretation. Nevertheless these findings, with those reported by Tramoni discussed previously, illustrate how the response override and fronto-hippocampal modulation hypotheses provide an interesting and productive lens through which to view real life cases of motivated forgetting.

Summary of Neural Basis of Memory Control

Recent years have seen the emergence of a neurobiological model of motivated forgetting that integrates this otherwise controversial process with widely accepted and fundamental mechanisms for the control of human behavior and thought. Response override is a universally acknowledged function of cognitive control, and the neural mechanisms underlying it have received extensive study. Retrieval suppression can be profitably viewed as a special case of this process, in which the function to be stopped is episodic memory retrieval, and the targets of control are representations of episodic experience supported in part by the hippocampus.

Studies of retrieval suppression with simple words, and emotional pictures have now consistently shown that suppressing awareness of an unwanted memory engages lateral prefrontal cortical regions overlapping with those involved in response override to modulate neural activity in the hippocampus. These conclusions have received converging support from electrophysiological research, which has established several indices of retrieval suppression, and the likely engagement of response override. The extent to which response override mechanisms are engaged predicts forgetting of the suppressed trace, and individual differences in the function of these systems appears to be related to how well people control unwanted memories. There is even some preliminary indication that fronto-hippocampal modulation may provide a model of some cases of psychogenic amnesia. Much work remains to be done, however, to identify the precise relationship between memory and motor response suppression processes, to identify the pathways by which lateral prefrontal cortex exerts influence on the hippocampus, and to understand the nature of the disruption induced by hippocampal modulation. Taken together, this work specifies a useful and specific neurobiological model that reinforces the utility of the response override framework for understanding motivated forgetting.

Building Retrieval Suppression as a Model of Motivated Forgetting

Thus far, our discussion has focused on the variety of useful discoveries that have been made in current research on retrieval suppression. Despite these interesting successes, the case for retrieval suppression as a mechanism of motivated forgetting is in a relatively early stage of development (Anderson & Levy, 2006). In the remainder of this article, we discuss important issues that remain to be addressed in future research to build a strong case for the role of retrieval suppression in motivated forgetting.

Generalization of Negative Control Effects to Ecologically Valid Memories

Research on retrieval suppression was, at the outset, motivated by the observation that continuously confronting inescapable retrieval cues appeared to be related to subjective reports of forgetting for childhood abuse. The observation that retrieval suppression causes both total control effects and negative control effects illustrates one way in which this surprising relationship may come about. When reminders lead to recollections that one is motivated to not think about, inhibitory control mechanisms have a detrimental impact on the retention of the suppressed memory.

One must acknowledge, however, that there is a considerable gap in the nature of the memories studied in laboratory work and those present in these real cases. Simple pairs of words provide a useful beginning for understanding retrieval suppression, but ultimately research must examine whether such mechanisms can induce forgetting of complex, multi-modal, emotional events personally relevant to the rememberer. Does retrieval suppression "scale up" to real events? The work of Depue and colleagues demonstrating negative control effects with face-scene pairs moves in the right direction. Nevertheless, even these stimuli are relatively constrained. If it could be shown that negative control effects occur for naturalistic episodic experiences, and autobiographical memories, the case for the relevance of retrieval suppression would be stronger.

It must be emphasized that there are reasons why experimentalists begin studying a process with simple memory items like words and photographs. With materials like these, one can carefully control what is encoded, as well as what strategies or processes people bring to bear. The process of generalizing mechanisms to complex, less controlled stimuli is likely to present challenges and complexities that are difficult to anticipate. As such, patience and persistence is required to evaluate whether this generalization is possible. Nevertheless, the fact that the present work was motivated by a perplexing but similar pattern in self reports of memory for abuse suggests that it may be possible to span this considerable gap, given imagination and persistence.

Persistence of the Negative Control Effect Over Time

If retrieval suppression underlies some cases of motivated forgetting, it suggests that forgetting can persist over extended periods. To understand how this occurs, more work must be done to examine how long negative control effects last, and whether their durability provides a reasonable model of these phenomena. If negative control effects only lasted 5 min, for example, one might question their relevance to motivated forgetting. However, if retrieval suppression can produce durable forgetting, or that forgetting can be sustained by other means, it would strengthen its relevance to motivated forgetting, and define the conditions under which these effects to occur.

Most research on the persistence of negative control effects has focused on the conventional procedure without instructions about how to control memory. The findings thus far indicate that negative control effects may last somewhere between one day and one week. Several factors remain unexplored, however, that may influence the impact of suppression on long-term retention. First, one must consider the cumulative effects of suppression over many repetitions spread out over time and how this may affect the durability of forgetting. As noted earlier the cumulative time suppressing an item in the Think/No-Think procedure is between 45 s and a minute, all within a single half an hour session. Real cases of memory control are likely to involve more protracted efforts, spread out over months or longer. These situations differ in the amount of suppression and in its schedule. Distributed, recurring efforts at suppression may have more enduring effects on the negative control effect, much like distributed repetition of memory items has far bigger effects on retention than do massed repetitions. Thus, estimates of the durability of negative control effects based on a small number of suppressions within a session may underestimate the longevity of the effect in real life cases. Clearly, this *distributed practice hypothesis* needs to be tested.

Second, the relevance of present efforts to estimate the durability of negative control effects to real cases of motivated forgetting may be limited by the test methodology. All current tests of the durability of negative control effects ask people to explicitly recall unwanted memories on the final test, a situation unlikely to occur in real settings. As Hertel, Large, Dahl, and Levy (2011) aptly argue, it is unlikely that someone motivated to exclude an unwanted memory from awareness would turn around and try to retrieve that memory. Rather, upon encountering cues to the unwanted memory, they will, if anything, be biased away from any such retrieval, especially given their efforts to develop alternative thoughts in relation to reminders. Thus, according to this *retrieval tendency hypothesis*, a better estimate of the impact of suppression on the control of awareness, in real terms, would estimate the spontaneous retrieval of the unwanted memory in response to a cue, when no instructions are given to recall anything (e.g., providing the first thought that comes to mind; Hertel et al.). Perhaps people never recall the unwanted items spontaneously when given reminders and always manage to think of something else first. In practical terms, this accomplishes the goal of keeping the unwanted memory from awareness. Indeed, as discussed later, spontaneous retrieval of alternative associations provides one way of reinstating negative control effects.

Third, one must consider that estimates of the average durability of negative control effects, based on a large sample may not reflect the durability exhibited by people who are exceptionally effective at suppressing memories. As discussed shortly, insufficient attention has been given to studying the extremes of memory control, and the manner in which the impact of suppression in those participants may differ from the typical effect. Such extremes may emerge because of ability or expertise. Expertise at retrieval suppression may reflect superior strategies for retrieval suppression, or strengthening of cognitive control through extensive practice. Thus, a better understanding of the durability of negative control effects and their implications for real cases requires studying people who are especially good at it.

The Extremes of Motivated Forgetting

The cases that started the recovered memory debate are ones in which people claim to forget disturbing experiences over many years. Many people find such cases difficult to believe because they defy the intuition that if something that unusual happened, we would remember it. Given these considerations, if some cases are real, they may indeed not be the norm. Perhaps the vast majority of people having such experiences would remember them, confirming the average person's intuition. If so, then cases in which abuse is truly forgotten might be extremes on a continuum, such that only people with strong cognitive control are capable of it.

If this *control ability hypothesis* is correct, there is an important disconnect in the relevance of the current laboratory approach to real cases. In laboratory studies, research focuses on the *average negative control effect*, collapsed over many people with widely varying control abilities. The characteristics of this sample are not representative of people likely to succeed at suppressing truly unpleasant and unusual memories. Arguably what research should be doing instead is trying to understand people who are hypereffective at suppression. Indeed, retrieval suppression need not be exceptionally powerful in all people. *Rather, all it takes for retrieval suppression to be an excellent model of recovered memories is for a small fraction of people to be profoundly good at it.*

One approach to conducting such research is to study individuals who recover memories of abuse after years of forgetting. Presumably if the abuse event can be corroborated as having truly occurred, individuals who forget may have better memory control abilities than people who also have corroborated abuse, but who always remembered it. If so, one might find larger negative control effects in such cases than in individuals who have had continuous memory of the abuse. Such an approach has been taken in related research by Geraerts and colleagues, who have studied thought suppression abilities in people with recovered memories (Geraerts, McNally, Jelicic, Merckelbach, & Raymaekers, 2008). Interestingly, people who recovered memories of abuse spontaneously, outside of therapy do in fact show superior thought suppression capability, consistent with this hypothesis.

Another approach would be to identify people who show large negative control effects, and study them to determine whether or not have characteristics that would be consistent with either enhanced cognitive control in general, or particularly effective strategies. Might effective suppressors show superior performance on stop signal reaction time tasks or other measures of executive function? Might they show more effective engagement of lateral prefrontal cortex during retrieval suppression? The systematic characterization of effective suppressors may be extremely helpful in identifying characteristics of individuals who might be especially prone to be good at memory control. It would also be helpful to know the proportion of the population that is capable of extremely effective retrieval suppression. If only a small fraction of individuals is capable of hyper-suppression, this may explain why people often think that this level of control over one's memory seems implausible.

Conditions of Memory Recovery

Surprisingly little work has focused on whether memories can be recovered, once they have been suppressed. To develop retrieval suppression as a model of motivated forgetting that can account for the forgetting of child abuse that is later accompanied by the recovery of the abuse, it would be helpful to explore whether recovery following suppression is possible, the conditions that trigger recovery, and the characteristics of memories that are recovered. If the conditions of recovery can be delineated in experimental work, it may help to understand when and how memories may be recovered in real cases.

Several conditions are likely to contribute to memory recovery, and it should be possible to clearly document these in laboratory studies. First, in general, the more times that one attempts to retrieve the same information, the more one recalls, even when one feels that one cannot recall any more, a phenomenon known as *hypermnesia* (Erdelyi & Kleinbard, 1978; Payne, 1987). Moreover, even when overall recall does not increase with repeated retrieval, previously unrecalled items often get recalled on later tests (but are balanced by forgetting of previously recalled items), a phenomenon known as *reminiscence*. Although some work has already shown that hypermnesia is possible for to-be-forgotten items in the directed forgetting procedure (Goernert & Wolfe, 1997; Goernert, 2005), no work has yet examined whether hypermnesia or reminiscense can also be found with retrieval suppression. This *reminiscence hypothesis* predicts that all or part of unwanted memories may be recoverable, given repeated efforts at retrieval, though, under such circumstances, one must also be concerned about the introduction of reconstructive errors that may distort memory (see, e.g., Henkel, 2004).

Second, the more cue information one provides, the more likely that retrieval may succeed, even if suppression has occurred. Although suppression ought to impair memory from a variety of cues, this does not mean that adding cuing information shouldn't help increase the chances that a suppressed memory can be recovered, at least in part. There have been elegant demonstrations of powerful cue-based recovery effects in experimental paradigms other than retrieval suppression (Smith & Moynan, 2008), but research has not yet examined how varying the number of cues influences items suffering from negative control effects. One possibility is that providing cues for baseline and suppression items simply raises overall performance in both conditions, leaving negative control effects unaffected. Another possibility is that negative control effects may differentially benefit from cues, resulting in a "release" effect. Regardless of which pattern is observed, however, if additional cues help participants recall items that would have been forgotten, it would suggest that encountering related cues in everyday life should increase the chances of a suppressed memory being recovered. Whether some cues might be more powerful in eliciting recovery than others is also a question of interest. For instance, reinstatement of spatial or emotional context may be important.

Third, the passage of time itself may contribute to memory recovery, as assumed by current attempts to study the longevity of negative control effects. On this view, items suffering from negative control effects may undergo a gradual change in state over time that increases their accessibility. For instance, inhibition may gradually dissipate over time. The idea that time may be an important factor predicting the release of inhibition owes its conceptual heritage to research on spontaneous recovery from extinction in research on classical conditioning (Pavlov, 1927, Rescorla, 2004), and on analogous recovery effects in episodic memory research on retroactive interference (Underwood, 1949, Brown, 1976, Wheeler, 1995). The passage of time has also been proposed to enhance reminiscence and hypermnesia effects in repeated recall, even when participants are fully occupied with other tasks in between repetitions, in a phenomenon called incubated reminiscence (Smith & Vela, 1991). Negative control effects may exhibit a similar release over time, though, as discussed previously, the issue needs further exploration.

Finally, the parameters that determine when a memory will be recovered may be different for real cases of motivated forgetting, if having a genuine motive for forgetting matters. For instance, reminders of an unpleasant experience such as abuse may be threatening during childhood, but as circumstances change and a person grows to be more self sufficient, secure, and independent of the abuser, feelings of threat that drive maintenance of memory control may subside. If the motive driving memory control no longer dominates, recovery may be possible. Addressing issues relating to motivation presents a challenge to studying memory control in the laboratory, as we discuss next.

The Role of Motivation in Motivated Forgetting

Real situations that drive motivated forgetting have a critical ingredient that all laboratory research on memory control lacks: motivation. As discussed at the outset, people do not need special incentives to control awareness of unpleasant memories, as they are naturally motivated to not dwell on memories that make them angry, fearful, anxious, sad, or embarrassed.

When we study memory control in the laboratory, we are arguably studying a pale reflection of what must occur when people have an emotional incentive to succeed. Participants in most studies have no personal motive to suppress response words, apart from agreeing to cooperate with us. Absent a real personal motive for controlling awareness, we cannot know how effectively findings capture what happens in real cases. Indeed, when a true motive for suppressing is absent, other naturally occurring motivations will dominate. For instance, many participants are naturally motivated to appear smart, clever, or competent, and these motives very often drive them to intentionally rehearse suppression items when they know they are not supposed to (as discussed earlier) because they suspect they will be tested. Thus, unless special precautions are taken to ensure that people don't view the study as being about memory, the forces of motivation run counter to what the paradigm tries to achieve. We try to solve this *problem of counter-motives* by framing the task as being about the *ability to ignore distracting things*. We repeatedly stress that we are assessing this ability, which aligns subjects' desires to appear clever and competent with our task goals.

Nevertheless, research on motivated forgetting would benefit if participants had a personal motive for controlling memory, apart from compliance. There are two approaches to incorporating motivation into research on retrieval suppression. The first would be to study participants who, based of diagnostic criteria or other known facts, would have a motive to suppress certain content. For instance, participants with social phobia arguably have greater motivation to suppress awareness of stimuli with social content, and so might show larger negative control effects for that material. The second would be to experimentally induce a desire to suppress certain contents. Whether a creative way to induce motives could be devised that was still ethical remains to be seen.

Integration with Research on Directed Forgetting

Although retrieval suppression is an important model situation for understanding motivated forgetting, another body of work addresses related issues: directed forgetting. Research on directed forgetting examines whether people can intentionally forget recently encountered information. For example, in the item-method directed forgetting procedure (Bjork, 1972), people are presented stimuli (e.g., words, pictures) one at a time, and are told that following each item, they will receive instructions directing them to either remember or forget it. After the list is completed, a final recall or recognition test is given. The typical finding with the item method is that participants can recall or recognize substantially more remember items than forget items. In contrast, in the list-method directed forgetting procedure, a similar instruction is adopted, though a whole list is presented before the participants receive the remember or forget instruction, at which point a second list is presented. Here too, memory for the first list is impaired, compared to a first list that participants are asked to remember (Bjork et al., 1998; Geiselman et al., 1983, Johnson, 1994; see Golding & MacLeod, 1998, for a review). In contrast, recognition memory for items forgotten with the list method is often intact, though not when recognition memory places greater demands on context memory (Sahakyan, Waldum, Benjamin, & Bickett, 2009).

Both retrieval suppression and directed forgetting represent cases in which an effort to not think about an event or set of events leads to diminished recall of the unwanted memories. Despite this apparent similarity, however, the implementation of mnemonic control in these situations may vary. For instance, some have attributed item method directed forgetting to intentional truncation of encoding processes. By this view, until participants receive the cue to remember or forget, subjects intentionally halt elaborative encoding until they know what they are supposed to do, elaborating the item further only if it is to be remembered (e.g., Basden, Basden, & Gargano, 1993). Others have argued for a role of cognitive control and response override in this procedure (Hourihan & Taylor, 2006), a hypothesis supported by both behavioral (Fawcett & Taylor, 2008) and imaging studies (Wylie, Fox, & Taylor, 2008) that document the dependency of the forget instruction on attention and cognitive control systems. Regardless of which mechanism is at play, this task best captures situations in which we may prematurely terminate thoughts about an unpleasant experience to limit the footprint of that experience in our memories. The list method directed forgetting effect, by contrast, has been attributed to both to inhibition of the first list (Geiselman et al., 1983), and also to intentional shifts in mental context between the first list and the second (Sahakyan & Kelley, 2002). In essence, list-method directed forgetting models the situation in which we try to get our mind off of something that has happened recently, by "changing gears." Retrieval suppression instead captures situations in which, encoding has already succeeded, and at some arbitrary point later a powerful reminder triggers an unwanted recollection. Given that the reminder cannot be escaped, mental context shift or truncated encoding are not viable options, and response override is likely to be more important. Thus, even though these tasks are superficially similar, memory control may be accomplished by different means and under different conditions.

An important goal of research on motivated forgetting is to understand the relationship between these different phenomena, the mechanisms they engage, and the situations they model. We would like to suggest the possibility that these tasks may all be viewed as engaging cognitive control, but perhaps targeted at different types of representations and processes. According to this *flexible control hypothesis* (Anderson, 2005), response override mechanisms may be flexibly targeted at different stages of memory, and at different processes. Item method directed forgetting may be a case of *encoding suppression*; list-method directed forgetting may reflect *temporal context suppression*; and negative control effects may reflect *retrieval suppression*, as we have discussed. This view is broadly compatible with the notion of response override as a general mechanism that can be targeted at different types of representations and processes. Alternative conceptualizations may be possible, however, and the important goal is to understand how these phenomena are related to one another.

Integration with Research on Thought Suppression

In apparent contradiction to the foregoing findings, a body of research on thought suppression has generally focused on the inefficacy of attempts to control thoughts. This research focuses on people's ability to suppress a single target thought over an extended period (usually 5 min). In the typical "white bear" paradigm (Wegner, Schneider, Carter, & White, 1987; see Wegner, 1994, Wenzlaff & Wegner, 2000 for reviews), participants are told to spend 5 min suppressing all thoughts about a target thought (e.g., white bears) and to otherwise think about what they wish. If, however, they happen to think about white bears in the interim, they should ring a bell to indicate that the white bear intruded. After the 5 min period ends, they are given an additional 5 min "expression" period, in which they are told to think about white bears. Two general findings are sometimes observed. First, compared to an expression period, thought suppression instructions greatly reduce the frequency of the unwanted thought, though it rarely eliminates thoughts of the white bear completely. Second, a period of expression that follows a period of suppression often results in many more thoughts about white bears in comparison to a period of expression that does not follow suppression. The latter finding suggests that, ironically, attempting to suppress the unwanted thought causes a rebound in its accessibility, making it more accessible than it otherwise would have been. The conclusion usually reached in this literature is that thought suppression is counterproductive, and may lead to heightened levels of intrusive thoughts.

Here again, what might seem to be similar situations may not be served by the same mechanism. A key difference between thought suppression and the other methods is that the former makes explicit reference to a particular forbidden thought that is the very object of the task to be performed. The participants' understanding of the task is that their goal is to not think about white bears. As long as the participants try to accomplish that goal, it will be impossible to achieve it because simply remembering what they are supposed to do requires them to violate the goal. This contrasts with retrieval suppression, for example, in that the latter simply asks participants to prevent awareness of the memory that goes with a certain cue, without making reference to what that memory is. The fact that the goal of retrieval suppression task does not incorporate the very thing that is to be avoided may be a crucial feature that predicts when effective suppression is and is not possible. We propose this *goal-integration theory* as an account of this discrepancy between work on retrieval suppression and thought suppression. This hypothesis needs to be carefully examined to see if can help to disentangle when efforts at suppression will be productive. A careful analysis of the differing situations captured by these tasks, and the mechanisms involved will likely prove to be extremely helpful in relating research on mental control to clinical settings.

Unconscious Influences of Suppressed Memories

One final issue concerns whether retrieval suppression influences implicit access to traces. Many clinicians, particularly those from the psychoanalytic tradition subscribe to the view that even when memories cannot be retrieved, they continue to exert an influence on behavior and thought unconsciously. The possibility that such influences exist is intriguing. Yet, most of the work conducted thus far on retrieval suppression has focused on intentional, explicit retrieval of suppressed memories. Might memories that are intentionally suppressed continue to exert influence on people's behavior on indirect memory tests? Understanding whether and how such indirect influences might arise is theoretically important, and could also have profound implications for understanding the characteristics and consequences of retrieval suppression in clinical settings.

At present, only one study has been conducted looking at implicit memory for recently suppressed materials (Kim & Yi, 2008). Surprisingly, this study found that even indirect tests like perceptual identification of pictures show negative control effects, suggesting that suppression is not limited to conscious access to a trace. Clearly, however, further work needs to be done to assess the generality of this effect. One issue of particular interest is whether emotional learning associated with an unwanted memory might be preserved even when episodic memory for the experience is impaired. Thus, even when people cannot remember the negative event associated with a stimulus, they may experience emotional reactions to the stimulus that lead them to behave differently. Similarly, other indirect measures such as gaze pattern or other motor actions may reveal persisting influences. The discovery of intact influences of a prior experience, despite impaired memory would be informative at both a theoretical and clinical level.

Beyond the Initial Act of Retrieval Suppression: How Memory Control Develops Over Time

Motivated forgetting is unlikely to be accomplished in a single cognitive act or even in a short time, particularly for complex events with emotional content. Rather, it may require sustained effort, particularly if a person is confronted with reminders. For these reasons, motivated forgetting may best be viewed as an ongoing process supported by adapting mechanisms that limit awareness of the experience. Much of what is studied in the think/no-think paradigm, however, concerns the initial phases of memory control when one encounters reminders to a recently experienced event. Yet, the understanding of motivated forgetting likely requires an appreciation of how retrieval suppression accumulates over time, and how a person's coping response may adapt, neither of which are easily studied in controlled experiments. Here we discuss ways in which memory control may develop over time.

The Intentionality Shift Theory

After an unpleasant event, many people confront challenges in memory control, particularly if reminders are inescapable. The memories are recent and accessible. Given motivation to control awareness, however, intrusions diminish with time and effort. It is thus unavoidable that living with the demand to control an unwanted memory forces a person to improve with practice, as happens with all skills. This improvement will take the form of one or more habitual cognitive or affective responses to unwelcome reminders that suppress the experience and redirect thought. If practice continues over years, people may get very well adapted to the task. This protracted practice is a critical feature of real cases of motivated forgetting that is not easily studied in the laboratory.

In our initial discussion of retrieval suppression, we suggested that memory control may shift from being intentional to unintentional, in part through a gradual shift in the approach people take (Anderson & Green, 2001). According to this *intentionality shift theory*, people initially emphasize direct suppression because reminders elicit the unwanted memory involuntarily. Excluding the trace from awareness may often require direct suppression. Over time, however, people associate diversionary thoughts to the reminder, and may learn to retrieve those thoughts and pre-empt retrieval of the unwanted memory. Those thoughts may be other ideas about the reminder that a person selectively retrieves both as a means of occupying momentary awareness, and as a way of self-inflicting retrieval induced forgetting. Thus, extensive practice with unwelcome reminders may be associated with a progression from direct suppression to something more akin to our original selective retrieval hypothesis of motivated forgetting (Anderson, 2001; Bjork et al., 1998).

A gradual shift from a direct suppression approach to selective retrieval may ultimately permit people to forget not only the unpleasant experience, but also the process of suppressing it. There are two mechanisms by which this type of *goal forgetting* may occur. First, shifting from direct suppression to retrieving diversionary thoughts allows for a change in the goal people have from intentional control to retrieval of particular thoughts. Although the initial purpose of retrieving distracting thoughts is to intentionally suppress retrieval, this goal may be forgotten over time. If retrieval of thought substitutes reinstates inhibition of the unwanted event or further exaggerates interference, the shift from intentional suppression to selective retrieval should facilitate unawareness of the mental actions people take to avoid awareness of the unwanted memory. Second, as people become more practiced in retrieving diversionary thoughts in response to reminders, retrieval may become relatively automatic. If memories of earlier efforts to suppress are themselves associated to the reminder, this shift to retrieving alternative thoughts may ultimately suppress memories of control as well.

Although the intentionality shift theory is speculative, it may account for an important feature of recovered memories that may at first blush seem hard to reconcile with the emphasis we have placed on intentional retrieval suppression: the fact that people not only forget the original experience, but also how they came to forget it. This forgetting of the cognitions that one has about ones memories, including cognitions about intentional forgetting, might be termed *metamemory amnesia*, which we discuss next. A complete account of motivated forgetting thus requires an explanation both for how the memory itself was forgotten, and how the forgetting itself was forgotten.

The Reinstatement Hypothesis

The foregoing description assumes that forgetting becomes increasingly successful as people practice. Although this may be true for minor unpleasantness of life, more traumatic experiences may not progress as smoothly. Rather, truly upsetting experiences may be characterized by periodic resurgences in which the experience, not altogether forgotten, intrudes again, either in response to diminished capacity, new powerful reminders to the experience, or spontaneous recovery. These periodic challenges demand that retrieval suppression be reinstated. This may take the form of a return to intentional suppression or, instead, a resumption of diversionary thoughts.

Undoubtedly remindings of the unwanted experience are unpleasant, as are thoughts about the experience of being reminded. For these reasons, reinstatement of suppression will not merely be targeted at the original experience, but also thoughts that one has about it during the period of reminding. As such, even when a person remembers the experience for a period of time, they may not remember the remembering on later occasions. The reasons for this metamemory amnesia are straightforward. If we remember our thoughts –whether about perceptions or other thoughts – it is because these thoughts are stored in episodic memory as part of the content of experience. If a new trace is stored that encodes our thoughts about the memory, this new trace will share much in common with the original memory and be a natural target for retrieval suppression.

The reinstatement process thus predicts the phenomenon that Jonathan Schooler and colleagues called the "forgot it all along" effect, in which a person claims to have never recalled an experience when they have (Schooler, Bendiksen, & Ambadar, 1997; Shobe & Schooler, 2001). Schooler recounts cases of people who are convinced that they recovered a memory for childhood abuse never before retrieved, only to be corrected another person, who points out that the experience had been discussed years earlier. This forgot-it-all-along (FIA) effect has been modeled in the laboratory by the forgot-it-all-along paradigm (Arnold & Lindsay, 2002; Geraerts, 2012, this volume; Geraerts, Arnold, Lindsay, Merckelbach, Jelicic, & Hauer, 2006). Although forgetting prior remembering has been explained in terms of context dependent memory, real cases could just as easily be explained by reinstatement of retrieval suppression. Importantly, although some have taken the forgetting of prior remembering as evidence for an alternative hypothesis to motivated forgetting, the present analysis demonstrates that this conclusion is not demanded by this phenomenon. Rather, periodic recoveries and reinstatements are to be expected based on retrieval suppression, as is metamemory amnesia.

The Influence of Other Forgetting Mechanisms Over Time

Although we have emphasized retrieval suppression, it is not the only means of controlling unwanted memories. One can also truncate elaborative encoding, avoid retrieval cues where possible, and change physical context (Baddeley, Eysenck, & Anderson, 2009). In real cases, a person will not rely exclusively on one mechanism, but will use any approach that succeeds. For instance, when a person intentionally stops a train of thought about an unpleasant experience, they are not only controlling their momentary affective state, but also limiting the encoding of elaborate traces that may pose fresh difficulties in memory control. By limiting encoding, a person reduces the integration of the unwanted thoughts with the rest of memory, increasing the potential for it to be forgotten (Anderson, 2001). This type of memory control is well modeled by item method directed forgetting, discussed earlier, which establishes that people can exert considerable influence over which experiences make it into memory.

When unpleasant experiences make it into memory, however, people will try to prevent retrieval from occurring. In this article, we have focused on cases in which reminders are inescapable and retrieval must be suppressed or redirected. The mechanisms engaged to control memory will likely be very different if reminders can be avoided altogether, however. Avoiding reminders eliminates the need to override retrieval or to retrain one's response to reminders. If retrieval suppression does not occur, then the consequences of retrieval suppression should also be avoided. Thus, avoiding reminders by changing physical contexts (e.g., moving to a different city or apartment) will probably work to reduce intrusions, but may not suppress the avoided memories if relevant cues do emerge. Hence, when people who have successfully avoided reminders in an initial context encounter reminders in a later and different context, they may experience full recollection of the unwanted memory (Brewin, 2012, this volume). Thus, cue avoidance and context shift deprive a person of a chance to retrain memory. This may be why abuse by a stranger more likely leads to continuous memory, whereas abuse by a parent is more likely to produce at least a partial forgetting of the abuse (Anderson, 2001; DePrince et al., 2012, this volume).

Truncated encoding and motivated context shifts may occur at different points in the development of a person's response to an unwanted memory. Truncated encoding may play a more important role early on, as a person strives to limit encoding and elaboration during or shortly after the experience. For instance, a person who tries to "remove themselves" psychologically from an unpleasant situation by focusing on entirely unrelated thoughts, or details of the physical environment is in effect is trying to redirect attention to other content to avoid encoding. Attempts to not dwell upon an event or think elaboratively about it afterwards serve a similar function. In contrast, for individuals who must live with inescapable reminders, motivated context shifts may occur later in the evolution of their response, when after a period of time such reminders are no longer present. For example, as a child matures into an adult, they will ultimately leave their home and perhaps move to a different city. Alternatively, the physical context may remain the same and a person may seek a shift in mental context by segmenting off whole periods of their past. When this type of context shift occurs, there is a qualitative change in the coping mechanisms: context shift makes retrieval suppression less relevant. As such, effects induced by retrieval suppression may subside (e.g., suppression will be released), although this change may go unnoticed, as reminders do not occur. This shift in physical (and likely emotional and mental) context sets the stage, potentially, for recovery of a forgotten memory, should the right cue appear. This process – the attempt to intentionally shift context to forget – is modeled by the list-method directed forgetting procedure of Robert and Elizabeth Bjork (Bjork, & Bjork, 2003; Bjork, 1989; Geiselman et al., 1983) as discussed above.

More broadly, retrieval suppression is not synonymous with motivated forgetting. Motivated forgetting is achieved when people do not recall aspects of their past because they have engaged mechanisms to limit access to those experiences. The nature of those mechanisms may vary as long as they serve the broader motive of limiting awareness. Moreover, the motivated forgetting process is likely to be temporally extended, with the mechanisms engaged shaped by practice over time, and by changing circumstances of the individual controlling their memory. Thus, an understanding of how motivated forgetting emerges will require the development of laboratory models of different processes, and the incorporation of those into a broader framework of adaptive memory.

Assessing the Role of Retrieval Suppression in Recovered Memories

So far, we have focused on the mechanisms of retrieval suppression and how these mechanisms contribute to motivated forgetting. Our focus was not on the recovered memory debate, because the theoretical and practical themes of motivated forgetting transcend it. The purpose of this symposium, however, is to reconsider the scientific evidence in relation to this debate. Here we reflect on the implications of retrieval suppression for the recovered memory debate, and whether it may be one factor contributing to some cases of recovered memories.

Before beginning, it bears emphasis that this research cannot prove that any one recovered memory is real, and, if real, whether it may have been caused by suppression. The inconvenient truth is that even if a recovered memory is real, we will never know with certainty how and why it was forgotten, because the past events that led to the forgetting are unobservable. Because people reporting recovered memories often do not remember efforts to forget, evidence for retrieval suppression will often be indirect. As such, our comments should be taken as assessments of what may be possible in general, with conclusions about individual cases left to an assessment of its particulars. With those thoughts in mind, we divide our comments into what can and cannot reasonably be said.

What Can Be Said

The most basic implication of this research is that it provides an existence proof of a process that could, in principle, explain real cases of motivated forgetting, including cases of recovered memories. The work demonstrates that when people repeatedly confront reminders to an unwanted memory and take mental action to limit awareness of that memory, processes are engaged that achieve at least two basic outcomes: (a) they deprive a memory of the normal facilitation it would enjoy, and (b) they disrupt retention of the excluded trace, compared to when no reminders appear. Both of these actions, on average, reduce long-term accessibility of the suppressed trace, relative to other experiences of a similar age, which have the chance to be spontaneously retrieved given reminders. Reductions in accessibility are likely to be accomplished by several mechanisms, including direct suppression and thought substitution. Regardless of how these reductions are accomplished, however, one can certainly no longer say that there is no way, in principle, for motivated forgetting of abuse experiences to occur.

Of course, the present work was conducted with simple laboratory materials on very short time scales, and so proper caution must be exercised in generalizing these findings to events with considerably more complexity, emotional content, and personal relevance. Indeed, although these findings establish a process that could, in principle, produce these experiences, we emphasize that they do not, as yet, demonstrate a connection between recovered memories and retrieval suppression. As discussed in the preceding section, far more work needs to be done to develop retrieval suppression as a model of motivated forgetting. Thus, what has been established here is more properly viewed as a foundation for scientific development, rather than a completed proof of a process underlying motivated forgetting of abuse experiences.

Having said this, there is reason for optimism that the development of this case may succeed. Our retrieval suppression hypothesis was initially inspired by the higher incidence of self-reported forgetting for people abused by a parent than by a stranger. This pattern, on its face, is highly counter-intuitive, and led us to hypothesize that there may be something important about having to confront inescapable retrieval cues, coupled with a motivation to control awareness. Indeed, a similarly counter-intuitive retention pattern has been observed in the laboratory under the theoretically hypothesized conditions. The fact that these conditions in the laboratory are associated with enhanced forgetting lends credence to that hypothesis, and suggests that we may have identified one important contributor to some reports of recovered memories. Nevertheless, much work remains to connect this situation to the mechanisms studied in the laboratory. Indeed, for that connection to succeed, we must also fully explore why people are more likely to report forgetting abuse when it was committed by a caregiver.

Apart from providing an existence proof, the current work also provides a framework that suggests important hypotheses about when one is more likely to observe continuous versus discontinuous memory for abuse, and, moreover, the characteristics of forgetting under different circumstances. For instance, the current framework suggests that motivated forgetting accomplished by factors other than retrieval suppression, such as motivated context shifts, may differ in its characteristics from retrieval suppression. For instance, whereas reinstating the context of abuse may elicit strong recollections of the memory for people using motivated context shifts, it may be less effective as a means of eliciting retrieval of memories forgotten through retrieval suppression. If retrieval suppression has been maintained over the years in response to repeated reminders, the memory should be less accessible from those reminders and others.

What Cannot Be Said

Although it may be possible to develop a model of motivated forgetting built on the present work, we must clarify implications that do not, at present, follow from this work. First, as should be apparent from our discussion, we do not claim that all cases of memory recovery need to be produced by retrieval suppression. As we have emphasized, there are likely to be many cognitive routes to achieving reduced accessibility of unwanted memories, some of which will involve retrieval suppression, others of which will not. Retrieval suppression seems more likely to contribute in cases where a person is forced to confront unwelcome reminders over a long time, and is motivated to control awareness. As such, care should be taken to not overgeneralize the relationship of these findings to all cases of recovered memories.

Second, the present hypothesis frames motivated forgetting as a gradual process that people get better at with practice. Moreover, the process begins as an intentional act. For these reasons, the present mechanism does not address cases where memories are forgotten abruptly via an unconscious defense mechanism. So, for instance, if someone abruptly forgets a violent action shortly after it is taken, and has no recollection of the event, this does not obviously fall out of the processes envisioned here. Nevertheless, retrieval suppression might be involved, as some of the cases discussed here illustrate. Accounting for such cases requires one to provide additional arguments to why a process that normally develops with practice can be applied abruptly with dramatic effect, and with accompanying metamemory amnesia.

Third, the present framework does not imply that memories recovered after retrieval suppression will be accurate. The idea that suppressed memories may be preserved for many years and recovered in pristine form, seems highly implausible. Indeed, research on related inhibitory phenomena such as retrieval-induced forgetting, indicate that memories suppressed by inhibitory processes are actually more susceptible to distortion via misinformation effects than memories that have not been inhibited (see MacLeod & Saunders, 2008, for a review). Thus, suppressing unwanted memories over a long time may fragment the experience and render it subject to distortion and reconstruction processes of the sort discussed in other contributions to this symposium. Thus, an understanding of the memorial consequences of motivated forgetting is likely to require consideration of retrieval suppression and distortion processes (Erdelyi, 2006).

Concluding Remarks

A basic truth of human nature is that people don't like to feel bad. If there was ever a law of human behavior that could be counted on, it's that when someone is an aversive state, they will usually try to remove themselves from it. Similarly undeniable is the fact that not everything in memory is pleasant. Unlike unpleasant physical circumstances, however, one cannot as easily escape one's unpleasant memories. Wherever we go, they are with us. If people can be counted on to remove themselves from unpleasant states and if conscious awareness of some memories makes us feel unpleasant, it follows that people must be motivated to limit conscious awareness of certain memories. A scientific theory of forgetting cannot ignore the impact of these powerful motivational forces on shaping the fate of experience in long-term memory. What we remember and what we forget of our life experience is driven as much or more by our goals to regulate our current emotional state as it is by the passive, incidental factors traditionally emphasized in cognitive psychology.

The evidence that human beings try to control what they remember in service of regulating their emotional state is readily seen in the behavior of individuals and societies. As individuals, we alter our worlds to prevent being reminded of unpleasant experiences; we throw away objects given to us and we change apartments or towns; as societies, we even tear down buildings (e.g., the library associated with the Columbine shooting) or build new ones (e.g., the Millennium tower) to control what and how we remember. When forced to live with reminders, however, our only choice is to adjust our inner landscape. In this article, we discussed how this adjustment occurs. People control unwanted memories by engaging systems evolved to inhibit habitual responses to inhibit memories, making them harder to remember. The mechanisms that achieve this function are not exotic special-purpose responses to trauma, but rather are applications of broad mechanisms that achieve cognitive control. Thus, the tools to understand motivated forgetting are readily available in the armamentarium of cognitive neuroscience. Understanding how motivational forces alter what we remember of our lives provides key insights into what makes us resilient and shapes us as people.

Acknowledgments Preparation of this article was supported by National Science Foundation grant 0643321. The authors would like to thank Robert Bjork, Steve Smith, Karl-Heinz Bauml, Lili Sahakyan, Tracy Taylor-Hemick, Paula Hertel, Jutta Joormann, Kepa Paz-Alanso, Roland Benoit, and Zara Bergstrom for useful comments on this manuscript.

Appendix A

The 32 published articles on which the meta-analysis in Fig. 3 (right panel) is based. Note that four published articles are not included either because they used different dependent measures or did not fully report recall data (see caption, Fig. 3).

Reference	Participants	Suppressed Material
Anderson, M. C. & Green, C., 2001	normals (n=96)	neutral words
Hertel, P. T. & Gerstle, M., 2003	controls (n=32) and dysphorics (n=32)	positive and negative words
Anderson, M. C. et al., 2004	normals (n=24)	neutral words
Hertel, P. T. & Calcaterra, G., 2005	normals (n=72)	neutral words
Joormann, J. et al., 2005	controls (n=24) and depressed (n=32)	neutral words
Wessel, I. et al., 2005	low (n=33) and high (n=35) dissociators	neutral words
Bulevich, J. B. et al., 2006	normals (n=66)	neutral words
Bergstrom, Z. M. et al., 2007	normals (n=31)	neutral words
Depue, B. E. et al., 2007	normals (n=16)	negative IAPS scenes
Kim, K. et al., 2007	repressors (n=29) and nonrepressors (n=46)	neutral and negative words
Lee, Y. et al., 2007	normals (n=82)	neutral words
Salame, P. & Danion, J., 2007	schizophrenics (n=23) and controls (n=24)	neutral words
Hertel, P. T. & Mahan, A., 2008	dysphoric (n=18) and nondysphoric (n=18)	words related and unrelated to cue
Bergstrom, Z. M. et al., 2009	normals (n=48)	neutral words
Hanslmayr, S. et al., 2009	normals (n=24)	neutral words
Hotta, C. & Kawaguchi, J., 2009	normals (n=24)	neutral words
Joormann, J. et al., 2009	controls (n=45) and MDDs (n=45)	negative words
Mecklinger, A. et al., 2009	normals (n=24)	neutral words
Paz-Alonso, P. M. et al., 2009	8-12 year olds (n=40) and normals (n=30)	neutral words
Tomlinson, T. D. et al., 2009	normals (n=84)	neutral words
Tramoni, E. et al., 2009	functional amnesia patient (n=1) and controls (n=12)	neutral words
Dieler, A. C. et al., 2010	normals (n=16)	positive, negative and neutral words
Hanslmayr, S. et al., 2010	normals (n=48)	neutral words
Hertel, P. & McDaniel, L., 2010	repressors (n=36) and nonrepressors (n=36)	negative words
Lambert, A. J. et al., 2010	normals (n=126)	neutral words
Lemoult, J. et al., 2010	normals (n=56)	neutral words
Norby, S. et al., 2010	normals (n=48)	neutral and negative words
Wessel, I. et al., 2010	morning and evening types (n=80)	neutral words
Anderson, M. C. et al., 2011	older adults (n=61) and younger adults (n=62)	neutral words
Meier, B. et al., 2011	normals (n=20)	neutral words
Murray, B. D. et al., 2011	older adults (n=79) and younger adults (n=87)	neutral words
Waldhauser, G. T. et al., 2011	high anxiety and low anxiety (total n=41)	neutral words

References

Adams, Z. W., Derefinko, K. J., Milich, R., & Fillmore, M. T. (2008). Inhibitory functioning across ADHD subtypes: Recent findings, clinical implications, and future directions. *Developmental Disabilities Research Reviews, 14*(4), 268–275. doi:10.1002/ddrr.37.

Allen, G. A., Mahler, W. A., & Estes, W. K. (1969). Effects of recall tests on long-term retention of paired associates. *Journal of Verbal Learning and Verbal Behavior, 8*(4), 463–470.

Anderson, M. C. (2001). Active forgetting: Evidence for functional inhibition as a source of memory failure. *Journal of Aggression, Maltreatment, and Trauma, 4*(2), 185–210.

Anderson, M. C. (2003). Rethinking interference theory: Executive control and the mechanisms of forgetting. *Journal of Memory and Language, 49*, 415–445.

Anderson, M. C. (2005). The role of inhibitory control in forgetting unwanted memories: A consideration of three methods. In C. MacLeod & B. Uttl (Eds.), *Dynamic cognitive processes* (pp. 159–190). Tokyo: Springer.

Anderson, M. C., Bjork, R., & Bjork, E. (1994). Remembering can cause forgetting: Retrieval dynamics in long-term memory. *Journal of Experimental Psychology: Learning, Memory, and Cognition, 20*(5), 1063–1087.

Anderson, M. C., & Green, C. (2001). Suppressing unwanted memories by executive control. *Nature, 410*, 366–369.

Anderson, M. C., Reinholz, J., Kuhl, B., & Mayr, U. (2011). Intentional suppression of unwanted memories grows more difficult as we age. *Psychology and Aging, 26*, 397–405.

Anderson, M. C., & Levy, B. J. (2006). Encouraging the nascent cognitive neuroscience of repression. *Behavioral and Brain Sciences, 29*(5), 511–513.

Anderson, M. C., Ochsner, K. N., Kuhl, B., Cooper, J., Robertson, E., Gabrieli, S. W., et al. (2004). Neural systems underlying the suppression of unwanted memories. *Science, 303*(5655), 232–235. doi:10.1126/science.1089504.

Anderson, M. C., & Spellman, B. A. (1995). On the status of inhibitory mechanisms in cognition: Memory retrieval as a model case. *Psychological Review, 102*(1), 68–100.

Anderson, M. C., & Weaver, C. (2009). Inhibitory control over action and memory. In L. R. Squire (Ed.), *The new encyclopedia of neuroscience* (pp. 153–163). Oxford: Elsevier Ltd. doi:10.1016/B978-008045046- 9.00421-6.

Arnold, M. M., & Lindsay, D. S. (2002). Remembering remembering. *Journal of Experimental Psychology: Learning, Memory, and Cognition, 28*, 521–529.

Aron, A. R., Fletcher, P. C., Bullmore, E. T., Sahakian, B. J., & Robbins, T. W. (2003). Stop-signal inhibition disrupted by damage to right inferior frontal gyrus in humans. *Nature Neuroscience, 6*(2), 115–116. doi:10.1038/nn1003.

Aslan, A., & Bäuml, K. T. (2010). Retrieval-induced forgetting in young children. *Psychonomic Bulletin and Review, 17*(5), 704–709. doi:10.3758/PBR.17.5.704.

Baddeley, A. D., Eysenck, M., & Anderson, M. C. (2009). *Memory*. Hove: Psychology Press.

Band, G. P., & van Boxtel, G. J. (1999). Inhibitory motor control in stop paradigms: Review and reinterpretation of neural mechanisms. *Acta Psychologica, 101*(2–3), 179–211.

Barkley, R. (1997). Behavioral inhibition, sustained attention, and executive functions: Constructing a unifying theory of ADHD. *Psychological Bulletin, 121*(1), 65–94.

Basden, B. H., Basden, D. R., & Gargano, G. J. (1993). Directed forgetting in implicit and explicit memory tests: A comparison of methods. *Journal of Experimental Psychology: Learning, Memory, and Cognition, 19*(3), 603–616.

Baumeister, R. (2003). Ego depletion and self-regulation failure: A resource model of self-control. *Alcoholism, Clinical and Experimental Research, 27*(2), 281–284. doi:10.1097/01.ALC.0000060879.61384.A4.

Baumeister, R., Bratslavsky, E., Muraven, M., & Tice, D. M. (1998). Ego depletion: Is the active self a limited resource. *Journal of Personality and Social Psychology, 74*(5), 1252–1265.

Bekker, E. M., Kenemans, J. L., & Verbaten, M. N. (2005). Source analysis of the N2 in a cued Go/NoGo task. *Cognitive Brain Research, 22*(2), 221–231. doi:10.1016/j.cogbrainres.2004.08.011.

Benjamin, A. (2010). In Benjamin Aaron (Ed.), *Successful remembering and successful forgetting: A festschrift in honor of Robert A. Bjork*. New York: Psychology Press.

Bergstrom, Z. M., Anderson, M. C., Buda, M., Simons, J., & Richardson-Klavehn, A. (submitted). Intentional retrieval suppression can conceal guilty knowledge in ERP memory detection tests.

Bergström, Z. M., de Fockert, J. W., & Richardson-Klavehn, A. (2009). ERP and behavioural evidence for direct suppression of unwanted memories. *NeuroImage, 48*(4), 726–737. doi:10.1016/j.neuroimage.2009.06.051.

Bergström, Z. M., Velmans, M., de Fockert, J., & Richardson-Klavehn, A. (2007). ERP evidence for successful voluntary avoidance of conscious recollection. *Brain Research, 1151*, 119–133. doi:10.1016/j.brainres.2007.03.014.

Bjork, R. A. (1972). Theoretical implications of directed forgetting. In A. W. Melton & E. Martin (Eds.), *Coding processes in human memory* (pp. 217–235). Washington, DC: Winston.

Bjork, R. A. (1975). Retrieval as a memory modifier. In R. Solso (Ed.), *Information processing and cognition: The Loyola Symposium* (pp. 123–144). Hillsdale, NJ: Lawrence Erlbaum Associates.

Bjork, R. A. (1989). Retrieval inhibition as an adaptive mechanism in human memory. In H. L. Roediger & F. I. M. Craik (Eds.), *Varieties of memory and consciousness: Essays in honour of Endel Tulving* (pp. 309–330). Hillsdale, NJ: Erlbaum.

Bjork, E. L., & Bjork, R. A. (2003). Intentional forgetting can increase, not decrease, the residual influences of to-be-forgotten information. *Journal of Experimental Psychology: Learning, Memory, and Cognition, 29*, 524–531.

Bjork, E. L., Bjork, R. A., & Anderson, M. C. (1998). Varieties of goal-directed forgetting. In J. M. Golding & C. M. MacLeod (Eds.), *Intentional forgetting: Interdisciplinary approaches* (pp. 103–137). Hillsdale, NJ: Erlbaum.

Bokura, H., Yamaguchi, S., & Kobayashi, S. (2001). Electrophysiological correlates for response inhibition in a Go/NoGo task. *Clinical Neurophysiology, 112*(12), 2224–2232.

Booth, J. R., Burman, D. D., Meyer, J. R., Lei, Z., Trommer, B. L., Davenport, N. D., et al. (2005). Larger deficits in brain networks for response inhibition than for visual selective attention in attention deficit hyperactivity disorder (ADHD). *The Journal of Child Psychology and Psychiatry, 46*(1), 94–111. doi:10.1111/j.1469-7610.2004.00337.x.

Brewin, C. R. (2012, this volume). A theoretical framework for understanding recovered memory experiences. In R. F. Belli (Ed.), *True and false recovered memories: Toward a reconciliation of the debate* (pp. 149–173). *Vol. 58: Nebraska Symposium on Motivation.* New York: Springer.

Brown, A. S. (1976). Spontaneous recovery and human learning. *Psychological Bulletin, 83*, 321–338.

Bulevich, J. B., Roediger, H. L., Balota, D. A., & Butler, A. C. (2006). Failures to find suppression of episodic memories in the think/no-think paradigm. *Memory & Cognition, 34*(8), 1569–1577.

Butler, A. J., & James, K. H. (2010). The neural correlates of attempting to suppress negative versus neutral memories. *Cognitive, Affective, & Behavioral Neuroscience, 10*(2), 182–194. doi:10.3758/CABN.10.2.182.

Cameron, C. (1993, April). *Recovering memories of childhood sexual abuse: A longitudinal report.* Paper presented at the Western Psychological Association convention, Phoenix, AZ, USA.

Carrier, M., & Pashler, H. (1992). The influence of retrieval on retention. *Memory & Cognition, 20*(6), 633–642.

Casey, B. J., Castellanos, F. X., Giedd, J. N., Marsh, W. L., Hamburger, S. D., Schubert, A. B., et al. (1997). Implication of right frontostriatal circuitry in response inhibition and attention-deficit/hyperactivity disorder. *Journal of the American Academy of Child and Adolescent Psychiatry, 36*(3), 374–383. doi:10.1097/00004583-199703000-00016.

Chan, J. C. K. (2009). Long-term effects of testing on the recall of nontested materials. *Memory, 18*(1), 49–57. doi:10.1080/09658210903405737.

Conroy, R., & Salmon, K. (2005). Selective postevent review and childrens' memory for nonreviewed materials. *Journal of Experimental Child Psychology, 90*(4), 185–207. doi:10.1016/j.jecp. 2004.11.004.

Conroy, R., & Salmon, K. (2006). Talking about parts of a past experience: The impact of discussion style and event structure on memory for discussed and nondiscussed information. *Journal of Experimental Child Psychology, 95*(4), 278–297. doi:10.1016/j.jecp. 2006.06.001.

DePrince, A., Brown, L., Cheit, R., Freyd, J., Gold, S. N., Pezdek, K., & Quina, K. (2012, this volume). Motivated forgetting and misremembering: Perspectives from betrayal trauma theory. In R. F. Belli (Ed.), *True and false recovered memories: Toward a reconciliation of the debate* (pp. 193–242). *Vol. 58: Nebraska Symposium on Motivation.* New York: Springer.

Depue, B. E., Banich, M. T., & Curran, T. (2006). Suppression of emotional and nonemotional content in memory: Effects of repetition on cognitive control. *Psychological Science, 17*(5), 441–447. doi:10.1111/j.1467-9280.2006.01725.x.

Depue, B. E., Burgess, G. C., Willcutt, E. G., Bidwell, L. C., Ruzic, L., & Banich, M. T. (2010). Symptom-correlated brain regions in young adults with combined-type ADHD: Their organization, variability, and relation to behavioral performance. *Psychiatry Research: Neuroimaging, 182*(2), 96–102. doi:10.1016/j.pscychresns.2009.11.011.

Depue, B. E., Burgess, G. C., Willcutt, E. G., Ruzic, L., & Banich, M. T. (2010). Inhibitory control of memory retrieval and motor processing associated with the right lateral prefrontal cortex:

Evidence from deficits in individuals with ADHD. *Neuropsychologia, 48*(13), 3909–3917. doi:10.1016/j.neuropsychologia.2010.09.013.

Depue, B. E., Curran, T., & Banich, M. T. (2007). Prefrontal regions orchestrate suppression of emotional memories via a two-phase process. *Science, 317*(5835), 215–219. doi:10.1126/science.1139560.

Detre, G. J., Natarajan, A., & Norman, K. A. (2010, November). *Moderate memory activation leads to forgetting in the Think-No Think paradigm.* Poster presented at the Annual Meeting of the Society for Neuroscience, San Diego, CA, USA.

Dieler, A. C., Plichta, M. M., Dresler, T., & Fallgatter, A. J. (2010). Suppression of emotional words in the Think/No-Think paradigm investigated with functional near-infrared spectroscopy. *International Journal of Psychophysiology, 78*(2), 129–135. doi:10.1016/j.ijpsycho.2010.06.358.

Donkers, F., & van Boxtel, G. J. M. (2004). The N2 in go/no-go tasks reflects conflict monitoring not response inhibition. *Brain and Cognition, 56*, 165–176.

Duzel, E., Cabeza, R., Picton, T. W., Yonelinas, A. P., Scheich, H., Heinze, H. J., et al. (1999). Task-related and item-related brain processes of memory retrieval. *Proceedings of the National Academy of Sciences, 96*, 1794–1799.

Eimer, M. (1993). Effects of attention and stimulus probability on ERPs in a Go/Nogo task. *Biological Psychology, 35*(2), 123–138.

Eldridge, L. L., Knowlton, B. J., Furmanski, C. S., Bookheimer, S. Y., & Engel, S. A. (2000). Remembering episodes: A selective role for the hippocampus during retrieval. *Nature Neuroscience, 3*, 1149.

Erdelyi, M. H. (1996). *The recovery of unconscious memories: Hypermnesia and reminiscence.* Chicago: The University of Chicago Press.

Erdelyi, M. H. (2006). The unified theory of repression. *Behavioral and Brain Sciences, 29*(5), 499–551. doi:10.1017/S0140525X06009113.

Erdelyi, M., & Kleinbard, J. (1978). Has Ebbinghaus decayed with time? The growth of recall (hypermnesia) over days. *Journal of Experimental Psychology: Human Learning and Memory, 4*(4), 275–289.

Falkenstein, M. (2006). Inhibition, conflict and the Nogo-N2. *Clinical Neurophysiology, 117*(8), 1638–1640. doi:10.1016/j.clinph.2006.05.002.

Falkenstein, M., Hoormann, J., & Hohnsbein, J. (1999). ERP components in Go/Nogo tasks and their relation to inhibition. *Acta Psychologica, 101*(2–3), 267–291.

Fawcett, J. M., & Taylor, T. L. (2008). Forgetting is effortful: Evidence from reaction time probes in an item-method directed forgetting task. *Memory & Cognition, 36*(6), 1168–1181.

Feldman-Summers, S., & Pope, K. S. (1994). The experience of 'forgetting' child abuse: A national survey of psychologists. *Journal of Consulting and Clinical Psychology, 3*, 626–639.

Ford, R. M., Keating, S., & Patel, R. (2004). Retrieval-induced foregetting: A developmental study. *Developmental Psychology, 22*(4), 5850–603.

Freyd, J. J. (1996). *Betrayal trauma: The logic of forgetting childhood abuse.* Cambridge, MA: Harvard University Press.

Freyd, J. J., DePrince, A. P., & Gleaves, D. (2007). The state of betrayal trauma theory: Reply to McNally – conceptual issues and future directions. *Memory, 15*, 295–311.

Freyd, J. J., Deprince, A. P., & Zurbriggen, E. L. (2006). Self-reported memory for abuse depends upon victim-perpetrator relationship. *Journal of Trauma & Dissociation, 2*(3), 5–15.

Friedman, D., & Johnson, R. (2000). Event-related potential (ERP) studies of memory encoding and retrieval: A selective review. *Microscopy Research and Technique, 51*(1), 6–28. doi:10.1002/1097-0029(20001001)51:1<6::AID-JEMT2>3.0.CO;2-R.

Garavan, H., Ross, T. J., Murphy, K., Roche, R. A. P., & Stein, E. A. (2002). Dissociable executive functions in the dynamic control of behavior: Inhibition, error detection, and correction. *NeuroImage, 17*(4), 1820–1829.

Garcia-Bajos, E., Migueles, M., & Anderson, M. C. (2009). Script knowledge modulates retrieval-induced forgetting for eyewitness events. *Memory, 17*(1), 92–103. doi:10.1080/09658210802572454.

Geiselman, R. E., Bjork, R. A., & Fishman, D. L. (1983). Disrupted retrieval in directed forgetting: A link with posthypnotic amnesia. *Journal of Experimental Psychology: General, 112*(1), 58–72.

Geraerts, E., Arnold, M. M., Lindsay, D. S., Merckelbach, H., Jelicic, M., & Hauer, B. (2006). Forgetting of prior remembering in people reporting recovered memories of childhood sexual abuse. *Psychological Science, 17*, 1002–1008.

Geraerts, E. (2012, this volume). Cognitive underpinnings of recovered memories of childhood abuse. In R. F. Belli (Ed.), *True and false recovered memories: Toward a reconciliation of the debate* (pp. 175–191). *Vol. 58: Nebraska Symposium on Motivation.* New York: Springer.

Geraerts, E., McNally, R. J., Jelicic, M., Merckelbach, H., & Raymaekers, L. (2008). Linking thought suppression and recovered memories of childhood sexual abuse. *Memory, 16*(1), 22–28. doi:10.1080/09658210701390628.

Goernert, P. (2005). Source-monitoring accuracy across repeated tests following directed forgetting. *British Journal of Psychology, 96*(2), 231–247.

Goernert, P. N., & Wolfe, T. (1997). Is there hypermnesia and reminiscence for information intentionally forgotten? *Canadian Journal of Experimental Psychology, 51*(3), 231–240.

Goldberg, L. R., & Freyd, J. J. (2006). Self-reports of potentially traumatic experiences in an adult community sample: Gender differences and test-retest stabilities of the items in a brief betrayal-trauma survey. *Journal of Trauma & Dissociation, 7*(3), 39–63.

Golding, J. M., & MacLeod, C. M. (1998). *Intentional forgetting: Interdisciplinary approaches.* Mahwah, NJ: Erlbaum.

Goodman, G. S., Ghetti, S., Quas, J. A., Edelstein, R. S., Alexander, K. W., Redlich, A. D., et al. (2003). A prospective study of memory for child sexual abuse: New findings relevant to the repressed-memory controversy. *Psychological Science, 14*, 113–118.

Goodmon, L. B., & Anderson, M. C. (2011). Semantic integration as a boundary condition on inhibitory processes in episodic retrieval. *Journal of Experimental Psychology: Learning, Memory, and Cognition, 37*(2), 416–436. doi:10.1037/a0021963.

Hagger, M. S., Wood, C., Stiff, C., & Chatzisarantis, N. L. D. (2010). Ego depletion and the strength model of self-control: A meta-analysis. *Psychological Bulletin, 136*(4), 495–525. doi:10.1037/a0019486.

Hanslmayr, S., Leipold, P., & Bauml, K. (2010). Anticipation boosts forgetting of voluntarily suppressed memories. *Memory, 18*, 252–257. doi:10.1080/09658210903476548.

Hanslmayr, S., Leipold, P., Pastötter, B., & Bäuml, K. (2009). Anticipatory signatures of voluntary memory suppression. *The Journal of Neuroscience, 29*(9), 2742–2747. doi:10.1523/JNEUROSCI.4703-08.2009.

Harnishfeger, K. K., & Pope, R. S. (1996). Intending to forget: The development of cognitive inhibition in directed forgetting. *Journal of Experimental Child Psychology, 62*(2), 292–315. doi:10.1006/jecp. 1996.0032.

Hasher, L., & Zacks, R. T. (1988). Working memory, comprehension, and aging: A review and a new view. In H. Bower (Ed.), *The psychology of learning and motivation* (Vol. 22, pp. 193–225). San Diego, CA: Academic.

Henkel, L. A. (2004). Erroneous memories arising from repeated attempts to remember. *Journal of Memory and Language, 50*, 26–46.

Henkel, L., & Koffman, K. J. (2004). Memory distortions in coerced false confessions: A source monitoring framework analysis. *Applied Cognitive Psychology, 18*(5), 567–588.

Hertel, P. T. (1994). Depressive deficits in memory: Implications of research and theory for memory improvement following traumatic brain injury. *NeuroRehabilitation, 4*, 143–150.

Hertel, P. T. (1998). Relation between rumination and impaired memory in dysphoric moods. *Journal of Abnormal Psychology, 107*(1), 166–172.

Hertel, P. T., Large, D., Dahl, E., & Levy, A. (2011). Suppression-induced forgetting on a free-association test.

Hertel, P. T., & Calcaterra, G. (2005). Intentional forgetting benefits from thought substitution. *Psychonomic Bulletin and Review, 12*(3), 484–489.

Hertel, P. T., & Gerstle, M. (2003). Depressive deficits in forgetting. *Psychological Science, 14*(6), 573–578.

Hertel, P., & Mahan, A. (2008). Depression-related differences in learning and forgetting responses to unrelated cues. *Acta Psychologica, 127*(3), 636–644. doi:10.1016/j.actpsy.2007.11.004.

Hertel, P., & McDaniel, L. (2010). The suppressive power of positive thinking: Aiding suppression-induced forgetting in repressive coping. *Cognition and Emotion, 24*(7), 1239–1249.

Hotta, C., & Kawaguchi, J. (2009). Self-initiated use of thought substitution can lead to long term forgetting. *Psychologia, 52*(1), 41–49.

Hourihan, K. L., & Taylor, T. L. (2006). Cease remembering: Control processes in directed forgetting. *Journal Of Experimental Psychology: Human Perception and Performance, 32*(6), 1354–1365. doi:10.1037/0096-1523.32.6.1354.

Huddleston, E., & Anderson, M.C. (in preparation). Retrieval suppression modulates activation in content-specific neocortical areas.

Hulbert, J. C., Anderson, M. C., & Kuhl, B. (in preparation). Enhanced inhibitory control over memory in people with extensive traumatic experience.

Hulbert, M. C., Shivde, G. S., & Anderson, M. C. (2011). Evidence against associative blocking as a cause of cue-independent retrieval-induced forgetting. *Experimental Psychology*.

Iversen, S., & Mishkin, M. (1970). Perseverative interference in monkeys following selective lesions of inferior prefrontal convexity. *Experimental Brain Research, 11*(4), 376–386.

Johnson, M. K. (1994). Binding complex memories: The role of reactivation and the hippocampus. In D. L. Schacter & E. Tulving (Eds.), *Memory systems* (pp. 311–350). Cambridge, MA: The MIT Press.

Johnson, R., Kreiter, K., Russo, B., & Zhu, J. (1998). A spatio-temporal analysis of recognition-related event-related brain potentials. *International Journal of Psychophysiology, 29*(1), 83–104.

Joormann, J., Hertel, P. T., Brozovich, F., & Gotlib, I. H. (2005). Remembering the good, forgetting the bad: Intentional forgetting of emotional material in depression. *Journal of Abnormal Psychology, 114*(4), 640–648. doi:10.1037/0021-843X.114.4.640.

Joormann, J., Hertel, P. T., Lemoult, J., & Gotlib, I. H. (2009). Training forgetting of negative material in depression. *Journal of Abnormal Psychology, 118*(1), 34–43. doi:10.1037/a0013794.

Joormann, J., Yoon, K. L., & Zetsche, U. (2007). Cognitive inhibition in depression. *Applied and Preventive Psychology, 12*, 128–139.

Karpicke, J. D., & Roediger, H. L. (2008). The critical importance of retrieval for learning. *Science, 319*(5865), 966–968. doi:10.1126/science.1152408.

Kikuchi, H., Fujii, T., Abe, N., Suzuki, M., Takagi, M., Mugikura, S., et al. (2010). Memory repression: Brain mechanisms underlying dissociative amnesia. *Journal of Cognitive Neuroscience, 22*(3), 602–613. doi:10.1162/jocn.2009.21212.

Kim, K., & Yi, D. (2008, November). Perceptual consequences of memory suppression. Poster presented at the Annual Meeting of the Society for Neuroscience, Washington, DC, USA.

Kim, K., Yi, D., Yang, E., & Lee, K. (2007). What makes repressors good suppressors? The effect of trait anxiety. *Korean Journal of Psychology, 26*, 261–277.

Kopp, B., Mattler, U., Goertz, R., & Rist, F. (1996). N2, P3 and the lateralized readiness potential in a nogo task involving selective response priming. *Electroencephalography and Clinical Neurophysiology, 99*(1), 19–27.

Lambert, A. J., Good, K. S., & Kirk, I. J. (2010). Testing the repression hypothesis: Effects of emotional valence on memory suppression in the think – no think task. *Consciousness and Cognition, 19*(1), 281–293. doi:10.1016/j.concog.2009.09.004.

Landauer, T. K., & Bjork, R. A. (1978). Optimum rehearsal patterns and name learning. In M. M. Gruneberg, P. E. Morris, & R. N. Sykes (Eds.), *Practical aspects of memory* (pp. 625–632). New York: Academic.

Lavric, A., Pizzagalli, D. A., & Forstmeier, S. (2004). When 'go' and 'nogo' are equally frequent: ERP components and cortical tomography. *The European Journal of Neuroscience, 20*(9), 2483–2488. doi:10.1111/j.1460-9568.2004.03683.x.

Lee, Y., Lee, H., & Tsai, S. (2007). Effects of post-cue interval on intentional forgetting. *British Journal of Psychology, 98*(2), 257–272. doi:10.1348/000712606X120410.

LeMoult, J., Hertel, P. T., & Joorman, J. (2010). Training the forgetting of negative words: The role of direct suppression and the relation to stress reactivity. *Applied Cognitive Psychology, 24,* 365–375.

Levy, B. J., & Anderson, M. C. (2002). Inhibitory processes and the control of memory retrieval. *Trends in Cognitive Sciences, 6*(7), 299–305.

Levy, B. J., & Anderson, M. C. (2008). Individual differences in the suppression of unwanted memories: The executive deficit hypothesis. *Acta Psychologica, 127*(3), 623–635. doi:10.1016/j.actpsy.2007.12.004.

Levy, B. J., & Wagner, A. D. (2011). Cognitive control and right ventrolateral prefrontal cortex: reflexive reorienting, motor inhibition, and action updating. *Annals of the New York Academy of Sciences, 1224,* 40–62.

Logan, G. D., Cowan, W., & Davis, K. (1994). On the ability to inhibit thought and action: A users' guide to the stop-signal paradigm. In D. D. Carr & T. H. Carr (Eds.), *Inhibitory processes in attention, memory, and language* (pp. 189–239). San Diego, CA: Academic.

Luria, A. R. (1966). *Higher cortical functions in man.* New York: Basic Books.

Lustig, C., Hasher, L., & Tonev, S. T. (2001a). Inhibitory control over the present and the past. *European Journal of Cognitive Psychology, 13,* 107–122.

MacDonald, A. W., Cohen, J. D., Stenger, V. A., & Carter, C. S. (2000). Dissociating the role of the dorsolateral prefrontal and anterior cingulate cortex in cognitive control. *Science, 288*(5472), 1835–1838.

MacLeod, M., & Macrae, C. (2001). Gone but not forgotten: The transient nature of retrieval-induced forgetting. *Psychological Science, 12*(2), 148–152.

MacLeod, M. D., & Saunders, J. (2008). Retrieval inhibition and memory distortion: Negative consequences of an adaptive process. *Current Directions in Psychological Science, 17*(1), 26–30.

Marx, B. P., Marshall, P. J., & Castro, F. (2008). The moderating effects of stimulus valence and arousal on memory suppression. *Emotion, 8*(2), 199–207. doi:10.1037/1528-3542.8.2.199.

McNally, R. J. (2007). Betrayal trauma theory: A critical appraisal. *Memory, 15,* 280–294.

Mecklinger, A., Parra, M., & Waldhauser, G. T. (2009). ERP correlates of intentional forgetting. *Brain Research, 1255*(C), 132–147. doi:doi:10.1016/j.brainres.2008.11.073.

Meier, B., König, A., Parak, S., & Henke, K. (2011). Suppressed, but not forgotten. *Swiss Journal of Psychology, 70*(1), 5–11. doi:10.1024/1421-0185/a000033.

Menon, V., Adleman, N. E., White, C. D., Glover, G. H., & Reiss, A. L. (2001). Error-related brain activation during a Go/NoGo response inhibition task. *Human Brain Mapping, 12*(3), 131–143.

Murray, B. D., Muscatell, K. A., & Kensinger, E. A. (2011). Effects of Emotion and Age on Performance During a Think/No-Think Memory Task Psychology and Aging in press.

Nigg, J. (2000). On inhibition/disinhibition in developmental psychopathology: Views from cognitive and personality psychology and a working inhibition taxonomy. *Psychological Bulletin, 126*(2), 220–246.

Nigg, J. (2001). Is ADHD a disinhibitory disorder? *Psychological Bulletin, 127*(5), 571–598. doi:10.1037//0033-2909.127.5.571.

Nørby, S., Lange, M., & Larsen, A. (2010). Forgetting to forget: On the duration of voluntary suppression of neutral and emotional memories. *Acta Psychologica, 133*(1), 73–80. doi:10.1016/j.actpsy.2009.10.002.

Norman, W., & Shallice, T. (1986). Attention to action. In R. J. Davidson, G. E. Schwartz, & D. Shapiro (Eds.), *Consciousness and self regulation: Advances in research and theory* (Vol. 4, pp. 1–18). New York: Plenum.

Ogle, C. M., & Paz-Alonso, P. M. (in preparation). Developmental changes in the suppression of emotional memories.

Oosterlaan, J., Logan, G. D., & Sergeant, J. A. (1998). Response inhibition in AD/HD, CD, comorbid AD/HD+CD, anxious, and control children: A meta-analysis of studies with the stop task. *Journal of Child Psychology and Psychiatry, 39*(3), 411–425.

Pavlov, I. P. (1927) *Conditioned reflexes* (G. V. Anrep, Trans.). London: Oxford University Press.

Payne, D. G. (1987). Hypermnesia and reminiscence in recall: A historical and empirical review. *Psychological Bulletin, 101*(1), 5–27. doi:10.1037/0033-2909.101.1.5.

Paz-Alonso, P. M., Ghetti, S., Wendelken, C., Anderson, M. C., & Bunge, S. (2011). Mnemonic control relies on a frontal-parietal-hippocampal network that is strengthened over childhood.

Paz-Alonso, P. M., Ghetti, S., Matlen, B. J., Anderson, M. C., & Bunge, S. A. (2009). Memory suppression is an active process that improves over childhood. *Frontiers in Human Neuroscience, 3*, 24. doi:10.3389/neuro.09.024.2009.

Quay, H. C. (1997). Inhibition and attention deficit hyperactivity disorder. *Journal of Abnormal Child Psychology, 25*(1), 7–13.

Racsmány, M., Conway, M. A., & Demeter, G. (2010). Consolidation of episodic memories during sleep: Long-term effects of retrieval practice. *Psychological Science, 21*(1), 80–85. doi:10.1177/0956797609354074.

Ramautar, J., Kok, A., & Ridderinkhof, K. (2004). Effects of stop-signal probability in the stop-signal paradigm: The N2/P3 complex further validated. *Brain and Cognition, 56*(2), 234–252. doi:10.1016/j.bandc.2004.07.002.

Rescorla, R. A. (2004). Spontaneous recovery. *Learning & Memory, 11*(5), 501–509. doi:10.1101/lm.77504.

Rubia, K., Overmeyer, S., Taylor, E., Brammer, M., Williams, S., Simmons, A., et al. (1999). Hypofrontality in attention deficit hyperactivity disorder during higher-order motor control: A study with functional MRI. *American Journal of Psychiatry, 156*, 891–896.

Rubia, K., Smith, A. B., Brammer, M. J., Tonne, B., & Taylor, E. (2005). Abnormal brain activation during inhibition and error detection in medication-naive adolescents with ADHD. *American Journal of Psychiatry, 162*, 1067–1075.

Sahakyan, L., & Kelley, C. (2002). A contextual change account of the directed forgetting effect. *Journal of Experimental Psychology: Learning, Memory, and Cognition, 28*(6), 1064–1072. doi:10.1037//0278-7393.28.6.1064.

Sahakyan, L., Waldum, E. R., Benjamin, A. S., & Bickett, S. P. (2009). Where is the forgetting with list-method directed forgetting in recognition? *Memory & Cognition, 37*(4), 464–476. doi:10.3758/MC.37.4.464.

Salamé, P., & Danion, J. (2007). Inhibition of inappropriate responses is preserved in the Think-No-Think and impaired in the random number generation tasks in schizophrenia. *Journal of the International Neuropsychological Society, 13*(2), 277–287. doi:10.1017/S1355617707070300.

Sasaki, K., Gemba, H., & Tsujimoto, T. (1989). Suppression of visually initiated hand movement by stimulation of the prefrontal cortex in the monkey. *Brain Research, 495*(1), 100–107.

Saunders, J., & MacLeod, M. D. (2002). New evidence on the suggestibility of memory: The role of retrieval-induced forgetting in misinformation effects. *Journal of Experimental Psychology: Applied, 8*(2), 127–142.

Schmajuk, M., Liotti, M., Busse, L., & Woldorff, M. G. (2006). Electrophysiological activity underlying inhibitory control processes in normal adults. *Neuropsychologia, 44*(3), 384–395. doi:10.1016/j.neuropsychologia.2005.06.005.

Schooler, J. W., Bendiksen, M., & Ambadar, Z. (1997). Taking the middle line: Can we accommodate both fabricated and recovered memories of sexual abuse? In M. Conway (Ed.), *Recovered Memories and False Memories*. Oxford: Oxford University Press.

Schultz, T. M., Passmore, J., & Yodor, C. Y. (2003). Emotional closeness with perpetrators and amnesia for child sexual abuse. *Journal of Child Sexual Abuse, 12*, 67–88.

Shobe, K. K., & Schooler, J. W. (2001). Discovering fact and fiction: Case-based analyses of authentic and fabricated memories of abuse. In G. M. Davies & T. Dalgleish (Eds.), *Recovered memories: Seeking the middle ground* (pp. 95–151). Chichester: Wiley.

Smith, M. (1993). Neurophysiological manifestations of recollective experience during recognition memory judgments. *Journal of Cognitive Neuroscience, 5*(1), 1–13.

Smith, M., & Guster, K. (1993). Decomposition of recognition memory event-related potentials yields target, repetition, and retrieval effects. *Electroencephalography and Clinical Neurophysiology, 86*(5), 335–343.

Smith, S. M., & Moynan, S. C. (2008). Forgetting and recovering the unforgettable. *Psychological Science, 19*(5), 462–468. doi:10.1111/j.1467-9280.2008.02110.x.

Smith, S. M., & Vela, E. (1991). Incubated reminiscence effects. *Memory & Cognition, 19*(2), 168–176.

Squire, L. R. (1992). Memory and the hippocampus: A synthesis from findings with rats, monkeys, and humans. *Psychological Review, 99*(2), 195–231.

Storm, B. C. (2010). Retrieval-induced forgetting and the resolution of competition. In A. Benjamin (Ed.), *Successful remembering and successful forgetting: A festschrift in honor of Robert A. Bjork* (pp. 89–105). New York: Psychology Press.

Storm, B. C., Bjork, E. L., Bjork, R. A., & Nestojko, J. F. (2006). Is retrieval success a necessary condition for retrieval-induced forgetting? *Psychonomic Bulletin and Review, 13*(6), 1023–1027.

Storm, B. C., & White, H. A. (2010). ADHD and retrieval-induced forgetting: Evidence for a deficit in the inhibitory control of memory. *Memory, 18*(3), 265–271. doi:10.1080/09658210903547884.

Tamm, L., Menon, V., Ringel, J., & Reiss, A. (2004). Event-related fMRI evidence of frontotemporal involvement in aberrant response inhibition and task switching in attention-deficit/hyperactivity disorder. *Journal of the American Academy of Child and Adolescent Psychiatry, 43*(11), 1430–1440. doi:10.1097/01.chi.0000140452.51205.8d.

Tandoh, K., & Naka, M. (2007). Durability of retrieval-induced forgetting. *Shinrigaku Kenkyu: The Japanese Journal of Psychology, 78*(3), 310–315.

Tomlinson, T. D., Huber, D. E., Rieth, C. A., & Davelaar, E. J. (2009). An interference account of cue-independent forgetting in the no-think paradigm. *Proceedings of the National Academy of Sciences of the United States of America, 106*(37), 15588–15593. doi:10.1073/pnas.0813370106.

Tramoni, E., Aubert-Khalfa, S., Guye, M., Ranjeva, J. P., Felician, O., & Ceccaldi, M. (2009). Hypo-retrieval and hyper-suppression mechanisms in functional amnesia. *Neuropsychologia, 47*(3), 611–624.

Trott, C. T., Friedman, D., Ritter, W., Fabiani, M., & Snodgrass, J. G. (1999). Episodic priming and memory for temporal source: event-related potentials reveal age-related differences in prefrontal functioning. *Psychology and Aging, 14*, 390–413.

Underwood, B. J. (1949). Proactive inhibition as a function of time and degree of prior learning. *Journal Of Experimental Psychology, 39*(1), 24–34.

van Boxtel, G. J., van der Molen, M. W., Jennings, J. R., & Brunia, C. H. (2001). A psychophysiological analysis of inhibitory motor control in the stop-signal paradigm. *Biological Psychology, 58*(3), 229–262.

Waldhauser, G.T., Johansson, M., & Lindgren, M. (submitted). The effects of intentional suppression on recognition memory.

Waldhauser, G. T., Johansson, M., Backstrom, M., & Mecklinger, A. (2011). Trait anxiety, working memory capacity, and the effectiveness of memory suppression. *Scandinavian Journal of Psychology, 52*(1), 21–27. doi:10.1111/j.1467-9450.2010.00845.x.

Wegner, D. M. (1994). Ironic processes of mental control. *Psychological Review, 101*, 34–52.

Wegner, D. M., Schneider, D. J., Carter, S., & White, T. (1987). Paradoxical effects of thought suppression. *Journal of Personality and Social Psychology, 53*, 5–13.

Wenzlaff, R. M., & Wegner, D. M. (2000). Thought suppression. In S. T. Fiske (Ed.), *Annual review of psychology* (Vol. 51, pp. 51–91). Palo Alto, CA: Annual Reviews.

Wessel, I., Huntjens, R. J. C., & Verwoerd, J. R. L. (2010). Cognitive control and suppression of memories of an emotional film. *Journal of Behavior Therapy and Experimental Psychiatry, 41*(2), 83–89. doi:10.1016/j.jbtep. 2009.10.005.

Wessel, I., Wetzels, S., Jelicic, M., & Merckelbach, H. (2005). Dissociation and memory suppression: A comparison of high and low dissociative individuals' performance on the Think-No Think task. *Personality and Individual Differences, 39*(8), 1461–1470.

Wheeler, M. A. (1995). Improvement in recall over time without repeated testing: Spontaneous recovery revisited. *Journal of Experimental Psychology: Learning, Memory, and Cognition, 21*(1), 173–184.

Wilding, E. L., Doyle, M. C., & Rugg, M. D. (1995). Recognition memory with and without retrieval of context: An event-related potential study. *Neuropsychologia, 33*(6), 743–767.

Wilding, E., & Rugg, M. (1996). An event-related potential study of recognition memory with and without retrieval of source. *Brain, 119*, 889–905.

Williams, L. M. (1994). Recall of childhood trauma: A propective study of women's memories of child sexual abuse. *Journal of Consulting and Clinical Psychology, 62*(6), 1177–81.

Wilson, S. P., & Kipp, K. (1998). The development of efficient inhibition: Evidence from directed-forgetting tasks. *Developmental Review, 18*(1), 86–123.

Wylie, G. R., Fox, J. J., & Taylor, T. L. (2008). Forgetting as an active process: An fMRI investigation of item-method directed forgetting. *Cerebral Cortex, 18*, 670–682.

Searching for Repressed Memory

Richard J. McNally

Abstract This chapter summarizes the work of my research group on adults who report either repressed, recovered, or continuous memories of childhood sexual abuse (CSA) or who report no history of CSA. Adapting paradigms from cognitive psychology, we tested hypotheses inspired by both the "repressed memory" and "false memory" perspectives on recovered memories of CSA. We found some evidence for the false memory perspective, but no evidence for the repressed memory perspective. However, our work also suggests a third perspective on recovered memories that does not require the concept of repression. Some children do not understand their CSA when it occurs, and do not experience terror. Years later, they recall the experience, and understanding it as abuse, suffer intense distress. The memory failed to come to mind for years, partly because the child did not encode it as terrifying (i.e., traumatic), not because the person was unable to recall it.

Keywords Dissociation • False memory • Repression • CSA

The controversy concerning reports of repressed and recovered memories of childhood sexual abuse (CSA) has been among the most bitter in the history of psychology and psychiatry (Brewin, 2003; McNally, 2003a). Two polarized interpretations of these reports have dominated the controversy, both presupposing that CSA counts as a psychologically traumatic experience.

According to the *repression perspective*, the mind protects itself by banishing memories of abuse precisely because they are so traumatic. Victims become incapable of recalling their abuse until it is psychologically safe to do so, often many years later. People ordinarily remember traumatic experiences all too well (Porter & Peace, 2007), as the syndrome of posttraumatic stress disorder (PTSD) so dramatically

R.J. McNally (✉)
Harvard University, Cambridge, MA, USA
e-mail: rjm@wjh.harvard.edu

R.F. Belli (ed.), *True and False Recovered Memories: Toward a Reconciliation of the Debate*, Nebraska Symposium on Motivation, DOI 10.1007/978-1-4614-1195-6_4, © Springer Science+Business Media, LLC 2012

illustrates (American Psychiatric Association [APA], 2000, pp. 463–468). Therefore, an apparent inability to remember trauma seemingly implies an inhibitory mechanism that blocks conscious access to memories of these events. If a person says that he or she remembered an episode of abuse after not having thought about it for years, then repression theorists suspect that the memory must have been repressed (e.g., Briere & Conte, 1993). Indeed, why else would someone forget a seemingly unforgettable experience?

These theorists sometimes use synonyms for *repression*, such as *traumatic amnesia*, *dissociative amnesia*, and *traumatic dissociative amnesia*, but the idea is the same: precisely *because* the experience was so emotionally traumatic, the person is *unable* to recall it. As Brown, Scheflin, and Hammond (1998) put it:

> when emotional material reaches the point of being
> traumatic in intensity – something that cannot be
> replicated in artificial laboratories – in a certain
> subpopulation of individuals, material that is too
> intense may not be able to be consciously processed and
> so may become unconscious and amnesic. (p. 97)

If repressed memories of CSA were functionally inert, then they would have little clinical relevance. However, repression theorists liken these memories to an undetected malignant tumor that silently poisons the emotional life of the unwitting victim. Victims may be entirely oblivious to their history of horrific trauma, thanks to "massive repression" (Herman & Schatzow, 1987, p. 12), yet suffer its psychological consequences nevertheless. As Breuer and Freud (1893/1955) put it, a repressed memory of sexual abuse "acts like a foreign body which long after its entry must continue to be regarded as an agent that is still at work" (p. 6).

Toxic memories of which the victim is entirely unaware may cause diverse psychological symptoms, according to repression theorists. This belief provided the justification for therapists using hypnosis, guided imagery, and other methods to exhume the memories (e.g., Courtois, 1992; Olio, 1989). As Brown et al. (1998) wrote:

> Because some victims of sexual abuse will repress their memories by dissociating them from
> consciousness, hypnosis can be very valuable in retrieving these memories. Indeed, for some
> victims, hypnosis may provide the only avenue to the repressed memories. (p. 647)

Once patients recover their memories, they can process them emotionally, and integrate them into the narrative of their lives.

Summarizing this perspective in his book, entitled *Repressed Memories*, Spiegel (1997) emphasized that

> the nature of traumatic dissociative amnesia is such
> that it is not subject to the same rules of ordinary
> forgetting; it is more, rather than less, common after
> repeated episodes; involves strong affect; and is
> resistant to retrieval through salient cues. (p. 6)

Hence, Spiegel holds that memory for trauma obeys different laws than those governing the encoding and recollection of other experiences. Ordinarily, the more often a type of event occurs, the better able a person is to remember having experienced that type of event, especially if it involved strong emotion. Repression theorists, however, believe otherwise.

Advocates of the *false memory perspective* hold that memories of abuse are not exempt from the principles that govern the encoding and recall of other emotional memories (e.g., Pendergrast, 1996). If sexual abuse counts as an emotionally traumatic experience, then stress hormones released during the event should ensure its memorability (McGaugh, 2003). Accordingly, if someone does report a prior inability to recall a seemingly traumatic experience, the person is likely mistaken about the event. These theorists suspect that imagery of the abuse does not correspond to a genuine event, but rather reflects an unintentional confabulation, especially if it surfaced only after the person has undergone recovered-memory therapy techniques such as hypnosis (Ceci & Loftus, 1994).

Historical Background

That a person could experience a psychologically traumatic event not involving physical insult to brain, be unable to recall the event, and later have it return to consciousness is an idea whose popularity began to flourish in 19th century Europe (Borch-Jacobsen, 2009, pp. 19–36). In fact, a comprehensive search of the worldwide medical, historical, and fictional literature failed to uncover a single recorded instance prior to the 19th century (Pope, Poliakoff, Parker, Boynes, & Hudson, 2007a). The authors of this study offered a $1,000 prize to anyone who could locate a case of dissociative amnesia prior to 1800.

I came closest to winning the prize (Carey, 2007), nearly qualifying with my case of Madame de Tourvel in Choderlos de Laclos's 1782 novel, *Les Liaisons Dangereuses*. Unfortunately for me, the pious Madame de Tourvel repressed the memory of her adultery and betrayal by her lover for a mere half hour before recovering it (Choderlos de Laclos (1782/1961, pp. 348–349). However, massive media publicity of the repressed memory challenge eventually generated a winner. The case appeared in J. B. Marsollier's *Nina*, a 1786 French opera (Pope, Poliakoff, Parker, Boynes, & Hudson, 2007b). This 18th century case does not invalidate Pope et al.'s (2007a) conclusion that claims about one's inability to remember trauma amount to a culturally shaped idiom of distress arising in Europe in the climate of Romanticism. The case in *Nina* merely moves the threshold back a few years.

Scrutinizing the work of Jean Charcot, Pierre Janet, and Sigmund Freud, the historian of psychiatry, Borch-Jacobsen, described "the birth of a true psychiatric myth, fated to a grand future: *the patient is entirely ignorant of the trauma that caused his symptoms*" (p. 30). Prior to Charcot developing this idea via his hypnotic work, his polysymptomatic hysteria patients "remembered quite clearly the psychic or mechanical shock that had triggered their hysterical paralyses and attacks. After, they would tend not to know the cause of their symptoms any longer; the era of 'dissociation of consciousness' and of 'repression' had begun" (p. 25). Unwittingly conveying his "completely new expectation, that of post-traumatic *amnesia*" (p. 25) to his suggestible patients during hypnosis, Charcot found exactly what he was seeking: seemingly dissociated memories of trauma.

Janet and Freud further promoted the concepts of traumatic dissociative amnesia and repression. Formulating his seduction theory of hysteria, Freud (1962) developed a therapeutic approach that constitutes a direct precursor of the late 20th century attempts to recover presumably repressed memories of CSA (Crews, 1995, pp. 216–218; McNally, 2007a). Freud believed that sexual abuse occurring during the preschool years, if repressed from consciousness, could later erupt into hysteria if the person encounters a triggering event after puberty. He believed that helping patients recover their repressed memories of abuse, enabling them to abreact their emotions, and encouraging them to express the trauma in words would cure their hysteria. Unfortunately, Freud's therapy failed to produce the predicted cures, and he quietly abandoned his seduction theory, replacing it with classical psychoanalysis (Israëls & Schatzman, 1993; McNally, 2003a, pp. 159–169).

The Aims of this Chapter

I have three aims in this chapter, whose title echoes that of one my colleague's books (Schacter, 1996). Schacter's book, *Searching for Memory*, was wide ranging, whereas my chapter chiefly concerns the search for evidence of repressed memories of trauma.

First, I examine the evidence that repression theorists adduce to support their claim that many trauma victims are incapable of remembering their most horrific experiences (e.g., Brown et al., 1998; Brown, Scheflin, & Whitfield, 1999). The devil is in the details, and scrutiny of their evidence and arguments shows that repression theorists seemingly misunderstand the very studies they cite in support of the authenticity of the phenomenon (McNally, 2003a, pp. 186–228; McNally, 2004, 2007b; Piper, Pope, & Borowiecki, 2000). In fact, an analysis of studies concerning corroborated traumatic events uncovered no convincing evidence that victims had forgotten, let alone repressed, their trauma (Pope, Oliva, & Hudson, 1999). There are isolated cases of people who seemingly forgot traumatic experiences, only to recall them later (Schooler, Bendiksen, & Ambadar, 1997). Yet at least in some of these cases, the evidence clearly shows that the victims had actually recalled their trauma during the time when they had mistakenly believed that it had never come to mind. That is, they had forgotten their prior recollections.

Second, the concept of repression has nevertheless inspired laboratory research. My colleagues and I have tested hypotheses about processes potentially relevant to encoding, remembering, and forgetting of sexual abuse. I describe these experiments, our results, and the strengths and limitations of the laboratory approach.

Third, ambiguities in the concept of trauma itself have contributed to the recovered memory controversy. Some of these are difficult to resolve, yet there are good reasons to believe that there is a third perspective on recovered memories in addition to the repression and false memory perspectives that can illuminate at least some cases of CSA. I close my chapter by elaborating on these issues.

What Does the Science Say About Repression of Trauma?

Brown, Scheflin, and Whitfield wrote "the burden of proof is on them [skeptics of repressed memories of trauma] to show that repressed memories do not exist" (1999, p. 125). This is an elementary error. Brown et al. have it exactly backwards: the burden of proof lies on those making the claim that people do repress their memories of trauma. It is logically impossible for anyone to prove the null hypothesis that something never occurs. Indeed, even if overwhelming evidence indicates that traumatic experiences are remembered all too well, this does not rule out the possibility that evidence for repressed memories of trauma may subsequently emerge.

In any event, repression theorists have cited many studies that they believe bolster the case for repressed memories of trauma. In the following sections, I examine their arguments and evidence. Unfortunately, their arguments often betray confusions about memory and trauma.

Confusing Posttraumatic Forgetfulness with an Inability to Remember the Trauma Itself

People exposed to traumatic events, especially those who develop PTSD, often report memory and concentration problems in everyday life. In fact, this problem was a formal diagnostic criterion for PTSD in the third edition of the *Diagnostic and Statistical Manual of Mental Disorders* (DSM-III; APA, 1980, p. 238). Unfortunately, repression theorists cite it as relevant to repression (e.g., Brown et al., 1999).

For example, Wilkinson (1983) interviewed survivors of the collapse of the skywalks in the lobby of Kansas City's Hyatt Regency Hotel. Using DSM-III criteria, he found that 88% of them reported "repeated recollections" of the horrific trauma, and 27% reported "memory difficulties."

These findings, however, have nothing to do with an inability to remember the trauma. Obviously, someone who has repeated recollections of a traumatic event is not someone who cannot remember the traumatic event. One must not confuse everyday forgetfulness that develops after exposure to trauma with an inability to remember the trauma itself.

Confusing Impaired Encoding with Amnesia for the Trauma

Among several changes occurring in the diagnostic criteria for PTSD between DSM-III and its revision (DSM-III-R; APA, 1987) was the replacement of memory and concentration problems with the very different symptom of inability to recall an important aspect of the trauma (Criterion C3). Inability to recall an important aspect of the trauma remained in the criteria set in DSM-IV (APA, 1994), including its text revision (DSM-IV-TR; APA, 2000).

Although repression theorists have argued that this symptom signifies amnesia for aspects of the trauma, it is, at best, deeply ambiguous. The claim that someone is unable to recall something presupposes that the person encoded it in the first place. Yet people do not encode every aspect of an experience into memory; their minds do not operate like videotape machines. This is especially true of rapidly unfolding traumatic events, such as an automobile accident or drive-by shooting.

Consider the phenomenon of weapon focus. During emotionally arousing events, the central aspects of the experience tend to capture the person's attention, often at the expense of the peripheral aspects. Hence, a person robbed at gunpoint may recall the details of the weapon, yet be unable to describe the face of the assailant. However, failure to recall the appearance of the robber need not signify amnesia for his face; it likely means that attention was riveted on the gun while the robbery was unfolding. Indeed, it makes no sense to say someone has "amnesia" for something if it never made it into memory in the first place.

Hence, we must not confuse a failure to encode with an inability to remember. The concept of repression presupposes that the person has encoded the experience, yet remains unable to recall it because defensive mechanisms of the mind block its recollection.

Interestingly, trauma survivors with PTSD seldom endorse this symptom anyway (Breslau, Reboussin, Anthony, & Storr, 2005; Rubin, Berntsen, & Bohni, 2008). Accordingly, the DSM-V committee should delete it from the revised criteria for PTSD (McNally, 2009a).

Confusing Psychogenic Amnesia with Repression of Trauma

Although the term "psychogenic amnesia" appears parenthetically as a clarifying phrase for the PTSD C3 criterion, it also refers to a rare syndrome whereby a person reports complete loss of his or her autobiographical memory (Kihlstrom & Schacter, 2000). People receiving this diagnosis report sudden, massive retrograde memory loss, including loss of one's personal identity. Calling it "psychogenic" amnesia merely denotes that no obvious "organic" cause occurred. There appears to be no obvious physical insult to the brain precipitating the syndrome. In fact, although stressful events do sometimes precede the emergence of psychogenic amnesia, many are not especially traumatic (e.g., death of a grandparent, job difficulties, and romantic disappointments). Memory usually returns spontaneously within a few weeks, often suddenly.

Although sometimes cited as relevant to recovered memories of CSA (e.g., Arrigo & Pezdek, 1997), the syndrome of psychogenic amnesia differs from the concept of traumatic dissociative amnesia in three important ways. First, autobiographical memory loss is global, and not specific to stressful events. Second, and most strikingly, the person loses, or claims to have lost, his or her personal identity. Third, antecedents to memory loss are not necessarily traumatic, and it is unclear whether they truly precipitate the emergence of the syndrome.

Confusing Organic Amnesia for Repression of Trauma

Some clinical theorists occasionally confuse cases of organic amnesia for psychic repression of trauma. For example, Brown et al. (1998) claimed that "Dollinger (1985) found that two of the 38 children studied after watching lightning strike and kill a playmate had no memory of the event" (pp. 609–610). These elementary school children had been playing soccer when the fatal thunderstorm abruptly began.

Brown et al., however, forgot to mention that side flashes from the main lightning bolt had struck both children, knocking them unconscious, and nearly killing them (Dollinger, 1985). Their amnesia for the lightning strike was due to a nearly fatal insult to the brain. Being struck by lightning would surely count as psychically as well as physically traumatizing, if one encoded the experience, which neither child did. Yet the psychic aspects of the disaster were insufficient to trigger amnesia for the event. Indeed, the children who were not struck by lightning remembered the disaster very well, and many suffered from posttraumatic symptoms (Dollinger, 1985).

Confusing Nondisclosure with Repression of Trauma

When questioned by survey interviewers, some adult survivors of childhood abuse fail to mention their abuse when explicitly asked about it (e.g., Widom & Morris, 1997). Despite the research team having consulted official records corroborating the abuse, the survey respondents did not disclose their experiences when the interviewers asked about a history of abuse. However, we must not equate a failure to disclose with an inability to remember. Although it is possible that the person has forgotten his or her childhood abuse, there are other reasons why a survey respondent might choose to deny it to a survey interviewer. Reluctance to discuss potentially embarrassing or upsetting experiences with a stranger might account for denial of abuse, as Femina, Yeager, and Lewis (1990) discovered when they re-interviewed nondisclosing abuse victims.

Confusing Childhood Amnesia with Repression of Trauma

People can recall few of their experiences occurring before the age of 4 or 5. Neurocognitive changes in brain maturation that support language and memory make it very difficult for older children and adults to recall events from their preschool years. Accordingly, if someone fails to recall an episode of molestation from these years, then we need not attribute this failure to memory repression. Because of normal childhood amnesia, nearly all events from these years will be lost forever. For example, in one survey of 129 women who had been medically assessed for sexual abuse during childhood, 16 denied ever having been sexually abused

(Williams, 1994). However, several of these women experienced molestation before the age of five. Hence, their denial of abuse is likely attributable to childhood amnesia rather than repression or an unwillingness to acknowledge their abuse to a survey interviewer.

Confusing Not Thinking About Abuse with Repression of Trauma

A common mistake is to confuse not thinking about something with an inability to remember it. In one influential questionnaire study, Briere and Conte (1993) found that 59% of adults in treatment for the effects of CSA answered affirmatively when questioned whether there had ever been "a time when you could not remember" (p. 24) the abuse. The authors interpreted this result as evidence for "sexual abuse-related repression" (p. 26). However, an affirmative reply to this question implies that the person had spent time trying unsuccessfully to remember his or her abuse. But if these patients had repressed all memories of their abuse, why would they try to recall it in the first place? I suspect that most patients interpreted this question as meaning, "Has there ever been a time when you did not think about your abuse?" Yet *not thinking about* one's abuse is not the same thing as being *unable* to recall it, and evidence for repression requires an *inability* to recall the abuse. It is entirely possible that these memories would have come to mind during the period of pre-sumptive repression had the person encountered reminders of the abuse.

Distinguishing between not thinking about something for a long time versus being unable to remember it has profound clinical implications. It is not a mere semantic quibble. If patients have not thought about their abuse for many years, then questions during a clinical intake interview will likely prompt recollection. On the other hand, if clinicians believe that patients often repress their memories of abuse, they may be inclined to engage in so-called recovered memory techniques to unlock the presumably repressed memories even when patients deny a history of abuse.

Research on People Reporting Recovered Memories

My colleagues, students, and I have been conducting research on trauma survivors since 1985 (e.g., McNally et al., 1987; Trandel & McNally, 1987). Most of these studies have concerned veterans, especially those from the Vietnam War. We have tackled the problem of trauma from the perspectives of psychometrics (Macklin et al., 1998; McNally & Shin, 1995), epidemiology (Engelhard et al., 2007; McNally, 2007c; McTeague, McNally, & Litz, 2004), and neuroimaging (Shin, Kosslyn, et al., 1997; Shin, McNally, et al., 1999). However, many of our experiments have con-cerned the application of cognitive paradigms to elucidate information-processing biases and abnormalities associated with PTSD (McNally, 1998, 2006). Using these methods, we have been investigating the cognitive psychology of people reporting recovered memories of CSA (McNally, 2003b).

Our migration into the recovered-memory controversy began after I had interviewed women who had responded to our newspaper advertisement that requested volunteers for a study on adult survivors of childhood sexual abuse. My Ph.D. student, Lisa Shin, was conducting a positron emission tomography (PET) study regarding the functional neuroanatomy of traumatic memory in women who had suffered sexual abuse as children and who either had or did not have PTSD (Shin et al., 1999). I was one of the clinicians conducting psychiatric diagnostic interviews to determine whether potential subjects qualified for the study. During the course of about 10 days, I assessed several women who had responded to our advertisement, but who remembered nothing about their abuse. Puzzled, I asked them why they responded to an ad that requested survivors of sexual abuse when they had no memories of sexual abuse. Each explained that she had been experiencing various symptoms (e.g., depressed mood, problems with men, drinking too much), and assumed that these otherwise inexplicable difficulties resulted from memories of sexual abuse which they could not remember. These women did not qualify for our PET study, which required autobiographical memories of abuse. However, they inspired our new program of research on recovered memories of CSA.

Shortly thereafter, I discussed my experiences with these interviewees with my colleague, Daniel Schacter. Curious what might happen if we were to advertise for subjects who believe they harbor inaccessible memories of abuse, we decided to embark upon a research program designed to elucidate cognitive functioning in these individuals. The Memory Wars were raging still, and yet cognitive scientists had yet to study the very people at the heart of the controversy. As it turned out, we had no shortage of subjects.

Our research program on recovered memories of sexual abuse involved successive waves of subjects. We recruited four groups of subjects (McNally, Clancy, Schacter, & Pitman, 2000a). The *repressed memory group* included women who suspected that they had been sexual abuse victims as a child despite their having no autobiographical memories of abuse. They inferred the presence of buried memories of abuse based on a diversity of psychological problems. These subjects were similar to those I excluded from the PET study. We used the *repressed memory* label because it captures their phenomenology, not because we believe they harbor repressed memories.

The *recovered memory group* included women who reported childhood sexual abuse, reported not having thought about their abuse for years, and reported having recalled it later in life. Unlike members of the repressed memory group, these subjects described at least one autobiographical memory of molestation. In our first wave of research, we did not endeavor to corroborate the memories reported by any of our subjects, and hence we did not know whether the memories reported by the recovered memory group, for example, were genuine memories or false memories.

The continuous memory group included women who said that they had never forgotten their sexual abuse. The control group included women who reported no history of sexual abuse.

In one of our early projects, we administered a battery of questionnaires to our subjects to characterize them in terms of personality and psychiatric symptoms (McNally et al., 2000a). We found that continuous memory subjects were indistinguishable from nonabused control subjects on measures of depression, stress, dissociation, negative affectivity, and positive affectivity. This was a bit surprising, and perhaps attributable to the fact that many continuous memory subjects had participated in counseling sessions and likely benefited from treatment, thereby experiencing symptom reduction.

Perhaps more strikingly, the group that had no memories of sexual abuse, but whose members believed they harbored repressed memories of abuse, scored higher on measures of depression, stress, dissociation, and negative affectivity, but not positive affectivity, than did members in the continuous memory group. The recovered memory group tended to score midway between the continuous memory and repressed memory groups on these measures.

There are at least two possible explanations for the significantly more distressed profile in the repressed memory group than in the continuous memory group. One possibility is that subjects in the repressed memory group were experiencing the psychological toll of having buried their memories of abuse, as Freud would have suspected. Another possibility is that their symptoms arose from diverse sources, and their inference that they harbored repressed memories reflected an "effort after meaning" – an attempt to make sense of distressing, otherwise inexplicable symptoms. We suspect that the second interpretation is the correct one.

Our group subsequently published a psychometric and clinical study on another wave of subjects (McNally, Perlman, Ristuccia & Clancy, 2006b). Although our primary focus in this research program has been memory phenomenology and its correlates, not psychiatric illness, we did conduct formal clinical interviews in this study.

This project involved men as well as women who reported sexual abuse during childhood. There were 42 repressed memory subjects, 38 recovered memory subjects, 92 continuous memory subjects, and 36 nonabused control subjects. In contrast to results in our previous study, all three groups reporting CSA scored similarly on measures of depression, anxiety, and dissociation, and higher than did the nonabused control group. The difference between the results of the two studies seemed attributable to a slightly less distressed repressed memory group and a substantially more distressed continuous memory group. For example, the mean Beck Depression Inventory (BDI; Beck & Steer, 1987) scores in the continuous memory group in the first and second studies were 5.0 and 14.5, respectively, whereas the corresponding scores in the repressed memory group were 21.1 and 16.5, respectively.

Using Foa and Tolin's (2000) interview, we found that 45% of the continuous memory subjects met current symptomatic criteria for PTSD, whereas 38% of the recovered memory subjects, 14% of the repressed memory subjects, and 3% of the nonabused control subjects did so. The referent trauma in the first two groups was CSA, whereas it was another trauma (e.g., automobile accident) for the groups without abuse memories.

We also conducted structured interviews for current major depressive disorder (MDD) as well as for the anxiety disorders. MDD was present in 15% of the continuous memory subjects, 8% of the recovered memory subjects, 13% of the repressed memory subjects, and 0% of the control subjects.

We also tested a hypothesis inspired by Freyd's betrayal trauma theory (Freyd, 1996; Freyd, DePrince, & Gleaves, 2007; DePrince et al., 2012, this volume; for a critique, see McNally, 2007d). According to this theory, children abused by a caretaker are more likely to develop amnesia for their abuse than are children abused by someone on whom they do not rely for food, shelter, and clothing. Children whose caretakers betray them by molesting them encounter a psychologically senseless situation. The very person who provides for their vital survival needs is violating them sexually. Freyd suggests that children resolve this conflict by developing amnesia for their abuse, thereby ensuring maintenance of the caretaking bond essential for physical survival. This theory implies that more subjects in the recovered memory group than in the continuous memory group would cite a primary caretaker as their abuser (e.g., parent, stepparent, foster parent). However, the proportion of subjects in each group reporting caretaker abuse was nearly identical: 20% in the continuous memory group and 21% in the recovered memory group.

Laboratory Research Relevant to False Memories

My students, colleagues, and I have conducted experiments designed to test hypotheses arising from both the false memory perspective and the repression perspective. In our first experiment, we tested whether women reporting recovered memories of CSA were more prone than were control subjects to experience memory distortion following guided imagery of possible childhood events (Clancy, McNally, & Schacter, 1999). We used the imagination-inflation paradigm of Garry, Manning, Loftus, and Sherman (1996). Subjects first rated their confidence regarding whether they had experienced certain events during childhood (e.g., finding a $10 bill in a parking lot). No event concerned abuse. At a later session, the experimenter conducted a guided imagery session whereby she had the subject close her eyes and vividly imagine what it would have been like to experience certain events in childhood.

We then readministered the original list of events, asking subjects to rate their confidence that the events had occurred to them during childhood. The false memory perspective implies that the recovered memory subjects would be especially vulnerable to the imagination inflation effect. That is, they should exhibit an increase in confidence that childhood events that they envisioned during the guided imagery session occurred relative to control events that they did not envision. However, the control subjects exhibited an imagination effect more than twice as great as that exhibited by the recovered memory subjects. Interestingly, several subjects in the recovered memory group asked us whether the purpose of the study was to see whether they would develop false memories about childhood in the laboratory. Their questions imply that the paradigm is too transparent, at least to subjects reporting recovered memories of abuse.

Subsequent studies provided data consistent with the false memory perspective. We found that women who report recovered memories of CSA exhibit false memory propensity in the laboratory relative to women who say they had never forgotten their abuse. In the Deese/Roediger/McDermott paradigm (Deese, 1959; Roediger & McDermott, 1995; for a review, see Gallo, 2010), recovered memory subjects are especially likely to "remember" having encountered critical lure words (e.g., sweet) that embody the gist of emotionally neutral word lists they did encounter (e.g., sugar, candy; Clancy, Schacter, McNally, & Pitman, 2000). These data do not mean that the recovered CSA memories of these subjects are false; they are merely *consistent* with this possibility.

Yet, using the DRM paradigm, we have also found that subjects whose recovered memories are almost certainly false likewise exhibit false memory propensity in the DRM paradigm. In these experiments, we tested subjects who reported recovered memories of space alien abduction (Clancy, McNally, Schacter, Lenzenweger, & Pitman, 2002) and past lives (Meyersburg, Gallo, Bogdan, & McNally, 2009). However, a British team failed to find heightened false memory propensity in the DRM paradigm in a group of subjects reporting contact with aliens (French, Santomauro, Hamilton, Fox, & Thalbourne, 2008). However, as Gallo (2010) observed, these subjects exhibited a strong trend for false recognition (but not false recall) and not all members of the group reported actual abduction by space aliens.

Finally, adults who report recovered memories of CSA tend to exhibit reality monitoring deficits on tasks requiring them to discriminate whether they had a seen a word or merely having imagined having seen it (McNally, Clancy, Barrett, & Parker, 2005). This finding is consistent with the possibility that recovered memory subjects may have difficulty discriminating memories of images ("fantasy") from memories of perceptions ("reality").

Despite performance similarities on the DRM false memory task among people who report recovered memories of CSA, space alien abduction, and past lives, the differences among these groups are at least as pronounced as any similarities (Clancy, 2005). For example, our abductees routinely mention encounters with aliens that appear to be episodes of isolated sleep paralysis accompanied by hypnopompic ("upon awakening") hallucinations of intruders in their bedroom (McNally & Clancy, 2005a; McNally, Lasko, Clancy, Macklin, Pitman, & Orr, 2004). Although adults reporting histories of CSA do experience sleep paralysis more often than do control subjects (McNally & Clancy, 2005b, 2006), they seldom connect the experience with abuse. Perhaps more importantly, people who report recovered memories of CSA tend to score higher than do alien abductees on measures of psychological distress (e.g., depression; McNally, Clancy, et al., 2000a; McNally, Perlman, et al., 2006b; McNally et al., 2004).

Laboratory Research Relevant to Recovered Memories

The child psychiatrist Lenore Terr (1991) suggested that sexually abused children sometimes cope by acquiring a dissociative, avoidant encoding style enabling them to disengage attention during abusive episodes and direct it elsewhere. Unable to escape physically from their abuser, they escape psychologically. The ability to attend to benign features of the environment, such as wallpaper patterns, and to pretend that one is somewhere else, may attenuate an otherwise emotionally overwhelming experience. Terr implies that dissociative encoding during abuse episodes may partly explain apparent amnesia for the abuse later in life. Although this encoding style may be adaptive if it helps the child cope emotionally with a very difficult, physically inescapable situation, it may have psychiatric consequences later in life.

To investigate these issues in the laboratory, we administered an item-cuing directed-forgetting task to three groups of women: CSA victims with PTSD, CSA victims without PTSD, and nonabused control subjects (McNally, Metzger, Lasko, Clancy, & Pitman, 1998). Subjects saw a series of words on a computer screen. There were three categories of words, varying in emotional valence. The trauma category included words such as *incest* and *molested*, the positive category included words such as *carefree* and *confident*, and the neutral category included household words, such *banister* and *mailbox*. Each word appeared for 2 s, replaced by a cue either to remember (RRRR) or to forget (FFFF) the previous word. Half of the words in each category were followed by remember cues and the others were followed by forget cues. We told subjects that we would test their memory for the RRRR word. However, after the encoding phase, we asked subjects to write down all the words they remembered having seen, regardless of whether a remember cue or a forget cue had followed the word.

A standard directed forgetting effect would entail better recall for RRRR words than for FFFF words. This effect results from subjects endeavoring to memorize a word, but then ceasing to do so when an FFFF cue follows it. Hence, superior recollection of RRRR words relative to FFFF words is attributable to better encoding of the former than the latter (Golding, 2005; Johnson, 1994). To the extent that subjects can disengage their attention from FFFF words, their memory for these items should be impaired.

Inspired by Terr's (1991) ideas about dissociating attention from threat cues, we predicted that CSA subjects, especially those suffering from PTSD, would exhibit superior ability to abort encoding of trauma words relative to other words and relative to nonabused control subjects. That is, their motivation to avoid thinking about abuse-related material and their acquired skill in dissociating their attention from such material would result in relatively poor memory for trauma words. (Incidentally, our interpretation of Terr implies that psychiatrically suffering CSA subjects should not only exhibit very poor recall of trauma words followed by forget instructions; they should also not exhibit enhanced remembering of trauma words followed by remember instructions. That is, their propensity to avoid processing cues related to trauma should tend to attenuate any heightened encoding that might otherwise occur for trauma words followed by remember instructions. Hence, although these subjects should recall trauma-forget words much less often than positive and neutral-forget words, they should not exhibit superior recall for trauma-remember words relative to positive and neutral-remember words).

The results, however, ran counter to prediction. Abuse victims with PTSD exhibited poor memory for positive and neutral words that they were supposed to remember, and they recalled trauma words quite well, including those they were supposed to forget. If anything, the trauma words seemed intrusive and all too memorable for the PTSD group.

Upon reflection, perhaps these results were not that surprising, Terr's ideas notwithstanding. After all, to qualify for a current diagnosis of PTSD, subjects had to have been recalling their abuse on a regular basis in the form of intrusive recollections, nightmares, psychophysiological reactions to reminders, and flashbacks. That is, hallmark symptoms of PTSD would have overridden any skill these subjects would have acquired with regard to dissociating their attention from abuse cues.

Terr's (1991) hypothesis might be most relevant to subjects who report having forgotten their abuse or who report still being incapable of recalling it. Hence, we replicated our directed-forgetting procedure, testing subjects who reported repressed memories, recovered memories, or no history of sexual abuse (McNally, Clancy, & Schacter, 2001). The results revealed normal memory functioning in the repressed and recovered memory groups. Contrary to expectation, they did not exhibit impaired memory for trauma words relative to positive and neutral words. They exhibited a directed forgetting effect by recalling more RRRR words than FFFF words, but word valence did not affect this pattern.

Inspired by Terr's (1991) work, these directed forgetting experiments concerned the capacity of subjects to abort encoding of words followed by an FFFFF cue, thereby impairing subsequent recall of these words. However, there is a paradox embedded in Terr's theory. If children thoroughly dissociate their attention during an abuse episode, then they will have encoded nothing about the event in the first place and thus will have nothing to recall later in life. Accordingly, Terr's dissociation hypothesis might explain why a victim might fail to remember an abuse episode, but it cannot also explain why someone would remember it vividly later in life. People cannot recall experiences that they failed to encode into memory (Roediger & Bergman, 1998). The recovered memory controversy concerns the recollection of forgotten abuse, not merely the forgetting of abuse.

Accordingly, retrieval inhibition (Bjork, 1989), not dissociative encoding, may be the relevant process in the forgetting of CSA. Perhaps victims encode CSA, but then some inhibition mechanism blocks access to these encoded memories. In fact, this hypothesis would seem to fit a repression account especially well. Indeed, amnesia for abuse presupposes that the victim has encoded the experience, but is *unable* to retrieve it because defensive mechanisms of the mind block its retrieval.

To investigate heightened retrieval inhibition of trauma-related words in repressed and recovered memory subjects, we used the list method for our next directed forgetting experiment (Golding, 2005; Johnson, 1994). In our experiment (McNally, Clancy, Barrett, & Parker, 2004), we tested four groups of subjects, both men as well as women. The groups comprised adults who reported either repressed memories, recovered memories, or continuous memories of CSA, or who reported no history of CSA. Adapting the procedure of Myers, Brewin, and Power (1998), we presented subjects with two lists on a computer screen, each consisting of a series of intermixed trauma-related and positive words. We asked subjects to rate each word on a seven-point emotional meaning scale that ranged from −3 (very negative) to +3 (very positive). Each word appeared on the screen for 3 s, and 5 s elapsed between successive words.

Halfway through the words, the experimenter said, "What you have done so far is practice. You can forget about those words. I will now show you the actual set of test words that I want you to rate in the same way you did for the practice words." Hence, the experimenter directed the subject to forget the first list of words, but she did not direct the subject to remember the subsequent words.

Immediately after the encoding phase, the subject spent 3 min on a filler task requiring him or her to complete 84 easy arithmetic problems. Following this task, the experimenter said, "Please write down as many words as you can remember seeing from BOTH lists." This surprise, free recall task lasted for 5 min.

The results indicated that all groups recalled more words from the second list than from the first list, and recalled more trauma words than positive words. However, contrary to our hypothesis, the repressed and recovered groups did not exhibit poor recall of trauma words relative to positive words from the first list relative to the continuous memory and nonabused control groups. All groups exhibited a retrieval inhibition effect, and all groups exhibited this effect for positive words more than for trauma words. Hence, we failed to confirm the hypothesis of heightened retrieval inhibition for trauma words in the repressed and recovered memory groups. Trauma words were remembered equally well by all groups.

DePrince and Freyd (2004) questioned whether our directed forgetting experiments enhance understanding of the encoding and forgetting of CSA. They pointed out that these studies involved selective, not divided, attention in that subjects encountered one stimulus word at a time. They argued that a proper test would require subjects to perform another task concurrently with one concerning processing of threat cues. They emphasized that those sexually molested children who exhibit attentional dissociation during abuse episodes endeavor to attend to anything other than the abuse itself. Hence, experiments that require processing of threat cues under divided attention are more relevant to the clinical phenomenon than are those requiring selective processing of threat cues

To investigate this issue, DePrince and Freyd (2004) recruited college students, including some who reported trauma histories, and had them perform a directed-forgetting task involving trauma and neutral words. However, in this experiment, subjects either encoded words under either selective or divided attention. Consistent with their hypothesis, they found that students scoring high on the Dissociative Experiences Scale (DES; Bernstein & Putnam, 1986) exhibited impaired recall of trauma words after having encoded them under divided, but not selective, attention conditions.

We endeavored to replicate DePrince and Freyd's experiment by testing subjects reporting either recovered or continuous memories of CSA or reporting no history of CSA (McNally, Ristuccia, & Perlman, 2005). Relative to subjects with continuous memories of abuse or no abuse history, those who report recovered memories of abuse should exhibit memory impairment for trauma words relative to neutral words when they have encoded words under divided, but not selective, attention conditions. Following DePrince and Freyd (2004), we presented intermixed trauma (e.g., *incest*) and neutral household words (e.g., *lamp*), one at a time, in four consecutive blocks. Each word appeared at center screen for 6 s. For each subject, two blocks of words appeared under selective attention conditions, and two blocks of words appeared under divided attention conditions. Under selective attention conditions, words appeared in black letters against a white background. Under divided attention conditions, words appeared against a white background, but randomly changed colors from red to blue and vice versa during the time they were on the screen. Hence, for example, the word *molested* might appear in blue letters for 2 s, switch to red letters for 1 s, and then switch back to blue letters for the final 3 s of the 6-s duration. For blocks involving divided attention, subjects had to press the space bar of the computer whenever a word changed color. Hence, they performed two tasks at once: encoding the word and tracking how many times it changed color. For each subject, instructions telling subjects to forget the words in the preceding block occurred after two blocks, whereas instructions telling subjects to remember the words in the preceding block occurred after the other two blocks.

A subsequent recall test, however, failed to detect the predicted recall deficits for trauma words encoded under divided attention among subjects reporting recovered memories. In fact, all three groups recalled more trauma words than neutral words, regardless of selective versus divided attention encoding conditions. Devilly et al. (2007) likewise failed to replicate the findings of DePrince and Freyd (2004), despite their testing college students who varied in dissociation proneness. Devilly et al.'s research prompted a critique by DePrince, Freyd, and Malle (2007) and a rebuttal by Devilly and Ciorciari (2007; DePrince et al., 2012, this volume, also comment on this laboratory research).

Our group conducted two additional experiments relevant to the concept of repression. Repression theorists hold that blocked memories of abuse may nevertheless affect the emotional life of CSA victims despite their being incapable of recalling their abuse. Accordingly, we tested whether repressed memory subjects might exhibit increased interference for trauma words in the emotional Stroop paradigm (McNally, Clancy, Schacter, & Pitman, 2000b). In this paradigm, subjects view words of varying emotional valence, and attempt to name the colors in which the words appear while ignoring the meanings of the words (Williams, Mathews, & MacLeod, 1996). Difficulty ignoring the meaning of word results in the subject taking longer to name its color. Patients with anxiety disorders (Bar-Haim, Lamy, Pergamin, Bakermans-Kranenburg, & van IJzendoorn, 2007), including those with PTSD (McNally, Kaspi, Riemann, & Zeitlin, 1990; McNally, Amir, & Lipke, 1996), exhibit slower color-naming of threat words relative to other negative words, positive words, and neutral words.

We administered a computerized emotional Stroop task to subjects reporting repressed, recovered, or continuous memories of CSA, or no history of CSA (McNally et al., 2000b). They named the colors of trauma words, positive words, and neutral words. Inconsistent with our hypothesis, patterns of Stroop interference in the repressed memory group were indistinguishable from that in the control group. Consistent with previous research, the severity of self-reported PTSD symptoms significantly predicted Stroop interference for trauma words, irrespective of group membership.

When people with depression attempt to recall specific memories in response to cue words (e.g., *happy*), they often experience difficulty doing so, recalling overgeneral memories instead (Williams et al., 2007). Most people can readily recall a specific memory, denoting an event that occurred on a certain day (e.g., "I was happy on the day my son was born"). However, people with depression often recall overgeneral memories that are either extended in time (e.g., "I was happy during my first year in college") or that denote a category of events (e.g., "I am always happy when I am playing golf"). Difficulty recalling specific memories from one's past predicts one's difficulty overcoming depression (Brittlebank, Scott, Williams, & Ferrier, 1993) and predicts one's difficulty solving problems (Evans, Williams, O'Loughlin, & Howells, 1992). Hence, the overgeneral memory phenomenon has important clinical implications. We found that patients with PTSD likewise exhibit difficulty recalling specific memories in this task (McNally, Litz, Prassas, Shin, & Weathers, 1994; McNally, Lasko, Macklin, & Pitman, 1995).

One hypothesis regarding overgeneral memory is that it reflects a person's attempt to avoid thinking about an emotionally painful past (Williams et al., 2007). Accordingly, we tested whether repressed and recovered memory subjects, in particular, would exhibit difficulty retrieving specific memories in response to either positive or negative cue words, relative to continuous memory subjects and subjects who report no CSA (McNally et al., 2006b). We thought that overgeneral memories would be especially common in the repressed and recovered memories when we asked them to recall a specific episode from childhood versus adolescence or adulthood.

We found that all groups found it easier to recall specific memories from adulthood than childhood. Consistent with our hypothesis, the repressed memory group recalled significantly fewer specific memories than the control group did. The recovered memory and continuous memory groups fell midway between the other two groups. The relative impairment in the repressed memory group concerned difficulties retrieving specific memories from childhood, not adulthood.

These results are consistent with the repression prediction. They are also consistent with another interpretation. Some theorists have suggested that poor overall memory for one's childhood may signify that one may harbor dissociated memories of trauma (e.g., Loewenstein, 1991). Hence, one's difficulty retrieving specific memories from one's childhood prompt some people to assume that psychological problems in their lives may arise from buried memories of trauma.

Strengths and Limitations of Laboratory Research

Our program of research has its strengths and weaknesses. In contrast to many investigators conducting research relevant to the Memory Wars, we have studied women and men recruited from the community who report continuous, recovered, or repressed memories of CSA, or who report no CSA history. Importantly, many of these community recruits have been in psychotherapy, but not with us. They are diverse, varying in age, sex, ethnicity, education, and social class (McNally et al., 2006a). Yet they were volunteers, and it is difficult to know how they might differ from their counterparts who do not volunteer for research on sexual abuse. This issue, of course, is relevant to all research, not just ours.

On the other hand, our subjects knew that they were volunteering for research on survivors of sexual abuse. It is difficult to tell whether this affected their responses to questionnaires or responses on experimental tasks. For example, consider our directed forgetting experiments. We assumed that the ability to disengage attention from words related to abuse is a developed skill that CSA survivors can deploy in the laboratory in the item-cuing studies. Likewise, we assumed that heightened retrieval inhibition is a well-practiced process detectable in the laboratory. These assumptions may not be correct. For example, it is possible that subjects in the recovered memory group are no longer able to keep information about abuse from intruding on awareness. Once the "latch of repression" is unlocked, it may be impossible for these individuals to avoid thinking about their abuse. On the other hand, if one assumes that the repressed memory group does harbor memories of CSA, which they still cannot access, then this group should certainly have exhibited enhanced retrieval inhibition for abuse words, but they did not.

Our laboratory research involved established paradigms from cognitive psychology, and it involved standardized stimulus materials. Yet we had to make assumptions here, too. For example, subjects encountered mere words semantically related to abuse, not personal memories of abuse per se. We assumed that encoding, forgetting, and recalling words related to abuse would tap processes relevant to the encoding, forgetting, and recalling of autobiographical memories of abuse. Despite their emotional significance, words such as *molested* are unlikely to have the evocative power as a vivid memory of one's own molestation. We assumed, though, that if someone cannot disengage attention from the word *molested*, then it seems unlikely that they could disengage attention from the genuine experience as it is occurring, their motivation to do so notwithstanding.

Trauma and Its Ambiguities

Canonical traumatic experiences are life-threatening events that incite overwhelming terror. They seem qualitatively different from the normal stressors and hassles of everyday life, and they alone presumably possess the capacity to produce the symptomatic profile of PTSD. These assumptions influenced the concept of trauma embodied in the DSM-III definition of PTSD.

It is entirely possible that a person exposed to subtraumatic stressors will develop the full range of PTSD symptoms, but fail to earn the diagnosis because the stressor fell short of qualifying as traumatic. Discomfort about denying these sufferers the PTSD diagnosis, and hence reimbursable treatment, motivated the expansion of the concept of trauma in later editions of the DSM. For example, the DSM-IV PTSD committee, of which I was a member, modified the text and criteria for the disorder, causing a conceptual bracket creep in the definition of what counts as a traumatic stressor (McNally, 2003c). Hence, people who experience intense fear, horror, or helplessness after merely learning about another person's exposure to danger now count as victims of trauma themselves, eligible for the diagnosis of PTSD. According to DSM-IV, a person no longer needs to be physically present at the scene of trauma, either as its direct victim or as witness, to qualify as a trauma survivor today (McNally & Breslau, 2008). This means that horrified citizens throughout America who watched television coverage of the September 11, 2001 terrorist attacks count as trauma survivors potentially diagnosable with PTSD just as much as those who nearly perished in the assault on the World Trade Center (Marshall et al., 2007).

The text accompanying the current criteria for PTSD explicitly certify CSA as a qualifying trauma, irrespective of threat of harm. According to DSM-IV-TR (APA, 2000), "For children, sexually traumatic events may include developmentally inappropriate sexual experiences without threatened or actual violence or injury" (p. 464). Reviewing the history of how mental health professionals and other experts have conceptualized sexual abuse, Davis (2005) concluded, "The PTSD framework as a general model for sexual abuse was by no means obvious" (p. 116). It is unclear how well it fits the trauma paradigm if violence or threat of violence is absent. Nevertheless, many clinicians, including me (e.g., McNally, 2003a, pp. 2–3), have used the term *survivor* of childhood sexual abuse. Calling someone a survivor implies that the person was in danger of losing his or her life (cf. cancer survivors and Holocaust survivors). Yet few victims of childhood sexual abuse were in mortal danger.

However, to note the oddity of calling someone a *survivor*, whose life was not endangered, does not minimize the moral reprehensibility of the sexual molestation of children. Yet people who question the survivor label or trauma label run the risk of being accused of minimizing sexual abuse, and unwittingly providing aid and comfort to pedophiles.

Unfortunately, conflation of moral and scientific issues is common in the field of traumatic stress studies. Indeed, unlike the other anxiety disorders, PTSD implies the moral categories of perpetrator and victim. In contrast, consider panic disorder. When someone develops panic attacks, no one is to blame. When someone develops PTSD, there is usually someone or something to blame. PTSD is morally complex in ways that the other anxiety disorders are not.

However, we must avoid confusing moral and scientific issues when considering trauma. Problems arise when we fail to distinguish between them. For example, the study of risk factors for PTSD was de facto taboo for many years, based on the mistaken notion that it amounted to blaming victims for their plight (McNally, 2009b).

Another example concerns the uproar occurring in response to Rind, Tromovitch, and Bauserman's (1998) meta-analytic study showing that many sexually abused children do not suffer long-term psychiatric consequences. While serving on the DSM-IV PTSD committee, I had completed the literature review of the then-small literature on childhood PTSD (McNally, 1993). Accordingly, Rind et al.'s findings surprised me as they did many clinicians. Yet the outrage at the authors who, after all, merely synthesized and interpreted the results of CSA studies done by others, was even more surprising, especially when it culminated in a formal Congressional condemnation of their peer-reviewed article in *Psychological Bulletin* (Lilienfeld, 2002).

I suspect that critics of Rind et al. feared that data showing that many sexually abused children are resilient and do not experience lasting harm would authorize pedophilia on the grounds of "no harm, no foul." Pedophiles surely would have enthusiastically drawn this normative conclusion from the data. Ironically, the reactions of both Rind et al.'s critics and the pedophiles indicate that both groups presupposed the validity of a utilitarian (consequentialist) ethics whereby the moral character of an action depends entirely on its consequences (Bentham, 1823/1948, p. 2). If the child receives no harm and the perpetrator receives pleasure, then sexual molestation is permissible, according to a consequentialist ethic. But one need not draw this appalling conclusion if one adheres to a deontological ethical system (Kant, 1785/1964, p. 34). That is, we can accept the fact that children are often resilient and still categorically condemn sexual contact between children and adults. Deontological ethics prohibit adults from using a child as a means to satisfy themselves sexually, irrespective of the psychiatric consequences for the child. Had Rind et al.'s critics been more Kantian and less utilitarian, the brouhaha over Rind et al.'s *Psychological Bulletin* article and its formal condemnation by Congress would have never occurred.

The recognition that CSA need not qualify as a canonical traumatic stressor that provokes terror and fear for one's life points to a third interpretation of recovered memories distinct from both the repression account and the false memory account (McNally & Geraerts, 2009). That is, one can reject the concept of repressed memories of trauma as lacking evidential support without assuming that all recovered memories of CSA must therefore be false memories.

In our research program, we have defined recovered memory subjects as people who report sexual abuse as a child, report not having thought about it for many years, and then report recalling it later in life (e.g., McNally et al., 2006a). This definition does not presuppose that the victim experienced the abuse as a terrifying trauma when it occurred, and nor does it presuppose that the memory of the abuse was inaccessible, thanks to repression or dissociation, during the long period of time when it apparently never came to mind.

Hence, there appear to be recovered memories of CSA that were neither traumatic nor previously repressed. In the typical case (Clancy & McNally, 2005/2006), the victim was about 7 years of age and failed to understand the experience as sexual or as abusive. The victim knew and trusted the perpetrator who neither threatened nor physically harmed the victim, who experienced confusion, disgust, or anxiety, but not terror. The abuse, often fondling, seldom occurred on more than one or a few occasions. The victim was able to avoid dwelling on this unpleasant, confusing experience precisely because it was not traumatic in the sense of being terrifying. He or she rarely disclosed it to other people, and hence did not discuss it with others. If the perpetrator died or moved away, the victim often lacked reminders of the experience to prompt recollection during the period when he or she did not think about the abuse. However, encounters with reminders in adulthood prompted recovery of the memory of CSA, and understanding it through the eyes of an adult often resulted in PTSD symptoms. For the first time, victims realized that someone, often someone they knew, loved, and trusted, had sexually exploited them.

In conclusion, although the repression account holds that people become incapable of recalling their abuse *because* it was so traumatic, our data suggest a different interpretation. People forget their abuse because it was not traumatic when it first occurred, even though it remains morally reprehensible nevertheless.

Susan Clancy's *The Trauma Myth*

This chapter mainly concerns our group's research on recovered memories of CSA. However, my former Ph.D. student and postdoctoral fellow, Susan Clancy (2009) has extended some of these themes to childhood sexual abuse in general in her book entitled *The Trauma Myth*. The focus of her book is continuous, not recovered, memories of CSA. She mentions recovered memories only in passing. Nevertheless, *The Trauma Myth* has sparked controversy reminiscent of the Memory Wars. Favorable book reviews have appeared in publications ranging from *People* magazine to *Science* magazine, but postings to Amazon.com and other Internet sites document sharply divided opinions about her central thesis. Ironically, some of her angriest critics are therapists, whereas many of her strongest supporters are abuse survivors themselves who say that Clancy truly understands their experience.

Her interviews with adults reporting histories of CSA have led her to conclude that the trauma model of sexual abuse is often incorrect. That is, many of her interviewees say that they did not experience the terror that accompanies violent, often life-threatening, canonical traumatic events, such as rape, combat, and so forth. They report that perpetrators were usually adults with whom they had a close relationship (e.g., teacher, grandfather). The perpetrators did not use threats, physical force, or other coercion. However, they did provide the victims with attention, nonsexual affection, and gifts. The victims, often in elementary school, were too young to understand that these trusted adults were sexually exploiting them. The children often experienced anxiety, confusion, and disgust, but their desire to maintain their relationship with the perpetrator led them to overlook the bizarre, secretive sexual experiences with the perpetrator. Sometimes lonely and starved for affection, these children were vulnerable for exploitation.

As the children grew older, they understood what had been happening to them. They reacted with feelings of shock and betrayal (cf. Freyd, 1996). Some of them disclosed the abuse to adults, but the responses they received were far from uniformly positive. Some adults disbelieved their reports, whereas others asked the children why they did not refuse to participate in the sexual activities. Others were supportive of the victims.

Ironically, partly because victims did not experience coercion, violence, and terror during the abuse itself, they become especially vulnerable to delayed psychological damage. Many of Clancy's interviewees told her that they felt somehow complicit in their abuse, believing that their failure to resist the authority of the adult abuser means that they had consented to sexual activity. As Clancy is quick to emphasize, youngsters cannot consent to things they do not understand, such as sexual activity with adults. Hence, the blame rests entirely with the perpetrators. Tragically, however, many of the victims were haunted by feelings of guilt and shame, believing that they were somehow responsible for what happened to them.

As Clancy emphasizes, had coercion been involved, victims would likely have experienced less guilt and shame later in life because it would be nearly impossible for victims to feel complicit in their own molestation. As a mother of three young daughters herself, Clancy felt intense anger at the perpetrators, yet was often surprised that the victims themselves were less angry about their betrayal than Clancy expected them to be. She suspects that irrational feelings of guilt, shame, and complicity might have muted their anger. The upshot is that sexual abuse has very damaging long-term psychological consequences even when, or perhaps especially when, the abuse was neither coercive or terror inducing.

Contrary to the implication of her book's title, Clancy stresses that some victims *do* experience coercive and violent sexual abuse in childhood. These victims clearly fit the trauma model and hence are at risk for developing acute PTSD. Her complaint is that traumatologists have too often assumed that CSA *always* counts as a terror-inducing trauma when it occurs. Because she suspects that the trauma model fits only a minority of cases, clinicians will misunderstand how CSA psychologically damages victims. The toxic emotion is not terror, as the trauma model implies, but shame and guilt however irrational these feelings may be. To say that CSA is often not traumatic when it occurs does not minimize the psychological damage it can subsequently cause. Indeed, traumatic events – experiences that threaten one's life and induce terror – are not the only kind of experience that can cause lasting psychological harm.

As Clancy acknowledges, the trauma model has served to underscore the seriousness of sexual abuse, putting it on the radar screen of society and clinical psychology. Unfortunately, it may misdirect clinical interventions for CSA victims for whom it does not apply. The model has roots in animal research on Pavlovian fear conditioning (e.g., Foa, Zinbarg, & Rothbaum, 1992), and accordingly has inspired efficacious treatments for rape-related PTSD such as prolonged imaginal exposure therapy that diminishes fear associated with traumatic memories (e.g., Foa & Rothbaum, 1998). Yet to the extent that negative self-referent emotions, such as shame and guilt, figure prominently in the clinical picture, exposure therapy may not be the best approach (Foa & McNally, 1996). Cognitive therapy (Ehlers et al., 2003) targeting guilt and shame may work best for CSA victims for whom the trauma model does not fit.

In conclusion, the moral reprehensibility of sexual abuse remains regardless of whether the victim experienced trauma at the time of its occurrence and regardless of extent or type of psychological damage occurring in its wake. On this point, all participants in the Memory Wars can agree.

References

American Psychiatric Association. (1980). *Diagnostic and statistical manual of mental disorders* (3rd ed.). Washington, DC: Author.
American Psychiatric Association. (1987). *Diagnostic and statistical manual of mental disorders* (3rd ed., rev.). Washington, DC: Author.

American Psychiatric Association. (1994). *Diagnostic and statistical manual of mental disorders* (4th ed.). Washington, DC: Author.

American Psychiatric Association. (2000). *Diagnostic and statistical manual of mental disorders – text revision* (4th ed.). Washington, DC: Author.

Arrigo, J. M., & Pezdek, K. (1997). Lessons from the study of psychogenic amnesia. *Current Directions in Psychological Science, 6*, 148–152.

Bar-Haim, Y., Lamy, D., Pergamin, L., Bakermans-Kranenburg, M. J., & van IJzendoorn, M. H. (2007). Threat-related attentional bias in anxious and nonanxious individuals: A meta-analytic study. *Psychological Bulletin, 133*, 1–24.

Beck, A. T., & Steer, R. A. (1987). *Beck depression inventory manual.* San Antonio, TX: Psychological Corporation.

Bentham, J. (1823/1948). *The principles of morals and legislation* (rev. ed.). New York: Hafner.

Bernstein, E. M., & Putnam, F. W. (1986). Development, reliability, and validity of a dissociation scale. *The Journal of Nervous and Mental Disease, 174*, 727–735.

Bjork, R. A. (1989). Retrieval inhibition as an adaptive mechanism in human memory. In H. L. Roediger III & F. I. M. Craik (Eds.), *Varieties of memory and consciousness: Essays in honor of Endel Tulving* (pp. 309–330). Hillsdale, NJ: Erlbaum.

Borch-Jacobsen, M. (2009). *Making minds and madness: From hysteria to depression.* Cambridge: Cambridge University Press.

Breslau, N., Reboussin, B. A., Anthony, J. C., & Storr, C. L. (2005). The structure of posttraumatic stress disorder: Latent class analysis in 2 community samples. *Archives of General Psychiatry, 62*, 1343–1351.

Breuer, J., & Freud, S. (1893/1955). On the psychical mechanism of hysterical phenomena: Preliminary communication. In J. Strachey (Ed. and Trans.), *The standard edition of the complete psychological works of Sigmund Freud* (Vol. 2, pp. 3–17). London: Hogarth Press.

Brewin, C. R. (2003). *Post-traumatic stress disorder: Malady or myth?* New Haven, CT: Yale University Press.

Briere, J., & Conte, J. (1993). Self-reported amnesia for abuse in adults molested as children. *Journal of Traumatic Stress, 6*, 21–31.

Brittlebank, A. D., Scott, J., Williams, J. M. G., & Ferrier, I. N. (1993). Autobiographical memory in depression: State or trait marker? *The British Journal of Psychiatry, 162*, 118–121.

Brown, D., Scheflin, A. W., & Hammond, D. C. (1998). *Memory, trauma treatment, and the law.* New York: Norton.

Brown, D., Scheflin, A. W., & Whitfield, C. L. (1999). Recovered memories: The current weight of evidence in science and in the courts. *Journal of Psychiatry and Law, 27*, 5–156.

Carey, B. (2007). A study of memory looks at fact and fiction. *New York Times*, February 2, A15 and A21.

Ceci, S. J., & Loftus, E. F. (1994). "Memory work": A royal road to false memories? *Applied Cognitive Psychology, 8*, 351–364.

Choderlos de Laclos, P.-A.-F. (1782/1961). *Les liaisons dangereuses* (P. W. K. Stone, Trans.). London: Penguin.

Clancy, S. A. (2005). *Abducted: How people come to believe they were kidnapped by aliens.* Cambridge, MA: Harvard University Press.

Clancy, S. A. (2009). *The trauma myth.* New York: Basic Books.

Clancy, S. A., & McNally, R. J. (2005/2006). Who needs repression? Normal memory processes can explain "forgetting" of childhood sexual abuse. *Scientific Review of Mental Health Practice, 4*, 66–73.

Clancy, S. A., McNally, R. J., & Schacter, D. L. (1999). Effects of guided imagery on memory distortion in women reporting recovered memories of sexual abuse. *Journal of Traumatic Stress, 12*, 559–569.

Clancy, S. A., McNally, R. J., Schacter, D. L., Lenzenweger, M. F., & Pitman, R. K. (2002). Memory distortion in people reporting abduction by aliens. *Journal of Abnormal Psychology, 111*, 455–461.

Clancy, S. A., Schacter, D. L., McNally, R. J., & Pitman, R. K. (2000). False recognition in women reporting recovered memories of sexual abuse. *Psychological Science, 11*, 26–31.

Courtois, C. A. (1992). The memory retrieval process in incest survivor therapy. *Journal of Child Sexual Abuse, 1*, 15–31.

Crews, F. (1995). *The memory wars: Freud's legacy in dispute.* New York: New York Review of Books.

Davis, J. E. (2005). *Accounts of innocence: Sexual abuse, trauma, and the self.* Chicago: University of Chicago Press.

Deese, J. (1959). On the prediction of occurrence of particular verbal intrusions in immediate recall. *Journal of Experimental Psychology, 58*, 17–22.

DePrince, A., Brown, L., Cheit, R., Freyd, J., Gold, S. N., Pezdek, K., & Quina, K. (2012, this volume). Motivated forgetting and misremembering: Perspectives from betrayal trauma theory. In R. F. Belli (Ed.), *True and false recovered memories: Toward a reconciliation of the debate* (pp. 193–242). *Vol. 58: Nebraska Symposium on Motivation.* New York: Springer.

DePrince, A. P., & Freyd, J. J. (2004). Forgetting trauma stimuli. *Psychological Science, 15*, 488–492.

DePrince, A. P., Freyd, J. J., & Malle, B. F. (2007). A replication by another name: A response to Devilly et al. (2007). *Psychological Science, 18*, 218–219.

Devilly, G. J., & Ciorciari, J. (2007). Conclusions in science when theory and data collide. *Psychological Science, 18*, 220–221.

Devilly, G. J., Ciorciari, J., Piesse, A., Sherwell, S., Zammit, S., Cook, F., et al. (2007). Dissociative tendencies and memory performance on directed-forgetting tasks. *Psychological Science, 18*, 212–217.

Dollinger, S. J. (1985). Lightning-strike disaster among children. *The British Journal of Medical Psychology, 58*, 375–383.

Ehlers, A., Clark, D. M., Hackmann, A., McManus, F., Fennell, M., Herbert, C., et al. (2003). A randomized controlled trial of cognitive therapy, a self-help booklet, and repeated assessments as early interventions for posttraumatic stress disorder. *Archives of General Psychiatry, 60*, 1024–1032.

Engelhard, I. M., van den Hout, M. A., Weerts, J., Arntz, A., Hox, J. J. C. M., & McNally, R. J. (2007). Deployment-related stress and trauma in Dutch soldiers returning from Iraq: Prospective study. *The British Journal of Psychiatry, 191*, 140–145.

Evans, J., Williams, J. M. G., O'Loughlin, S., & Howells, K. (1992). Autobiographical memory and problem-solving strategies of parasuicide patients. *Psychological Medicine, 22*, 399–405.

Femina, D. D., Yeager, C. A., & Lewis, D. O. (1990). Child abuse: Adolescent records vs. adult recall. *Child Abuse & Neglect, 14*, 227–231.

Foa, E. B., & McNally, R. J. (1996). Mechanisms of change in exposure therapy. In R. M. Rapee (Ed.), *Current controversies in the anxiety disorders* (pp. 329–343). New York: Guilford Press.

Foa, E. B., & Rothbaum, B. O. (1998). *Treating the trauma of rape: Cognitive-behavioral therapy for PTSD.* New York: Guilford.

Foa, E. B., & Tolin, D. F. (2000). Comparison of the PTSD symptom scale-interview version and the clinician-administered PTSD scale. *Journal of Traumatic Stress, 13*, 181–191.

Foa, E. B., Zinbarg, R., & Rothbaum, B. O. (1992). Uncontrollability and unpredictability in posttraumatic stress disorder: An animal model. *Psychological Bulletin, 112*, 218–238.

French, C. C., Santomauro, J., Hamilton, V., Fox, R., & Thalbourne, M. A. (2008). Psychological aspects of the alien contact experience. *Cortex, 44*, 1387–1395.

Freud, S. (1962). The aetiology of hysteria. In: J. Strachey (Ed. and Trans.), *The standard edition of the complete works of Sigmund Freud* (Vol. 3, pp. 191–221). London: Hogarth Press.

Freyd, J. J. (1996). *Betrayal trauma: The logic of forgetting childhood abuse.* Cambridge, MA: Harvard University Press.

Freyd, J. J., DePrince, A. P., & Gleaves, D. H. (2007). The state of betrayal trauma theory: Reply to McNally – conceptual issues and future directions. *Memory, 15*, 295–311.

Gallo, D. A. (2010). False memories and fantastic beliefs: 15 years of the DRM illusion. *Memory & Cognition, 38*, 833–848.

Garry, M., Manning, C. G., Loftus, E. F., & Sherman, S. J. (1996). Imagination inflation: Imagining a childhood event inflates confidence that it occurred. *Psychonomic Bulletin and Review, 3*, 208–214.

Golding, J. M. (2005). Directed forgetting tasks in cognitive research. In A. Wenzel & D. C. Rubin (Eds.), *Cognitive methods and their application to clinical research* (pp. 177–196). Washington, DC: American Psychological Association.

Herman, J. H., & Schatzow, E. (1987). Recovery and verification of memories of childhood sexual trauma. *Psychoanalytic Psychology, 4*, 1–14.

Israëls, H., & Schatzman, M. (1993). The seduction theory. *History of Psychiatry, 4*, 23–59.

Johnson, H. M. (1994). Processes of successful intentional forgetting. *Psychological Bulletin, 116*, 274–292.

Kant, I. (1785/1964). *Groundwork of the metaphysic of morals* (H. J. Paton, Trans.). New York: Harper Torchbooks.

Kihlstrom, J. F., & Schacter, D. L. (2000). Functional amnesia. In F. Boller & J. Grafman (Eds.), *Handbook of neuropsychology* (2nd ed., Vol. 2, pp. 409–427). Amsterdam: Elsevier Science.

Lilienfeld, S. O. (2002). When worlds collide: Social science, politics, and the Rind et al. (1998) child sexual abuse meta-analysis. *American Psychologist, 57*, 176–188.

Loewenstein, R. J. (1991). An office mental status examination for complex chronic dissociative symptoms and multiple personality disorder. *Psychiatric Clinics of North America, 14*, 567–604.

Macklin, M. L., Metzger, L. J., Litz, B. T., McNally, R. J., Lasko, N. B., Orr, S. P., et al. (1998). Lower precombat intelligence is a risk factor for posttraumatic stress disorder. *Journal of Consulting and Clinical Psychology, 66*, 323–326.

Marshall, R. D., Bryant, R. A., Amsel, L., Suh, E. J., Cook, J. M., & Neria, Y. (2007). The psychology of ongoing threat: Relative risk appraisal, the September 11 attacks, and terrorism-related fears. *American Psychologist, 62*, 304–316.

McGaugh, J. L. (2003). *Memory and emotion: The making of lasting memories*. New York: Columbia University Press.

McNally, R. J. (1993). Stressors that produce DSM-III-R posttraumatic stress disorder in children. In J. R. T. Davidson & E. B. Foa (Eds.), *Posttraumatic stress disorder: DSM-IV and beyond* (pp. 57–74). Washington, DC: American Psychiatric Press.

McNally, R. J. (1998). Experimental approaches to cognitive abnormality in posttraumatic stress disorder. *Clinical Psychology Review, 18*, 971–982.

McNally, R. J. (2003a). *Remembering trauma*. Cambridge, MA: Belknap Press/Harvard University Press.

McNally, R. J. (2003b). Recovering memories of trauma: A view from the laboratory. *Current Directions in Psychological Science, 12*, 32–35.

McNally, R. J. (2003c). Progress and controversy in the study of posttraumatic stress disorder. *Annual Review of Psychology, 54*, 229–252.

McNally, R. J. (2004). The science and folklore of traumatic amnesia. *Clinical Psychology: Science and Practice, 11*, 29–33.

McNally, R. J. (2006). Cognitive abnormalities in post-traumatic stress disorder. *Trends in Cognitive Sciences, 10*, 271–277.

McNally, R. J. (2007a). Do certain readings of Freud constitute "pathological science"? A comment on Boag (2006). *Review of General Psychology, 11*, 359–360.

McNally, R. J. (2007b). Dispelling confusion about traumatic dissociative amnesia. *Mayo Clinic Proceedings, 82*, 1083–1087.

McNally, R. J. (2007c). Revisiting Dohrenwend et al.'s Revisit of the national Vietnam veterans readjustment study. *Journal of Traumatic Stress, 20*, 481–486.

McNally, R. J. (2007d). Betrayal trauma theory: A critical appraisal. *Memory, 15*, 280–294.

McNally, R. J. (2009a). Can we fix PTSD in DSM-V? *Depression and Anxiety, 26*, 597–600.

McNally, R. J. (2009b). Posttraumatic stress disorder. In P. H. Blaney & T. Millon (Eds.), *Oxford textbook of psychopathology* (2nd ed., pp. 176–197). Oxford: Oxford University Press.

McNally, R. J., Amir, N., & Lipke, H. J. (1996). Subliminal processing of threat cues in posttraumatic stress disorder? *Journal of Anxiety Disorders, 10*, 115–128.

McNally, R. J., & Breslau, N. (2008). Does virtual trauma cause posttraumatic stress disorder? *American Psychologist, 63*, 282–283.

McNally, R. J., & Clancy, S. A. (2005a). Sleep paralysis, sexual abuse, and space alien abduction. *Transcultural Psychiatry, 42*, 113–122.

McNally, R. J., & Clancy, S. A. (2005b). Sleep paralysis in adults reporting repressed, recovered, or continuous memories of childhood sexual abuse. *Journal of Anxiety Disorders, 19*, 595–602.

McNally, R. J., & Clancy, S. A. (2006). Sleep paralysis and recovered memories of childhood sexual abuse: A reply to Pendergrast. *Journal of Anxiety Disorders, 20*, 538–540.

McNally, R. J., Clancy, S. A., Barrett, H. M., & Parker, H. A. (2004). Inhibiting retrieval of trauma cues in adults reporting histories of childhood sexual abuse. *Cognition and Emotion, 18*, 479–493.

McNally, R. J., Clancy, S. A., Barrett, H. M., & Parker, H. A. (2005). Reality monitoring in adults reporting repressed, recovered, or continuous memories of childhood sexual abuse. *Journal of Abnormal Psychology, 114*, 147–152.

McNally, R. J., Clancy, S. A., Barrett, H. M., Parker, H. A., Ristuccia, C. S., & Perlman, C. A. (2006a). Autobiographical memory specificity in adults reporting repressed, recovered, or continuous memories of childhood sexual abuse. *Cognition and Emotion, 20*, 527–535.

McNally, R. J., Clancy, S. A., & Schacter, D. L. (2001). Directed forgetting of trauma cues in adults reporting repressed or recovered memories of childhood sexual abuse. *Journal of Abnormal Psychology, 110*, 151–156.

McNally, R. J., Clancy, S. A., Schacter, D. L., & Pitman, R. K. (2000a). Personality profiles, dissociation, and absorption in women reporting repressed, recovered, or continuous memories of childhood sexual abuse. *Journal of Consulting and Clinical Psychology, 68*, 1033–1037.

McNally, R. J., Clancy, S. A., Schacter, D. L., & Pitman, R. K. (2000b). Cognitive processing of trauma cues in adults reporting repressed, recovered, or continuous memories of childhood sexual abuse. *Journal of Abnormal Psychology, 109*, 355–359.

McNally, R. J., & Geraerts, E. (2009). A new solution to the recovered memory debate. *Perspectives on Psychological Science, 4*, 126–134.

McNally, R. J., Kaspi, S. P., Riemann, B. C., & Zeitlin, S. B. (1990). Selective processing of threat cues in posttraumatic stress disorder. *Journal of Abnormal Psychology, 99*, 398–402.

McNally, R. J., Lasko, N. B., Clancy, S. A., Macklin, M. L., Pitman, R. K., & Orr, S. P. (2004). Psychophysiological responding during script-driven imagery in people reporting abduction by space aliens. *Psychological Science, 15*, 493–497.

McNally, R. J., Lasko, N. B., Macklin, M. L., & Pitman, R. K. (1995). Autobiographical memory disturbance in combat-related posttraumatic stress disorder. *Behaviour Research and Therapy, 33*, 619–630.

McNally, R. J., Litz, B. T., Prassas, A., Shin, L. M., & Weathers, F. W. (1994). Emotional priming of autobiographical memory in post-traumatic stress disorder. *Cognition and Emotion, 8*, 351–367.

McNally, R. J., Luedke, D. L., Besyner, J. K., Peterson, R. A., Bohm, K., & Lips, O. J. (1987). Sensitivity to stress-relevant stimuli in posttraumatic stress disorder. *Journal of Anxiety Disorders, 1*, 105–116.

McNally, R. J., Metzger, L. J., Lasko, N. B., Clancy, S. A., & Pitman, R. K. (1998). Directed forgetting of trauma cues in adult survivors of childhood sexual abuse with and without posttraumatic stress disorder. *Journal of Abnormal Psychology, 107*, 596–601.

McNally, R. J., Perlman, C. A., Ristuccia, C. S., & Clancy, S. A. (2006b). Clinical characteristics of adults reporting repressed, recovered, or continuous memories of childhood sexual abuse. *Journal of Consulting and Clinical Psychology, 74*, 237–242.

McNally, R. J., Ristuccia, C., & Perlman, C. A. (2005). Forgetting of trauma cues in adults reporting continuous or recovered memories of childhood sexual abuse. *Psychological Science, 16*, 336–340.

McNally, R. J., & Shin, L. M. (1995). Association of intelligence with severity of posttraumatic stress disorder symptoms in Vietnam combat veterans. *The American Journal of Psychiatry, 152*, 936–938.

McTeague, L. M., McNally, R. J., & Litz, B. T. (2004). Prewar, war-zone, and postwar predictors of posttraumatic stress disorder in female Vietnam veteran health care providers. *Military Psychology, 16*, 99–114.

Meyersburg, C. A., Bogdan, R., Gallo, D. A., & McNally, R. J. (2009). False memory propensity in people reporting recovered memories of past lives. *Journal of Abnormal Psychology, 118*, 399–404.

Myers, L. B., Brewin, C. R., & Power, M. J. (1998). Repressive coping and the directed forgetting of emotional material. *Journal of Abnormal Psychology, 107*, 141–148.

Olio, K. A. (1989). Memory retrieval in the treatment of adult survivors of sexual abuse. *Transactional Analysis Journal, 19*, 93–100.

Pendergrast, M. (1996). *Victims of memory: Incest accusations and shattered lives* (rev. ed.). London: HarperCollins.

Piper, A., Jr., Pope, H. G., Jr., & Borowiecki, J. J., III. (2000). Custer's last stand: Brown, Scheflin, and Whitfield's latest attempt to salvage "dissociative amnesia. *Journal of Psychiatry and Law, 28*, 149–213.

Pope, H. G., Jr., Oliva, P. S., & Hudson, J. I. (1999). Repressed memories: The scientific status. In D. L. Faigman, D. H. Kaye, M. J. Saks, & J. Sanders (Eds.), *Modern scientific testimony: The law and science of expert testimony* (Vol. 1, Pocket part, pp. 115–155).St. Paul, MN: West Publishing.

Pope, H. G., Jr., Poliakoff, M. B., Parker, M. P., Boynes, M., & Hudson, J. I. (2007a). Is dissociative amnesia a culture-bound syndrome? Findings from a survey of historical literature. *Psychological Medicine, 37*, 225–233.

Pope, H. G., Jr., Poliakoff, M. B., Parker, M. P., Boynes, M., & Hudson, J. I. (2007b). The authors' reply. *Psychological Medicine, 37*, 1067–1068.

Porter, S., & Peace, K. A. (2007). The scars of memory: A prospective, longitudinal investigation of the consistency of traumatic and positive emotional memories in adulthood. *Psychological Science, 18*, 435–441.

Rind, B., Tromovitch, P., & Bauserman, R. (1998). A meta-analytic examination of assumed properties of child sexual abuse using college samples. *Psychological Bulletin, 124*, 22–53.

Roediger, H. L., III, & Bergman, E. T. (1998). The controversy over recovered memories. *Psychology, Public Policy, and Law, 4*, 1091–1109.

Roediger, H. L., III, & McDermott, K. B. (1995). Creating false memories: Remembering words not presented in lists. *Journal of Experimental Psychology. Learning, Memory, and Cognition, 21*, 803–814.

Rubin, D. C., Berntsen, D., & Bohni, M. K. (2008). A memory-based model of posttraumatic stress disorder: Evaluation basic assumptions underlying the PTSD diagnosis. *Psychological Review, 115*, 985–1011.

Schacter, D. L. (1996). *Searching for memory: The brain, the mind, and the past.* New York: Basic Books.

Schooler, J. W., Bendiksen, M., & Ambadar, Z. (1997). Taking the middle line: Can we accommodate both fabricated and recovered memories of sexual abuse? In M. A. Conway (Ed.), *Recovered memories and false memories* (pp. 251–292). Oxford: Oxford University Press.

Shin, L. M., Kosslyn, S. M., McNally, R. J., Alpert, N. M., Thompson, W. L., Rauch, S. L., et al. (1997). Visual imagery and perception in posttraumatic stress disorder: A positron emission tomographic investigation. *Archives of General Psychiatry, 54*, 233–241.

Shin, L. M., McNally, R. J., Kosslyn, S. M., Thompson, W. L., Rauch, S. L., Alpert, N. M., et al. (1999). Regional cerebral blood flow during script-driven imagery in childhood sexual abuse-related PTSD: A PET investigation. *The American Journal of Psychiatry, 156*, 575–584.

Spiegel, D. (1997). Foreword. In D. Spiegel (Ed.), *Repressed memories* (pp. 5–11). Washington, DC: American Psychiatric Press.

Terr, L. C. (1991). Childhood trauma: An outline and overview. *The American Journal of Psychiatry, 148*, 10–20.

Trandel, D. V., & McNally, R. J. (1987). Perception of threat cues in posttraumatic stress disorder: Semantic processing without awareness? *Behaviour Research and Therapy, 25*, 469–476.

Widom, C. S., & Morris, S. (1997). Accuracy of adult recollections of childhood victimization: Part 2. Childhood sexual abuse. *Psychological Assessment, 9*, 34–46.

Wilkinson, C. B. (1983). Aftermath of a disaster: The collapse of the Hyatt Regency Hotel skywalks. *The American Journal of Psychiatry, 140*, 1134–1139.

Williams, J. M. G., Barnhofer, T., Crane, C., Hermans, D., Raes, F., Watkins, E., et al. (2007). Autobiographical memory specificity and emotional disorder. *Psychological Bulletin, 133*, 122–148.

Williams, J. M. G., Mathews, A., & MacLeod, C. (1996). The emotional Stroop task and psychopathology. *Psychological Bulletin, 120*, 3–24.

Williams, L. M. (1994). Recall of childhood trauma: A prospective study of women's memories of child sexual abuse. *Journal of Consulting and Clinical Psychology, 62*, 1167–1176.

A Theoretical Framework for Understanding Recovered Memory Experiences

Chris R. Brewin

Abstract If recovered memory experiences appear counter-intuitive, this is in part due to misconceptions about trauma and memory, and to a failure to adopt a comprehensive model of memory that distinguishes personal semantic memory, autobiographical event memory, and memory appraisal. Memory performance is generally superior when events, including traumas, are central to identity. Prolonged trauma in childhood, however, can produce severe identity disturbances that may interfere with the encoding and later retrieval of personal semantic and autobiographical event information. High levels of emotion either at encoding or recall can also interfere with the creation of coherent narrative memories. For example, high levels of shock and fear when memories are recovered unexpectedly may lead to the experience of vivid flashbacks. Memory appraisals may also influence the sense that an event has been forgotten for a long time. Recovered memories, although unusual, do not contradict what we know about how memory works.

Keywords Childhood • Forgetting • Identity • Trauma

Introduction

Why has the idea that memories of trauma can be forgotten and then recovered attracted the controversy it has? Why have eminent clinicians and academics, not all of whom are experts on trauma and memory, felt qualified to join the advisory boards of false memory societies and lend their considerable weight to assertions that are either empirically unsupported or even run contrary to expert opinion? Undoubtedly one reason has been the framing of the debate in terms of mysterious

C.R. Brewin (✉)
University College London, England, UK
e-mail: c.brewin@ucl.ac.uk

R.F. Belli (ed.), *True and False Recovered Memories: Toward a Reconciliation of the Debate*, Nebraska Symposium on Motivation, DOI 10.1007/978-1-4614-1195-6_5, © Springer Science+Business Media, LLC 2012

and unverifiable processes, such as "repression" or "dissociative amnesia", rather than an observable phenomenon, "forgetting". Although dissociative processes are familiar to clinicians working in the trauma field, the phenomena are poorly understood and are rarely encountered in everyday life or, of course, in the laboratory. Use of unclear terms like "repression" by clinicians has invited skepticism from some experimental psychologists. Perhaps as a result, claimed forgetting of abuse has often been invalidated by linking it to the discredited process of "repression". In logic this is the 'straw person' fallacy.

Examples of the conflation of forgetting with repression are provided by Loftus and Davis (2006), who noted: "Most fundamentally, to demonstrate that memories can be repressed and later recovered, at least three things must be verified: (a) that the abuse did take place, (b) that it was forgotten and inaccessible for some period of time, and (c) that it was later remembered" (p. 471), and "Yet over the past couple of decades, many persons have reported having experienced massive abuse that was repressed and recovered, which raises the question of whether some or all such "memories" might be false" (p. 475). A recent edition of the False Memory Syndrome Foundation Newsletter (2010, Vol 19, no. 1, p. 1) similarly notes "Belief in the historical accuracy of "recovered repressed memories" continues its journey through our culture, its passage sometimes marked by incidents that seem discouraging, as though no progress had been made....a legal decision in Minnesota reinforces the understanding that there is a lack of scientific evidence for the theory of repressed and recovered memories".

Another reason for the controversy has been the widespread acceptance of a false premise, namely that traumatic events are not forgotten (see, for example, McNally, 2012, this volume). Typical claims include: "Traumatic events—those experienced as overwhelmingly terrifying at the time of their occurrence—are highly memorable and seldom, if ever, forgotten" (McNally, 2005); "Memories for trauma are distinctive, long-lasting, and easily retrieved" (Shobe & Kihlstrom, 1997). Although traumas are sometimes unforgettable, particularly by people suffering from posttraumatic stress disorder (PTSD), the evidence that they are invariably better remembered than non-traumas in healthy populations is equivocal (Brewin, 2007). To make this point more concrete, a landmark study found that only about a quarter of personally experienced and significant life events that were entered into monthly records were recalled when participants were given similar checklists at the end of a 10-month period (Raphael, Cloitre, & Dohrenwend, 1991). Desirable events and events involving significant loss were better recalled, but the effects were modest, and there was no advantage for events involving illness or injury.

Another, much smaller-scale, study found that participants recalled only half their visits to HMOs over the previous year, even when these were for serious events involving a problem that had a high probability of resulting in a major infection, debility, or death if not treated by a medical professional (Means & Loftus, 1991). Non-recurring events were better recalled than recurrent events but the effect, like that for seriousness, was not significant with the low numbers. Schraedley and colleagues investigated the effects of depression on reporting of traumatic events over an interval of 1 year (Schraedley, Turner, & Gotlib, 2002). Whereas worsening of mood did not affect reporting, improvement in mood led to significantly fewer events being reported at the second time point. The results of these studies are consistent in emphasizing that, although traumatic events are likely to be better recalled than non-traumatic ones, a high degree of forgetting can be expected.

This culturally sanctioned myth concerning memory for trauma has led to several deductions that, although logically incorrect, may apply some of the time. For example, one deduction is that if the event was forgotten, it cannot have been traumatic. It *is* plausible that in some cases a forgotten event, such as child sexual molestation, may not have been understood and hence not experienced as traumatic at the time (Loftus, Garry, & Feldman, 1994; DePrince et al., 2012, this volume; McNally, 2003; McNally, 2012, this volume), although it may have been frightening, painful, and unpleasant. Another deduction is that if an apparently traumatic event was forgotten, it may not have occurred at all. There is indeed evidence that some recovered 'memories' do pertain to events that have been suggested or imagined, and do not correspond to reality (Loftus & Davis, 2006; McNally, 2003). A third deduction is that if a traumatic event appears to have been forgotten, the person may be mistaken about having forgotten it. This is supported by Schooler's observations that some individuals who claim to have forgotten trauma memories had in fact had conversations about the supposedly forgotten events in the recent past. This he termed the "forgot-it-all-along" effect (Schooler, 2001; see also Geraerts, 2012, this volume).

If traumas *are* often forgotten, how are we to explain this? The notion that "ordinary forgetting" (Loftus, Garry, et al., 1994) is a sufficient explanation implies that there is a satisfactory understanding of what forgetting is. But "ordinary forgetting" does not account for the fact that negative events tend to be forgotten more readily than positive ones (Walker, Skowronski, & Thompson, 2003). Moreover, traditional accounts of forgetting largely based on group studies of word list learning in the laboratory cannot be assumed to be adequate. For example, such studies focused mainly on passive forgetting and were not designed to account for stimuli or experiences a person actively wanted to forget. To understand recovered memory experiences, therefore, it is first necessary (a) to carefully document the phenomena themselves, (b) to have a model of memory that can accommodate the range of relevant observations, (c) to consider how disturbances produced by trauma, such as PTSD, can affect memory, and (d) to take due cognizance of individual differences in memory processing. Only then is an adequate understanding likely to emerge.

The Phenomenology of Recovered Trauma Memories

The starting point for any consideration of the recovered memory controversy must be a description of the phenomenon itself. Too often this description is based on unsubstantiated claims that caricature the data and skew the nature of the argument that follows. Among the facts that surveys of recovered trauma memories have established are that they are not just concerned with sexual abuse but also include medical procedures, other child maltreatment, and witnessing violence or death (Andrews et al., 1999; Elliott, 1997; Feldman-Summers & Pope, 1994; Melchert, 1996). They do not just occur within a therapeutic context, but are often retrieved spontaneously (Andrews et al., 1995; Elliott & Briere, 1995; Feldman-Summers & Pope, 1994). Corroborative evidence of varying quality is often available, particularly when the memories have been recovered spontaneously outside of therapy (Andrews et al., 1999; Chu, Frey, Ganzel, & Matthews, 1999; Feldman-Summers & Pope, 1994; Geraerts et al., 2007; Williams, 1995). Finally, the degree of reported amnesia varies considerably, from total forgetting to some basic knowledge of the trauma being retained despite forgetting of many salient facts and episodes (Andrews et al., 2000; Elliott & Briere, 1995; Gold, Hughes, & Hohnecker, 1994; Harvey & Herman, 1994; Loftus, Polonsky, & Fullilove, 1994; Malmo & Laidlaw, 2010).

What is it like to recover a trauma memory that has been forgotten? There are no data from general population samples, which is a major drawback. In case studies and clinical samples the experience often appears to be accompanied by shock or surprise, and the majority of memories tend to be similar to those reported by patients with PTSD: they are fragmented, accompanied by high levels of emotion, and experienced as a reliving of the original event (Andrews et al., 2000; Hunter & Andrews, 2002; Malmo & Laidlaw, 2010; van der Hart, Bolt, & van der Kolk, 2005). Individuals recovering memories have used words and phrases like "stunned", "complete chaos in my emotions", "just this extreme emotion of fear and disbelief", "it was literally like a brick wall just hit me…I just started crying and screaming uncontrollably" (Schooler, 2001). This occurred despite evidence that, as noted above, in a subset of individuals the memories had in fact been previously recalled and even discussed with relatives.

In the Andrews et al. (2000) study the most commonly reported single trigger within therapy was a therapeutic technique although these accounted for less than half the instances of reported memory recovery. The most common triggers prior to therapy were events involving the client's children, or children reaching the same stage of development as the client was at the time of the supposed trauma, followed closely by events involving physical contact with the client, or physical danger to the client or another known person. Other studies have noted that even when clients are in therapy the triggers to memory recovery often occur outside sessions (Malmo & Laidlaw, 2010).

This, then, is the little we know about the experience of recovering a trauma memory. The variety in these accounts suggests that a number of different processes may be at work and that a broad approach to understanding memory will be needed.

A Model of Memory

It is convenient to enumerate three main aspects of memory: *capacity*, *content*, and *process*. *Capacity* refers to individual variability in the amount of information that can be learned, manipulated, and either recalled or used in some other way, and in the efficiency with which this can be done: Measures include standardized tests of verbal and non-verbal learning, working memory capacity, and prospective memory. *Content* refers to what is remembered: Examples include semantic memory (memory for facts), episodic memory (memory for events), and autobiographical memory (memory for facts and events concerning the self). Memory *processes* may be described at a number of levels, including the molecular, neuropsychological, cognitive, and social. Cognitive processes are traditionally considered in terms of encoding, storage, and retrieval functions (for example, voluntary versus involuntary recall), but need to be expanded to consider active attempts to enhance or suppress memory. There is also an important role for judgment and appraisal, and for individual differences in the way memory is used.

These more subjective appraisal functions are critical in evaluating the operation and integrity of memory and arriving at conclusions about the source and veridicality of what comes to mind (Burgess & Shallice, 1996). The source-monitoring framework (Johnson, Hashtroudi, & Lindsay, 1993; Johnson, Raye, Mitchell, & Ankudowich, 2012, this volume) also emphasizes the central role of memory decisions involving the attribution of retrieved information to a source, for example actual or imagined. Understanding recovered memory experiences principally draws on knowledge and theory about the interplay of memory content and process, including appraisal.

An important subset of memory content concerns the self, and Conway (Conway, 2005) has proposed a hierarchical model of autobiographical memory in which overarching semantic knowledge about the self is at the apex. This conceptual level also contains information about overall themes, lifetime periods, and general events. At this level sits the knowledge that one has visited Istanbul, has three sisters, or has a father who sells insurance. This kind of knowledge is central to a person's identity and has been argued to be immediate, as opposed to episodic memory which requires a search (Tulving, 1983). It is now thought that individuals have a collection of multiple 'selves' that are experienced at different times and in different contexts (Harter, Bresnick, Bouchey, & Whitesell, 1997; Markus, & Sentis, 1982). These overlapping ways in which we experience our own identity correspond to a set of related structures in long-term memory that contain some constant features of the self (overarching semantic knowledge) but also contain information relating to the self at specific ages and in the performance of specific roles. Conway has made the valuable proposal that at any one time information is processed by a "working self", a limited subset of self-related memory structures analogous to the limited working memory system.

This higher-level content about the self needs to be distinguished from voluntary memory for specific autobiographical periods and episodes, the construction of which is typically accompanied by more detailed contextual information including time and place. As noted by Conway (Conway & Pleydell-Pearce, 2000), this level can be divided into schematic memory for sequences of similar experiences, in which recall may largely consist of a general summary of what typically happened, and memory for single specific events. Strategic mechanisms such as rehearsal and directed forgetting exist to influence these episodic memories in the service of the

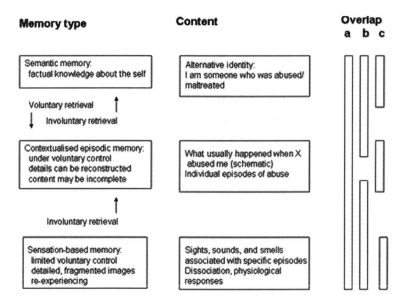

Fig. 1 Hierarchical organization of autobiographical memory in someone who knows he or she is an abuse survivor

person's goals. At the third level there is sensation-based information relating to individual events in the form of images that are automatically retrieved in response to internal or external cues (Brewin, Dalgleish, & Joseph, 1996; Brewin, Gregory, Lipton, & Burgess, 2010; Conway, 2009). Unlike contextualized episodic memories, these lower-level images are not subject to direct strategic control, and may be hard to access except in the presence of very specific cues.

Figure 1 illustrates this hierarchical organization of autobiographical memory using the example of someone who has always known they were abused as a child. The overarching self-narrative contains semantic information about being abused, maltreated, or however the person chooses to describe these experiences to themselves. At the next level down are schematic and individual episodic memories of abuse episodes, which can be voluntarily retrieved if desired but may also be retrieved automatically by internal or external reminders. At the level below are detailed sensory images of these events, linked to emotions such as fear and shame as well as patterns of physiological arousal. There is limited control over their retrieval, which occurs as a result of internal or external stimuli that match their content.

At the right of Fig. 1 are bars representing different degrees of overlap in autobiographical memory for abuse. The first bar (a) indicates that the person is fully aware of all episodes, detailed images, and emotions, and has good access to them. The second bar (b) indicates that the person is aware of some episodes of abuse, but that there are additional episodes and linked images and emotions that they are unaware of. The third bar (c) indicates that autobiographical memory is fragmented, with the person being aware of little more than the fact of having been abused, and being unable to recall specific episodes. Likewise, episodic memories are not integrated with detailed images and emotional reactions.

Trauma and Personal Semantic Memory

It has been proposed that traumatization invariably involves structural changes to the personality to varying degrees (van der Hart, Nijenhuis, & Steele, 2005). Following the British psychologist Charles Myers (Myers, 1940), van der Hart and colleagues distinguished between the apparently normal part of the personality (ANP), driven by the action systems of daily life, and the emotional part of the personality (EP) driven by defensive action systems evoked by traumatic experiences including anxiously attached or avoidant attachment styles. Primary structural dissociation, characteristic of simple PTSD, involves alternation between the ANP and the EP, when the latter is elicited by trauma reminders. Secondary and tertiary structural dissociation involve greater degrees of fragmentation of the ANP and EP associated with repeated childhood or adult trauma. Similarly, it has been argued that episodic memories of trauma represent a threat to the coherence of the conceptual self and therefore tend to remain unintegrated with it (Conway, 2005).

Consistent with these theories, a large community survey found that reports of childhood abuse were associated with large perceived gaps in memory for childhood periods (Edwards, Fivush, Anda, Felitti, & Nordenberg, 2001). This phenomenon has been frequently reported (Malmo & Laidlaw, 2010). More specifically, personal semantic memory seems to be impaired in women reporting childhood abuse, even though episodic memory remains comparatively intact (Hunter & Andrews, 2002; Stokes, Dritschel, & Bekerian, 2008). In the study by Hunter and Andrews, women with recovered memories of childhood abuse, compared to those who had never been abused, found it harder to recall facts about their childhoods, such as home addresses and names of teachers, friends, and neighbors.

Effects of trauma on identity have also been addressed in the developmental literature. Exposure to abuse in childhood is associated from a very young age with dissociation, a fragmented identity (internal conflict between multiple selves), speaking less about internal states, and the development of a false self whereby there is a large discrepancy between the self presented to the outside world and the self experienced as "real" or "authentic" (Beeghly & Cicchetti, 1994; Crittenden & Dilalla, 1988; Ogawa, Sroufe, Weinfield, Carlson, & Egeland, 1997). In addition to the lack self-awareness, there are disruptions to the continuity of the self over time and to the sense of possessing an integrated self (Harter, 1998). In young adults exposure to violence is associated with discrepancies between who people feel they are and who they feel they ought to be (Brewin & Vallance, 1997).

Identity fragmentation is the defining characteristic of dissociative identity disorder, a condition often linked to experiencing severe levels of trauma (Lewis, Yeager,

Table 1 PTSD status and change in military veterans' perceptions of the world (adapted from Brewin, Garnett, et al., 2011)

	Physical disability% (n = 33)	PTSD% (n = 108)
No change	39	9
A small change	30	18
A large change	30	74

Swica, Pincus, & Lewis, 1997; Sar, Akyuz, & Dogan, 2007; Xiao et al., 2006). Both in this disorder (Dorahy et al., 2009) and in PTSD (Brewin & Patel, 2010), this fragmentation is often manifested in the form of hearing one's thoughts as voices, some of which are negative and accusatory. Enduring personality change after catastrophic experience is also recognized as a diagnostic category in the International Classification of Diseases, and more complex forms of PTSD have been described as involving an assault on the personality amounting to a form of 'mental death' (Ebert & Dyck, 2004).

With respect to traumatic events themselves, it has been argued that they are often highly memorable and can form turning points in people's construction of their own identity (Pillemer, 1998). Higher levels of posttraumatic symptoms are associated with seeing such events as a key to identity (Berntsen & Rubin, 2006). Consistent with this, 7–8 months after the 2005 London bombings, 61% of a sample of Londoners reported both positive and negative changes in their relation to the world and 23% in how they felt about themselves (Rubin, Brewin, Greenberg, Simpson, & Wessely, 2005).

As shown in Table 1, UK war veterans diagnosed with PTSD, compared to those with physical disabilities, saw service-related trauma as bringing about significant changes in their perception of the world and their relation to it (Brewin, Garnett, & Andrews, 2011). Veterans frequently repeated the belief that they were now seeing the world as it really was – "my blinkers have been taken off now" – and that the reality is that the world is not benign. Feelings of isolation and strangeness were compounded by a feeling of there being a stigma to having been in the armed forces: "the only people I have any time for really are people of the ex-service community; I just feel as though they're the only people that I trust".

Table 2 from the same study shows that war veterans also saw service-related trauma as bringing about significant changes in their perception of themselves. One veteran described how he found it difficult to look people in the eye: "because of my face, because my whole body's image and my facial image have been destroyed". For a number of veterans there was the sense of having been changed fundamentally, as a person, for the worse: the idea of having been tainted and diminished morally. Some veterans complained of an emotional numbing, having less ability and volition to express emotion. For example, one said: "Kissing the kids like, I can't kiss the kids. I can't hug my children; I find that difficult to be honest".

Given this apparent role of trauma memories in identity formation, it is of great interest that numerous longitudinal and retrospective studies have now found that a substantial proportion of people reporting child sexual abuse (somewhere between

Table 2 PTSD status and change in military veterans' perceptions of themselves (adapted from Brewin, Garnett, et al., 2011)

	Physical disability% (n=33)	PTSD% (n=108)
No change	27	4
A small change	33	12
A large change	39	84

15% and 60%) say they have had periods in their lives (often lasting for several years) when they had less memory of the abuse or could not remember that it had taken place (Brewin & Andrews, 1998; Brown, Scheflin, & Whitfield, 1999; Goodman, Quas, & Ogle, 2009). These answers, which we may call "subjective inaccessibility judgements", seem to indicate that there is a problem in accessing the fact of the abuse, not just details of the episodes; in other words, personal semantic memory is involved. The events have apparently not been central to the person's identity.

On what basis are people able to conclude that they have forgotten abuse or other traumas? It has been suggested that when people claim they had periods when they could not remember the trauma they may not mean they had forgotten the events but simply not thought about them (McNally, 2003; McNally, 2012, this volume). Of course some studies have asked more probing questions, such as "Was there ever a period when you would not have remembered this event, even if you were asked about it directly?" Although some individuals still agree that they would not have remembered (Ghetti et al., 2006; Joslyn, Carlin, & Loftus, 1997), answers to this kind of hypothetical question are far from compelling, to say the least. McNally argues that for statements concerning forgetting to make sense, individuals must have tried to think about the trauma but failed.

An alternative possibility has been identified from studies in which people have specifically been asked whether or not an event has happened to them. Researchers have suggested that there are two main ways in which a person reaches a conclusion that an event has *not* happened (Gallo, Bell, Beier, & Schacter, 2006). They may search for and retrieve logically inconsistent information that rules out event occurrence. Alternatively, they may use a distinctiveness heuristic: The more distinctive the event, the more likely they believe they would be able to retrieve a corresponding memory and hence, finding none, the more willing they are to say it did *not* happen (Ghetti, 2003; Strack & Bless, 1994).

This account of deciding about event non-occurrence can be applied to judgments of the subjective inaccessibility of childhood abuse memories. As people will probably not have been specifically questioned about them, they will not have had the opportunity to retrieve inconsistent information. By default, therefore, the account suggests the operation of a heuristic, namely that some facts, such as one's hair color or how many siblings one has, are so distinctive that they should be part of an ever-present personal semantic knowledge. If one cannot immediately recall being aware of having been abused, therefore, the inference is that it must have been forgotten.

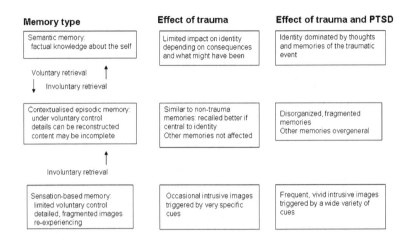

Fig. 2 Effects of trauma and PTSD on different levels of autobiographical memory

One of the many weaknesses in this literature is the relative absence of comparisons of reported amnesia for abuse with amnesia for other traumatic and non-traumatic events from the same life period. One exception is evidence that partial and complete amnesia are also reported in connection with non-traumatic childhood events such as attending summer camps (Read & Lindsay, 2000). Attendance at summer camps would seem less likely than abuse to be represented in semantic memory, and so it would be surprising if retrieving memories of such events was accompanied by the same degree of shock and surprise as has been reported for childhood abuse. Nevertheless, these findings caution against assuming that reported amnesia for child abuse is as distinctive as has been claimed and therefore requiring of special explanation.

Summary. Exposure to repeated trauma, particularly in childhood, affects the coherence and integrity of identity and is associated with corresponding deficits in personal semantic memory. These deficits may enhance the ease with which traumatic events including abuse can be forgotten. The distinctiveness heuristic may also contribute to some people's willingness to agree they had forgotten an episode of abuse and to the shock often associated with recovery. In PTSD traumatic events appear to become much more central to sufferers' identity, an effect shown in the upper part of Fig. 2.

Trauma and Autobiographical Event Memories

Although, as noted earlier, there is little evidence that trauma and non-trauma memories behave differently in healthy populations, PTSD has a profound effect on memory. PTSD patients have general difficulties with episodic memories for neutral material (Brewin, Kleiner, Vasterling, & Field, 2007), and in recalling specific details of events they have personally experienced (Moore & Zoellner, 2007). When it comes to personal trauma memories, both PTSD patients (Brewin et al., 1996) and individuals describing trauma memories recovered after a lengthy period of time (Andrews et al., 1999, 2000) have identified intrusive, emotion-laden memories and flashbacks.

A flashback is a form of memory characterized by a vivid sensory image, usually visual but not necessarily so. They tend to consist of fragmented snapshots or series of images, come to mind involuntarily, and are experienced as happening again in the present (Brewin, 2007; Ehlers, Hackmann, & Michael, Ehlers 2004). In flashbacks the recall of traumatic images appears to be disconnected from contextual information that normally associates a sensory memory with awareness of a corresponding time and place (Brewin, Gregory, et al., 2010). They can vary from relatively mild (there is a transient sense of the event reoccurring in the present) to extreme (the person loses all connection with their current autobiographical self and present surroundings while reexperiencing the memory). Importantly, these intrusions do not invariably reproduce an event that actually took place (Hackmann, Ehlers, Speckens, & Clark, 2004; Reynolds & Brewin, 1998), and reminders of imagined events can also elicit strong physiological arousal.

According to the dual representation theory of PTSD (Brewin et al., 1996), the disorder is caused by a failure to form a complete contextualized autobiographical memory of the traumatic event. These contextualized memories are referred to as "verbally accessible memories" in the theory. This is not the same as the concept of a "narrative" memory that contains a verbal account of the trauma (Van der Kolk & Fisler, 1995). Rather, the key idea is that information needs to receive sufficient conscious attention at encoding for contextualization to occur, and this would incidentally make it available for the construction of a narrative if required. The theory proposes that in PTSD important information is only represented in the form of images ("situationally accessible memories"), and that their lack of context is responsible for memories being experienced as flashbacks. Contextualization, achieved for example by trauma-focused cognitive- behavior therapy, conversely results in the corresponding images becoming harder to retrieve. A revised version of the theory (Brewin, Gregory, Lipton & Burgess (2010) grounds these observations in specific neural processes, proposing that information is contextualized by the ventral visual stream connecting the occipital with medial and inferior temporal areas. Flashbacks are thought to be produced by processing that occurs predominantly in the dorsal visual stream, connecting the occipital and parietal cortex, insufficiently modulated by ventral stream processing.

Although PTSD patients experience vivid involuntary imagery and retain excellent memory for the fact of the trauma having happened to them (Rubin, Berntsen, & Bohni, 2008), there is considerable evidence that these patients have difficulties in deliberately bringing to mind coherent, well-integrated autobiographical memories of the traumatic event (Harvey & Bryant, 1999; Jelinek, Randjbar, Seifert, Kellner, & Moritz, 2009). These difficulties have often been found to be related to self-reported dissociation either during or after the traumatic event (Brewin, 2007).

Moreover, impaired voluntary trauma memory predicts the course of the disorder (Halligan, Michael, Clark, & Ehlers, 2003; Jones, Harvey, & Brewin, 2007). Perhaps not surprisingly, therefore, retrospective recall of traumatic events is not invariably stable but can be affected by symptom levels (Engelhard, van den Hout, & McNally, 2008; Giosan, Malta, Jayasinghe, Spielman, & Difede, 2009; Heir, Piatigorsky, & Weisaeth, 2009). Thus, the more severe the person's current PTSD symptoms, the more intense they will tend to describe their emotions and dissociative reactions at the time of trauma.

One of the puzzling aspects of recovered trauma memories is how the intense associated emotions were suppressed or went unnoticed, often for long periods of time. Were these emotions necessarily present at encoding? A common assumption, based on the typical definition of a trauma as an event that is overwhelming, is that emotional arousal, flashbacks, and other symptoms reflect the encoding of the event under extremely high arousal. These symptoms are immediate but essentially normal responses that usually disappear of their own accord. PTSD is typically understood as reflecting an inappropriate persistence of these responses (Yehuda & Ledoux, 2007). Must we assume therefore that people who recover trauma memories experienced intense emotions, high arousal, and reexperiencing around the time of the original events?

This standard view of how PTSD develops does not readily account for the fact that many onsets are delayed. Recent research using a variety of approaches including growth curve modeling (Bonanno et al., 2008; Bonanno, Rennicke, & Dekel, 2005) suggests that there are four common patterns to posttraumatic responses: symptom levels that are high initially and remain high (chronic pattern), symptoms that are high initially and then fall (recovery pattern), symptoms that are low initially and remain low (resilient pattern), and symptoms that are low initially and then rise (delayed onset pattern). Consistent with this, a recent systematic review found that delayed onset posttraumatic disorder accounted for approximately 15% of civilian and 38% of military PTSD cases (Andrews, Brewin, Philpott, & Stewart, 2007).

This assumption that disordered responding starts immediately post-trauma is also reflected in most biological research on PTSD, which models the disorder by exposing laboratory animals to fear-inducing situations and measuring their initial learning in terms of changes in hormones, neurotransmitters, gene transcription factors, and other processes. This conditioning model is relevant to normal fear responses but is unsuitable both for explaining why such responses to a traumatic event fail to subside in a minority of those exposed, and for explaining delayed onsets (Yehuda & Ledoux, 2007). Following the suggestions of Post and colleagues (Post, Weiss, & Smith, 1995), there is now considerable evidence for a gradually unfolding process of sensitization that occurs in the weeks and months post-trauma (Griffin, 2008; Shalev et al., 2000).

It has been argued that PTSD involves both associative fear memories, relevant to explaining the reexperiencing symptoms of PTSD, and nonassociative fear memories (e.g., sensitization), relevant to explaining hyperarousal (Siegmund & Wotjak, 2006). Animal experiments have provided evidence that the two processes are functionally distinct (Siegmund & Wotjak, 2007a, 2007b). Sensitization, which

Table 3 Dissociative and emotional trauma reactions in military veterans with immediate onset PTSD, delayed onset PTSD, and no PTSD (adapted from Andrews et al., 2009)

	Immediate onset PTSD (n=40)	Delayed onset PTSD (n=63)	No PTSD (n=39)	Sig
Fear, helplessness or horror (PTSD A2)	85% a	81% a	53% b	***
Peritraumatic dissociation	5.9 a	4.5 b	3.4 b	***
Anger at time of trauma	3.1 a	2.5 b	2.2 b	*
Shame at time of trauma	2.5 a	1.8 b	1.3 b	***
Anger about trauma now	3.3 a	2.6 b	1.7 c	***
Shame about trauma now	2.7 a	2.2 a	1.3 b	***

Means & % with different subscripts differ significantly
$*p<.05; ***p<.001$

Table 4 Acquisition of PTSD symptoms over time in military veterans with immediate and delayed onset PTSD (adapted from Andrews et al., 2009). Values reflect mean number of cumulative symptoms

	Immediate onset PTSD (n=40)	Delayed onset PTSD (n=63)
Before any service trauma	.22	.33
Before main trauma in service	.40	.90
Within 6 months of main trauma	3.70	3.83
More than 6 months after main trauma	–	6.89
At PTSD onset	10.52	10.52

may involve structural remodelling in the amygdala, requires an extended time course and thus may provide a good account of the delayed onset of symptoms. Consistent with this position, hyperarousal appears to be important in predicting the way PTSD symptoms develop over time (Marshall, Schell, Glynn, & Shetty, 2006; Schell, Marshall, & Jaycox, 2004).

A recent study comparing immediate and delayed onset PTSD in war veterans (Andrews, Brewin, Stewart, Philpott, & Hejdenberg, 2009) found that they were similar in their amount of trauma exposure, and in the number and type of symptoms they reported at onset. At the time of the trauma, however, the immediate onset group reported significantly more peritraumatic dissociation, anger, and shame than those with delayed onsets, suggesting that they were overwhelmed by the intensity of the event in ways that went beyond fear, helplessness, and horror (see Table 3). The delayed-onset group, in contrast, differed in showing a gradual accumulation of symptoms that began earlier and continued to build up steadily throughout their military career. Table 4 shows that they already had significantly more symptoms than the immediate onset group prior to the main traumatic event they reported experiencing in service. They were more likely to report major depressive disorder and alcohol abuse prior to PTSD onset, which was generally triggered by a (non-military) severe life stressor. Table 5 shows that these stressors occurred significantly more often than in a control group of veterans with physical disabilities. As with the animal research reviewed above, Andrews and colleagues concluded

Table 5 Life stress in 12 months before onset in delayed-onset veterans and a comparable period in veterans with no PTSD (adapted from Andrews et al., 2009)

	Delayed onset PTSD (n=63) (%)	No PTSD (n=39) (%)	sig
Presence of a severe stressor	77	32	***
Presence of an 'independent' severe stressor	57	24	**
Presence of PTSD A1 trauma	11	18	ns
Presence of a minor stressor	45	58	ns

% with different subscripts differ significantly
**p<.01; ***p<.001

that the immediate and delayed onset presentations implicated different etiological mechanisms, one emphasizing the impact of the critical traumatic event on memory and one involving a more general and progressive sensitization.

Summary. Episodic trauma memories tend not to be distinctive in healthy populations, but have special features in people who either have PTSD or who have featured in clinical and case studies of recovered memory (see Fig. 2). These groups report vivid sensory imagery combined with poorly organized, fragmented narrative memories that may change over time. There is evidence that vivid reexperiencing does not always reflect being overwhelmed with emotion at encoding but may develop as a result of progressive sensitization. This is consistent with the observation that some memories recovered in adulthood can be experienced as vivid flashbacks even though this symptom was not previously recalled as having been present in childhood.

Trauma and Memory Appraisal

As we have seen in our discussion of semantic memory, judgments of forgetting often involve an inferential process. There have been a number of suggestions that faulty memory appraisal may be involved when people identify gaps in their memory for childhood experiences. It has been demonstrated (Belli, Winkielman, Read, Schwarz, & Lynn, 1998; Read & Lindsay, 2000) that when assessing the integrity of their memory for childhood, people rely partly on the ease or difficulty with which they can bring instances to mind. In the experiment by Belli et al., participants were asked to report four, eight, or twelve events from when they were 5–7 and 8–10 years old, after which they had to evaluate the adequacy of their childhood memory. Those who were instructed to retrieve more events paradoxically rated their childhood memory as worse than the groups who had to retrieve fewer events, at least in part because they attributed the difficulty of the task to deficiencies in their memory.

On the basis of these reports, it has been suggested (Belli et al., 1998; Winkielman, Schwarz, & Belli, 1998) that psychotherapy patients' reports of incomplete childhood memory might be a mistaken consequence of difficulty in trying to recall large numbers of events, rather than reflecting genuine problems with memory.

Despite this evidence that memory judgments may sometimes be mistaken, there is also reason to think that they are sometimes accurate. One study investigated whether ordinary individuals who judge themselves to have a bad memory for their childhood do in fact score more poorly on a standardized test of autobiographical memory (Brewin & Stokou, 2002). They found that a group who thought they had poor memory for childhood did score worse than a control group on tests of memory for both the facts and events of their own life. A more recent study has similarly reported that subjectively identified memory problems did not correlate with suggestibility or false recollections, and that participants were accurate in estimating their objective memory performance (Van Bergen, Jelicic, & Merckelbach, 2009).

A number of studies have tested whether trauma exposure or PTSD result in another type of appraisal problem, the mistaken belief that one has previously encountered a novel item. The Deese-Roediger-McDermott (DRM) paradigm measures the tendency to falsely recall that an associated item (e.g., 'sleep') was presented in a list of thematically related words (e.g., 'bed', 'pillow', 'dream'). The results so far with verbal and visual versions of this task have been inconsistent (Bremner, Shobe, & Kihlstrom, 2000; Brennen, Dybdahl, & Kapidzic, 2007; Jelinek, Hottenrott, Randjbar, Peters, & Moritz, 2009; Zoellner, Foa, Brigidi, & Przeworski, 2000).

The DRM paradigm was also used to explore memory recovery mechanisms by testing four groups of participants: women reporting recovered memories of childhood sexual abuse, women who believed that they were sexually abused as children but who could not recall this abuse (the "repressed" group), women who were sexually abused as children and always remembered the abuse, and women with no history of childhood sexual abuse (Clancy, Schacter, McNally, & Pitman, 2000; McNally, 2012, this volume). The results suggested that the recovered-memory group was more prone to false recognition than the other groups. More recently it has been shown that increased false recall and recognition are specific to people who recovered abuse memories in the context of suggestive therapy, and are not evident in people who recovered their memories spontaneously (Geraerts, 2012, this volume; Geraerts et al., 2009).

Based on the suggestions of Schooler (Schooler, 2001), the program of research conducted by Geraerts and colleagues (Geraerts, 2012, this volume; Geraerts et al., 2009) confirmed a different kind of appraisal problem that appears to typify those that recover memories spontaneously. Unlike participants who recalled abuse memories after suggestive therapy, or who had continuous memories of abuse, or who had not been abused at all, those with spontaneously recalled abuse were particularly likely to forget they had previously retrieved a word in another context (groups were similar in judging words retrieved in the same context). The authors suggested that having the experience of spontaneously recovering a memory reflects a more general deficit in the appraisal of previous recall attempts. In other words, the experience illustrates an illusion of forgetting rather than actual forgetting.

Summary. There is little evidence that trauma exposure or PTSD are in general reliably associated with memory appraisal problems. Recent research indicates that people who recover abuse memories spontaneously and those who recover them after suggestive therapy have distinct memory appraisal deficits.

Individual Differences in Memory Processes

In addition to evidence that trauma and PTSD differentially affect semantic and episodic forms of memory, it is important to recognize that there are great individual differences, not just in memory capacity but in memory process and memory appraisal. It is implausible, therefore, that trauma will have uniform effects on memory.

Repressive coping style. This style, despite its name, is only indirectly related to the concept of repression as used by psychotherapists. It is defined as a tendency to score simultaneously low on a measure of trait anxiety but high on a measure of social desirability (Weinberger, Schwartz, & Davidson, 1979). A large body of research has found that 'repressors' defined in this way have difficulty in recalling unhappy autobiographical memories. For example, given 60 s to recall as many childhood memories as possible, repressors recalled significantly fewer unhappy memories than non-repressors, and that their age at the time of the first unhappy memory they recalled was substantially greater. In contrast, there were no differences in recalling positive memories (Davis & Schwartz, 1987). This pattern has been replicated with memory for stories, and it has been shown that repressors are better able to deliberately forget negative, but not positive, material (Myers & Brewin, 1995; Myers, Brewin, & Power, 1998). Crucially, this does not seem to be because repressors have enjoyed happier, more problem-free lives: In fact, they reported significantly more hostility, more indifference and less closeness in their relationships with their fathers, making this possibility very unlikely (Myers & Brewin, 1994).

Attachment style. It has been proposed that individuals with an avoidant attachment style, who are fearful and dismissive of intimate relationships, defensively inhibit the processing of negative or attachment-related information. In one study, avoidant individuals recalled fewer emotional events and took longer to retrieve those they did recall, particularly events related to sadness and anxiety. They also rated their memories as less emotionally intense and the events as having occurred at an older age than those recalled by nonavoidant participants (Mikulincer & Orbach, 1995). In a recent study memory for documented instances of child abuse was assessed in victims approximately 13 years later. When the abuse was more severe, those with an avoidant attachment style were less likely to recall accurate details of their experiences (Edelstein et al., 2005). These memory deficits did not appear to result from a tendency to minimize what had happened. Non-avoidant individuals, in contrast, tended to recall more severe abuse better.

Summary. There is good evidence that some individuals are more adept than others at selectively forgetting negative material. At present it is unclear whether possession of these coping and attachment styles is related to an increased likelihood of having recovered memory experiences. The findings do, however, emphasize that generalizations about trauma and memory should be treated with great caution, and that early experiences may influence in unexpected ways the accessibility of negative information.

Explaining Recovered Memory

Contrary to the widespread myth that traumatic events are seldom if ever forgotten, much trauma is not remembered until something happens to bring it to mind. As is the case for non-traumatic events, availability for recall will depend on how well the events are represented within personal semantic memory (Williams, Stiles, & Shapiro, 1999). Particularly when it comes to childhood trauma, it is hazardous to impose adult assumptions about what should or should not be recalled. Over and above issues about the salience of the events, extensive trauma in childhood is associated with complexity and fragmentation in the self system, such that there are impoverished levels of semantic knowledge concerning the self and more scope for the existence of parallel self-representations in which specific trauma memories feature weakly if at all. The great variability in the amount and extent of amnesia reported in the context of recovered memory experiences is consistent with this multiplicity of representations.

What will determine if a trauma does become part of the person's overarching semantic knowledge about themselves? Family recognition, discussion, and explanation, and consequences that are explicitly linked to the trauma, such as changing schools or being taken into care, are all likely to generate associative links between the trauma and other aspects of the person's life, thus cementing the events within overarching semantic knowledge. Consistent with this, reported rates of forgetting child abuse are substantially lower when there have been legal proceedings nearer to the time at which the abuse occurred. Conversely, secrecy, lack of understanding, and the absence of any social interaction or obvious consequences, will produce representations with fewer associative links to other life experiences. To this must be added attempts to consciously forget frightening, hurtful, or embarrassing events (Anderson et al., 2004; Anderson & Huddleston, 2012, this volume; Levy & Anderson, 2008). Considering also that some individuals appear particularly adept at deliberately forgetting negative events, we can see that even highly arousing experiences may come to be represented in memory within limited contexts that are subsequently rarely accessed.

Figure 3 illustrates a possible set of processes underlying a genuine recovered memory experience that occurs spontaneously rather than as a result of suggestive therapy (Geraerts, 2012, this volume Geraerts et al., 2009). Let us assume that secrecy and fear of disclosure have led to the development of alternative identities, only one of which contains any knowledge about the abuse he or she experienced in childhood. The identity without this knowledge is in everyday use and generally dominant. Exposure to unexpected triggering events or thoughts leads to the involuntary retrieval of autobiographical abuse memories or specific images related to the abuse accompanied by high levels of emotion (see also Anderson & Huddleston, 2012, this volume). This in turn leads to the involuntary retrieval of the alternative identity with knowledge of the abuse. Many, if not most, recovered memory experiences may not elicit the shock that has been noted in case studies and clinical samples. When shock does occur, this is likely to be because of two linked reasons.

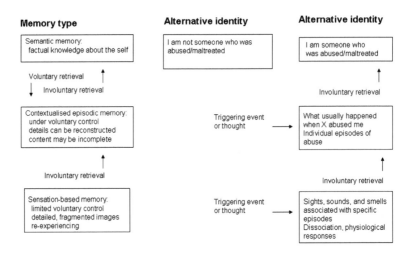

Fig. 3 A possible set of processes underlying a recovered memory experience

First, sensation- and emotion-rich representations may be involuntarily accessed for the first time in many years, bringing with them intense feelings such as fear and shame. There are numerous instances of traumatic memories changing over time, and it is clear that experiencing a vivid recovered memory does not imply that the same emotions were necessarily experienced when the event was encoded. There are a number of mechanisms that may result in memories being re-encoded with much greater affect, leading to the generation of flashbacks when there may have been none before. First, the strength of a conditioned response may be greatly affected by subsequent information that alters the aversiveness of the original unconditioned stimulus. This is known as UCS revaluation (Davey, 1989). Thus learning that the original aversive experience was much more heinous, or involved much greater betrayal, than had hitherto been believed, would be expected to produce much stronger emotional and physiological reactions. Second, memories and their accompanying emotions may be amplified when they are revisited later in a very negative mood state (van Giezen, Arensman, Spinhoven, & Wolters, 2005). Third, a gradual build-up of arousal may produce the conditions for the formation and intrusion of highly emotional memories, usually following further severe stress (Andrews et al., 2009).

The second reason why there may be shock at memory recovery is the discovery that events regarded now as very significant were not represented in overarching semantic memory, thus contradicting basic assumptions about memory as well as a dominant self-narrative or self-theory (Harter, 1998). People who believed that trauma or abuse should always be remembered, yet cannot recall specifically thinking about it, will be more shocked, and also more likely to agree that they must have forgotten it. Even if the recovered memories are not initially accompanied by intense emotion, there will be unforeseen, and possibly profound, implications for the person's self-concept, and for their relationships with family and friends. This may invest the memory recovery with the status of a turning point, generating further intense emotions that sustain high levels of arousal and increase the risk of PTSD.

The existence of the "forgot-it-all-along" effect (Schooler, 2001) is a useful reminder that memory recovery need not be a dramatic experience or personal turning point. Let us imagine that at some point a person has retrieved an identity containing semantic knowledge of their abuse or trauma, but that this identity has limited access to specific event memories of abusive episodes (illustrated by overlap bars b and c in Fig. 1). As a result, this person may only retrieve schematic representations of "what usually happened", characterized by suppression of negative emotions that were dangerous or unacceptable (DePrince et al., 2012, this volume; Freyd, 1996). This information may feature in a conversation without leading to the retrieval of more detailed, sensation- and affect-laden records. In the absence of these markers of significance, there may be no reason to identify the traumatic events as of such importance that they need to be represented at the level of overarching semantic knowledge concerning the self. Thus the information will remain linked to a specific, occasionally-retrieved 'self', and the conversation will soon be forgotten.

Another factor influencing the memorability of previous recall is whether events have come to mind as the result of a deliberate search or as the result of being cued (Padilla-Walker & Poole, 2002). In these experiments, participants first had to learn a series of sentences and then free recall them. Following a distraction task they were asked to generate the sentences again, and say whether or not they had remembered them on the previous occasion. Participants who were asked to free recall the sentences on the second occasion were more likely to remember their prior recalls than participants who performed a recognition task or were cued with a picture. These results suggest that when trauma memories have been recovered spontaneously, or cued by some reminder, memory for previous recollection will be less accurate, provided that in the previous recollection they did not produce feelings of shock or surprise and were not subsequently incorporated into overarching semantic knowledge.

In light of our accumulating empirical and theoretical understanding, genuine recovered memory experiences no longer appear as bizarre or counter-intuitive as they have been painted by those who are skeptical of their occurrence. The field has not been well-served by much of the existing literature, which has uncritically embraced a variety of myths, logical errors, and false assumptions, and adopted a simplistic approach to what are complex and fascinating memory phenomena. Understanding these experiences forces us to confront the complexity of memory and of the forces that shape it. The study of recovered memory has taught us about how limited our knowledge is of forgetting and of the representation of trauma, and about the danger of ignoring phenomena that are more clearly documented in the clinic than in the laboratory. But it has also taught us that some mental events are so compelling that reality and fantasy become confused, and that there are continuing dangers from ill-informed therapists employing suggestive procedures and failing to exercise a proper independence concerning the veracity of mental experiences. The only certain conclusion is that there is a great deal more to learn in the future.

References

Anderson, M. C., & Huddleston, E. (2012, this volume). Towards a cognitive and neurobiological model of motivated forgetting. In R. F. Belli (Ed.), *True and false recovered memories: Toward a reconciliation of the debate* (pp. 53–120). *Vol. 58: Nebraska Symposium on Motivation*. New York: Springer.

Anderson, M. C., Ochsner, K. N., Kuhl, B., Cooper, J., Robertson, E., Gabrieli, S. W., et al. (2004). Neural systems underlying the suppression of unwanted memories. *Science, 303*(5655), 232–235.

Andrews, B., Brewin, C. R., Ochera, J., Morton, J., Bekerian, D. A., Davies, G. M., et al. (1999). Characteristics, context and consequences of memory recovery among adults in therapy. *British Journal of Psychiatry, 175*, 141–146.

Andrews, B., Brewin, C. R., Ochera, J., Morton, J., Bekerian, D. A., Davies, G. M., et al. (2000). The timing, triggers and qualities of recovered memories in therapy. *British Journal of Clinical Psychology, 39*, 11–26.

Andrews, B., Brewin, C. R., Philpott, R., & Stewart, L. (2007). Delayed-onset posttraumatic stress disorder: A systematic review of the evidence. *American Journal of Psychiatry, 164*(9), 1319–1326.

Andrews, B., Brewin, C. R., Stewart, L., Philpott, R., & Hejdenberg, J. (2009). Comparison of immediate-onset and delayed-onset posttraumatic stress disorder in military veterans. *Journal of Abnormal Psychology, 118*(4), 767–777.

Andrews, B., Morton, J., Bekerian, D. A., Brewin, C. R., Davies, G. M., & Mollon, P. (1995). The recovery of memories in clinical practice: Experiences and beliefs of British Psychological Society practitioners. *Psychologist, 8*, 209–214.

Beeghly, M., & Cicchetti, D. (1994). Child maltreatment, attachment, and the self system - emergence of an internal state lexicon in toddlers at high social risk. *Development and Psychopathology, 6*(1), 5–30.

Belli, R. F., Winkielman, P., Read, J. D., Schwarz, N., & Lynn, S. J. (1998). Recalling more childhood events leads to judgments of poorer memory: Implications for the recovered false memory debate. *Psychonomic Bulletin & Review, 5*(2), 318–323.

Berntsen, D., & Rubin, D. C. (2006). The centrality of event scale: A measure of integrating a trauma into one's identity and its relation to post-traumatic stress disorder symptoms. *Behaviour Research and Therapy, 44*(2), 219–231.

Bonanno, G. A., Ho, S. A. Y., Chan, J. C. K., Kwong, R. S. Y., Cheung, C. K. Y., Wong, C. P. Y., et al. (2008). Psychological resilience and dysfunction among hospitalized survivors of the SARS epidemic in Hong kong: A latent class approach. *Health Psychology, 27*(5), 659–667.

Bonanno, G. A., Rennicke, C., & Dekel, S. (2005). Self-enhancement among high-exposure survivors of the September 11th terrorist attack: Resilience or social maladjustment? *Journal of Personality and Social Psychology, 88*(6), 984–998.

Bremner, J. D., Shobe, K. K., & Kihlstrom, J. F. (2000). False memories in women with self-reported childhood sexual abuse: An empirical study. *Psychological Science, 11*(4), 333–337.

Brennen, T., Dybdahl, R., & Kapidzic, A. (2007). Trauma-related and neutral false memories in war-induced posttraumatic stress disorder. *Consciousness and Cognition, 16*(4), 877–885.

Brewin, C. R. (2007). Autobiographical memory for trauma: Update on four controversies. *Memory, 15*(3), 227–248.

Brewin, C. R., & Andrews, B. (1998). Recovered memories of trauma: Phenomenology and cognitive mechanisms. *Clinical Psychology Review, 18*(8), 949–970.

Brewin, C. R., Dalgleish, T., & Joseph, S. (1996). A dual representation theory of posttraumatic stress disorder. *Psychological Review, 103*(4), 670–686.

Brewin, C. R., Garnett, R., & Andrews, B. (2011). Trauma, mental health, and identity change in veterans with PTSD or physical Injury. *Psychological Medicine, 41*(8), 1733–1740.

Brewin, C. R., Gregory, J. D., Lipton, M., & Burgess, N. (2010). Intrusive images in psychological disorders: Characteristics, neural mechanisms, and treatment implications. *Psychological Review, 117*, 210–232.

Brewin, C. R., Kleiner, J. S., Vasterling, J. J., & Field, A. P. (2007). Memory for emotionally neutral information in posttraumatic stress disorder: A meta-analytic investigation. *Journal of Abnormal Psychology, 116*(3), 448–463.

Brewin, C. R., & Patel, T. (2010). Auditory pseudohallucinations in United Kingdom war veterans and civilians with posttraumatic stress disorder. *Journal of Clinical Psychiatry, 71*(4), 419–425.

Brewin, C. R., & Stokou, L. (2002). Validating reports of poor childhood memory. *Applied Cognitive Psychology, 16*(5), 509–514.

Brewin, C. R., & Vallance, H. (1997). Self-discrepancies in young adults and childhood violence. *Journal of Interpersonal Violence, 12*(4), 600–606.

Brown, D., Scheflin, A. W., & Whitfield, C. L. (1999). Recovered memories: The current weight of the evidence in science and in the courts. *Journal of Psychiatry & Law, 27*, 5–156.

Burgess, P. W., & Shallice, T. (1996). Confabulation and the control of recollection. *Memory, 4*(4), 359–411.

Chu, J. A., Frey, L. M., Ganzel, B. L., & Matthews, J. A. (1999). Memories of childhood abuse: Dissociation, amnesia, and corroboration. *American Journal of Psychiatry, 156*, 749–755.

Clancy, S. A., Schacter, D. L., McNally, R. J., & Pitman, R. K. (2000). False recognition in women reporting recovered memories of sexual abuse. *Psychological Science, 11*(1), 26–31.

Conway, M. A. (2005). Memory and the self. *Journal of Memory and Language, 53*(4), 594–628.

Conway, M. A. (2009). Episodic memories. *Neuropsychologia, 47*(11), 2305–2313.

Conway, M. A., & Pleydell-Pearce, C. W. (2000). The construction of autobiographical memories in the self-memory system. *Psychological Review, 107*(2), 261–288.

Crittenden, P. M., & Dilalla, D. L. (1988). Compulsive compliance - the development of an inhibitory coping strategy in infancy. *Journal of Abnormal Child Psychology, 16*(5), 585–599.

Davey, G. C. L. (1989). UCS revaluation and conditioning models of acquired fears. *Behaviour Research and Therapy, 27*(5), 521–528.

Davis, P. J., & Schwartz, G. E. (1987). Repression and the inaccessibility of affective memories. *Journal of Personality and Social Psychology, 52*, 155–162.

DePrince, A., Brown, L., Cheit, R., Freyd, J., Gold, S. N., Pezdek, K., & Quina, K. (2012, this volume). Motivated forgetting and misremembering: Perspectives from betrayal trauma theory. In R. F. Belli (Ed.), *True and false recovered memories: Toward a reconciliation of the debate* (pp. 193–242). *Vol. 58: Nebraska Symposium on Motivation*. New York: Springer.

Dorahy, M. J., Shannon, C., Seagar, L., Corr, M., Stewart, K., Hanna, D., et al. (2009). Auditory hallucinations in dissociative identity disorder and schizophrenia with and without a childhood trauma history similarities and differences. *Journal of Nervous and Mental Disease, 197*(12), 892–898.

Ebert, A., & Dyck, M. J. (2004). The experience of mental death: The core feature of complex posttraumatic stress disorder. *Clinical Psychology Review, 24*(6), 617–635.

Edelstein, R. S., Ghetti, S., Quas, J. A., Goodman, G. S., Alexander, K. W., Redlich, A. D., et al. (2005). Individual differences in emotional memory: Adult attachment and long-term memory for child sexual abuse. *Personality and Social Psychology Bulletin, 31*(11), 1537–1548.

Edwards, V. J., Fivush, R., Anda, R. F., Felitti, V. J., & Nordenberg, D. F. (2001). Autobiographical memory disturbances in childhood abuse survivors. *Journal of Aggression, Maltreatment & Trauma, 4*, 247–263.

Ehlers, A., Hackmann, A., & Michael, T. (2004). Intrusive re-experiencing in post-traumatic stress disorder: Phenomenology, theory, and therapy. *Memory, 12*(4), 403–415.

Elliott, D. M. (1997). Traumatic events: Prevalence and delayed recall in the general population. *Journal of Consulting and Clinical Psychology, 65*, 811–820.

Elliott, D. M., & Briere, J. (1995). Posttraumatic stress associated with delayed recall of sexual abuse: A general population study. *Journal of Traumatic Stress, 8*, 629–647.

Engelhard, I. M., van den Hout, M. A., & McNally, R. J. (2008). Memory consistency for traumatic events in Dutch soldiers deployed to Iraq. *Memory, 16*(1), 3–9.

Feldman-Summers, S., & Pope, K. S. (1994). The experience of forgetting childhood abuse: A national survey of psychologists. *Journal of Consulting and Clinical Psychology, 62*, 636–639.

Freyd, J. J. (1996). *Betrayal trauma: The logic of forgetting childhood abuse*. Cambridge, MA: Harvard University Press.

Gallo, D. A., Bell, D. M., Beier, J. S., & Schacter, D. L. (2006). Two types of recollection-based monitoring in younger and older adults: Recall-to-reject and the distinctiveness heuristic. *Memory, 14*(6), 730–741.

Geraerts, E. (2012, this volume). Cognitive underpinnings of recovered memories of childhood abuse. In R. F. Belli (Ed.), *True and false recovered memories: Toward a reconciliation of the debate* (pp. 175–191). *Vol. 58: Nebraska Symposium on Motivation*. New York: Springer.

Geraerts, E., Lindsay, D. S., Merckelbach, H., Jelicic, M., Raymaekers, L., Arnold, M. M., et al. (2009). Cognitive mechanisms underlying recovered-memory experiences of childhood sexual abuse. *Psychological Science, 20*(1), 92–98.

Geraerts, E., Schooler, J. W., Merckelbach, H., Jelicic, M., Hauer, B. J. A., & Ambadar, Z. (2007). The reality of recovered memories - corroborating continuous and discontinuous memories of childhood sexual abuse. *Psychological Science, 18*(7), 564–568.

Ghetti, S. (2003). Memory for nonoccurrences: The role of metacognition. *Journal of Memory and Language, 48*(4), 722–739.

Ghetti, S., Edelstein, R. S., Goodman, G. S., Cordon, I. M., Quas, J. A., Alexander, K. W., et al. (2006). What can subjective forgetting tell us about memory for childhood trauma? *Memory & Cognition, 34*(5), 1011–1025.

Giosan, C., Malta, L., Jayasinghe, N., Spielman, L., & Difede, J. (2009). Relationships between memory inconsistency for traumatic events following 9/11 and PTSD in disaster restoration workers. *Journal of Anxiety Disorders, 23*(4), 557–561.

Gold, S. N., Hughes, D., & Hohnecker, L. (1994). Degrees of repression of sexual abuse memories. *American Psychologist, 49*, 441–442.

Goodman, G. S., Quas, J. A., & Ogle, C. M. (2009). Child maltreatment and memory. *Annual Review of Psychology, 61*, 325–351.

Griffin, M. G. (2008). A prospective assessment of auditory startle alterations in rape and physical assault survivors. *Journal of Traumatic Stress, 21*(1), 91–99.

Hackmann, A., Ehlers, A., Speckens, A., & Clark, D. M. (2004). Characteristics and content of intrusive memories in PTSD and their changes with treatment. *Journal of Traumatic Stress, 17*(3), 231–240.

Halligan, S. L., Michael, T., Clark, D. M., & Ehlers, A. (2003). Posttraumatic stress disorder following assault: The role of cognitive processing, trauma memory, and appraisals. *Journal of Consulting and Clinical Psychology, 71*(3), 419–431.

Harter, S. (1998). The effects of child abuse on the self-system. *Journal of Aggression, Maltreatment and Trauma, 2*, 147–169.

Harter, S., Bresnick, S., Bouchey, H. A., & Whitesell, N. R. (1997). The development of multiple role-related selves during adolescence. *Development and Psychopathology, 9*(4), 835–853.

Harvey, A. G., & Bryant, R. A. (1999). A qualitative investigation of the organization of traumatic memories. *British Journal of Clinical Psychology, 38*, 401–405.

Harvey, M. R., & Herman, J. L. (1994). Amnesia, partial amnesia, and delayed recall among adult survivors of childhood trauma. *Consciousness and Cognition, 3*, 295–306.

Heir, T., Piatigorsky, A., & Weisaeth, L. (2009). Longitudinal changers in recalled perceived life threat after a natural disaster. *British Journal of Psychiatry, 194*(6), 510–514.

Hunter, E. C. M., & Andrews, B. (2002). Memory for autobiographical facts and events: A comparison of women reporting childhood sexual abuse and non-abused controls. *Applied Cognitive Psychology, 16*(5), 575–588.

Jelinek, L., Randjbar, S., Seifert, D., Kellner, M., & Moritz, S. (2009). The organization of autobiographical and nonautobiographical memory in posttraumatic stress disorder (PTSD). *Journal of Abnormal Psychology, 118*(2), 288–298.

Jelinek, L., Hottenrott, B., Randjbar, S., Peters, M. J., & Moritz, S. (2009). Visual false memories in post-traumatic stress disorder (PTSD). *Journal of Behavior Therapy and Experimental Psychiatry, 40*(2), 374–383.

Johnson, M. K., Hashtroudi, S., & Lindsay, D. S. (1993). Source monitoring. *Psychological Bulletin, 114*, 3–28.

Johnson, M. K., Raye, C. L., Mitchell, K. J., & Ankudowich, E. (2012, this volume). The cognitive neuroscience of true and false memories. In R. F. Belli (Ed.), *True and false recovered memories: Toward a reconciliation of the debate* (pp.15–52). *Vol. 58: Nebraska Symposium on Motivation*. New York: Springer.

Jones, C., Harvey, A. G., & Brewin, C. R. (2007). The organisation and content of trauma memories in survivors of road traffic accidents. *Behaviour Research and Therapy, 45*(1), 151–162.

Joslyn, S., Carlin, L., & Loftus, E. F. (1997). Remembering and forgetting childhood sexual abuse. *Memory, 5*(6), 703–724.

Levy, B. J., & Anderson, M. C. (2008). Individual differences in the suppression of unwanted memories: The executive deficit hypothesis. *Acta Psychologica, 127*(3), 623–635.

Lewis, D. O., Yeager, C. A., Swica, Y., Pincus, J. H., & Lewis, M. (1997). Objective documentation of child abuse and dissociation in 12 murderers with dissociative identity disorder. *American Journal of Psychiatry, 154*(12), 1703–1710.

Loftus, E. F., & Davis, D. (2006). Recovered memories. *Annual Review of Clinical Psychology, 2*, 469–498.

Loftus, E. F., Garry, M., & Feldman, J. (1994). Forgetting sexual trauma - what does it mean when 38% forget? *Journal of Consulting and Clinical Psychology, 62*(6), 1177–1181.

Loftus, E. F., Polonsky, S., & Fullilove, M. T. (1994). Memories of childhood sexual abuse: Remembering and repressing. *Psychology of Women Quarterly, 18*, 67–84.

Malmo, C., & Laidlaw, T. S. (2010). Symptoms of trauma and traumatic memory retrieval in adult survivors of childhood sexual abuse. *Journal of Trauma & Dissociation, 11*(1), 22–43.

Markus, H., & Sentis, K. (1982). The self in social information processing. In J. Suls (Ed.), *Psychological perspectives on the self* (Vol. 1, pp. 41–70). Hillsdale, N.J.: Lawrence Erlbaum.

Marshall, G. N., Schell, T. L., Glynn, S. M., & Shetty, V. (2006). The role of hyperarousal in the manifestation of posttraumatic psychological distress following injury. *Journal of Abnormal Psychology, 115*(3), 624–628.

McNally, R. J. (2003). *Remembering trauma*. Cambridge, MA: Harvard University Press.

McNally, R. J. (2005). Debunking myths about trauma and memory. *Canadian Journal of Psychiatry-Revue Canadienne De Psychiatrie, 50*(13), 817–822.

McNally, R. J.. (2012, this volume). Searching for repressed memory. In R. F. Belli (Ed.), *True and false recovered memories: Toward a reconciliation of the debate* (pp. 121–147). *Vol. 58: Nebraska Symposium on Motivation*. New York: Springer.

Means, B., & Loftus, E. F. (1991). When personal history repeats itself - decomposing memories for recurring events. *Applied Cognitive Psychology, 5*(4), 297–318.

Melchert, T. P. (1996). Childhood memory and a history of different forms of abuse. *Professional Psychology-Research and Practice, 27*, 438–446.

Mikulincer, M., & Orbach, I. (1995). Attachment styles and repressive defensiveness - the accessibility and architecture of affective memories. *Journal of Personality and Social Psychology, 68*(5), 917–925.

Moore, S. A., & Zoellner, L. A. (2007). Overgeneral autobiographical memory and traumatic events: An evaluative review. *Psychological Bulletin, 133*(3), 419–437.

Myers, C. S. (1940). *Shell shock in France 1914–1918*. Cambridge: Cambridge University Press.

Myers, L. B., & Brewin, C. R. (1994). Recall of early experience and the repressive coping style. *Journal of Abnormal Psychology, 103*, 288–292.

Myers, L. B., & Brewin, C. R. (1995). Repressive coping and the recall of emotional material. *Cognition & Emotion, 9*, 637–642.

Myers, L. B., Brewin, C. R., & Power, M. J. (1998). Repressive coping and the directed forgetting of emotional material. *Journal of Abnormal Psychology, 107*, 141–148.

Ogawa, J. R., Sroufe, L. A., Weinfield, N. S., Carlson, E. A., & Egeland, B. (1997). Development and the fragmented self: Longitudinal study of dissociative symptomatology in a nonclinical sample. *Development and Psychopathology, 9*(4), 855–879.

Padilla-Walker, L. M., & Poole, D. A. (2002). Memory for previous recall: A comparison of free and cued recall. *Applied Cognitive Psychology, 16*(5), 515–524.

Pillemer, D. B. (1998). *Momentous events, vivid memories*. Cambridge, MA: Harvard University Press.

Post, R. M., Weiss, S. R. B., & Smith, M. D. (1995). Sensitization and kindling: Implications for the evolving neural substrates of post-traumatic stress disorder. In M. J. Friedman, D. S. Charney, & A. Y. Deutch (Eds.), *Neurobiological and clinical consequences of stress: From normal adaptation to post-traumatic stress disorder* (pp. 203–224). Philadelphia, PA: Lippincott-Raven.

Raphael, K. G., Cloitre, M., & Dohrenwend, B. P. (1991). Problems of recall and misclassification with checklist methods of measuring stressful life events. *Health Psychology, 10*(1), 62–74.

Read, J. D., & Lindsay, D. S. (2000). "Amnesia" for summer camps and high school graduation: Memory work increases reports of prior periods of remembering less. *Journal of Traumatic Stress, 13*(1), 129–147.

Reynolds, M., & Brewin, C. R. (1998). Intrusive cognitions, coping strategies and emotional responses in depression, post-traumatic stress disorder and a non-clinical population. *Behaviour Research and Therapy, 36*(2), 135–147.

Rubin, D. C., Berntsen, D., & Bohni, M. K. (2008). Memory-based model of posttraumatic stress disorder: Evaluating basic assumptions underlying the PTSD diagnosis. *Psychological Review, 115*(4), 985–1011.

Rubin, G. J., Brewin, C. R., Greenberg, N., Simpson, J., & Wessely, S. (2005). Psychological and behavioural reactions to the bombings in London on 7 July 2005: Cross sectional survey of a representative sample of Londoners. *British Medical Journal, 331*(7517), 606–611.

Sar, V., Akyuz, G., & Dogan, O. (2007). Prevalence of dissociative disorders among women in the general population. *Psychiatry Research, 149*(1–3), 169–176.

Schell, T. L., Marshall, G. N., & Jaycox, L. H. (2004). All symptoms are not created equal: The prominent role of hyperarousal in the natural course of posttraumatic psychological distress. *Journal of Abnormal Psychology, 113*(2), 189–197.

Schooler, J. W. (2001). Discovering memories of abuse in the light of meta-awareness. *Journal of Aggression, Maltreatment and Trauma, 4*, 105–136.

Schraedley, P. K., Turner, R. J., & Gotlib, I. H. (2002). Stability of retrospective reports in depression: Traumatic events, past depressive episodes, and parental psychopathology. *Journal of Health and Social Behavior, 43*(3), 307–316.

Shalev, A. Y., Peri, T., Brandes, D., Freedman, S., Orr, S. P., & Pitman, R. K. (2000). Auditory startle response in trauma survivors with posttraumatic stress disorder: A prospective study. *American Journal of Psychiatry, 157*(2), 255–261.

Shobe, K. K., & Kihlstrom, J. F. (1997). Is traumatic memory special? *Current Directions in Psychological Science, 6*(3), 70–74.

Siegmund, A., & Wotjak, C. T. (2006). Toward an animal model of posttraumatic stress disorder. *Annals of the New York Academy of Sciences, 1071*, 324–334.

Siegmund, A., & Wotjak, C. T. (2007a). Hyperarousal does not depend on trauma-related contextual memory in an animal model of posttraumatic stress disorder. *Physiology & Behavior, 90*(1), 103–107.

Siegmund, A., & Wotjak, C. T. (2007b). A mouse model of posttraumatic stress disorder that distinguishes between conditioned and sensitised fear. *Journal of Psychiatric Research, 41*(10), 848–860.

Stokes, D. J., Dritschel, B. H., & Bekerian, D. A. (2008). Semantic and episodic autobiographical memory recall for memories not directly associated with childhood sexual abuse. *Journal of Family Violence, 23*(6), 429–435.

Strack, F., & Bless, H. (1994). Memory for nonoccurrences - metacognitive and presuppositional strategies. *Journal of Memory and Language, 33*(2), 203–217.

Tulving, E. (1983). *Elements of episodic memory*. Oxford: Oxford University Press.

Van Bergen, S., Jelicic, M., & Merckelbach, H. (2009). Are subjective memory problems related to suggestibility, compliance, false memories, and objective memory performance? *American Journal of Psychology, 122*(2), 249–257.

van der Hart, O., Bolt, H., & van der Kolk, B. A. (2005). Memory fragmentation in dissociative identity disorder. *Journal of Trauma & Dissociation, 6*(1), 55–70.

van der Hart, O., Nijenhuis, E. R. S., & Steele, K. (2005). Dissociation: An insufficiently recognized major feature of complex posttraumatic stress disorder. *Journal of Traumatic Stress, 18*(5), 413–423.

Van der Kolk, B. A., & Fisler, R. (1995). Dissociation and the fragmentary nature of traumatic memories - overview and exploratory study. *Journal of Traumatic Stress, 8*(4), 505–525.

van Giezen, A. E., Arensman, E., Spinhoven, P., & Wolters, G. (2005). Consistency of memory for emotionally arousing events: A review of prospective and experimental studies. *Clinical Psychology Review, 25*(7), 935–953.

Walker, W. R., Skowronski, J. J., & Thompson, C. P. (2003). Life is pleasant - and memory helps to keep it that way! *Review of General Psychology, 7*(2), 203–210.

Weinberger, D. A., Schwartz, G. E., & Davidson, R. J. (1979). Low-anxious, high-anxious, and repressive coping styles: Psychometric patterns and behavioral and physiological responses to stress. *Journal of Abnormal Psychology, 88*, 369–380.

Williams, J. M. G., Stiles, W. B., & Shapiro, D. A. (1999). Cognitive mechanisms in the avoidance of painful and dangerous thoughts: Elaborating the assimilation model. *Cognitive Therapy and Research, 23*(3), 285–306.

Williams, L. M. (1995). Recovered memories of abuse in women with documented child sexual victimization histories. *Journal of Traumatic Stress, 8*, 649–673.

Winkielman, P., Schwarz, N., & Belli, R. F. (1998). The role of ease of retrieval and attribution in memory judgments - judging your memory as worse despite recalling more events. *Psychological Science, 9*(2), 124–126.

Xiao, Z. P., Yan, H. Q., Wang, Z., Zou, Z., Xu, Y., Chen, J., et al. (2006). Trauma and dissociation in China. *American Journal of Psychiatry, 163*(8), 1388–1391.

Yehuda, R., & Ledoux, J. (2007). Response variation following trauma: A translational neuroscience approach to understanding PTSD. *Neuron, 56*(1), 19–32.

Zoellner, L. A., Foa, E. B., Brigidi, B. D., & Przeworski, A. (2000). Are trauma victims susceptible to "false memories"? *Journal of Abnormal Psychology, 109*(3), 517–524.

Cognitive Underpinnings of Recovered Memories of Childhood Abuse

Elke Geraerts

Abstract Recent research on recovered memories of childhood sexual abuse has shown that there are at least two types of recovered memory experiences: those that are gradually recovered within the context of suggestive therapy and those that are spontaneously recovered, without extensive prompting or explicit attempts to reconstruct the past. These recovered memory experiences have different origins, with people who recover memories through suggestive therapy being more prone to forming false memories, and with people who report spontaneously recovered memories being more prone to forgetting prior instances of remembering. Additionally, the two types of recovered memory experiences are linked to differences in corroborative evidence, implying that memories recovered spontaneously, outside of suggestive therapy, are more likely to correspond to genuine abuse events. This chapter highlights the background of the recovered memory debate, summarizes recent studies with individuals reporting recovered memory experiences and points towards applications in the justice system and in clinical practice.

Keywords Cognitive mechanisms • False memories • Recovered memory • Suppression

Can people forget an emotionally traumatic event such as childhood sexual abuse (CSA)? Is it possible that such memories are being blocked from consciousness and is it possible that we might recall them many years later? In the past decade, this issue has led to a controversy within the fields of psychology and psychiatry, with the veracity of such recovered memories often being a reason for discussion (for a review, see e.g., Brewin, 2007; McNally & Geraerts, 2009). On one side of this debate, there are scholars who claim that the most traumatic memories can be

E. Geraerts (✉)
Erasmus University Rotterdam, Rotterdam, the Netherlands
e-mail: geraerts@fsw.eur.nl

R.F. Belli (ed.), *True and False Recovered Memories: Toward a Reconciliation of the Debate*, Nebraska Symposium on Motivation, DOI 10.1007/978-1-4614-1195-6_6,
© Springer Science+Business Media, LLC 2012

blocked from awareness (e.g., Brown, Scheflin, & Hammond, 1998). On the other side of the debate are researchers who have long studied the fallibility of memory and who state that traumatic memories are imprinted in memory and are very rarely forgotten. Also, they point out that there are clear reasons to be cautious in interpreting recovered memories (e.g., Ceci & Loftus, 1994; Kihlstrom, 2004; McNally, 2003). That is, when people remember, they may engage in reconstructing an experience, thereby adding details to a memory that may not have taken place. Additionally, people sometimes confuse the source of their memories. For example, events that were seen in a movie, heard in a story or even imagined may be confused with events that have truly happened. Such confusion is especially dangerous when people enter certain forms of therapy aimed at recovering memories. The use of therapeutic techniques as hypnosis, guided imagery, dream interpretation, and other suggestive treatments may create a situation in which it may be difficult for a person to distinguish fact from fiction (Loftus & Davis, 2006).

Unlike most controversies in psychology, this one has spread far beyond the clinic and laboratory: It has influenced legislation and outcomes in civil suits and criminal trials (Geraerts, Raymaekers, & Merckelbach, 2008). Famous cases of recovered memory have received intense media attention because of their legal implications. Also, fictionalized cases often appear in films or books with a recovered memory as a main plot device. For example, the popular book by Nicci French, *The Memory Game* (1997), describes how the main character Jane Crane recovers memories from her childhood, instigated by suggestive techniques of her therapist. Based on these memories Crane falsely accuses her father in law of having committed a murder. Clearly, stories such as this one influence people's opinion about the veracity of recovered memories and the contribution of therapy.

The purpose of this chapter is to discuss how cognitive studies on forgetting and false memories are relevant to the debate surrounding recovered memories. In particular, recent research examining the cognitive functioning of people reporting recovered CSA memories will be reviewed. This line of research encourages the assumption of a balanced view of recovered memories: Recovered memories are not all true or all false. Instead, one should inspect the context of recovery and the cognitive mechanism involved in a recovered memory in order to evaluate its veracity.

Forgetting

Although it sounds counterintuitive to most people, it is helpful to forget. For instance, without a way of screening out our unwanted thoughts and memories, we would be overwhelmed by all of the information surrounding us. As a result, people are motivated to forget. Motivated forgetting refers to the idea that not all of our forgetting is haphazard but may instead be related to our motives and intentions. Psychologists have studied this phenomenon with a method known as the directed forgetting procedure, in which participants are instructed to forget recently encoded materials.

Directed Forgetting

There are two variants of the directed forgetting procedure, and each targets somewhat different psychological processes (for reviews, see Anderson, 2005; Golding, 2005). In a typical procedure of *item method directed forgetting*, subjects view a series of words, to be encoded for a later memory test. Immediately following each word, subjects receive an instruction to either continue to remember the word, or to forget it. After completion of the list, subjects are given a test of all to-be-remembered *and* to-be-forgotten words. The typical result in this paradigm is that final test performance for to-be-forgotten words is significantly impaired, relative to to-be-remembered items, which are recalled quite well. This result may be due to an encoding deficit for to-be-forgotten words. Subjects may rehearse the words until they receive an instruction to either remember or forget the word. At this point, they either terminate encoding and rehearsal when having received an instruction to forget, or continue to rehearse the word when instructed to remember the word (Basden, Basden, & Gargano, 1993).

In contrast to the item method, *list method directed forgetting* presents the forget instruction halfway through the list. The instruction is unexpected and therefore subjects are likely to continue their best efforts to encode the words right until the forget instruction is given. A final test is then given and subjects are asked to disregard the earlier instruction to forget, and to remember as much as they can. In this procedure, it is unlikely that subjects rely on a strategy in which they do not encode the words in the first part of the list. That is, they do not receive any mention that they will have to forget anything until the entire first half of the list has been presented, and therefore have every apparent motive to encode items as effectively as possible. The results from this list method suggest that this procedure does not rely on motivated encoding deficits, but rather a retrieval deficit (Basden et al., 1993). Consistent with this idea, list method directed forgetting effects typically disappear when recognition memory is tested, showing that forgotten items remain intact in memory. Accordingly, this method shows that when people are no longer inclined to remember recently encountered and well-encoded events, they can intentionally lower the accessibility of those events.

Is there any evidence that such processes can be engaged to forget emotional experiences? Amanda Barnier and co-workers (2007) examined this issue by exploring whether subjects would show directed forgetting of recently recalled autobiographical memories. They asked subjects to generate a personal memory in response to 24 different cue words. The cue words were designed to elicit neutral, positive and negative autobiographical memories. Importantly, after the first 12-item word list was presented, subjects either received an instruction to forget the previous items as being simply practice, or that they should remember them, as they might be asked to recall the memories later on. Subjects then generated another 12 memories in response to 12 new cue words. Next, subjects were asked to mention all of the memories that they had generated in both lists. In several experiments, Barnier et al. found solid directed forgetting effects. These effects occurred for neutral, positive as well as for negative memories. Hence, it seems that directed forgetting effects can take place for autobiographical memories.

Several studies have begun to investigate directed forgetting in people with post-traumatic stress disorder (for a review, see Geraerts & McNally, 2008), as well as recovered memories of abuse (this chapter). Also, several other paradigms have been developed to examine how people attempt to push unwanted memories out of awareness (see Anderson & Huddleston, 2012, this volume).

Repressive Coping

Research on motivated forgetting has shown that people are able to push unwanted memories out of mind. Interestingly, some people are so skilled at pushing memories out of mind, that they are especially good at forgetting unhappy experiences. So-called "repressors" tend to recall fewer negative events from their lives (Myers & Brewin, 1994) and report low levels of anxiety and stress, even when physiological measures indicate strong emotional reactions to a certain person or situation. Myers and colleagues (Myers, Brewin, & Power, 1998) examined whether repressors are skilled at inhibiting retrieval by using a directed forgetting procedure in which subjects had to study pleasant or unpleasant words. Results showed that repressors were more adept than nonrepressors at using retrieval inhibition to block recall of recently studied unpleasant words, even though there were no differences between the two groups in blocking recall of pleasant words.

Repressors have also been found to be superior to nonrepressors in intentionally suppressing personal emotional events from their past. Barnier, Levin, and Maher (2004) made use of a thought suppression paradigm (see Wegner, Schneider, Carter, & White, 1987) to examine this issue. Repressors and nonrepressors were instructed to identify a recent event that made them either proud or embarrassed during an imagining period. After this period, they were told either to avoid thinking about this event or to think of anything at all. Finally, in the expression period, subjects were instructed to think of anything. Subjects monitored occurrence of the target thought throughout these periods. For the proud event, all subjects avoided target thoughts when instructed to suppress them. However, for the embarrassing event, repressors reported fewer thoughts than nonrepressors, even when *not* instructed to suppress them. Moreover, regardless of instructions, repressors did not show an increase in thoughts related to the embarrassing event after having suppressed this event, an effect that is typically found in this task (i.e., the post-suppression rebound effect). It seems like repressors are natural suppressors, skilled in avoiding negative thoughts about an embarrassing event. But does such a repressive coping style come with a cost? May natural repressors experience more unwanted intrusions in the days after having intentionally avoided such thoughts?

My colleagues and I (Geraerts, Merckelbach, Jelicic, & Smeets, 2006) examined this issue by instructing repressors to keep a 7-day diary reporting their positive and negative intrusions, after having suppressed these intrusions in the lab, similar to the study of Barnier and colleagues. Repressors showed fewer negative intrusions than nonrepressors in the laboratory session. Over the 7-day period, however, they reported the *highest* number of negative intrusions. These results seem to suggest that repressive coping might indeed be adaptive in the short run, leading to fewer unwanted thoughts. In the long run, though, having a repressive coping style seems maladaptive, increasing the frequency of intrusions even more. Recently, research in my laboratory also found that repressors show overgeneral memories for negative autobiographical events. That is, when asked to retrieve a negative memory, repressors are not able to list specific details of the events, relative to nonrepressors, and relative to the retrieval of positive events (Geraerts, Dritschel, Kreplin, Rasmussen, & Waddington, 2010). This overgeneral retrieval style has been linked to depressive symptoms as well (Williams et al., 2007). Clearly, these findings seem to suggest that a repressive coping style is *not* the most sensible way for coping with emotionally negative events.

False Memories

It is clear from the research described above that people can forget unwanted memories. Besides forgetting, people sometimes come up with details that never happened to them. Indeed, memory more closely resembles a synthesis of experiences than a replay of a videotape (Schacter, 2001). In the most dramatic instance, people may even come to believe memories of experiences that never occurred to them. In some cases these false memories pertain to traumatic events, such as childhood abuse.

At first sight, the idea that someone would remember a traumatic experience that has never occurred seems rather unlikely. Yet, people have recollected all sorts of unlikely events. To name just a few examples: Individuals claim to have recovered memories of satanic ritual abuse (Scott, 2001), previous lives (Geraerts, Wanmaker, & Dijkstra, 2011; Meyersburg, Bogdan, Gallo, & McNally, 2009), and even abduction by space aliens (Clancy, 2005). Most of these memories have surfaced with the encouragement of mental health professionals.

Types of False Memory Paradigms

The controversy regarding the possibility of such false memories, especially memories of CSA, has sparked great interest in memory distortion among cognitive psychologists. These psychologists have conducted at least three types of relevant studies. The first began to appear before the debate over false memories, whereas the other two emerged in response to it. The first type of study relates to how misinformation given to subjects after they witness an event may distort their memory for details of the event. Studies of Elizabeth Loftus have shown that giving witnesses misleading information after an event can distort their memory reports of that event.

The so-called *misinformation effect* occurs when subjects believe having seen items that were misleadingly suggested (for a review, see Loftus, 2005).

The second type of false memory study involves the creation of false memories of having encountered certain stimuli. A study by Henry Roediger and Kathleen McDermott (1995) inspired considerable research on this type of false memory. Reviving a task introduced by James Deese (1959), they conducted a study that involved what has come to be known as the Deese-Roediger-McDermott (DRM) paradigm. Their work showed that it is surprisingly easy to create false memories among college students in the laboratory. In their experiments, subjects studied a list of words that are strong semantic associates of a word not presented on the list – the *critical lure*. This lure captures the gist of the entire list. For example, one list contained words related to the topic of sleep, such as *bed, rest, awake, tired,* and *dream.* However, the word *sleep* was not mentioned. Roediger and McDermott tested whether subjects would "remember" having heard words that had been only suggested, not presented (i.e., the critical lures), like *sleep.* Intriguingly, on subsequent tests, many of their subjects falsely recalled and recognized having seen these critical lures. Subsequent DRM studies have shown how easily false memories develop in the laboratory and how long lasting they can be in a variety of subject populations (for a review, see Gallo, 2006).

The third type of false memory study examined whether it is possible to implant false autobiographical memories. Researchers have falsely suggested to people that they had experienced a childhood event when in fact it never happened. Examples include being lost in a shopping mall for an extended period of time, being hospitalized overnight, and spilling a punch bowl at a family wedding (Hyman, Husband, & Billings, 1995; Loftus & Pickrell, 1995). In each of these studies a significant minority of subjects came to accept all or part of the suggestion. Interestingly, highly emotional false events have been suggested as well: People have been persuaded that they experienced awful events as children, such as almost having drowned (Heaps & Nash, 2001) or having been a victim of a vicious animal attack (Porter, Yuille, & Lehman, 1999). Taken together, these studies show the power of this type of suggestion. It has led many subjects to believe or sometimes even remember in detail events that did not occur. Across many studies that now have used this procedure, about 30% of subjects on average have created either partial or complete false memories (Lindsay, Hagen, Read, Wade, & Garry, 2004).

Another witty technique for planting false memories involves the use of fake photographs (Wade, Garry, Read, & Lindsay, 2002). Wade and colleagues showed subjects a doctored photograph consisting of a real photograph of the subject and a relative pasted into a prototype photograph of a hot-air balloon. Importantly, family members confirmed that the event never occurred. By the end of the experiment, consisting of three interviews, about 50% of the subjects had partially or clearly remembered the false hot-air balloon ride.

These studies and many more like them clearly show that people can develop false beliefs and memories for events that did not happen to them. But might such false beliefs and memories have repercussions on attitudes and behavior? Studies from Bernstein, Laney, Morris, and Loftus (2005) provide some clues: They falsely suggested to their subjects that they had become ill after eating a certain food (e.g., hard-boiled eggs, strawberry ice cream) when they were children and found that this false suggestion increased subjects' confidence that the critical item had indeed happened. Moreover, these false beliefs had consequences for their subjects, such as decreased self-reported preference for the target food and an increased anticipated behavioral avoidance of the target food.

These studies demonstrate that false beliefs can influence attitudes. A recent study examined whether false beliefs or memories can also produce real changes in *behavior* (Geraerts, Bernstein, et al., 2008). In this study, it was suggested to subjects that, as children, they had become ill after eating egg salad. After this manipulation, a significant minority of subjects came to believe they had experienced this event. More importantly, this newfound autobiographical belief was accompanied by a significantly lower consumption of egg salad sandwiches, both immediately and 4 months after the false suggestion. Indeed, other work now also seems to suggest that false memories can indeed have behavioral consequences (Scoboria, Mazzoni, & Jarry, 2008).

Applying False Memory Paradigms

Clearly, a large collection of studies on the creation of false memories has conclusively shown that misinformation can distort memory reports, non-presented stimuli can be lured into memory, and suggestions may make people incorrectly believe to have experienced a childhood event when they actually did not. To what extent are these conclusions relevant to the question of whether people develop false memories of traumatic events?

Pezdek and Lam (2007) for example, claim that it is inappropriate to generalize directly from false memory research that did not involve planting entirely new events in memory (e.g., falsely remembering non-presented words in the DRM paradigm) to real world situations that do involve planting entirely new events in memory. They point out that it has not been shown that the mechanisms that operate in a DRM paradigm apply to memory for planting entirely new events in memory, especially memory for childhood abuse (see also DePrince et al., 2012, this volume). Yet, objections to laboratory demonstrations of the misinformation effect as irrelevant to the real world of psychotherapy may have less force nowadays than they originally did as researchers have responded to these objections by showing that it is possible to implant false memories of a diversity of experiences (for a review, see Wade et al., 2007). Also, cognitive and personality measures such as working memory capacity and dissociative experiences, are correlated with the propensity to make memory errors. Likewise, individuals' sensitivity to the DRM effect has been found to correlate positively with individuals' sensitivity to false memories in different paradigms, including false autobiographical memories (for a review, see Gallo, 2006). Moreover, and ironically, the most impressive demonstrations of the creation of false memories have arisen in clinical settings, not in the laboratory. If one considers that trivial manipulations in the laboratory can create memory distortion, these effects may be even more pronounced in the context of suggestive therapy in which therapist and patient join forces to uncover memories of abuse. Over many sessions, and with the aid of techniques such as guided imagination and hypnosis, false memories of childhood sexual abuse have arisen.

Laboratory Studies of Persons with Recovered Memories

One outstanding aspect of the recovered memory debate has been the absence of any research on cognitive functioning of people reporting recovered memories. Until recently, scholars on both sides of the debate have argued their case by relying on evidence from either clinical experience, surveys of abuse survivors, or studies with college students (McNally, 2003). Laboratory studies on the cognitive functioning of people reporting recovered memories have been surprisingly lacking. Only recently have researchers begun to examine how people with recovered CSA memories perform on tests of forgetting, as well as tests of false memories.

Directed Forgetting

Some clinical theorists like Leone Terr (1991) maintain that sexually abused children cope by developing an avoidant encoding style that enables them to disengage their attention from threatening cues, thereby impairing their memory for these cues. If people reporting recovered memories have indeed acquired this cognitive style, then this should be evident in the laboratory. As the item method directed forgetting (see above) taps encoding abilities, McNally and colleagues examined the ability of people with recovered CSA memories to forget trauma-related words (McNally, Clancy, & Schacter, 2001; see also McNally, 2012, this volume). Subjects were shown a series of words on a computer screen, one at a time. Each word appeared for 2 s and was replaced by a cue instructing the subject either to remember or to forget the previous word. Three categories of words were used: trauma-related (e.g., *abuse*), positive (e.g., *sociable*), and neutral (e.g., *banister*). Immediately after this encoding phase, subjects were asked to write down as many words as they could remember, regardless of the original instructions to forget or remember. Interestingly, McNally et al. found *normal* memory functioning in the recovered memory group. That is, they recalled to-be-remembered words more often than to-be-forgotten words, regardless of word valence. Moreover, they showed neither worse nor better memory for trauma-related words relative to control subjects without a history of abuse. So, people with recovered memories did not exhibit the predicted superior ability to avoid the encoding of material related to abuse.

Might their reported forgetting of childhood abuse be attributed to superior retrieval inhibition instead of avoidant encoding? To examine this possibility, both

McNally's and my laboratory used the list method directed forgetting procedure (see above). Subjects were told they were taking part in an emotional judgment task, with no hint that they had to remember words. After presentation of the first list, they were then told that what they had had been just practice and they could forget about those words. The second word list was than presented for which subjects were asked to rate the emotionality of each word. In a surprise recall task, subjects were asked to recall as many words as possible from *both* lists. Both laboratories found that subjects recalled more words from the second list than from the first list which had been followed by the forget instruction. Also, all groups recalled trauma words more often than positive words. Interestingly, people reporting recovered CSA memories did not exhibit superior forgetting of trauma versus positive words, relative to control subjects (Geraerts, Smeets, Jelicic, van Heerden, & Merckelbach, 2006; McNally, Clancy, Barrett, & Parker, 2004). This finding suggests that people with recovered memories are not superior at inhibiting retrieval of trauma-related words. So, again no support for the idea that people with recovered memories of CSA are better forgetters of trauma cues than are people who report either never forgetting their abuse or report never having been abused.

Creating False Memories

Might it be the case then that scholars do have a point in arguing that at least some recovered memories might be false recollections, often induced by suggestive therapeutic techniques? Is it that people reporting recovered memories – or at least some of them – may be more prone to developing false memories, and is this evident in the laboratory? To address this possibility, McNally's and my laboratory used the DRM paradigm (see above) to elicit false memories in people reporting recovered memories. In doing so, the idea was tested that people reporting recovered CSA memories would be more prone to falsely remembering and recognizing non-presented words. That is, they would have more difficulty differentiating between what they really saw and what was automatically activated due to the presentation of semantically related words. As hypothesized, we found that as a group, people with recovered CSA memories more often falsely recalled and recognized the non-presented critical lures, relative to people with continuous CSA memories, and people with no history of abuse (Clancy, Schacter, McNally, & Pitman, 2000).

Despite clear demonstrations of this DRM effect, Freyd and Gleaves (1996) questioned whether results on this task could be related to real world examples of false memories. They correctly pointed out that false memories often involve highly emotional events such as childhood abuse, whereas the DRM paradigm typically involves neutral words. As a result, the frequency of false recall or recognition in the DRM paradigm may be lowered when trauma-related material would be used, as these words are more distinctive. My colleagues and I tested this prediction by including trauma-related material in the DRM paradigm as well. Lists were centred on critical lures such as assault and abuse. Results showed that false recall and recognition performance was higher in individuals with recovered CSA memories. This effect was especially profound in the recognition modality (Geraerts, Smeets, Jelicic, van Heerden, & Merckelbach, 2005).

What do these findings tell us about the authenticity of reports of recovered abuse memories? Several researchers have suggested that deficits in source monitoring may lead to false memories. People with such deficits are prone to making incorrect judgements about the origins or sources of information (Johnson, Hashtroudi, & Lindsay, 1993; Johnson, Raye, Mitchell, & Ankudowich, 2012, this volume). Relating this to the DRM paradigm, one needs to make a distinction between what was presented and what was activated besides the presented material (i.e., critical lures). That is, the presentation of semantically associated words may activate a gist (a general idea about the concept of the list), which makes it possible for individuals to rely more on memory for this gist than on the verbatim memory traces of the presented material (Brainerd & Reyna, 1998). Accordingly, when subjects think of the critical lure at study because it automatically comes to mind, at test they must differentiate between these memories of the gist versus memories of the studied words. The above results suggest that at least some individuals with recovered memories may have a source monitoring deficit for all types of material, whether the content is neutral or trauma-related (see also, McNally, Clancy, Barrett, & Parker, 2005). They may be more likely to accept a memory of the gist as being a genuine memory. So, it seems plausible that at least some of those with recovered memories developed false memories of abuse via a subtle interaction between already existing source monitoring difficulties and suggestive therapeutic techniques.

A Step Outside the Laboratory

This kind of work in the laboratory may lead one to conclude that recovered memories are sometimes fictitious. On the other hand, work outside the laboratory has also shown that the opposite may happen, that recovered memories may reflect genuine abuse events. Jonathan Schooler and colleagues (e.g., Schooler, Bendiksen, & Ambadar, 1997; Shobe & Schooler, 2001) published several case descriptions of individuals who experienced the discovery of apparently long-forgotten memories of abuse. Memories that were all recovered outside the context of therapy. Importantly, corroborative information was found for these cases. In some of these cases something fascinating was found: The partners of the women who reported a recovered memory experience mentioned that their spouses had talked about the abuse, *prior* to the alleged recovered memory experience. Schooler et al. proposed that such cases demonstrate a forgot-it-all-along (FIA) mechanism, which can lead to the forgetting of prior instances of recollecting a past event. During the recovered memory experience, the traumatic event may be recalled in a qualitatively different way from past occasions of remembering it. For example, it may be recalled more completely, more episodically, or as abuse per se rather than as some more innocent category of childhood event. As such a recollection is often paired with shock and surprise, individuals' assessment of their prior knowledge may be influenced. They might reason, "If I am this shocked and surprised now, then I must have completely forgotten about the experience" (p. 283). Hence, these case studies put forward the possibility that at least some recovered memories reflect genuine abuse episodes about which people simply forgot their prior thoughts.

Forgetting Prior Remembering

Is it possible that some people with recovered memories are not truly recalling the abuse event for the first time in years, but are forgetting prior cases of thinking about it? If so, how would this forgetting of prior recall come about? To explore this possibility, my colleagues and I (Geraerts, Arnold, et al., 2006) investigated whether people reporting recovered memories were more likely to underestimate their prior remembering. In a FIA task, subjects with recovered or continuous memories of abuse were asked to generate an autobiographical memory from their childhood in response to each of 25 cue phrases describing common childhood events (e.g., being home alone, going to the dentist). For some events, they were asked to focus on emotionally positive aspects of the event, but for others, they were instructed to concentrate on the negative aspects. Two months later subjects returned to the laboratory and generated the same memories. This time, however, subjects were instructed to retrieve the events in the same emotional frame as before, but for other events, they were instructed to retrieve the event in the opposite emotional frame. So, for example, if they had recalled "being home alone without parents" in a positive light during the first visit (e.g., having lots of freedom), they recalled the same event again, but focused on the negative aspects (e.g., being afraid of a thunderstorm or feeling lonely). Finally, subjects returned to the lab for a third time 2 months later and recalled all of the events yet again. Now subjects had to recall each event in the same emotional frame in which they had recalled it during their first visit. Critically, after recalling each of the memories, subjects told the experimenter whether or not they had recalled that same memory during the second visit. Would people be able to remember having recalled the event during the second visit? Would this depend on whether it was recalled in the same "emotional context" both then and now? Interestingly, when the emotional framing on the final visit differed from the one on the second visit, subjects showed a pronounced tendency to forget having remembered the event during that second visit, relative to when the emotional framing remained the same. So, simply shifting the way that people thought about the very same memory (whether positively or negatively) from one occasion to the next made them forget thinking about the memory before. Strikingly, this tendency was significantly greater for people reporting recovered memories than it was for people reporting continuously available memories, or people without any history of abuse.

So it seems that one reason why people may have a recovered memory experience is that they simply forget having remembered the event before, just as was observed in the case studies reported by Schooler et al. (1997). They may forget prior cases of remembering if, for example, the mental context when they are having their recovered memory experience differs dramatically from the mental context on prior occasions in which they thought of the event. By this view, it's not that people have forgotten the event all those years; it is that they simply can't remember having previously remembered the experience.

Two Types of Recovered Memory Experiences

When we review these laboratory findings, we can see different interpretations of recovered memories. People with recovered memories show an increased tendency towards false memory formation. In contrast, they also show pronounced underestimation of prior remembering. How can these phenomena be integrated? Careful inspection of recovered memory experiences suggests that they reveal themselves as two qualitatively different types; and that additional investigation of these types appears to provide an answer. In one type, people come to realize that they are abuse survivors, commonly attributing current life difficulties to their forgotten memories of CSA. In this type of recovered memory experience, abuse events are mostly slowly recalled over time, often instigated by suggestive therapeutic techniques such as guided imagery, dream interpretation, and hypnosis. In the other type of recovered memory experience, people are unexpectedly reminded of events that they believe they had not thought about for many years. Mostly, individuals recollect the abuse when encountering salient retrieval cues (e.g., a book or movie in which CSA is clearly depicted, being in the same setting as where the abuse happened, or events involving the person's children; see also Brewin, 2012, this volume, and Anderson & Huddleston, 2012, this volume, for issues pertaining to spontaneous recovery of CSA). This kind of recollection clearly differs from the one in which the person is gradually recalling the abuse, often in the course of suggestive therapy. If so, one expects it to be easier to find corroborative evidence for spontaneously recovered memories than for memories recovered through suggestive therapy.

To examine this issue, my colleagues and I invited subjects who had always remembered the abuse, had a recovered memory of it that took place during suggestive therapy, or had a recovered memory spontaneously, outside of therapy (Geraerts et al., 2007). After filling out a questionnaire about their memory of the abuse events, subjects were queried systematically about sources of corroboration. Independent raters who were blind to group assignment then, based on the sources provided by the participants, sought to determine if the abuse could be corroborated. A memory was considered corroborated if either (a) another individual reported learning about the abuse within a week after it happened, (b) another individual reported having been abused by the same perpetrator, or (c) the perpetrator admitted to committing the abuse. Strikingly, memories that were recovered spontaneously, outside of therapy, were corroborated at a rate (37%) that was quite comparable to that observed for people with continuously accessible memories of abuse (45%).

In contrast, memories recovered through suggestive therapy could not be corroborated (0%). Although the lack of corroboration does not imply that these recovered memories are false, it does recommend caution in interpreting memories recovered in suggestive therapy.

Differing Origins of Recovered Memory Experiences

The foregoing findings suggest that recovered memories may originate in different ways for people who recollect the abuse event spontaneously, and for those who recall it through suggestive therapy. We hypothesized that memories recalled through suggestive therapy may be more likely to be the product of suggestion, a possibility consistent with (but not demanded by) the lack of corroboration. People recalling memories spontaneously, by contrast, may have recalled the event previously, but may have simply forgotten the fact that they have recalled it before. To examine these possibilities, my colleagues and I tested people with spontaneously recovered memories, people with memories recovered through suggestive therapy, and people with continuously available memories on a simplified version of the above mentioned forgot-it-all-along task (Geraerts et al., 2009). Strikingly, only those subjects who had recovered their memories spontaneously showed exaggerated forgetting of prior remembering; subjects who recovered their memories in suggestive therapy or subjects with continuous memories showed no such pattern. When tested on a simple false memory task (DRM task), however, only people who recovered their memories in suggestive therapy showed exaggerated false memory formation; neither the spontaneously recovered group nor people with continuous access to their memories showed such a pattern.

These results strongly support the idea that memories recovered in suggestive therapy and recovered spontaneously may have fundamentally different origins. As a group, people who report having recovered their memories in suggestive therapy generally show a pronounced tendency to incorrectly claim that they have experienced events when they have demonstrably not experienced them as measured by the DRM test. To the extent that this pattern on the DRM task is indicative of a broader deficit in monitoring the source of one's memories, this finding suggests that such reports of recovered memories should be viewed with a cautious eye, as they may reflect an interaction of suggestive therapy with pre-existing source monitoring deficits. In contrast, people who believe they have spontaneously recovered a memory of CSA show no evidence at all of heightened susceptibility to the creation of false memories. This group does, however, show a pronounced tendency to forget prior incidences of remembering when those prior retrievals have taken place in a different retrieval context. So, even when prior accessibility of simple events studied in the laboratory can be objectively demonstrated, this group, as a whole, was significantly more likely to deny having remembered those events on previous occasions. These findings suggest that this group, as a whole, may simply be failing to remember their prior thoughts about a *genuine* incidence of CSA.

Conclusion

The debate about recovered memories of childhood abuse has received a great deal of attention, in part because of concern over the possibility that some proportion of recovered memory experiences may be false. Accordingly, cognitive researchers have examined how people may forget certain experiences on the one hand, and how people may come to remember events that have not happened to them on the other hand. Research on the cognitive functioning of people reporting recovered CSA memories has yielded evidence for at least two types of recovered memory experiences, each with their specific origin.

False recovered memories might arise when people participate in prolonged periods of trying to recollect an abuse event, instigated by highly suggestive memory recovery techniques. False memories of abuse have indeed been induced by such techniques, emphasizing the role of suggestion and source monitoring errors in shaping what people believe has happened to them. When a suggestive therapist is convinced of the existence of repressed abuse memories, and when a client starts to remember certain events, it may become difficult to comprehend that the memory may not be real, particularly when it provides a suitable explanation for current symptomatology. Indeed, memories of CSA that are recovered in suggestive therapy appear, in general, to be less open to corroboration in comparison to memories that are recovered spontaneously outside of therapy. Although the lack of corroboration does not indicate that a recovered memory is false, research suggests that people recovering memories under such circumstances are in fact more suggestible. This pattern of results raises the possibility that some of these recovery events may not reflect real abuse, but rather the unintentional result of overly suggestive therapeutic techniques. Other types of therapy that do not involve suggestion are not necessarily subject to this concern (see e.g., Andrews et al., 1999; Brewin, 2012, this volume). Thus, some cases of recovered memories may in fact be false memories that are, in effect, unwittingly implanted by therapists who actually intend to help the patient.

On the other hand, some recovered memories of sexual abuse have proven to be real events that can be corroborated, sometimes even with a confession of the perpetrator. Indeed, memories recovered spontaneously appear to be corroborated at the same rate as continuously accessible memories, suggesting that many of these experiences reflect real abuse events. People recovering memories under these circumstances exhibit an especially pronounced tendency to forget their prior experiences of remembering, and also show superior ability to suppress thoughts about anxious autobiographical memories.

Research on cognitive mechanisms underlying recovered memories has advanced our understanding on the validity of recovered memory reports and how such memories come about. Now that the recovered memory debate is decreasing in intensity and divergence, it will be important that research findings on recovered memories will be applied in the justice system and in clinical practice. Exciting future research on recovered memories on a wide range of empirical and theoretical fronts will only continue to advance our understanding of recovered memories and will hopefully yield a broader image of how one can determine on several levels the (in)accuracy of such memories.

Acknowledgment Elke Geraerts was supported by a grant from the Netherlands Organization for Scientific Research (NWO 451 07 004).

References

Anderson, M. C. (2005). The role of inhibitory control in forgetting unwanted memories: A consideration of three methods. In C. MacLeod & B. Uttl (Eds.), *Dynamic cognitive processes* (pp. 159–190). Tokyo: Springer.

Anderson, M. C., & Huddleston, E. (2012, this volume). Towards a cognitive and neurobiological model of motivated forgetting. In R. F. Belli (Ed.), *True and false recovered memories: Toward a reconciliation of the debate* (pp. 53–120). *Vol. 58: Nebraska Symposium on Motivation*. New York: Springer.

Andrews, B., Brewin, C. R., Ochera, J., Morton, J., Bekerian, D. A., Davies, G. M., et al. (1999). Characteristics, context and consequences of memory recovery among adults in therapy. *The British Journal of Psychiatry, 175*, 141–146.

Barnier, A. J., Conway, M. A., Mayoh, L., Speyer, J., Avizmil, O., & Harris, C. B. (2007). Directed forgetting of recently recalled autobiographical memories. *Journal of Experimental Psychology: General, 136*, 301–322.

Barnier, A. J., Levin, K., & Maher, A. (2004). Suppressing thoughts of past events: Are repressive copers good suppressors? *Cognition and Emotion, 18*, 513–531.

Basden, B. H., Basden, D. R., & Gargano, J. G. (1993). Directed forgetting in implicit and explicit memory tests: A comparison of methods. *Journal of Experimental Psychology: Learning, Memory, and Cognition, 19*, 603–616.

Bernstein, D. M., Laney, C., Morris, E. K., & Loftus, E. F. (2005). False beliefs about fattening foods can have healthy consequences. *Proceedings of the National Academy of Sciences, 102*, 13724–13731.

Brainerd, C. J., & Reyna, V. F. (1998). When things that were never experienced are easier to 'remember' than things that were. *Psychological Science, 9*, 484–489.

Brewin, C. R. (2007). Autobiographical memory for trauma: Update on four controversies. *Memory, 15*, 227–248.

Brewin, C. R. (2012, this volume). A theoretical framework for understanding recovered memory experiences. In R. F. Belli (Ed.), *True and false recovered memories: Toward a reconciliation of the debate* (pp. 149–173). *Vol. 58: Nebraska Symposium on Motivation*. New York: Springer.

Brown, D., Scheflin, A. W., & Hammond, D. C. (1998). *Memory, trauma treatment, and the law*. New York: Norton.

Ceci, S. J., & Loftus, E. F. (1994). 'Memory work': A royal road to false memories? *Applied Cognitive Psychology, 8*, 351–364.

Clancy, S. A. (2005). *Abducted: How people come to believe they were kidnapped by aliens*. Cambridge, MA: Harvard University Press.

Clancy, S. A., Schacter, D. L., McNally, R. J., & Pitman, R. K. (2000). False recognition in women reporting recovered memories of sexual abuse. *Psychological Science, 11*, 26–31.

Deese, J. (1959). On the prediction of occurrence of particular verbal intrusions in immediate recall. *Journal of Experimental Psychology, 58*, 17–22.

DePrince, A., Brown, L., Cheit, R., Freyd, J., Gold, S. N., Pezdek, K., & Quina, K. (2012, this volume). Motivated forgetting and misremembering: Perspectives from betrayal trauma theory. In R. F. Belli (Ed.), *True and false recovered memories: Toward a reconciliation of the debate* (pp. 193–242). *Vol. 58: Nebraska Symposium on Motivation*. New York: Springer.

French, N. (1997). *The Memory Game*. Londen: William Heinemann.

Freyd, J. J., & Gleaves, D. F. (1996). "Remembering" words not presented in lists: Relevance to the current recovered/false memory controversy. *Journal of Experimental Psychology: Learning, Memory, and Cognition, 22*, 811–813.

Gallo, D. A. (2006). *Associative illusions of memory. False memory research in DRM and related tasks*. New York: Psychology Press.

Geraerts, E., Arnold, M. M., Lindsay, D. S., Merckelbach, H., Jelicic, M., & Hauer, B. (2006). Forgetting of prior remembering in persons reporting recovered memories of childhood sexual abuse. *Psychological Science, 17*, 1002–1008.

Geraerts, E., Bernstein, D. M., Merckelbach, H., Linders, C., Raymaekers, L., & Loftus, E. F. (2008). Lasting false beliefs and their behavioral consequences. *Psychological Science, 19*, 749–753.

Geraerts, E. Dritschel, B., Kreplin, U., Miyagawa, L., & Waddington, J. (in press). Reduced specificity of negative autobiographical memories in repressive coping. *Journal of Behavior Therapy and Experimental Psychiatry*.

Geraerts, E., Lindsay, D. S., Merckelbach, H., Jelicic, M., Raymaekers, L., Arnold, M. M., et al. (2009). Cognitive mechanisms underlying recovered memory experiences of childhood sexual abuse. *Psychological Science, 20*, 92–98.

Geraerts, E., & McNally, R. J. (2008). Forgetting unwanted memories: Directed forgetting and thought suppression methods. *Acta Psychologica, 127*, 614–627.

Geraerts, E., Merckelbach, H., Jelicic, M., & Smeets, E. (2006). Long term consequences of suppression of intrusive thoughts and repressive coping. *Behaviour Research and Therapy, 44*, 1451–1460.

Geraerts, E., Raymaekers, L., & Merckelbach, H. (2008). Recovered memories of childhood sexual abuse: Current findings and their legal implications. Invited review paper. *Legal and Criminological Psychology, 13*, 165–176.

Geraerts, E., Schooler, J. W., Merckelbach, H., Jelicic, M., Hauer, B. J. A., & Ambadar, Z. (2007). The reality of recovered memories: Corroborating continuous and discontinuous memories of childhood sexual abuse. *Psychological Science, 18*, 564–567.

Geraerts, E., Smeets, E., Jelicic, M., Merckelbach, H., & van Heerden, J. (2006). Retrieval inhibition of trauma-related words in women reporting repressed or recovered memories of childhood sexual abuse. *Behaviour Research and Therapy, 44*, 1129–1136.

Geraerts, E., Smeets, E., Jelicic, M., van Heerden, J., & Merckelbach, H. (2005). Fantasy proneness, but not self-reported trauma is related to DRM performance of women reporting recovered memories of childhood sexual abuse. *Consciousness and Cognition, 14*, 602–612.

Geraerts, E., Wanmaker, S., & Dijkstra, K. (2011). False memory propensity before and after suggestive therapy: A study in individuals recovering previous lives. Manuscript in preparation. Submitted for publication

Golding, J. M. (2005). Directed forgetting tasks in cognitive research. In A. Wenzel & D. C. Rubin (Eds.), *Cognitive methods and their application to clinical research* (pp. 177–196). Washington, DC: American Psychological Association.

Heaps, C. M., & Nash, M. (2001). Comparing recollective experience in true and false autobiographical memories. *Journal of Experimental Psychology: Learning, Memory, and Cognition, 27*, 920–930.

Hyman, I. E., Husband, T. H., & Billings, F. J. (1995). False memories of childhood experiences. *Applied Cognitive Psychology, 9*, 181–195.

Johnson, M. K., Hashtroudi, S., & Lindsay, D. S. (1993). Source monitoring. *Psychological Bulletin, 114*, 3–28.

Johnson, M. K., Raye, C. L., Mitchell, K. J., & Ankudowich, E. (2012, this volume). The cognitive neuroscience of true and false memories. In R. F. Belli (Ed.), *True and false recovered memories: Toward a reconciliation of the debate* (pp. 15–52). *Vol. 58: Nebraska Symposium on Motivation*. New York: Springer.

Kihlstrom, J. F. (2004). An unbalanced balancing act: Blocked, recovered, and false memories in the laboratory and clinic. *Clinical Psychology: Science and Practice, 11*, 34–41.

Lindsay, D. S., Hagen, L., Read, J. D., Wade, K. A., & Garry, M. (2004). True photographs and false memories. *Psychological Science, 15*, 149–154.

Loftus, E. F. (2005). Planting misinformation in the human mind: A 30-year investigation of the malleability of memory. *Learning & Memory, 12*, 361–366.

Loftus, E. F., & Davis, D. (2006). Recovered memories. *Annual Review of Clinical Psychology, 2*, 469–498.

Loftus, E. F., & Pickrell, J. E. (1995). The formation of false memories. *Psychiatric Annals, 25*, 720–725.

McNally, R. J. (2003). *Remembering trauma*. Cambridge, MA: Belknap Press/Harvard University Press.

McNally, R. J., Clancy, S. A., Barrett, H. M., & Parker, H. A. (2004). Inhibiting retrieval of trauma cues in adults reporting histories of childhood sexual abuse. *Cognition & Emotion, 18*, 479–493.

McNally, R. J., Clancy, S. A., Barrett, H. M., & Parker, H. A. (2005). Reality monitoring in adults reporting repressed, recovered, or continuous memories of childhood sexual abuse. *Journal of Abnormal Psychology, 114*, 147–152.

McNally, R. J., Clancy, S. A., & Schacter, D. L. (2001). Directed forgetting of trauma cues in adults reporting repressed or recovered memories of childhood sexual abuse. *Journal of Abnormal Psychology, 110*, 151–156.

McNally, R. J. & Geraerts, E. (2009). A new solution to the recovered memory debate. *Perspectives in Psychological Science 4*, 126–134.

Meyersburg, C. A., Bogdan, R., Gallo, D. A., & McNally, R. J. (2009). False memory propensity in people reporting recovered memories of past lives. *Journal of Abnormal Psychology, 118*, 399–404.

Myers, L. B., & Brewin, C. R. (1994). Recall of early experience and the repressive coping style. *Journal of Abnormal Psychology, 103*, 288–292.

Myers, L. B., Brewin, C. R., & Power, M. J. (1998). Repressive coping and the directed forgetting of emotional material. *Journal of Abnormal Psychology, 107*, 141–148.

Pezdek, K., & Lam, S. (2007). What research paradigms have cognitive psychologists used to study "False memory", and what are the implications of these choices? *Consciousness and Cognition, 16*, 2–17.

Porter, S., Yuille, J. C., & Lehman, D. R. (1999). The nature of real, implanted, and fabricated memories or emotional childhood events. Implications for the recovered memory debate. *Law and Human Behavior, 23*, 517–537.

Roediger, H. L., III, & McDermott, K. B. (1995). Creating false memories: Remembering words not presented in lists. *Journal of Experimental Psychology: Learning, Memory, and Cognition, 21*, 803–814.

Schacter, D. L. (2001). How the mind forgets and remembers. In *The seven sins of memory*. Boston: Houghton Mifflin.

Schooler, J. W., Bendiksen, M. A., & Ambadar, Z. (1997). Taking the middle line: Can we accommodate both fabricated and recovered memories of sexual abuse? In M. Conway (Ed.), *False and recovered memories* (pp. 251–292). Oxford: Oxford University Press.

Scoboria, A., Mazzoni, G., & Jarry, J. (2008). Suggesting childhood food illness results in reduced eating behavior. *Acta Psychologica, 128*, 304–309.

Scott, S. (2001). *The politics and experience of ritual abuse: Beyond disbelief*. Buckingham, UK: Open University Press.

Shobe, K. K., & Schooler, J. W. (2001). Discovering fact and fiction: Case-based analyses of authentic and fabricated memories of abuse. In G. M. Davies & T. Dalgleish (Eds.), *Recovered memories: Seeking the middle ground* (pp. 95–151). Chichester: John Wiley & Sons.

Terr, L. C. (1991). Childhood traumas: An outline and overview. *The American Journal of Psychiatry, 148*, 10–20.

Wade, K. A., Garry, M., Read, J. D., & Lindsay, D. S. (2002). A picture is worth a thousand lies. Using false photographs to create false childhood memories. *Psychonomic Bulletin & Review, 9*, 597–603.

Wade, K. A., Sharman, S. J., Garry, M., Memon, A., Mazzoni, G., Merckelbach, H., et al. (2007). False claims about false memory research. *Consciousness and Cognition, 16*, 18–28.

Wegner, D. M., Schneider, D. J., Carter, S. R., & White, T. I. (1987). Paradoxical effects of thought suppression. *Journal of Personality and Social Psychology, 53*, 5–13.

Williams, J. M. G., Barnhofer, T., Crane, C., Hermans, D., Raes, F., Watkins, E., et al. (2007). Autobiographical memory specificity and emotional disorder. *Psychological Bulletin, 133*, 122–148.

Motivated Forgetting and Misremembering: Perspectives from Betrayal Trauma Theory

Anne P. DePrince, Laura S. Brown, Ross E. Cheit, Jennifer J. Freyd, Steven N. Gold, Kathy Pezdek, and Kathryn Quina

Abstract Individuals are sometimes exposed to information that may endanger their well-being. In such cases, forgetting or misremembering may be adaptive. Childhood abuse perpetrated by a caregiver is an example. Betrayal trauma theory (BTT) proposes that the way in which events are processed and remembered will be related to the degree to which a negative event represents a betrayal by a trusted, needed other. Full awareness of such abuse may only increase the victim's risk by motivating withdrawal or confrontation with the perpetrator, thus risking a relationship vital to the victim's survival. In such situations, minimizing awareness of the betrayal trauma may be adaptive. BTT has implications for the larger memory and trauma field, particularly with regard to forgetting and misremembering events. This chapter reviews conceptual and empirical issues central to the literature on memory for trauma and BTT as well as identifies future research directions derived from BTT.

A.P. DePrince (✉)
University of Denver, Denver, CO, USA
e-mail: Anne.DePrince@du.edu

L.S. Brown
Fremont Community Therapy Project, Seattle, WA, USA

R.E. Cheit
Brown University, Providence, RI, USA

J.J. Freyd
University of Oregon, Eugene, OR, USA

S.N. Gold
Nova Southeastern University, Fort Lauderdale, FL, USA

K. Pezdek
Applied Cognitive Psychology, Claremont Graduate University, Claremont, CA, USA

K. Quina
University of Rhode Island, Providence, RI, USA

R.F. Belli (ed.), *True and False Recovered Memories: Toward a Reconciliation of the Debate*, Nebraska Symposium on Motivation, DOI 10.1007/978-1-4614-1195-6_7, © Springer Science+Business Media, LLC 2012

Keywords Abuse • Betrayal trauma • Memory

Historically, traumatic responses have been understood as tied to experiences of fear at the time or in the aftermath of the trauma (see DePrince & Freyd, 2002a, 2002b). The emphasis on fear as the dominant response in understanding traumatic responses, including memory for the event, makes intuitive sense. Fear-inducing events often involve life-threat, activating a cascade of physiological and emotional responses, such as those seen among survivors diagnosed with PTSD. The traumatic event itself and the cascade of responses all seem as if they would be quite memorable. Further, the very use of the word *trauma* implies that events should be memorable. The word *trauma* comes from the Greek term for a wound. Physical wounds often leave visible scars. Even if not frightening or terribly painful, a physical wound seems unforgettable simply because a physical trace remains present and knowable.

However, clinical and research accounts have documented trauma survivors' reports of forgetting trauma and trauma-related information as well as misremembering events as less traumatic than they actually were since the nineteenth century (see Herman, 1992). As reviewed in this chapter, the literature on forgetting has expanded significantly in recent years to consider multiple facets of the phenomenon of forgetting, most often in terms of characteristics of individual abuse victims/survivors (e.g., survivors' age at the time of the event) and the veracity of victims'/survivors' memories. Betrayal trauma theory (BTT; Freyd, 1996) provides an important framework for expanding beyond an emphasis on the characteristics of individual survivors and fear to consider the dynamic and complex interpersonal contexts in which abuse often takes place, particularly familial abuse.

At its heart, "BTT is an approach to conceptualising trauma that points to the importance of social relationships in understanding post-traumatic outcomes, including reduced recall" (Freyd, DePrince, & Gleaves, 2007, p. 297; see also Freyd, 1994, 1996, 2001). Initially offered as a framework for understanding *why* victims of abuse would be motivated to forget the abuse or abuse-related information (Freyd, 1996), "the phrase *betrayal trauma* refers to a social dimension of trauma, independent of the individual's reaction to the trauma" (Freyd et al., 2007, p. 297). According to the original framing of BTT, the degree to which the abuse event represents a betrayal by a trusted, needed other person mediates the manner in which abuse-related information is processed and remembered (Sivers, Schooler, & Freyd, 2002). Freyd, Klest, and DePrince (2010) describe BTT as providing

> a theoretical framework for understanding the impact of interpersonal traumas in which the victim trusts, depends upon, or feels close to the perpetrator...The victim of a betrayal trauma has a profound conflict between the usual need to be aware of betrayal (and thus to confront or withdraw from the betrayer) and the particular need to maintain a close relationship with a significant attachment figure (and thus to maintain proximity and closeness). According to betrayal trauma theory, the victim is likely to respond to such violations by avoiding awareness of the betrayal in the service of maintaining the relationship. Avoidance of awareness may lead to some degree of forgetting of the betrayal trauma (p. 20).

Introduced by Jennifer Freyd in 1994, BTT grew up, so to speak, in a particular socio-political context. The same socio-political context that influenced the initial conceptualization and ongoing development of BTT has also influenced the field more generally – driving not only the questions of the day, but the methods used and the interpretations made by cognitive scientists. In this chapter, we first turn to a discussion of forgetting and misremembering, including the empirical evidence documenting that forgetting abuse does occur. We then turn to reviewing empirical and theoretical work on BTT, placing this work in the larger context of the literature on trauma and memory. We next address several issues that are relevant to BTT, but for which the theory does not imply a particular stance (e.g., processes by which memories are recovered; veracity of recovered memories; trauma therapy). We then take a step back to consider the socio-political context in which research on forgetting (and misremembering) is situated to inform discussion our closing discussion of the contributions BTT makes to future research directions.

Forgetting and Misremembering

Defining Terms

The title of this chapter highlights both forgetting and misremembering. We deliberately chose two terms to capture the phenomena of knowledge isolation for abuse. Drawing on the framework articulated by Freyd et al. (2007), *knowledge isolation* refers to the diverse ways information can be hidden from awareness. With the term forgetting, we invoke Freyd's concept of "unawareness", which describes situations in which abuse-related information is inaccessible to conscious recall (Freyd et al. 2007). The term is not used to imply a particular mechanism by which the inaccessibility arose. In fact, understanding the mechanisms by which forgetting occurs is a separate question from documenting the phenomenon of and motivations for forgetting. BTT is primarily concerned with the latter. Misremembering is a term we use to reflect knowledge isolation that involves biases to remember autobiographical events as more positive (or less negative) than they were. Such reconstruction of events in memory offers a strategy by which victims abused by people on whom they depend may be able to minimize or isolate knowledge about the abuse.

Two things should be noted before reviewing evidence regarding motivations for forgetting and misremembering. First, researchers and the public have primarily concerned themselves with questions related to the *absence* of information rather than other forms of knowledge isolation that may help people cope with and survive certain forms of trauma, particularly abuse by close others. Complete forgetting of abuse-related information has garnered the majority of attention (and controversy) in the research literature. However, BTT argues that knowledge isolation can also take the form of misremembering.

Second, BTT's focus on the *social context* in which abuse occurs highlights that the field has focused scrutiny nearly exclusively on *victim* reports of forgetting. For example, research questions have most often been framed to identify which victims/ survivors forget and why; the processes by which victim forgetting and remembering occur; as well as criteria by which we deem believable victim memories among people who claim to have forgotten for some period of time. This body of work has largely – albeit often implicitly – biased scrutiny of victim memory to the exclusion of scrutiny of offender memory. For example, one rarely (if ever) hears about research on forgetting, misremembering, or even false memories in offenders who protest that they did not commit abuse. Surely individual abusers have motivation to forget and/or misremember abuse (as well as perhaps society; see Herman, 1992 for a related discussion on societal denial of trauma and abuse). In fact, such motivation must in most instances be quite strong; the person who can avoid remembering harming a child is denying criminal actions. Thus, we will highlight opportunities to extend research on victim memory to address important questions about offender memory.

Methodological Issues in Research on Victim Forgetting

Several methodological issues should be considered when reviewing data on survivors' forgetting for abuse. First, research on forgetting and misremembering of trauma is difficult, as the phenomena themselves beg important questions about methods and participants. For example, how do you measure a memory that is not accessible (or was never encoded) for a private event that was not witnessed by anyone but the perpetrator, as is the case for many abuse experiences? Who are the best participants for studies on forgetting and misremembering: people who report having forgotten and now remember; people who we have some reason to believe they were abused and now forget; or another group altogether? Thus, an important challenge faced by the field is to study rigorously something that has been naturalistically observed for so long, but appears to fit poorly into previously developed memory paradigms.

Second, self-reports of memory for personal events, no matter how banal, are not objective. Even the most skilled researcher cannot verify the accuracy of participants' memories, nor be certain that participants are forthcoming in their self-reports. Descriptions of personal experience are filtered through each participant's own interpretations, even for events in the recent past; memories from childhood are particularly subject to elaboration and interpretation through an adult's cognitive capabilities (e.g., Sloutsky & Fisher, 2004). Events that are well-remembered may be omitted or deemed too insignificant, or too difficult, to report. And a large body of laboratory research demonstrates that misremembering of details in a short film is common, even when the major event is correctly recalled (e.g., Loftus, 1975).

Third, difficulties with self-report are only magnified when the memory is for a traumatic event. Among other challenges, researchers have documented underreporting of trauma (Smith et al., 2000; Ullman, 2007), particularly sexual assault and abuse. For example, as recently reviewed by Belknap (in press), some estimates suggest that as few as 8–10% of women report their rape experiences to law enforcement. While a higher proportion of people may disclose their experiences to researchers when they are asked about victimization than they spontaneously disclose to law enforcement, certainly not all do. In addition, researchers must grapple with and acknowledge limitations of research related to a complex range of situations, such as participants' failure to define (and thus report) an experience as "abuse" (Koss, 1993) as well as a lack of detail when traumatic experiences are described (Lindbolm & Gray, 2010).

Fourth, the previous three issues intersect with the challenges of studying memory outside the lab, particularly autobiographical memory. The practice of drawing conclusions about individual experiences from lab experiments, addressed early on by Sears (1936), remains a problem, particularly in the face of social pressures to discount abuse survivors (Freyd & Gleaves, 1996; Herman, 1992) and to privilege researcher voices (which may or may not be survivor voices) over lay survivor voices, which lack the tonalities or the authority of the academy or the laboratory (Freyd & Quina, 2000). Writing about a project to document abuse in an institution that housed developmentally disabled girls and young women, Malacrida (2006) notes that "…like many other survivor narratives, filled with hidden stories of physical, sexual, economic, psychological, medical and legal abuse, and like other survivor stories about these kinds of abuse, the potential for discrediting these memories is high" (p. 406). The author goes on to note that "From Sigmund Freud, whose patients' reports of sexual abuse from male relatives were so discounted as to form the basis of his theory of oedipal desire and penis envy, to current debates over 'false memory syndrome' that continue to keep vulnerable individuals from disclosing the harms done to them, relatively powerful social actors have consistently had the capacity to discredit and silence the memories of those in the margins" (p. 406).

For many of us doing research on forgetting and misremembering, we inherently have an impact on the legitimacy afforded to survivors' voices from the margins. Researchers are afforded great social power to legitimize viewpoints, referred to as cognitive authority (for related discussion, see Freyd, 1997). Rightly or wrongly, from cable news to magazines, researchers are often credited with the ability to identify Truth. In individual survivor cases, though, this is a power we simply do not have. Thus, our field faces numerous potential pitfalls in terms of what science can tell us about the truth of any one person's experiences. Even when we focus in on some piece of the puzzle of forgetting and misremembering that seems "objective", such as reaction times or imaging data or a checklist of remembered words from a list, it is incumbent on us to interpret that work in the particular socio-political context in which we labor. Currently, the context continues to be one where researcher voices are privileged over survivor voices. The legitimacy offered to researchers comes with a responsibility to approach research on forgetting and misremembering with tremendous humility, honesty, and open-mindedness, and with full awareness that our conclusions have an impact on the extent to which survivors' voices on the margins are further legitimized or diminished (Freyd & Quina, 2000).

Research Findings on Victim Forgetting Generally

Given the myriad challenges in research on forgetting (e.g., victim under-reporting, difficulty defining and measuring constructs), the consistency with which forgetting (including failure to report or recall all or part of an abusive experience) is reported across studies is actually quite impressive. While the percentages of participants who report forgetting varies with the methods, definitions, and populations sampled, a diverse range of research studies and case reports consistently reveal a substantial proportion of adult survivors who experience a period of partial or complete forgetting for childhood abuse.

Though physical and emotional abuse have been linked to forgetting (as have other traumatic events, such as exposure to war), childhood sexual abuse (CSA) generally leads to greater disruption (Elliott, 1997); therefore, we focus on CSA in this review. Table 1 provides a brief snapshot of studies that have reported memory disruptions among CSA survivors. Across studies, several factors emerge in terms of links to increased memory disruption. While the factors are discussed in turn, these factors often co-occur within a single victim, and a predictor which may be statistically significant must nonetheless be interpreted in the larger context of the abusive dynamic.

Also indicated in Table 1, many studies suggest the experience of forgetting is not usually an all-or-nothing amnesia. In fact, most studies describe a continuum between complete forgetting and always remembering, here referred to as "partial forgetting." (e.g., Crowley, 2007; Gold, Hughes, & Swingle, 1999). Examples include forgetting some of the abusive incidents but not all; remembering physical abuse but not sexual abuse; or experiencing confusion about details of the original experience. Furthermore, the memory itself may be piecemeal, and may involve more primal senses such as taste or odor, feelings of pressure or touch memories, with or without accompanying visual, auditory, or narrative memory (Stoler, 2001).

Clinical versus Non-clinical Samples. Among 30 women in long-term treatment for severe and enduring abuse, Crowley (2007) found that 33% reported partial forgetting, while 47% reported complete forgetting. Gold et al. (1999) found rates of 37% and 27% for partial and complete forgetting, and Briere and Conte (1993) reported forgetting in 59% of 450 men and women in treatment. In contrast, Epstein and Bottoms (2002) and Freyd, DePrince, and Zurbriggen (2001) each found that only 14% of college students who reported childhood sexual abuse also reported forgetting, and Melchert (1996) and Melchert and Parker (1997) reported rates of 18% and 20%, respectively. Studies using national samples report slightly higher rates, between 30% and 52% (Elliott & Briere, 1995; Fish & Scott, 1998; Fivush & Edwards, 2004; Wilsnack, Wonderlich, Kristjanson, Vogeltanz-Holm, & Wisnack, 2002).

Table 1 Rates of forgetting for CSA across representative research studies

Study	Sample	% forgetting CSA	Factors increasing forgetting
Allard (2009)	79 Japanese male and female students; 53% reporting medium – and 47% reporting high – betrayal abuses	68% across types of trauma	Greater for high and medium than for low betrayal
Briere and Conte (1993)	450 men and women in therapy	59%	Earlier onset and more enduring abuse
Chu et al. (1999)	74 women inpatients reporting CSA	26% partial 34% complete	Earlier age of onset. (Earlier age also associated with PTSD and elevated DES scores.)
Couacaud (1999)	112 women	59%	
Crowley (2007)	30 women patients with severe, long term CSA from multiple abusers	33% partial 47% complete	Abuse perpetrated by caretaker
Dale and Allen (1998)	24 outpatients, 12 therapists, men and women, reporting CSA	16.5% partial 30% complete (overlapping categories due to multiple abuses)	
Elliott and Briere (1995)	152 women, 70 men reporting CSA in national stratified random sample	22% "some period" (partial) 20% complete	More threats, more distressing experience; earlier mean age of onset for complete than for partial group. No effect of age at onset, duration, frequency, penetration, incest, number of abusers, use of force
Epstein and Bottoms (2002)	104 college women reporting CSA	14%	Greater for abuse by trusted caregiver with betrayal (45%) and trusted caregiver plus shame (28%)
Feldman-Summers and Pope (1994)	24 male, 46 female APA members reporting CSA	53% for abuse by relative 44% for abuse by nonrelative	Greater number of abuses Nonsignificant tendency for age of onset and duration of abuse

(continued)

Table 1 (continued)

Study	Sample	% forgetting CSA	Factors increasing forgetting
Fish and Scott (1998)	135 male and female members of American Counseling Association reporting CSA	52%	Secrecy demanded by abuser Did not tell anyone
Fivush and Edwards (2004)	12 women reporting CSA by family member	50%	
Freyd et al. (2001)	74 college students reporting CSA	14%	Perpetrated by caretaker, regardless of age of onset or duration
Ghetti, et al. (2006)	137 women involved in legal proceedings for CSA as children; prospective study.	15%	More severe abuse, less involvement with legal system
Gold et al. (1999)	167 female outpatients	37% partial 37% complete	Younger at time of abuse
Goodman, et al. (2003)	175 young adults (141 females) involved in legal proceedings for CSA as children; prospective study.	19% did not disclose or denied ever being victim; 3 said charges were false	Younger at time of abuse, more severe abuse, less maternal support
Grassian and Holtzen (1996), reported in Herman and Harvey (1997)	42 men and women abused by same priest	47%	
Herman and Harvey (1997)	77 women in therapy	17% partial 16% complete	
Loftus, et al. (1994)	55 women in outpatient substance abuse treatment	12% some aspects of event 19% complete	No effect of incest, violence
Melchert (1996); Melchert and Parker (1997)	College women (n=72 and 110)	18% and 20%	Perpetrated by trusted caregiver (parent or stepparent); experienced betrayal
Melchert (1999)	25 college students reporting CSA	32%	More incidents, greater severity; no effect of age of onset
Schultz et al. (2003)	82 college women reporting CSA	38%	Family substance abuse, multiple perpetrators, emotional closeness to abuser.

Stoler (2001)	26 adult women reporting CSA	58%	Younger at age of abuse, more closely related to abuser
Widom and Morris (1997)	75 women with documented CSA histories, prospective study	32% did not report in interview 20 years later	Under 5 years old; Perpetrator an older person against their will
Williams (1995)	129 women with hospital records of CSA, prospective study	38% did not report; 16% had earlier period of forgetting	Younger at onset of abuse
Wilsnack, et al. (2002)	106 women reporting CSA from a national probability sample	26.5% (intrafamilial) 31.2% extrafamilial	Less support from mother

Clinical studies may in part reflect a bias in recruiting clients from agencies that specialize in treating trauma-related issues, who have self-selected as needing intervention with their recovery process. However, it is also the case that survivors who seek clinical intervention are often those with more traumatic experiences and more difficulties overcoming the myriad of symptoms associated with those experiences. Indeed, severe sexual abuse has been associated with higher levels of a wide range of symptoms, including PTSD and dissociative disorders, both of which have as symptoms memory disruptions. Chu, Frey, Ganzel, and Matthews (1999) reported that among 70 women inpatients reporting child sexual abuse, those with an earlier age of onset not only experienced greater memory disruption, but also were more likely to be diagnosed with PTSD and to score higher on the Dissociative Experiences Scale (DES). Although not analyzed with the rest of their data, Goodman et al. (2003) noted that in a subsample, those who reported forgetting also had higher DES scores. These findings are consistent with the relationship between peri-traumatic dissociation of combat, motor vehicle or disaster trauma and the development later of more serious symptoms of PTSD than in similarly trauma-exposed individuals with no dissociative symptoms (DePrince, Chu, & Visvanathan, 2006; Marmar et al., 1994; Koopman, Classen, & Spiegel 1994; Ursano et al., 1999). Further, these findings are consistent with BTT insofar as BTT implicates dissociation as potentially important to unawareness (Freyd, 1996).

Abuse Severity. As noted, while forgetting has been reported for other childhood abuses (physical and emotional), the level of disruption tends to be greater for CSA (e.g., Epstein & Bottoms, 2002; Melchert, 1999). Within CSA comparisons, the rate of forgetting is greater for those abused by an older person against their will (Widom & Morris, 1997) and in those whose court documents reveal more severe assaults (Ghetti et al., 2006). Interestingly, Melchert (1999) found that while survivors of more severe abuse reported more disruption for memory of their abusive experience(s), general childhood memory was not affected by abuse severity. Expanding the definition of severity to include the terror associated with the abusive experience, Elliott and Briere (1995) found that more threats made to the child by the abuser and more distress reported at the time of the abuse were predictors of memory disruption, while the use of force and penetration were not.

Age of Abuse Onset. Several studies suggest that very young children are more likely to forget abuse (e.g., Loftus, Garry, & Feldman, 1994; Widom & Morris, 1997; Williams, 1995), although such associations are not always observed (e.g., Melchert, 1999). Inconsistencies in observing associations between age and memory suggest that "age of onset" is probably not a singular predictor. For example, Elliott and Briere (1995) did not find that age of onset was an overall predictor of forgetting, but did observe that those reporting complete amnesia were on average younger at the time of the abuse onset than those with partial amnesia.

Early onset of sexual abuse is likely to be confounded with other characteristics of the abusive experience. For example, abuse by a family member or caregiver often starts at a young age and continues for some period of time (Courtois, 2010), which would then bring into play confounding factors of more severe types of abuse, greater betrayal, less protection from other family members, and the like. Briere and

Conte (1993) make this distinction, noting more memory disruptions among those with earlier onset *and* more enduring abuse. Furthermore, family dynamics that either support the child in resuming a normal life or fail to acknowledge the abuse or support the child (e.g., Ullman, 2007) may interact with other aspects of development (e.g., developing memory systems) to influence memory for the event.

Betrayal Trauma Theory

From a Focus on Individual Characteristics to Social Motivations

As noted previously, BTT focuses on motivations for forgetting, placing the individual victim in a social context to consider the influence of the victim-perpetrator relation. The theory predicts that closer victim-perpetrator relationships will be more strongly related to forgetting and misremembering. A host of studies now document links between the victim-perpetrator relationship and reports of forgetting across multiple data sets collected in diverse samples (e.g., undergraduates, community, help-seeking). Among undergraduates, Freyd et al. (2001) reported that physical and sexual abuse perpetrated by a caregiver was related to higher levels of self-reported memory impairment for the events compared to non-caregiver abuse. In another sample of 174 college students, those who reported memory loss for child sexual abuse were more likely to experience abuse by people who were well-known to them, compared to those who did not have memory loss (Sheiman, 1999). Further, in Epstein and Bottoms' (2002) sample of college women reporting CSA, rates of forgetting jumped dramatically higher, from an overall 14%, for those women who reported their perpetrator had been a trusted caregiver and that they had experienced betrayal (45%) or felt shame (28%).

Supporting BTT, Freyd (1996) reported on re-analyses from several data sets that showed that incestuous abuse was more likely to be forgotten than non-incestuous abuse, including a prospective sample derived from childhood visits to an emergency room and later assessed by Williams (1994, 1995). Similarly, retrospective samples assessed by Cameron (1993) and Feldman-Summers and Pope (1994) also link incestuous abuse to reports of forgetting. In addition, research by Schultz, Passmore, and Yoder (2003) as well as a doctoral dissertation by Stoler (2001) documented similar results. Schultz et al. (2003) noted in their abstract: "Participants reporting memory disturbances also reported significantly higher numbers of perpetrators, chemical abuse in their families, and closer relationships with the perpetrator(s) than participants reporting no memory disturbances." Similarly Stoler (2001) noted in the abstract to a dissertation: "Quantitative comparisons revealed that women with delayed memories were younger at the time of their abuse and more closely related to their abusers."

Stoler recruited 26 adult women who had been sexually abused as children, and found that 15 (58%) reported a period of forgetting. In qualitative interviews, the women reporting a period of forgetting described their relationship with the abuser in ambiguous or even positive terms: a father or stepfather who was well-liked by others, who was kind and loving during the daytime while abusive at night. In contrast, women with continuous memories reported either no ongoing relationship with the abuser, or an always-distrustful, negative dynamic: a neighbor, a father who was abusive with everyone. The family dynamic also differentiated the two groups. Forgetters described initial attempts to tell someone which were met with no action at best or negative consequences at worst, while others just said simply they knew they could not tell anyone. Women with continuous memories, on the other hand, were more likely to have told someone and to have been supported, even when the abuse did not stop.

Two prospective studies (Goodman et al., 2003; Williams, 1995) examined links between children's perceived level of support from their mothers and reporting, documenting that that less perceived support was associated with failure to report the abusive experience in subsequent interviews. Fish and Scott (1998) surveyed 432 members of the American Counseling Association and found that among those reporting CSA, forgetting was greater for those who had kept the abuse a secret, either because of threats from the abuser or because they were not able to tell anyone. These studies point to another aspect of CSA: the family dynamic in which abuse takes place matters for outcomes. In particular, treatment by non-abusive family members can also be harmful. Whitmire, Harlow, Quina and Morokoff (1999) found that among adult women, a history of CSA was strongly associated with a more negative family environment while growing up. Herman (1981) found that women incest survivors described their mothers as unable or unwilling to protect them, in contrast to women with fathers they felt were potential abusers but who had not acted that out.

More recently, research relevant to BTT has been extended cross-culturally. Allard (2009) studied betrayal in a sample of Japanese college students. Participants were asked to describe their full range of traumas, as well as the level of betrayal associated with each. These traumas were subsequently categorized according to level of betrayal (high, medium, and low), with sexual abuse among the high-betrayal acts. Allard reported that forgetting was more often reported for those experiences that were also experienced as high and medium betrayal than low.

Not surprisingly given the complexity of issues involved in studying forgetting of abuse, several studies report data that have been interpreted as inconsistent with BTT. For example, Goodman et al. (2003) reported that they failed to find a statistically significant relationship between betrayal trauma and memory impairment in a sample of adults who had been involved in child abuse prosecution cases during childhood. However, involvement in child abuse protection cases meant that the abuse was discovered and likely discussed repeatedly with the victims. Repeated discussion of the event and other consequences of disclosure (e.g., removal of the offender) are likely to affect memory and victim functioning, making the Goodman sample quite different from those reviewed above. In addition to the unusual nature of this sample, it is not clear whether there was simply insufficient statistical power to detect any relationship between betrayal trauma exposure and memory (see Zurbriggen & Becker-Blease, 2003).

Recent work by Lindblom and Gray (2010) points to the importance of considering the means by which researchers assess forgetting as well as the importance of BTT to understanding motivation. The studies described above largely involved participants' beliefs about their memories – that is, whether memories had ever been forgotten and if so, to what degree (an important exception to this tendency is work by Williams (1995), who compared women's reports of life experiences to documented abuse from an emergency room 17 years earlier). Lindblom and Gray measured narrative detail provided by a sample of undergraduates who met Criterion A of the PTSD diagnosis and who rated the abuse as their most distressing trauma. The authors operationalized memory in terms of word count in the narrative; perhaps because it is a highly variable measure and perhaps because of their small number of participants, word count was not significantly associated with most of their predictors. They found "more betrayal was associated with less detailed trauma narratives (p. 1)"; however, they concluded their results could be explained by factors other than BTT, such as survivor age, PTSD avoidance symptoms, and gender. Freyd, Klest, and DePrince (2010) pointed out that several problems with that conclusion. For example, it is not obvious that BTT would predict that memory for betrayal traumas should lead to the use of fewer words (even though a negative relationship between betrayal and avoidance was observed in these data). In addition, other research now suggests that betrayal trauma may mediate gender-PTSD links (Tang & Freyd, in press). Perhaps most importantly, though, Lindblom and Gray (2010) treat PTSD-Avoidance as unrelated to BTT, while Freyd et al. (2010) note that avoidance is indeed a form of unawareness. Further, Lindblom and Gray (2010) assessed memory in terms of the current narratives provided by college students, implicitly assuming that unawareness (as tapped by their word count measure) would continue into young adulthood when the pressure to maintain abusive attachments is presumably less than in childhood. BTT does not require indefinite unawareness – rather, the theory describes motivation for forgetting in the context of attachment and survival goals, which will of course change over time as relationships change.

In contrast to Lindblom and Gray (2010), O'Rinn, Lishak, Muller, and Classen (under review) interviewed 110 treatment-seeking women, all of whom reported histories of childhood sexual abuse (and many of whom reported histories of childhood physical or emotional abuse as well). Women who reported abuse by a parental figure (a high betrayal trauma) reported greater feelings of betrayal than women abused by a non-parental figure. Further, women who reported abuse by a parental figure also reported greater recovery of memories than those abused by a non-parental figure, though the groups did not differ in their reports of the clarity of memories. The question of how abuse survivors' own assessment of their betrayal, as measured by O'Rinn and colleagues, relates to outcomes is an interesting one. BTT suggests that abuse survivors will be less aware of betrayal while it is ongoing, processes that studies of adult survivors of childhood abuse are less likely to tap. As noted in considering Lindbolm and Gray's (2010) findings, the BTT framework does not directly address victim/survivor responses once the abuse has ended. DePrince, Chu, and Pineda (2011) take up these issues in work examining women's perceptions of betrayal by abusive intimate partners. They found that, consistent with BTT, less awareness of betrayal was associated with higher dissociation for recent abuse. Thus, researchers should consider the current abusive context in interpreting findings, particularly if there is no longer dependence between the victim and perpetrator.

Disentangling Motivation and Mechanism

BTT lays out issues related to the *motivation* for victim forgetting; the theory was not developed to identify or require particular cognitive mechanisms by which forgetting occurs. Indeed, explications of the mechanisms should be examined separately from those of the motivations for their occurrence. However, while BTT does not specify mechanisms by which forgetting can or must occur, the theory can certainly inform work related to mechanisms. For example, Anderson (e.g., Anderson, 2001; Anderson et al., 2004; Anderson & Huddleston, 2012) has conducted extensive work on inhibitory processes in memory, drawing specifically on BTT. As early as 2001, Anderson noted: "The proposal offered here is that betrayal traumas are much more likely to create circumstances conducive to retrieval-induced forgetting, and thus suppression, than are cases of stranger abuse" (p. 202). In addition, the study by Lindblom and Gray (2010) described above may point to the importance of avoidance mechanisms that could contribute to awareness.

Given links between dissociation and familial abuse, it has been reasonable to evaluate the role that dissociation may play in relation to unawareness and betrayal. In his seminal book on the development of dissociation, Putnam (1997) notes that the "relationship to the perpetrator emerged as a powerful predictor of pertinent outcome measures" (p. 50) in his longitudinal research with sexually abused girls. Indeed, Putnam talks at great length about the interactions of the family environment and developmental processes in the development of dissociation.

Several datasets link dissociation and betrayal traumas. For example, Chu and Dill (1990) reported that childhood abuse by family members (both physical and sexual) was significantly related to increased dissociation scores (as measured by the Dissociative Experiences Scale) in psychiatric inpatients. However, abuse by nonfamily members was not significantly associated with dissociation. Plattner et al. (2003) report that they found significant correlations between symptoms of pathological dissociation and intrafamilial (but not extrafamilial) trauma in a sample of delinquent juveniles. Freyd, Klest, and Allard (2005) and Goldsmith, Freyd, and DePrince (in press) report that high betrayal trauma exposure predicts dissociative symptoms in chronically ill participants and college students respectively. DePrince (2005) reported that the presence (versus absence) of betrayal trauma before the age of 18 was associated with pathological dissociation and with revictimization after age 18. In a study of mothers and school-aged children, maternal dissociation was significantly and positively related to maternal betrayal trauma history (Chu & DePrince, 2006). In particular, the number of betrayal trauma types to which women had been exposed predicted higher levels of dissociation. Further, mothers who reported exposure to one or more betrayal traumas reported significantly higher dissociation scores than mothers who reported no betrayal trauma exposure. In addition, children exposed to betrayal trauma events also had higher dissociation scores than their peers without betrayal trauma exposure. Finally, both mothers' and children's histories of betrayal trauma exposures were found to significantly predict children's dissociation. Hulette, Kaehler, and Freyd (2011) report similar intergenerational effects for mothers and children with betrayal trauma histories.

In addition, still other studies demonstrate links between familial experiences more generally and dissociation. For example, Mann and Sanders (1994) reported that dissociation was associated with parental rejection and inconsistency in applying discipline among boys (N=40). In a longitudinal study, Ogawa, Sroufe, Weinfield, Carlson, and Egeland (1997) observed that disorganized or avoidant attachment styles in child in relation to their mothers increased the risk for developing dissociation in adolescence. Interestingly, higher levels of dissociation were linked to decreased likelihood of disclosing childhood sexual abuse in a sample of young adults who had participated in criminal justice proceedings related to the abuse approximately 10 years earlier (Goodman et al., 2003), demonstrating the complex inter-relationships among factors in this line of research. To the extent that dissociation is linked to decrease likelihood of disclosure of CSA, this has an effect on the phenomenon we can observe in the lab.

Given links between dissociation and disruptions in memory (e.g., Putnam, 1997) and/or decreased disclosure of abuse (e.g., Goodman et al., 2003) in applied research, many researchers (including Freyd and her colleagues) have turned to basic laboratory tasks to examine dissociation and cognitive functioning with the hope that such a line of work could inform models of forgetting. Freyd and her colleagues have repeatedly documented links between high levels of dissociation and alterations in basic cognitive processing in the lab (e.g., Freyd et al., 1998; DePrince & Freyd, 2001, 2004; DePrince, Freyd, & Malle, 2007). Several researchers other than Freyd have also documented links between dissociation and alterations in attention and memory. Some of this work documents links directly between dissociation and disruptions in memory in the lab, such as work by Moulds and Bryant (2002). Moulds and Bryant compared participants diagnosed with Acute Stress Disorder (ASD; which is partially characterized by dissociative symptoms; see Spiegel & Cardeña, 1991) with non-traumatized participants on a directed forgetting task, where participants were directed to remember some words and forget others; and later tested on all words. The ASD group had poorer recall of to-be-forgotten trauma-related words than the non-traumatized group. In a replication and extension, Moulds and Bryant (2005) found that membership in a trauma-exposed ASD group was associated with reduced recall compared to trauma-exposed-no-ASD and no-trauma groups. In addition to the specific example offered in Moulds and Bryant's research, many studies conducted by researchers other than Freyd document links between dissociation and alterations in memory and attention function in the lab, including but not limited to: Chiu et al. (2010), Chiu, Yeh, Huang,

Wu, and Chiu (2009), DePrince, Weinzierl, and Combs (2008), De Ruiter, Phaf, Veltman, Kok, and Van Dyck (2003), De Ruiter, Phaf, Elzinga, and Van Dyck 2004, Dorahy, Irwin, and Middleton 2004, Dorahy, Middleton, and Irwin, 2005, Elzinga et al. (2007), Simeon (2006) and Veltman et al. (2005).

While some have argued or implied that specific failures to document forgetting in laboratory tasks (e.g., that involve memorizing lists of words) diminishes the validity of BTT (e.g., Devilly et al., 2007; McNally, 2012) or of forgetting for abuse altogether, such arguments simply do not make sense (see, e.g., Freyd et al., 2007). Failure to identify mechanisms in the lab does not mean that phenomena do not exist in the real world; rather, failure to identify mechanisms in the lab simply means researchers have not yet identified and/or manipulated conditions in the lab in a way that reflects the real world. Brewin (2007) notes problems with some of the critiques leveled based on laboratory findings:

> More recent evidence…indicates that dissociative reactions at the time of the trauma are linked both with a disturbance in voluntary trauma memories and with an increased risk of involuntary trauma memories. Individuals with high levels of dissociative symptoms are less likely to disclose previously documented abuse in their childhoods (Goodman et al., 2003), and are superior at forgetting trauma words (Moulds & Bryant, 2002, 2005). DePrince and Freyd (2001, 2004) conducted directed forgetting experiments with healthy volunteers who were low or high in trait dissociation, requiring them to forget neutral and trauma-related words. They reported that the high dissociators were superior at forgetting trauma words, but only when they were distracted by having a secondary cognitive task. McNally Ristuccia, and Perlman (2005) conducted a similar experiment with groups of individuals reporting continuous memories of sexual abuse, recovered memories of abuse, or no abuse, but failed to support the prediction that the recovered memory group would be better at forgetting trauma words under divided attention conditions. However, it is not clear whether McNally et al.'s recovered memory group reported more betrayal trauma or were more highly dissociative, the two factors identified as critical by DePrince and Freyd. (p. 241)

Brewin (2007) goes onto note: "These results are consistent with clinical views about the importance of defensive mental processes that affect attention and memory. Although there is little firm evidence yet to link these processes to the forgetting of trauma, there is ample reason to believe they are clinically relevant and will repay additional clinical and experimental investigation" (p. 241).

In recent years, Freyd and her colleagues have documented important links between betrayal trauma exposure and a range of negative outcomes. For example, Freyd, Klest, and Allard (2005) found that a history of betrayal trauma was strongly associated with physical and mental health symptoms, including dissociative symptoms, in a sample of ill individuals. Goldsmith et al. (in press) reported similar results in a sample of college students. In addition, Reichmann-Decker, DePrince, and McIntosh (2009) found that women who reported exposure to high-betrayal abuse (compared to those who did not report such exposure) showed alterations in basic, automatic emotional processes in the lab that were consistent with caregiving-maintenance goals in an abusive environment.

Several other researchers have also documented links between exposure to traumas high in betrayal and negative outcomes. For example, Edwards, Freyd, Dube,

Anda, and Felitti (in press) used data from the second wave collected as part of the Adverse Childhood Experiences (ACE) Study (Felitti et al., 1998) to test the hypothesis that social betrayal is harmful to a variety of health outcomes. In particular, Edwards et al. compared adults whose abuser was a family member or non-relative living in the home to those whose abuser was a family friend, relative living outside the home, or a stranger on several health outcomes. Participants in this second wave included slightly less than 7,000 of the original ACE sample (N = 17,337). A total of 3,100 (17.4%) participants reported one form of childhood sexual abuse (fondling, attempted intercourse, or intercourse) and also identified their abuser. As reviewed by Freyd et al. (2007), Edwards and colleagues documented that "Of sexual abuse survivors, 32% reported exposure to events high in betrayal, defined as an abuser who was a family or nonfamily member living in the home. High-betrayal abuse was related to depression, anxiety, suicidality, panic, and anger. High-betrayal participants had poorer health functioning on the SF-36 role-physical, role-emotional, and social functioning scales than low-betrayal victims." The Edwards et al. study is in line with other research that suggests abuse perpetrated by caregivers is associated with worse outcomes than non-caregiver abuse. For example, Atlas and Ingram (1998) reported that, in a sample of 34 hospitalized adolescents (aged 14–17 years), sexual distress was associated with histories of abuse by family members as compared to no abuse or abuse by a non-family member, whereas post-traumatic stress was not. Turell and Armsworth (2003) compared sexual abuse survivors who self-mutilate with those who do not. The authors reported that self-mutilators were more likely to have experienced familial relative to non-familial abuse. Using a sample of trauma survivors, Kelley (2009) compared the impact of perceptions of life threat and perceptions of betrayal in predicting PTSD. Kelley found a modest association between life threat and PTSD and a strong association between betrayal and PTSD. Using a sample of college student participants, Kaehler and Freyd (2009) found an association between high and medium betrayal trauma exposure and borderline personality characteristics. These results were replicated for women in an adult community sample, whereas men showed a different pattern (Kaehler & Freyd, in press).

Misremembering: The Literature on False Events in Memory

BTT focuses not only on forgetting, but also misremembering abuse as a means by which victims maintain attachments to abusive others on whom they depend (Freyd, 1998). We turn now to research on the conditions under which memory errors occur, particularly errors of misremembering or reconstruction. We will briefly review the literature on "false memories" to identify the kinds of memory errors people make as well as the conditions under which those errors are most likely to occur. While this literature has often been used to question the validity of victims' memories, we extend discussion to consider the implications of this work for misremembering abuse events as more positive (or less negative) than they were.

Cognitive Components Underlying the Construction of False Memories

We turn first to examining the cognitive conditions under which false events are more or less likely to be planted in memory. As recently as 2009, Bernstein and Loftus reported that "Many cases of allegedly recovered memories have turned out to be false memories implanted by well-meaning therapists who use suggestion and imagination to guide the search for memories" (p. 372). Their conclusion was based primarily on the results of Loftus and Pickrell (1995) who reported that 25% of their 24 participants remembered either "fully or partially," a false childhood event (i.e., being lost in a shopping mall) that was suggested by a close relative. However, it is clear that all life events are not equally likely to be planted in memory. What types of events are relatively more or less likely to be planted in memory and what are the cognitive operations that underlie this process?

In a model first proposed by Pezdek, Finger, and Hodge (1997), it was predicted that a necessary condition for planting a suggested event in memory is that the suggested event must first be considered true. Accordingly, *plausible* events – those perceived as having a high probability of occurrence for individuals in the cohort tested – should be more likely to be suggestively planted in memory than implausible events. In fact, studies by Pezdek et al. (1997) with adults and Pezdek and Hodge (1999) with children confirmed this prediction: plausible false events (e.g., being lost in a shopping mall) were more likely to be suggestively planted in memory than implausible false events (e.g., receiving a rectal enema).

The effect of plausibility can likely account for the finding that imagining oneself performing an event increases individuals' belief that the event had actually occurred to them (Garry & Polaschek, 2000; Mazzoni & Memon, 2003). Imagining oneself performing an event – like actually experiencing the event or viewing a doctored up photograph of oneself performing an event (Wade, Garry, Read, & Lindsay, 2002) – serves to increase the perceived plausibility of the event. However, Pezdek, Blandón-Gitlin, and Gabbay (2006a) reported that whereas imagining plausible events increased people's belief that the event had occurred to them, imagining implausible events had no effect on people's autobiographical beliefs.

Although plausible events are more likely to be suggestively planted in memory than implausible events, what makes an event plausible, and plausible to whom? When conveying to participants what the plausibility of an event is, the instructions indicate the prevalence rate of the event for individuals in a specific reference group. Blandón-Gitlin and Pezdek (under review) tested the hypothesis that when the reference group upon which the reported prevalence ratings are based has more in common with an individual, the group will be more likely to affect the individual's own autobiographical beliefs and memories than when the reference group has less in common with the individual, even if the individual is literally a member of both groups. In this study with college students, knowing the prevalence rate of a target event among "other college students like you" (i.e., *cohort plausibility*) affected participants' own autobiographical beliefs significantly more than did knowing the prevalence rate of "adults in a nationwide poll" (i.e., *general plausibility*). In light of the fact that the likelihood of forgotten memories of child sexual abuse has been reported to be a relatively implausible event both personally and in cohort members (Pezdek & Blandón-Gitlin, 2008), the results of this study suggest that the probability of planting a false memory of sexual abuse, for example in therapy, is likely to be low except when it is suggested that this event is likely to have occurred to other people who have much in common with the client. Simply knowing that rates of sexual abuse are relatively high in the general population is not likely to lead an individual to believe that they themselves may have been sexually abused.

According to the model of Pezdek et al. (1997), once an event is judged to be true, details of the generic script for the event as well as details from related episodes of the event are "transported" in memory and used to construct a memory for the suggested false event. It should thus be the case that the more one knows about a suggested event (that is, the greater the corpus of an individual's relevant background knowledge), the more likely it is that the suggested event will be incorporated into memory. To test this component of the model, Pezdek, Blandon-Gitlin, Lam, Hart, and Schooler (2006b) independently manipulated plausibility (the prevalence rate for the target event was described as high or low) and background knowledge (detailed descriptive information about the target event was presented or not). The main effect of each of these factors significantly affected individuals' beliefs that the target event had occurred to them in childhood. Similar results have been reported by others, including Mazzoni, Loftus, and Kirsch (2001). However, it is important to note that the background information provided only influenced people's beliefs about an event that was more consonant with their personal experiences. For example, if background details are presented about a target event administered in a hospital, and the individual knows that she was never in the hospital as a child, providing this background information is not likely to affect her belief that the suggested target event had occurred to her. These findings suggest that gaining knowledge about sexual abuse may be more likely to produce false memories of sexual abuse if one possesses relevant experiences to which that knowledge might apply. For example, gaining knowledge about sexual abuse might be more likely to influence the memories of individuals who recall dysfunctional relationships to which additional sexual details could be added, and be less likely to influence memories of individuals without dysfunctional childhood relationships.

The final major cognitive component underlying the construction of false events in memory occurs when the source of a suggested event is misattributed to that of an event actually experienced. When this occurs, a suggested event is likely to be erroneously judged to have actually occurred. However, these source misattribution errors do not always transpire. Once a memory for a suggested false event has been constructed, can it be discriminated from a memory for an event actually experienced? Yes, usually so. According to Johnson, Foley, Suengas, and Raye (1988), (see also Johnson, Raye, Mitchell, & Ankudowich, 2012), and more current research recently reviewed by Lindsay (2009), memories for experienced events are stored and embedded in memory within an elaborate informational network that typically includes a significant quantity of perceptual details (e.g., color, sound, and smell) and contextual information (e.g., time and place). On the other hand, memories for imagined or otherwise non-experienced events typically include less perceptual and contextual information and rather have more information about the cognitive processes that produced them. In fact, among the seven studies in which the phenomenal characteristics of memory for perceived versus suggested or imagined events were reviewed by Pezdek and Taylor (1999), in the majority of these studies, participants' (a) ratings of their confidence, (b) their ratings of the sensory clarity of their memories, and (c) the verbosity of their memory descriptions were significantly higher for perceived than for non-perceived events.

Recently, Blandón-Gitlin, Pezdek, Lindsay, and Hagan (2009) extended these findings to assess whether accounts of true events could be discriminated from accounts of suggested events that were believed to be true. Using the criterion-based content analysis (CBCA) and CBCA-trained judges, CBCA scores (as well as self-report memory measures) were significantly higher for accounts of true events than suggested events. However, for participants with "full" memories for the suggested event, there was no significant difference in ratings between conditions. Thus, although memories for true events can generally be discriminated from memories for false events, for a subset of individuals in the Blandón-Gitlin et al. (2009) study, those who had developed specially compelling false memories for events that were believed to have been experienced, CBCA ratings of these memories were similar to those of memories for true events actually experienced.

Suggestively Changing a Memory Rather than Planting a New Memory

The majority of research on memory suggestibility has used a three-stage procedure that dates back to the mid-1970s (Loftus, 1975; Loftus, Miller, & Burns, 1978; Pezdek, 1977). In this classic approach, individuals view a sequence of slides, a videotape, or a film of an event (often a traffic accident or a robbery) in the *presentation stage*. In the *suggestion stage*, the individuals are read a narrative or are asked some questions that intentionally mislead them about the identity of the target item (the misled condition), or they do not receive the misleading information (the control condition). In the *test stage*, participants are given a recognition or recall test for the original event. If memory for the target events is more accurate in the control condition than in the misled condition, this is taken as evidence for the suggestibility effect; that is, individuals have been misled by the post-event information in the suggestion phase. This is a robust effect: across numerous studies over the past 35-years, differences of 20–30% between performance on misled and control items have generally been reported.

This research on the suggestibility of memory is often used to support the claim that it is relatively easy to suggestively influence memory, to mislead people to believe that an event has occurred when it in fact has not. However, there is an important difference between the structure of this generalization claim and the structure of the source experiments on suggestibility. Whereas most of the suggestibility studies are structured such that event A occurs, event B is suggested, and memory is tested for A versus B, in the generalization claim regarding planting entirely new memories, A never occurs, A is suggested, and memory is tested for A versus not-A. In the first case, memory for an event that actually occurred is changed. In the second case, memory for an event that did not occur is planted. In the few studies that have used a procedure that involves suggestively planting (rather than changing) details that never occurred (e.g., Lane, & Zaragoza, 2007; Zaragoza, & Lane, 1994), what was suggested was a detail in an event sequence and not an entirely new event that had never occurred.

What evidence is there that planting event memories and changing event memories involve different cognitive processes and have different probabilities of occurrence? Pezdek and Roe (1997) tested 4-year old and 10-year old children on their relative vulnerability to suggestibility for changed, planted, and erased memories. Each child was touched in a specific way, or they were not touched at all, and it was later suggested that a different touch, a completely new touch, or no touch at all had occurred. The suggestibility effect occurred only in the changed memory condition, but not in the planted or erased memory condition. This finding is consistent with the false memory model of Pezdek et al. (1997) mentioned above. According to this model, a false memory for an event is constructed from details of the generic script for the event as well as details from related episodes of the event. In suggestively changing a memory for an event that actually occurred, memory for what transpired would remain intact with the exception of the altered details which would replace or over-ride the relevant details in memory. In suggestively planting a whole new memory, all of the details used to construct the suggested event in memory would be transported from the generic script for the event and from related episodes. The resulting memory would thus be more similar to the original memory in the changed than the planted memory condition, and thus more likely to be held as true. Thus, although it is relatively easy to change memory for a detail of an event that did occur, it is relatively more difficult to plant a memory for an event that did not occur.

Constructing Memories: Implications for Misremembering

What evidence is there that autobiographical memory is constructed rather than simply being a recording of one's life experiences, and what factors affect this constructive process? Significant evidence suggests that the onset of autobiographical memory begins with the onset of language (Nelson, 1993a), and parent–child talk about present and past life events affects how children remember these events (Nelson, 1993b). Tessler and Nelson (1994) reported a study in which three and a half year old children were observed during a museum visit with their mothers. The mother–children conversations were recorded. Children were interviewed in their homes 1 week later and asked to tell what they remembered of the visit to the museum. No child in either group recalled (free recall or prompted recall) any objects that had been seen but not talked about in a parent–child conversation; the parent–child conversation was a necessary condition for children's memory. Further, the content and style of each child's conversation tended to mirror that of his or her mother's conversation. Similar results have been reported by Fivush (1991).

These results supports Nelson's model of memory development. According to this model, talk between adults and children serves to structure children's experience, and this talk is internalized in the children's mental representation and subsequent recall of the experience. Thus, the way that adults construe events experienced by a child, and convey that construal to the child through language, affects how the event is remembered by the child. Accordingly, children's memory for the events of their life – their autobiographical memory – could relatively easily be socially constructed by the parent–child conversations that occur regarding these events. For example, consistent with BTT, conversations with parents, relatives, and older siblings could easily misconstrue the troubling events of one's childhood to have been happy events, and explain how troubling events could be *misremembered or reconstructed* otherwise.

The broader literature on memory errors in laboratory tasks (see DePrince, Allard, Oh, & Freyd, 2004) has important implications for misremembering. One of the most widely used tasks to study memory errors has been the Deese-Roediger-McDermott (DRM) paradigm. In the DRM, participants are asked to study a list of related words. During a later recognition task, a critical lure – a related word that was not presented with the original list – is presented. The sorts of memory errors in which a word that is related but was not presented is recalled – have been described as "false memories" and used to try to understand the risk for and experience of false memories for abuse. Indeed, in various studies with participants who report continuous versus discontinuous memories for abuse, the DRM paradigm is used to assess memory function, and presumably vulnerability for "false memories".

For example, Geraerts et al. (2009), (see also Geraerts, 2012) used the DRM as well as another task to estimate prior remembering in a sample of 120 adults who were classified into four groups: participants with spontaneously-recovered memories (recalled outside of therapy); recovered-in-suggestive-therapy memories; continuous memories; and control group (no reported abuse history). The groups did not differ in rates of overall correct recall of words presented during the DRM task. However, participants with recovered-in-suggestive-therapy memories were more likely to erroneously recall (and recognize) critical lures (that is, a related but not studied word) than participants in the other three groups. The same pattern was reported for recognition memory (though recognition memory was not independent of recall). The authors conclude:

> As a group, people who believed that they had recovered a memory of CSA through suggestive therapeutic techniques showed a pronounced tendency to incorrectly claim that they had experienced events that they had not really experienced, as measured by a simple cognitive test of false memory formation. To the extent that this pattern on the DRM task is indicative of a broader deficit in monitoring the source of one's memories, this finding suggests that such reports of recovered memories should be viewed with a cautious eye, as they may reflect the unwitting interaction of suggestive therapy with preexisting deficits in source memory (p. 96).

Importantly, the "events" that the participants erroneously said they *recognized* were lures; that is, items closely related to words in the list they had in fact studied. Geraerts and colleagues interpret these findings as evidence that the participants' autobiographical memories for abuse should be viewed skeptically, particularly when recalled in therapy.

At least two issues affect interpretation and generalization of these findings. First, Geraerts et al. (2009) data seem to speak less to the problem of erroneously "remembering" a whole new autobiographical memory of a life event that did not occur (e.g., falsely remembering CSA in the context of the reality of a lifetime of pleasant to positive experiences) and more to the importance of studying how people may come to *misremember* details that are related to what they actually experienced. If people in suggestive therapy tend to misremember details of events (in the case of this research, words) that they actually experienced, it remains unclear what implications this has for understanding the accuracy of CSA memories generally (see Freyd & Gleaves, 1996). Second, these data are not representative of all memories recalled in therapy. In fact, the authors focus on a subgroup that they describe as having received suggestive therapy. Thus, we must be cautious not to use these data to impugn memories of CSA generally or those recalled in non-suggestive therapy.

These findings also highlight important questions about the meaning of different types of memory errors in laboratory tasks. The recovered-memories-in-suggestive-therapies group was as accurate as the other groups in terms of correctly recalling the studied words; however, they mis-recalled related words that were not actually presented. Thus, is it not just as reasonable to argue that these findings suggest that participants are actually accurate with regard to the gist of an event, making errors in the details of the event? By analogy to autobiographical memories, then, is it not just as reasonable to argue that these participants are more likely to make errors in details, but to be accurate about the gist of the event (in this case, that CSA occurred)?

Interestingly, much of the research on errors in details for memories, such as the findings presented by Geraerts and colleagues, has focused on possible implications for memory errors in terms of falsely recalling abuse. An equally important question raised by this research, though, is: if some people are prone to misremembering details of actual events, are these people more likely to misremember childhoods that involved abuse as more positive (and less abusive) than they were? Misremembering abusive events may help an individual to maximize unawareness for abuse by a trusted/needed other. If one misremembers an abusive childhood as more positive than it was, this might help short-term survival goals (as described by BTT); however, resolving the psychological and physical consequences of abuse when one misremembers childhood as positive may be confusing to adults trying to make meaning of their experiences.

The literature on source monitoring errors (see Johnson, 2006; Johnson, Raye, Mitchell, & Ankudowich, 2012) is very relevant to how misremembering may contribute to victims' unawareness. As noted by Johnson (2006), "Memories are attributions that we make about our mental experiences based on their subjective qualities, our prior knowledge and beliefs, our motives and goals, and the social context (p. 760)". Johnson's work points to the importance of similarity in source memory errors, noting that "…the most compelling false memories seem to come from importation of features from real memories of actually perceived events rather than from imagination alone (p. 762)." Indeed, the source monitoring literature provides extensive documentation that these sorts of memory errors are more likely to occur when the erroneously recalled information is closely, semantically tied to a real experience. Thus, source monitoring errors may not explain for false memories of abuse in families that did not actually involve some degree of abusive behaviors (as the false information would be too different from the true information). However, this literature may have important implications for misremembering the abuse and/ or abusive family context as more positive/less negative than reality. As noted by Freyd et al. (2007) and Stoler (2001), abusive family contexts often comprise a mix of abusive and caring acts directed at children. Thus, abuse and care are closely tied experiences, providing a context that increases the likelihood of source monitoring errors. Given the survival motivations described by BTT, the same processes that contribute to source monitoring errors may facilitate victims to misremember the family context as more positive that it was.

Could victims misremember childhoods as more positive than they actually were thereby minimizing awareness of abuse? Freyd (1996) writes, "It is generally noted that human beings have a bias toward positive memories…Waldfogel (1948) discovered that adults are more likely to forget unpleasant childhood memories than pleasant ones. Wagenaar (1986) found a similar effect when he studied autobiographical memory" (p. 112–113). Similarly, Greenhoot, McClosky, and Glisky (2005) documented more positive misremembering of childhood by adolescents known to have experienced or witnessed family violence.

Thus, several pieces of evidence suggest that positive misremembering is possible. First, humans (including even violence-exposed teens) have a positivity memory bias. Second, memory errors are more likely to occur when the error is semantically-related to reality (e.g., stimuli presented in DRM and source monitoring paradigms). Third, it is easier to suggestively change a true memory than to plant an entirely new false memory (e.g., Pezdek & Roe, 1997). Fourth, abusive family contexts often also include positive experiences (e.g., Stoler, 2001). Thus, memory processes are amenable to misremembering in ways that can facilitate victim awareness of positive information and unawareness of abuse. Consistent with BTT, victims may misremember family experiences as more positive than they were to minimize awareness of abuse and therefore maintain necessary attachments.

Recovered Memories

BTT is agnostic about when and how memories are "recovered" (for research on potential mechanisms of memory recovery, see inhibitory mechanisms; see Anderson, 2001; Anderson & Huddleston, 2012). However, Freyd (1998) has written

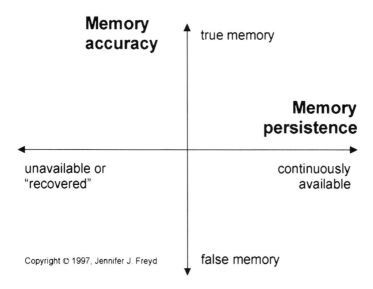

Fig. 1 Schematic depiction of two conceptually separable dimensions of memory that are often confused with one another in the context of the debate about recovered memories of abuse (Figure Copyright Jennifer J. Freyd, 1997. Reprinted with permission)

about the problematic conflation of the concepts of memory accessibility and accuracy. In particular, as illustrated in Fig. 1, Freyd (1998) argues that memory accuracy and accessibility are conceptually independent of one another. An inaccurate memory could be continuously available to someone; and an accurate memory could be unavailable for a period of time (see Freyd et al., 2007 for further discussion). Similarly, the fact that some survivors experience continuous (even intrusive) memories of corroborated traumatic events does not disprove the fact that some survivors experience unawareness (and later awareness) of corroborated recovered memories. Because the accuracy of recovered memories has important implications for the literature on trauma and memory generally as well as implications for BTT, we turn now to consider two central issues. First, what is the evidence (from both legal cases and psychological research) for the question of whether recovered memories can be accurate? And second, what role might trauma therapy play (if any) in the accurate recall of recovered memories?

Accuracy of Recovered Memories: Corroboration Research

In a recent review, Erdelyi (2010) summarizes the state of memory research as follows:

> The research literature since Ebbinghaus has shown unmistakably that—terminology aside—memory for materials "not thought of"/"excluded"/"repressed"/"suppressed"/"inhibited"/"cognitively avoided"/"dissociated"/"censored"/"rejected" from consciousness declines over time.

This rule presumably applies regardless of the motive for the exclusion or the person's consciousness of the exclusion. Thus, successful repression (it is not always successful) should yield amnesia. It has also been shown, as we have seen, that retrieval effort can at least partially reverse the amnesic trend of memory and produce hypermnesia.

Thus, both defensive repression (repression used to avoid upsetting memories, with consequent amnesia) and the recovery of such repressed memories should be obvious and universally accepted in scientific psychology. (Erdelyi, 2010, p. 630).

While a rich history of memory research now documents that unawareness and later recall are possible, considerable dialogue still surrounds the veracity of recovered memories. For better and sometimes worse (as discussed elsewhere, because of problems such as lack of witnesses, fallibility of offender memory), researchers have tended to treat corroboration of recovered memories as the gold standard by which to evaluate the veracity of those memories. As we review below, a substantial number of survivors obtained evidence to support that the abuse on which their recovered memories were based indeed took place. These cases document, therefore, that accurate recall of recovered memories is in fact possible (though, at this juncture, such cases do not help to describe the conditions under which accurate recall is most likely).

It is important, however, to put the issue of corroboration into perspective: a lack of corroboration for trauma does not mean the claim is false.[1] Not all CSA survivors attempt to corroborate their traumatic memories, and among those who do, not all are able to find any evidence, due to the circumstances, deaths of perpetrators and other family members, and the like. The focus on corroborated cases of recovered memory should not be conflated with an expectation that such evidence should exist in every case. An examination of corroborated cases of recovered memory can nevertheless be useful, since the sheer number of these cases disproves the extreme position that such cases do not exist. Furthermore, corroboration has been documented for victims with both continuous and recovered memories of the abuse.

No accepted definition for the term corroboration exists in the fields of psychology or law. In both psychology and law contexts, various kinds of evidence might be considered corroborative, and in turn, corroborative evidence can provide differing levels of proof. If corroboration is defined in the strictest ways, cases with corroboration are unusual, but available. In evaluating the difficulties in classifying abuse allegations in the Child Protective Service context, Herman (2005) notes that sometimes "there is absolutely clear and convincing corroborative evidence that abuse has occurred." In his view, the four best kinds of corroborative evidence are: medical, documentary, eyewitness, and confession. The same categories of evidence appear in many other studies.

---

[1] Until the 1980s, some states required corroboration from external witnesses to proceed with charges of rape, based on the assumption that women and children were prone to lying about sexual assault. These unreasonable requirements frequently prevented women and children from testifying about their own abuse, even when the event had just recently occurred and memories were fresh. Advocacy groups that today dismiss uncorroborated reports of recovered memory are adopting a similar position, often accompanied by the suggestion that women and children experience "false memories," or worse yet, lie about abuse.

As strong as these types of evidence might appear, it is important to note there are potential exceptions to each one. Only some kinds of medical evidence are considered *diagnostic* of sexual abuse; many medical findings are considered *indicative* or *supportive* but not *diagnostic*. Confessions can be false and eyewitness testimony can be erroneous. Documentary evidence, such as photographs or videotapes, would seem to be the strongest evidence of all, but even videotapes can be contested in various ways. Couacaud (1999) addressed these concerns by grouping types of corroboration according to the degree of external validation potentially available. High corroboration involved evidence that could potentially be examined independently, such as court records, medical records, police records, documentary evidence. Medium corroboration comprised statements from friends, family, or other victims. An example might be a childhood friend who corroborates that he or she was told about the abuse at the time. One could verify whether the friend made that claim, but there is no way of verifying whether it was true in the first instance. The lowest form of corroboration in Couacaud's (1999) study of 112 adult, female sexual abuse survivors was evidence that the perpetrator abused others. That kind of evidence is often excluded in criminal cases because its probative value is considered lower than its potential to suggest guilt by association, but it is generally allowed in family court.

Evidence from Legal Cases: The Recovered Memory Project

The Recovered Memory Project (Cheit, 1998; www.recoveredmemory.org), an internet-based archive of corroborated cases of recovered memory, was created in part to address the claim that corroborated cases did not exist. Launched in 1997, the archive is a collection of cases that disprove this claim. The archive currently contains 101 cases of recovered memory with corroborative evidence varying from extremely strong to circumstantial. The accumulation of cases and the lack of criticisms of most cases in the Archive provide compelling evidence that recovered memories can be later recalled accurately.[2]

An example of strong corroborative evidence is Julie Herald's recovered memory of sexual abuse by her uncle, Dennis Hood. Herald presented a taped telephone conversation in which her uncle indicated that she "had been the only one". Further, Two therapists testified that at a meeting in their offices, Hood admitted sexually abusing Herald (Fields, 1992). The jury verdict assessing compensatory and punitive damages against Hood was upheld by the Ohio Supreme Court.

---

[2]An additional impetus was the claim by a television documentary producer for PBS that after almost a year of research she could find "only one case where a claim of recovered memory could be backed up by anything more substantial than a woman and her therapist believing it so" (Johnson, 1995, p. C3).

Another example of strong corroboration is Peter VanVeldhuizen's memories of childhood sexual abuse from 1966 to 1968 by Reverend J. Van Zweden of the Netherlands Reformed Congregation Church in Iowa. VanVeldhuizen did not recall the abuse until February 1991, while undergoing psychotherapy. To avoid litigation, VanVeldthuizen agreed to submit the claim and all related evidence to the Institute for Christian Conciliation. VanVeldhuizen introduced a variety of corroborating evidence, including testimony that Rev. Van Zweden sexually abused his grandson and eyewitness testimony to one of the incidents of sexual abuse of Peter VanVeldhuizen by Rev. Van Zweden. The mediator concluded that "Peter has more than met the highest biblical standard of proof, which is actually required only in capital offenses, namely, that the sin be confirmed by the testimony of at least two witnesses." This case is particularly notable because VanVeldhuizen's access to his highly corroborated memories returned during therapy.

The archive also contains cases with lower levels of corroboration. An example of a case with circumstantial corroboration is Marilyn VanDerbur, a former Miss America. Her memories were corroborated by her sister, Gwen Mitchell, who had continuous memory of similar abuse and long thought that she "was the only one" sexually abused in the family (Germer, 1991). The corroborative evidence is not direct proof, but it is one of the three types of corroborative evidence incorporated into the framework adopted by Geraerts et al. (2007).

The only other significant critique of the archive to date involves McNally (2003), who noted that Archive is an "important step toward providing the evidence for recovered memory of traumas" but raised a concern about the financial motives that might cause people with continuous memory of abuse to claim recovered memory.[3] According to McNally, "state laws seldom permit people to file suit against alleged perpetrators unless the memories were entirely repressed" and concluded that this "is a serious problem" (p. 223) for the civil cases in the archive. McNally's critique was based on an incorrect view of the law. Many states that allow for civil claims for recovered memory also allow for claims by those who had continuous memory but only recently comprehended the wrongful nature of the abuse. There is no incentive to claim recovered memory in states that also have "comprehension-based" statutes of limitation (Cheit & Jaros, 2002). Given that a comprehension-based claim is not subject to the same controversy as a recovered-memory claim, the incentives would be *against* making a claim of recovered memory in those states. Williams (2000) did a careful survey of these differences in state statutes and concluded that there were only six jurisdictions (including the District of Columbia) that were "recovered-memory only." Thus, McNally's "serious problem" applies to only a handful of cases in the Archive.

As further evidence against a "serious problem" of financial motives in the Archive, the Archive includes several criminal cases that did not involve any civil claim for damages. There are also civil cases where the claimant did not expect to

---

[3]Piper (1999) challenged the factual basis of seven of the original 44 case; however, even these seven cases are factually defensible (see queryCheit, 1999).

Table 2 Reports of memory corroboration by CSA survivors

Study	Sample	% obtaining corroboration
Chu et al. (1999)	19 women reporting complete amnesia for CSA who attempted corroboration	89%
Couacaud (1997)	112 women	46% (delayed recall) 65% (continuous recall)
Feldman-Summers and Pope (1995)	24 male, 46 female APA members reporting CSA	46.9%, across types of abuses
Geraerts et al. (2007)	57 adults (45 women) reporting discontinuous memories of CSA; 71 adults (55 women) reporting continuous memories	37% (discontinuous, recovered outside therapy); 45% (continuous); 0% (discontinuous, "suggestive therapy")
Hardt and Rutter (2004)	Review of eight studies	Concludes "retrospective reports of serious abuse/neglect/conflict are sufficiently valid to be usable" (see their Table 1)
Herman and Shatzow (1987)	53 outpatients and former patients	74%, not different from those with continuous memories
Melchert (1999)	38 college students reporting CSA	50% "some form"
Stoler (2001)	26 community women reporting CSA	86% (delayed memories); 46% (continuous memories)

collect anything, including a few from the "recovered-memory only" states. There are also cases where the recovered memory could never be subject to a financial claim, including cases involving war trauma or murder. McNally did not acknowledge or examine the myriad cases in the Archive that contradict his concern.

Evidence from Research Studies on Recovered Memories

In addition to the Archive, clinical and survey research provide important evidence to demonstrate that corroboration of recovered memories of child sexual abuse can occur, although most of these studies rely on self-reports and have not applied as strict standards (see Table 2). One of the earliest studies to examine corroboration of recovered memories was conducted by Herman and Shatzow (1987). Among 53 female outpatients who had participated in short-term therapy groups for incest survivors, 64% did not have full recall of the sexual abuse. However, 74% of the women were able to obtain confirmation of the abuse from another source. Schooler (1994) later reported on a personal communication with lead author Judith Herman, who indicated that the corroboration rates did not vary significantly by whether the memory was continuous or not.

Dalenberg (1996) found that "memories of abuse were found to be equally accurate whether recovered or continuously remembered" (p. 229). Using a prospective method, Williams (1995) investigated the memories of women who, 17 years earlier as children, had been admitted into a hospital emergency room for sexual assault. Williams noted that: "In general, the women with recovered memories had no more inconsistencies in their accounts than did the women who had always remembered. (p. 660)". Williams commented further: "In fact, when one considers the basic elements of the abuse, their retrospective reports are remarkably consistent with what had been reported in the 1970s" (p. 662).

Feldman-Summers and Pope (1994) also examined the presence of corroboration among participants who reported recovered memory for child sexual abuse. Almost half (46.9%) of the participants who reported recovered memories (n=32) were able to find corroborating evidence. Further, 15% of the participants reported more than one type of corroboration. Couacaud (1997) found similar results: among adult women reporting a period of time when they could not recall some or all of an experience of CSA. 46% found corroborating evidence, compared to 65% of those who reported continuous memory.

Stoler (2001) found that almost twice as many – 86% – of women who reported a period of forgetting had corroborated their memories through another victim or a family member, compared to 46% of the women with continuous memories. Her qualitative interviews revealed that women who had recovered memories were more likely to attempt corroboration, since their memories were unexpected, confusing, and in some cases, incomplete.

Schooler and his colleagues added to this literature with a "corroborated case study" method that involved a detailed factual investigation of the circumstances and corroboration surrounding reported cases of recovered memory. Schooler et al. (1997) found evidence that some participants who reported recovered memory of abuse had apparently forgotten that they reported the abuse to someone else at an earlier date. This finding demonstrates the inadequacy of dichotomous categories that classify memories as either continuous or long-forgotten. Given that the cases all involved some form of corroboration, this research also contradicts the extreme position that trauma is always memorable and that reports of recovered memory of sexual abuse are always fictitious.

Geraerts et al. (2007), Geraerts (2012) also examined the presence or absence of corroborative evidence in a laboratory study that involved 128 participants, 57 of whom reported indicated that there was "a time when you were completely unaware that you had ever been a victim of abuse, and that you later came to remember that you were abused" (p. 565). Of those 57, only 16 (28%) indicated that they recovered access to memories during therapy. Relying on three types of corroborative evidence (another person reported learning of the abuse soon after it occurred, reported abuse by the same alleged perpetrator, or reported having committed the abuse), the authors found that the corroboration rate for memories recovered outside of therapy did not differ from the corroboration rate for those continuous abuse memories. The authors reported significantly more corroborative evidence for memories recovered outside of therapy than for memories reported to have been gradually recovered in therapy; however, the authors acknowledge that criteria for corroboration applied in the study do not prove the accuracy of the underlying memory beyond a reasonable doubt. That is, this evidence does not indicate that the memories recovered outside of therapy were necessarily more accurate than those recovered in therapy. Since only a small proportion of their sample recovered memories in therapy, and most of their sample was adults reporting less severe assault (fondling and oral sex without strong fear), it is difficult to draw conclusions about memory reliability based on lack of corroboration from their data.

Implications of Trauma Therapy for Recovered Memories

One of the issues that has fueled contention in the field over issues of forgetting and remembering is the allegation that therapists "implant" false memories of trauma, especially of childhood sexual abuse (CSA), in clients with no such history (e.g., Bernstein & Loftus, 2009). Because claims about therapy have played a prominent role in questions about the phenomena of forgetting and misremembering, we turn now to a brief discussion of treatment issues that are relevant to evaluating claims about memory from the empirical literature. The approach to treatment that was purportedly responsible for this phenomenon was "recovered memory therapy" (RMT). One puzzling aspect of this claim is that there is no established form of psychological treatment corresponding to this term. As Scheflin (1999) noted, "there are no known schools of recovered memory, no conferences on how to practice recovered memory therapy, nor are there any textbooks on the topic" (p. 2).

Scheflin's (1999) observation points to a source of continuing frustration for experts in the treatment of CSA-related problems. Careful inspection of the literature on the treatment of CSA survivors will show that memory uncovering is not currently advocated as a central treatment strategy (see, e.g., Briere, 1996; Chu, 1998; Cloitre et al., 2006; Courtois, 2010; Gill, 1988; Gold, 2000). In fact, this has been the case since the development of treatment approaches for this population first emerged in the late 1980s. One of the earliest comprehensive works on therapy for survivors of CSA, *Healing the Incest Wound* (Courtois, 1988), contained a mere two-paragraph section titled "Recounting the Incest." Even within this brief segment, Courtois explicitly stated that exhaustive disclosure of abuse details is *not* required for effective treatment. She does mention that it is not unusual for memories of abuse to arise during the course of therapy, but the clear implication is that this phenomenon occurs spontaneously rather than being a purposeful aim of treatment.

Although rhetoric in the recovered memory debate has implied that most traumatic memories characterized by delayed recall emerge in treatment, empirical research strongly contradicts this claim. In a national probability sample, Wilsnack et al. (2002) observed that less than 15% of previously-forgotten CSA memories had been recovered during the course of therapy. Elliott (1997) reported that in a survey of a community sample of 505 adults, 72% reported having experienced some form of trauma, and of these 32% reported some degree of delayed recall.

Among 12 cues for delayed recall, the most common was a media presentation (54%) and the *least common* was psychotherapy (14%). Her findings not only indicate that delayed recall is much more often triggered outside of the context of therapy than within it, but also demonstrates that recovered memory is a phenomena that occurs in every type of trauma, not just in CSA.

What, then, do therapists with expertise in psychological trauma focus on in treatment, if not encouraging clients to access to memories of abuse or other forms of trauma that were previously inaccessible? When trauma practitioners do address traumatic memories, it is usually not to foster the emergence of incidents that were not previously retrieved. Rather, most often recollections of trauma that the client already knows about are targeted for systematic exposure. Although there is a range of variations on this basic technique, such as prolonged exposure (PE; Foa & Rothbaum, 1998), eye movement desensitization and reprocessing (EMDR: Shapiro, 2001) and traumatic incident reduction (French & Harris, 1999), all are based on the principle that when a fear response has been conditioned to a particular stimulus, substantial efforts are commonly made to avoid that conditioned stimulus (CS). In this case the CS is the thinking about traumatic event and encountering stimuli that are associated with that event. By intentionally and systematically confronting the memory of the traumatic event, the fear response (in traumatic events, the fight/flight reflex) is eventually extinguished (Foa & Rothbaum, 1998). It is generally agreed among trauma therapists that when conducting exposure-based intervention approaches, it is not necessary to press for any more traumatic material than the client already remembers. While additional details may spontaneously emerge during the exposure process, whatever the client has retained is sufficient to serve as the target of exposure.

For some time now, trauma specialists have recognized that in clients with CSA histories, who often experienced repeated instances of molestation over a prolonged period of time, processing of traumatic memories, either through exposure or other means, should neither be the initial nor the most central focus of treatment. Rather, particularly in individuals with repeated or prolonged trauma, therapy should be "phase-oriented," unfolding as a three-stage process (Courtois, 2010; Courtois, Ford & Cloitre, 2009; Herman, 1992). The first stage centers on the establishment of *safety and stabilization*. Part of the initial assessment is aimed at determining whether the trauma is, in fact, over or whether the client continues to be endangered. A common example of the latter circumstance is someone who presents for therapy while still ensnared in a relationship marked by domestic violence. Rather than encouraging the processing of the still-being-experienced trauma in the battering relationship, the first order of business is to foster the development of a safety plan so that if violence erupts again the client is equipped to get away and escape to a secure place whether the violent partner is not likely to be able to follow. Where the trauma is not currently continuing, the primary goal of this first stage of therapy is to help the client stabilize, e.g., by teaching methods for reduction of anxiety and other forms of chronic distress, bolstering and expanding the client's coping skills, and, to the extent possible, establishing or enhancing adaptive occupational and social functioning.

We are ultimately left, however, with a seemingly glaring contradiction. The mainstream literature on trauma treatment does not advocate suggestive or leading therapeutic practices, and for quite some time now have often explicitly discouraged them (see, e.g., Chu, 1998; Courtois, 2001; Gold & Brown, 1997). And yet, Geraerts et al. (2009), (see also Geraerts 2012) were able to identify respondents who recovered memories of CSA in therapy that used leading and suggestive approaches very different from those described above, which raises two important issues. First, Geraerts et al. research is not epidemiological in nature. Their sample was one of convenience, not a random sample of people in therapy. Thus, their research tells us that people report therapy that involved suggestive techniques, but not about how generalizable these findings are to the public at large nor how their particular findings extend to people who recall memoires of abuse in therapy that was not suggestive.

The second issue is how to explain that suggestive therapy is taking place at all. Sadly, despite an extensive body of literature documenting that traumatic experiences and trauma-related disorders are highly prevalent (Gold, 2004), training in empirically validated and widely accepted treatment methods among experts in psychological trauma remains limited. Coverage of this area in most graduate programs in the helping professions is minimal to non-existent (Courtois & Gold, 2009; Miller, Coonrod, Brady, Moffitt, & Bay, 2004).

This observation points to a painful irony at the core of the recovered memory controversy. Detractors of trauma therapy have long accused practitioners of using intervention tactics that are suggestive and likely to implant false recollections of CSA in their clients. We would argue, however, that it is not therapists who are knowledgeable about and skilled in treatments in trauma psychology who engage in these practices. The mainstream literature on the subject does not promote such interventions. On the contrary, it explicitly discourages their use. Instead the literature emphasizes intervention strategies aimed at augmentation of present-day coping and adaptation as the initial and primary focus of treatment, particularly for survivors of prolonged CSA. Taken as a whole, the body of evidence suggests that it is clinicians who have *not* been adequately educated in trauma psychology that are at risk for employing suggestive approaches to therapy. What is called for, therefore, is not the suppression of trauma therapy, but just the opposite. In order to reduce the use of suggestive techniques while meeting the needs of survivors for mental health services which effectively address their trauma-related difficulties, much more extensive incorporation of mainstream, empirically grounded approaches to trauma training into the core curriculum of graduate education for mental health practitioners is indicated (Courtois & Gold, 2009).

Before Moving Forward, Taking a Look Back: The Historical Context for Studying Memory Processes

We have reviewed empirical and theoretical work on forgetting and misremembering trauma, particularly CSA. The research and clinical work that shapes this literature did not take place in a scientific vacuum – rather, this work developed in a very specific socio-political and historical context. Thus, before describing future research directions derived from BTT, we first take a look back to examine the socio-political and historical context that has influenced research to date. This context is important for understanding and interpreting where we have been – and perhaps even more important for setting the course for future research.

Our generation is not the first to be fascinated by memory puzzles. In fact, the complexity of memory has captures researchers' attention since the inception of psychology as a discipline. Factors influencing recall, limitations, and techniques for improving memory were well established with early research (e.g., Carmichael, Hogan, & Walter, 1932; Ebbinghaus, 1885; Miller, 1956; Sears, 1936). Of particular interest to researchers have been questions related to the conditions under which memories are flawed. For example, Bransford and Franks (1971) demonstrated misremembering of complex sentences when participants were presented with shorter sentences containing overlapping words and semantic meaning, sparking debate about methodological issues such as mode of presentation (Flagg & Reynolds, 1977). In a series of early studies, Loftus and her colleagues (e.g., Loftus, 1975) demonstrated misremembering of specific objects in fast-moving films of an auto accident or enactments of a classroom disruption, particularly when viewers were questioned with misleading cues.

These early demonstrations of memory fallibility largely relied on verbal or visual stimuli, such as lists of words or brief movies, shown under controlled conditions in laboratory settings or classrooms. Failures in individuals' memories for personal events were discussed in clinical and case studies, especially the psychoanalytic literature of Charcot, Janet and Freud (see Herman, 1992). These studies involved naturalistic observations, often of people whose basic human rights to safety and dignity had been violated through interpersonal violence committed by the people closest to them. After World War I, clinical reports of memory disruptions related to "war neurosis" began to appear, drawing the attention of a wider audience of professionals. Sears (1936) reviewed evidence for memory repression and dissociation after diverse traumatic experiences, including war, drawing from both research and clinical sources. While he attempted to bring together these two diverse types of information, he also acknowledged the necessary divide between research data and individual experiences. The phenomena of forgetting and misremembering combat experiences were widely accepted after World War II. In fact, after veterans returned from Vietnam reporting disruptions in memory processes (both intrusive and dissociative), Posttraumatic Stress Disorder (PTSD) was introduced into the Diagnostic and Statistical Manual of Mental Disorders-III (DSM III, American Psychiatric Association, 1980). The PTSD diagnosis included a criterion of memory impairment then and has retained this criterion through to the current DSM IV TR, (American Psychiatric Association, 2000).

Interpersonal Violence and the Socio-Political Context of Trauma Memory

In the 1970s, adult survivors of sexual abuse and rape began to speak out, much as their counterparts who had survived combat in the Vietnam War also began to speak out (see Herman, 1992 for a review). Survivors of rape and abuse did so in non-therapeutic contexts for the most part; the earliest collections of autobiographical writing by adult survivors of childhood abuse emerged from political and literary contexts (e.g., Angelou, 1969; Armstrong, 1978; Bass & Thornton, 1983). Following behind the survivors, the mental health disciplines began to acknowledge the impacts of childhood sexual abuse (CSA; Courtois, 1988; Herman, 1981; Quina & Carlson, 1989). As the experience of childhood abuse was moved by professionals from its grass-roots feminist political and consciousness-raising context into a medical-psychological one, the diagnosis of PTSD was applied to traumatized abuse survivors.

The subsequent groundswell of research on trauma, including child abuse, forever changed the field's view of trauma exposure. At first defined as *an event outside the realm of usual human experience* in DSM III, the very definition of trauma had to be changed in the next edition to reflect the fact that a vast majority of Americans report exposure to some form of trauma in their lifetimes (Davidson & Foa, 1991). Indeed, research in the 1980s and 1990s documented that exposure to interpersonal traumas, including child physical and sexual abuse, is far more common than previously believed. Contemporary, well-executed epidemiological studies indicate that approximately 80% of *youth* already report at least one lifetime incident of victimization; 15% of youth report lifetime maltreatment exposure (Finkelhor, Ormrod, & Turner, 2009). Approximately 10–11% of youth ages 3–11 report exposure to multiple forms of victimization, which Finkelhor and colleagues describe as poly-victimization. These numbers are particularly startling insofar as they involve youth; the rates of exposure for these young people may go even higher as they continue to develop into adulthood and experience new traumatic events as they age. In fact, other researchers have documented that violence early in life begets exposure to additional violence (e.g., Classen, Palesh, & Aggarwal, 2005; DePrince, 2005), pointing to the complexity and severity of the reality of abuse for many young people.

Some of those CSA survivors writing their stories in the early 1980s reported that the memories of their abuse had surfaced unexpectedly, sometimes after decades of being unaware of their existence (e.g., Armstrong, 1978; Bass & Thornton, 1983; Butler, 1978). Clinicians working with CSA survivors began to report that clients had recovered memories of CSA as a matter of course in their practices. As noted, many clinicians had long observed delayed recall in survivors of other traumas; however, reports of CSA were often dismissed as fantasy-driven. As feminist therapy changed the *social* context of understanding psychology and effective therapy in the 1980s, and as survivors began breaking their silence and connecting with others who could corroborate their reports, clinicians began to accept the veracity of CSA reports, including those once forgotten (Pope & Brown, 1996). It is in this context that BTT offered an important way to understand why CSA might be associated with forgetting.

As the enormity of both CSA and attendant memory difficulties became apparent, perpetrators began to be held legally and morally accountable, often years later after victims were grown and able to speak out. In some cases, charges of CSA occurred after the survivor remembered the abuse following a period of forgetting.

Perhaps in response to a new demand for accountability (e.g., in the courts), some began to question the reliability of recovered memories, and even the possibility that forgetting and remembering could occur. "False memory" became the subject of academic and legal debate for the next two decades [for reviews, see the report of the American Psychological Association Working Group on Investigation of Memories for Childhood Abuse (Alpert et al., 1996); special issues of *Consciousness & Cognition* (1994, volume 3, issues 3–4) and *Ethics & Behavior* (1995, volume 8, issue 2)].

During this period, organizations arose dedicated to discrediting survivors' delayed memories and targeting therapists who had witnessed survivors' stories when memories of CSA emerged. A "false memory syndrome" (FMS) narrative portrayed clients as the suggestible victims of unscrupulous or naïve therapists (see, e.g., Olio & Cornell, 1998; Pope, 1997). Since so many (though not all) of those who reported delayed recall for abuse memories were women, it was noted that the undertones of the FMS narrative appeared to include covertly sexist, and often overtly anti-feminist sentiments (see Brown, 1996). The circumstances of CSA made it all too easy to discount survivors' stories out of hand. Unlike combat (and other traumas more commonly experienced by men than women), where the trauma is public and therefore witnessed by those who can corroborate events, the only other witness to CSA is often the perpetrator.

Balancing Perspectives on Trauma Memory

Thankfully, the majority of researchers and clinicians have moved largely beyond the extreme positions of the past two decades, with wide acceptance of reports of memory disruptions in adult CSA survivors, observed in men and women after emotional, physical and/or sexual abuse in diverse samples (see Table 1). While there continue to be lawsuits against therapists in which expert witnesses testify that it is impossible for a childhood trauma to be unavailable to memory and then return to conscious recall, one of the genuinely positive results of the so-called memory wars has been the flourishing of solid research on forgetting, misremembering, and remembering abuse.

As the field embarks on the creation of high-quality psychological science to enhance understanding of issues of forgetting and misremembering, it is important to keep conversations rooted in the socio-political context in which abuse occurs. As researchers asking questions about memory for trauma, we are necessarily also asking questions that have bearing on issues central to basic human rights, which are violated when children are abused. In her now-classic text, *Trauma and Recovery*, Judith Herman (1992) captures poignantly the complex socio-political context in which society (including scientists) react and respond to human-induced traumas such as child abuse:

> To study psychological trauma means bearing witness to horrible events. When the traumatic events are of human design, those who bear witness are caught in the conflict between the victim and the perpetrator. It is morally impossible to remain neutral in this conflict. The bystander is forced to take sides. It is very tempting to take the side of the perpetrator. All the perpetrator asks is that the bystander do nothing. He appeals to the universal desire to see, hear, and speak no evil. The victim, on the other hand, asks the bystander to share the

burden or pain. The victim demands action, engagement, and remembering. After every atrocity one can expect to hear the same predictable apologies: it never happened, the victim lies, the victim exaggerates, the victim brought it on herself and in case there is time to forget the past and move on. The more powerful the perpetrator, the greater is his prerogative to name and define reality and the more completely his arguments prevail. In the absence of strong political movements for human rights, the active process of bearing witness inevitably gives way to the active process of forgetting. Repression, dissociation and denial are phenomena of a social as well as individual consciousness. (p. 8).

Questions of forgetting and misremembering cut to the heart of how society views and evaluates victims' and survivors' voices. The science that we produce is informed by and consumed in a particular socio-political context, one that has most often privileged the voice and reality of the offender over the voice and reality of the victim. Offenders are commonly members of the dominant groups of a culture; they are overwhelming male, they are adults when their victims are children, they are often situated in positions that are accorded institutional reverence and respect—parent, teacher, coach, priest. They carry the privilege of their social position, which includes the power to be believed by those around them, to be found credible, rational, and right.

Victims, conversely, are usually among the most vulnerable members of our society. They are children; many of them are girls. Many of the boys, according to the most recent research, are gender non-conforming or gay (Balsam, Rothblum, & Beauchaine, 2005). They may be emotionally dysregulated and engage in self-destructive behaviors, such as abusing substances and sometimes their own bodies, (either because they were abused or because perpetrators seek out victims with such attributes who are less likely to be believed; Salter, 2003). A few survivors, lacking interventions or support, find their lives spiral into further vulnerability, including a lack of education, addictions, sex work, and incarceration (Farley & Barkan, 1998; Quina & Brown, 2008; Zierler, Feingold, Laufer, Velentgas, & Mayer, 1991). Thus, victims are easy to discount or disbelieve, particularly relative to more powerful abusers.

Today, cognitive scientists have developed sophisticated research paradigms to ask incisive questions about forgetting and misremembering, and are contributing greatly to our understanding of traumatic memory. Memory is subject to error and false accusations sometimes do occur. However, it is incumbent on researchers who study forgetting and misremembering to simultaneously acknowledge the reality of child abuse in our society. CSA is a violation of the basic human rights of a child. Like all such violations, attempts will be made by its perpetrators to cover it up. As Sears' (1936) admonishments remind us, researchers also need to remember that the results of a laboratory study do not always neatly line up with the experiences of a child experiencing nightly rape by a parent, or an adult recalling such childhood experiences.

Using BTT to Frame New Directions of Inquiry

As reviewed in the previous section, the field has come to recognize the reality of child abuse experienced by a significant minority of the population and the very real consequences for memory for abuse. In the context of this larger literature on memory for abuse, BTT provides a useful framework for understanding conditions under

Table 3 Contributions of BTT to existing research and future directions

Contributions of existing BBT-related research
- Motivations for unawareness
- Documenting reports of forgetting
- Cognitive correlates of betrayal trauma exposure
- Physical and psychological correlates of betrayal trauma exposure

Future directions of BTT-related research
- Non-offending parent (or bystander) memory
- Perpetrator memory
- Application of memory error research to unawareness for betrayal (e.g. misremembering abuse/abusive contexts as more positive than they were)
- Re-conceptualization child abuse traumas in terms of betrayal (rather than primarily fear)

which forgetting and misremembering may occur. For example, while much of the literature on forgetting has assumed forgetting is amotivational, caused simply by passive processes such as decay (see Freyd, 1996), BTT describes a motivation for forgetting and misremembering. Though BTT does not specify mechanisms by which forgetting occurs, the theory sets the stage for several lines of inquiry that have now provided fruitful information for the field. Several studies now document cognitive correlates of betrayal and dissociation as well as deleterious outcomes related to betrayal traumas (see Table 3 for examples of correlates).

BTT also provides a framework for future directions in research. We turn now to describing some of these future directions (see summary in Table 3).

Non-offending Parent and Perpetrator Memory. As noted earlier in this manuscript, researchers have focused almost universally focused on victims' memory accuracy, to the exclusion of memory accuracy among non-offending family members and/or perpetrators. Given that victims' memory accuracy is sometimes evaluated by looking for corroboration with other family members and/or potential victims, it is critically important that researchers focus on memory processes among these individuals. Like the victim, non-offending others in family systems where abuse occurs may experience similar pressure to remain unaware, particularly non-offending parents. Researchers have yet to identify the conditions under which non-offending parents may respond similarly to victims, forgetting or misremembering abuse against children to maintain their own attachment with the offender. Research should evaluate the degree to which economic, emotional, and/or legal dependence on the offending parent may motivate unawareness in non-offending parents. To the extent that non-offending parents may be unaware of abuse because of their own dependence on the offender, their reports should not be used to corroborate the accuracy of victim reports. In addition to implications for research on corroboration, non-offending parents' unawareness can have an important effect on the safety and well-being of the child victim as the non-offending parent is likely to be less of a resource in ending and/or seeking out interventions to address the deleterious consequences of the abuse.

Similarly, researchers have yet to focus substantial effort on understanding the motivation to forget and misremember among offenders (see Becker-Blease &

Freyd, 2007 for a rare exception). Extending research to focus on offender memory is an essential directional shift, expanding to focus on the reliability perpetrators' memories. Offenders have overwhelming legal (as well as perhaps social and financial) motivations to indict victim memory. Like non-offending parents' memories, offender memories and motivations for unawareness have critically important implications for corroboration studies. The extent to which an offender forgets, misremembers, or lies about his or her actions has a direct bearing on the ability of the victim to corroborate the abuse. Thus, corroboration studies must be applied carefully to victim memory, as they can too easily be used to impugn victim memory while (implicitly) failing to question offender (and bystander) memories.

Misremembering. As researchers studying memory errors continue to document the conditions under which memory errors are likely to occur (e.g., when reality is similar to errors; when errors involve related information; see Geraerts, 2012; Geraerts et al., 2009; Johnson, 2006; Johnson et al., 2012), BTT offers a framework for considering how those processes may result in errors with regard to details about abusive experiences and/or misremembering of abusive families as more positive than perhaps they were. While much of the research derived from the betrayal trauma theory framework has focused on forgetting, BTT points to the need for additional research into how victims may *misremember* abuse and/or abusive contexts as more positive than they were to serve underlying attachment goals related to unawareness. Research paradigms that focus on errors in memory seem especially relevant to future research on misremembering (e.g., the DRM and source monitoring tasks). To date, evidence on memory errors in the DRM and source monitoring literature have largely been applied to the questions of how false memories for abuse that did not really happen could develop. However, given the similarity required to elicit source monitoring errors (e.g., a critical lure that is closely related to what was actually viewed by the participant is erroneously recognized in the DRM), these paradigms may actually be poised to inform misremembering. For example, in a complex family dynamic where information related to abuse and positive care from a caregiver are both presented to a child victim, that child may be more likely to misremember or reconstruct related, positive events that did not occur.

Fear or Relational Betrayal? BTT points to the need for research that considers deeply the social context in which traumas occur. To date, research has focused extensively on individual differences in fear when conceptualizing the harm caused by trauma. In fact, early focus in the trauma field on the sequelae of one-time events, sometimes referred to as Type 1 traumas (see Terr, 1990; e.g., as firestorms, earthquakes, combat traumas, and crime victimization), prioritized emphasis on experiences that often involved overwhelming fear. Type 1 traumas differ from most traumas high in betrayal (particularly child sexual abuse) in important ways. Type 1 traumas tend to be one-time events that involve witnesses and *do not* occur behind closed doors in isolation. Type 1 events do not necessarily involve larger familial and social dysfunction, whereas much child sexual abuse (e.g., incestuous abuse) does. While Type 1 traumas can be disruptive to illusions about personal safety and invulnerability (e.g., Janoff-Bulman, 1992), they are rarely experiences that inherently undermine victims' close attachment relationships at periods in development when such dependent attachments are necessary for survival.

Complementing the emphasis on fear in deleterious trauma responses, BTT provides a lens through which to consider also the role that social betrayal plays in responses to traumas (see DePrince & Freyd, 2002a, 2002b). By focusing on the relational contexts in which betrayal occurs, BTT shifts the paradigm to encourage research questions about wounds to attachment engendered by the violation of basic care-giving contracts between adults and children. Indeed, stories of forgotten (and later remembered) abuse are frequently characterized as confusing, disorienting, complicated situations in which a family member introduced sexual contact into a relationship in which a child was dependent for care, protection, and love (see Clancy, 2010, for one in-depth analysis of this kind of relational trauma). BTT points out that relational betrayals require management of the awareness of betrayal balanced against management of necessary attachment(s); and argues for the importance of examining consequences of such betrayals on attachment and cognitive processes.

BTT may have important connections to the growing literature on complex trauma responses, such as complex PTSD. Complex PTSD, first conceptualized by Herman (1992), has received increased attention in recent years (Courtois & Ford, 2009). Complex PTSD emphasizes the damage to multiple systems caused by chronic, interpersonal traumas that occur during development. In particular, complex PTSD has been proposed to include problems in: affect and impulse regulation; attention and consciousness; self perception; relations with others; somatic functioning; and systems of meaning (see Dorahy et al., 2009; Ford 1999; Herman, 1992; Taylor, Asmundson, Carleton, 2006). The chronic, interpersonal traumas that are believed to lead to complex PTSD, such as familial sexual abuse, include significant betrayals. Thus, BTT provides a roadmap for encouraging critically important research questions about the role that betrayal and attachment play in serious post-traumatic responses, such as complex PTSD. Where the field previously privileged fear narratives, BTT requires consideration of relational frames.

Future research should continue to improve on the operationalization and measurement of a continuum of betrayal. For example, relative to other abuse perpetrated by someone on whom a child depends, familial *sexual* abuse appears to be unique in several ways. First, familial sexual abuse stands apart from usual relationships between adults and children in contrast to physical and emotional abuse, which can occur on a continuum with other, more accepted behaviors in adult–child relationships. Thus, sexual abuse can involve dynamics in which offenders designate sexual abuse as "special", weaving it into a larger relational narrative that can be especially confusing for children. For example, cuddling can morph into sexual touch; sexual abuse can feel arousing to the child. Second, for some sexual abuse survivors, the sexual abuse experience may not necessarily be frightening at the time (relative to experiences of physical assault, for example), but may involve confusing and conflicting information (see Clancy, 2010, for one in-depth analysis of a relational trauma, and McNally, 2012, for similar notions regarding delayed shock and betrayal). Third, adults who sexually abuse children are likely aware that the actions are criminal (or at least disapproved of by most people) and cannot be justi-fied in the way that people may justify severe physical punishment or emotional abuse. Sexually abusive perpetrators may, consequently, behave in ways that com-municate to the child that something is amiss, leading to overt or covert demands for secrecy. The veil of secrecy enforced by perpetrators serves as a potent suggestion to forget the abuse (see Veldhuis & Freyd, 1999). The degree to which perpetrators demand secrecy may differ in important ways across forms of abuse, even within a close victim-perpetrator relationship.

Summary and Conclusion

For nearly 20 years now, researchers (in their labs) and clinicians (in their therapy offices) have studied the experience of remembering and forgetting childhood abuse. In 1994, the clinician members of the APA Working Group on Recovered Memory pointed out that the absence of a science of memory for trauma did not equate with an absence of reality of forgetting and later recollection of memories for abuse. Indeed, survivors of childhood abuse, particularly sexual abuse, have continued to report forgetting and misremembering, regardless of the accuracy of lab models try-ing to account for the phenomenon. The outcry that such delayed recall must be impossible has died down, although it has not become completely silent. The sci-ence that facilitates our comprehension of the mechanisms of forgetting, misre-membering, and later recall has matured.

Also for nearly two decades, cognitive scientists have considered how to study effectively and understand experiences of remembering and forgetting. The contro-versy of the so-called memory wars reflected how ill-informed the field was in the early 1990s regarding the biological, psychological, psycho-social, and existential dynamics of childhood maltreatment, particularly abuse by caregivers. The research reviewed in this chapter demonstrates how cognitive science studies that begin with a thorough understanding of the dimensions of childhood traumatic experience (e.g., relational and attachment perspectives, human rights violations inherent in child abuse) can inform both researchers and clinicians seeking to understand moti-vations and mechanisms by which forgetting and misremembering occur.

References

Allard, C. (2009). Prevalence and sequelae of betrayal trauma in a Japanese student sample. *Psychological Trauma: Theory, Research, Practice, and Policy, 1*(1), 65–77.

Alpert, J. L., Brown, L. S., Ceci, S. J., Courtois, C. A., Loftus, E. F., & Ornstein, P. A. (1996). *Working group on investigation of memories for childhood abuse: Final report.* American Psychological Association. Retrieved July 19, 2010 from http://www.apa.org/pi/families/resources/preface.pdf.

American Psychiatric Association. (1980). *Diagnostic and statistical manual of mental disorders III* (3rd ed.). Washington, DC: Author.

American Psychiatric Association. (2000). *Diagnostic and statistical manual of mental disorders IV-TR*. (4th ed., text revision). Washington, DC: Author.

Anderson, M. C. (2001). Active forgetting: Evidence for functional inhibition as a source of memory failure. *Journal of Aggression, Maltreatment, & Trauma, 4*, 184–210.

Anderson, M. C., & Huddleston, E. (2012). Towards a cognitive and neurobiological model of motivated forgetting. In R. F. Belli (Ed.), *True and false recovered memories: Toward a reconciliation of the debate* (pp. 53–120). *Vol. 58: Nebraska Symposium on Motivation*. New York: Springer.

Anderson, M. C., Ochsner, K. N., Kuhl, B., Cooper, J., Robertson, E., Gabrieli, S. W., et al. (2004). Neural systems underlying the suppression of unwanted memories. *Science, 303*, 232–235.

Angelou, M. (1969). *I know why the caged bird sings*. New York: Random House.

Armstrong, L. (1978). *Kiss Daddy goodnight: A speak-out on incest*. New York: Hawthorn Books.

Atlas, J. A., & Ingram, D. M. (1998). Betrayal trauma in adolescent inpatients. *Psychological Reports, 83*, 914.

Balsam, K. F., Rothblum, E. D., & Beauchaine, T. P. (2005). Victimization over the life span: A comparison of lesbian, gay, bisexual and heterosexual siblings. *Journal of Consulting and Clinical Psychology, 73*(3), 477–487.

Bass, E., & Thornton, L. (Eds.). (1983). *I never told anyone: Writings by women survivors of sexual abuse*. New York: Harper & Row.

Becker-Blease, K. A., & Freyd, J. J. (2007). Dissociation and memory for perpetration among convicted sex offenders. *Journal of Trauma & Dissociation, 8*(2), 69–80.

Belknap, J. (2010). Rape: Too hard to report and too easy to discredit victims." *Violence Against Women, 16*(12):1335–1344.

Bernstein, D. M., & Loftus, E. F. (2009). The consequences of false memories for food preferences and choices. *Perspectives on Psychological Science, 4*, 135–139.

Blandón-Gitlin, I., & Pezdek, K. (under review). Reference group affects perceived plausibility and autobiographical beliefs.

Blandón-Gitlin, I., Pezdek, K., Lindsay, S. D., & Hagan, L. (2009). Criteria-Based content analysis of true and suggested accounts of events. *Applied Cognitive Psychology, 23*, 901–917.

Bransford, J. D., & Franks, J. J. (1971). The abstraction of linguistic ideas. *Cognitive Psychology, 2*(4), 331–350.

Brewin, C. R. (2007). Autobiographical memory for trauma: Update on four controversies. *Memory, 15*, 227–248.

Briere, J. N. (1996). *Therapy for adults molested as children: Beyond survival*. (rev. 2nd ed.). New York: Springer.

Briere, J. N., & Conte, J. R. (1993). Self-reported amnesia for abuse in adults molested as children. *Journal of Traumatic Stress, 6*(1), 21–31.

Brown, L. S. (1996). On the construction of truth and falsity: Whose memory, whose history. In K. Pezdek & W. Banks (Eds.), *The recovered memory/false memory debate* (pp. 341–354). New York: Academic.

Butler, S. (1978). *Conspiracy of silence: The trauma of incest*. San Francisco: Volcano Press.

Cameron, C. (1993). Recovering memories of child hood sexual abuse: A longitudinal report. Paper presented at the Western Psychological Association Convention, Phoenix, Arizona.

Carmichael, L., Hogan, H. P., & Walter, A. A. (1932). An experimental study of the effect of language on the reproduction of visually perceived form. *Journal of Experimental Psychology, 15*, 73–86.

Cheit, R. E. (1998). Consider this, skeptics of recovered memory. *Ethics & Behavior, 8*(2), 141–160.

Cheit, R. E., & Jaros, C. (2002). Beyond memory: Child abuse and the statute of limitations. In M. Minow (Ed.), *Breaking the cycle of hatred: Memory, law, and repair* (pp. 170–187). Princeton, NJ: Princeton University Press.

Motivated Forgetting and Misremembering...   235

Chiu, C., Yeh, Y., Huang, Y., Wu, Y., & Chiu, Y. (2009). The set switching function of nonclinical dissociators under negative emotion. *Journal of Abnormal Psychology, 118*, 214–222.

Chiu, C., Yeh, Y., Huang, C., Wu, Y., Chiu, Y., & Lin, C. (2010). Unintentional memory inhibition is weakened in non-clinical dissociators. *Journal of Behavior Therapy and Experimental Psychiatry, 41*, 117–124.

Chu, J. A. (1998). *Rebuilding shattered lives: The responsible treatment of complex post-traumatic stress and dissociative disorders*. New York: John Wiley & Sons.

Chu, A. T., & DePrince, A. P. (2006). Development of dissociation: Examining the relationship between parenting, maternal trauma and child dissociation. *Journal of Trauma & Dissociation, 7*(4), 75–89.

Chu, J. A., & Dill, D. L. (1990). Dissociative symptoms in relation to childhood physical and sexual abuse. *The American Journal of Psychiatry, 147*, 887–892.

Chu, J. A., Frey, L. M., Ganzel, B. L., & Matthews, J. (1999). Memories of childhood abuse: Dissociation, amnesia, and corroboration. *The American Journal of Psychiatry, 156*(5), 740–755.

Clancy, S. A. (2010). *The trauma myth: The truth about the sexual abuse of children—and its aftermath*. New York: Basic Books.

Classen, C. C., Palesh, O. G., & Aggarwal, R. (2005). Sexual revictimization: A review of the empirical literature. *Trauma, Violence & Abuse, 6*(12), 103–129.

Cloitre, M., Cohen, L. R., & Karestan, C. K. (2006a). *Treating survivors of childhood abuse: Psychotherapy for the interrupted life*. New York: Guilford.

Cloitre, M., Cohen, L. R., & Karestan, C. K. (2006b). *Treating survivors of childhood abuse: Psychotherapy for the interrupted life*. New York: Guilford.

Couacaud, K. L. (1999). Recall of childhood sexual abuse: Abuse characteristics and clarity of memory. Dissertation Abstracts International, 59(7), 3686B. (UMI No. AAM9839235).

Couacaud, K. L. (1999). Recall of childhood sexual abuse: Abuse characteristics and clarity of memory (Doctoral dissertation, Pacific Graduate School of Psychology, 1999). *Dissertation Abstracts International, 59*(7-B), 3686.

Courtois, C. A. (1988). *Healing the incest wound: Adult survivors in therapy*. New York: W. W. Norton and Company.

Courtois, C. A. (2001). Implications of the memory controversy for clinical practice: An overview of treatment recommendations and guidelines. *Journal of Child Sexual Abuse, 9*(3), 183–210.

Courtois, C. A. (2010). *Healing the incest wound: Adult survivors in therapy* (2nd ed.). New York: W. W. Norton and Company.

Courtois, C. A., & Ford, J. D. (Eds.). (2009). *Treating complex traumatic stress disorders: An evidence-based guide*. New York: Guilford Press.

Courtois, C. A., Ford, J. D., & Cloitre, M. (2009). Best practices in psychotherapy for adults. In C. A. Courtois & J. D. Ford (Eds.), *Treating complex traumatic stress disorders: An evidence-based guide* (pp. 82–103). New York: Guildford Press.

Courtois, C. A., & Gold, S. N. (2009). The need for inclusion of psychological trauma in the professional curriculum: A call to action. *Psychological Trauma: Theory, Research, Practice and Policy, 1*(1), 3–23.

Crowley, M. S. (2007). Memories of childhood sexual abuse: Narrative analyses of types, experiences, and processes of remembering. *Journal of Interpersonal Violence, 22*(9), 1095–1113.

Dale, P., & Allen, J. (1998). On memories of childhood abuse: A phenomenological study. *Child Abuse & Neglect, 22*(8), 799–812.

Dalenberg, C. J. (1996). Accuracy, timing and circumstances of disclosure in therapy of recovered and continuous memories of abuse. *Journal of Psychiatry & Law, 24*(2), 229–275.

Davidson, J. R. T., & Foa, E. B. (1991). Diagnostic issues in posttraumatic stress disorder: Considerations for the DSM-IV. *Journal of Abnormal Psychology, 100*(3), 346–355.

de Ruiter, M. B., Phaf, R. H., Elzinga, B. M., & van Dyck, R. (2004). Dissociative style and individual differences in verbal working memory span. *Consciousness and Cognition, 13*, 821–828.

de Ruiter, M. B., Phaf, R. H., Veltman, D. J., Kok, A., & van Dyck, R. (2003). Attention as a characteristic of nonclinical dissociation: An event-related potential study. *NeuroImage, 19,* 376–390.

DePrince, A. P. (2005). Social cognition and revictimization risk. *Journal of Trauma & Dissociation, 6,* 125–141.

DePrince, A. P., Allard, C. B., Oh, H., & Freyd, J. J. (2004). What's in a name for memory errors? Implications and ethical issues arising from the use of the label "false memory" for errors in memory for details. *Ethics & Behavior, 14,* 201–233.

DePrince, A.P., Chu, A.T., & Pineda, A. (2011). Links between specific posttrauma appraisals and three forms of trauma-related distress. *Psychological Trauma: Theory, Research, Practice, and Policy.* doi:10.1037/a0021576.

DePrince, A. P., Chu, A., & Visvanathan, P. (2006). Dissociation and posttraumatic stress disorder. *PTSD Research Quarterly, 17*(1), 1–3.

DePrince, A. P., & Freyd, J. J. (2001). Memory and dissociative tendencies: The roles of attentional context and word meaning in a directed forgetting task. *Journal of Trauma & Dissociation, 2,* 67–82.

DePrince, A. P., & Freyd, J. J. (2002a). The harm of trauma: Pathological fear, shattered assumptions or betrayal? In J. Kauffman (Ed.), *Loss of the assumptive world* (pp. 71–82). New York: Taylor and Francis.

DePrince, A. P., & Freyd, J. J. (2002b). The intersection of gender and betrayal in trauma. In R. Kimerling, P. C. Oumette, & J. Wolfe (Eds.), *Gender and PTSD* (pp. 98–113). New York: Guilford Press.

DePrince, A. P., & Freyd, J. J. (2004). Forgetting trauma stimuli. *Psychological Science, 15,* 488–492.

DePrince, A. P., Freyd, J. J., & Malle, B. F. (2007). A replication by another name: A response to Devilly et al. (2007). *Psychological Science, 18,* 218–219.

DePrince, A. P., Weinzierl, K. M., & Combs, M. D. (2008). Stroop performance, dissociation, and trauma exposure in a community sample of children. *Journal of Trauma & Dissociation, 9*(2), 209–223.

Devilly, G. T., Ciorciari, J., Piesse, A., Sherwell, S., Zammit, S., Cook, F., et al. (2007). Dissociative tendencies and memory performance on directed-forgetting tasks. *Psychological Science, 18,* 212–217.

Dorahy, M. J., Irwin, H. J., & Middleton, W. (2004). Assessing markers of working memory function in dissociative identity disorder using neutral stimuli: A comparison with clinical and general population samples. *The Australian and New Zealand Journal of Psychiatry, 38,* 47–55.

Dorahy, M. J., Middleton, W., & Irwin, H. J. (2005). The effect of emotional context on cognitive inhibition and attentional processing in dissociative identity disorder. *Behaviour Research and Therapy, 43,* 555–568.

Dorahy, M. J., Corry, M., Shannon, M., MacSherry, A., Hamilton, G., McRobert, G., Elder, R., & Hanna, D. (2009). Complex PTSD, interpersonal trauma and relational consequences: Findings from a treatment receiving Northern Irish sample. *Journal of Affective Disorders, 112,* 71–80.

Ebbinghaus, H. (1885/1913). *Memory: A contribution to experimental psychology* [H. A. Ruger & C. E. Bussenius, Trans.]. New York: Columbia University.

Edwards, V. J., Freyd, J. J., Dube, S. R., Anda, R. F., & Felitti, V. J. (in press). Health outcomes by closeness of sexual abuse perpetrator: A test of betrayal trauma theory. *Journal of Aggression, Maltreatment & Trauma.*

Elliott, D. M. (1997). Traumatic events: Prevalence and delayed recall in the general population. *Journal of Consulting and Clinical Psychology, 65,* 811–820.

Elliott, D. M., & Briere, J. (1995). Posttraumatic stress associated with delayed recall of sexual abuse: A general population study. *Journal of Traumatic Stress, 8*(4), 629–647.

Elzinga, B. M., Ardon, A. M., Heijnis, M. K., de Ruiter, M. B., van Dyck, R., & Veltman, D. J. (2007). Neural correlates of enhanced working memory performance in dissociative disorder: A functional MRI study. *Psychological Medicine, 37,* 235–245.

Epstein, M. A., & Bottoms, B. L. (2002). Explaining the forgetting and recovery of abuse and trauma memories: Possible mechanisms. *Child Maltreatment, 7*(3), 210–225.

Erdelyi, M. H. (2010). The ups and downs of memory. *American Psychologist, 65,* 623–633.

Farley, M., & Barkan, H. (1998). Prostitution, violence and posttraumatic stress disorder. *Women & Health, 27,* 37–49.

Feldman-Summers, S., & Pope, K. S. (1994). The experience of "forgetting" childhood abuse: A national survey of psychologists. *Journal of Consulting and Clinical Psychology, 62*(3), 636–639.

Felitti, V. J., Anda, R. F., Nordenberg, D., Williamson, D. F., Spitz, A. M., Edwards, V., et al. (1998). The relationship of adult health status to childhood abuse and household dysfunction. *American Journal of Preventive Medicine, 14,* 245–258.

Fields, R. (1992, July 25). Witness says she felt confusion and guilt; Memory of sex abuse comes back by observing daughter, court is told. *Akron Beacon Journal,* p. C1.

Finkelhor, D., Turner, H., & Ormrod, R. (2009). Lifetime assessment of poly-victimization in a national sample of children and youth. *Child Abuse & Neglect, 33*(7), 403–411.

Fish, V., & Scott, C. G. (1998). Childhood abuse recollections in a nonclinical population: Forgetting and secrecy. *Child Abuse & Neglect, 23*(8), 791–802.

Fivush, R. (1991). The social construction of personal narratives. *Merrill-Palmer Quarterly, 37,* 59–82.

Fivush, R., & Edwards, V. J. (2004). Remembering and forgetting childhood sexual abuse. *Journal of Child Sexual Abuse, 13*(2), 1–19.

Flagg, P. W., & Reynolds, A. G. (1977). Modality of presentation and blocking in sentence recognition memory. *Memory & Cognition, 5*(1), 111–115.

Foa, E. B., & Rothbaum, B. O. (1998). *Treating the trauma of rape: Cognitive-behavioral therapy for PTSD.* New York: Guilford Press.

Ford, J. (1999). PTSD and disorders of extreme stress following warzone military trauma: Comorbid but distinct syndromes? *Journal of Consulting and Clinical Psychology, 67,* 3–12.

French, G. D., & Harris, C. J. (1999). *Traumatic incident reduction (TIR).* Boca Raton, FL: CRC Press.

Freyd, J. J. (1994). Betrayal trauma: Traumatic amnesia as an adaptive response to childhood abuse. *Ethics & Behavior, 4*(4), 307–329.

Freyd, J. J. (1996). *Betrayal trauma: The logic of forgetting childhood abuse.* Cambridge, MA: Harvard University Press.

Freyd, J. J. (1997). Violations of power, adaptive blindness, and betrayal trauma theory. *Feminism & Psychology, 7,* 22–23.

Freyd, J. J. (1998). Science in the memory debate. *Ethics & Behavior, 8*(2), 101–113.

Freyd, J. J. (2001). Memory and dimensions of trauma: Terror may be 'all-too-well temembered' and betrayal buried. In J. R. Conte (Ed.), *Critical issues in child sexual abuse: Historical, legal, and psychological perspectives* (pp. 139–173). Thousand Oaks, CA: Sage.

Freyd, J. J., DePrince, A. P., & Gleaves, D. (2007). The state of betrayal trauma theory: Reply to McNally (2007) – conceptual issues and future directions. *Memory, 15,* 295–311.

Freyd, J. J., DePrince, A. P., & Zurbriggen, E. L. (2001). Self-reported memory for abuse depends upon victim-perpetrator relationship. *Journal of Trauma & Dissociation, 2,* 5–17.

Freyd, J. J., & Gleaves, D. (1996). "Remembering" words not presented in lists: Relevance to the current recovered/false memory controversy. *Journal of Experimental Psychology. Learning, Memory, and Cognition, 22*(3), 811–813.

Freyd, J. J., Klest, B., & Allard, C. B. (2005). Betrayal trauma: Relationship to physical health, psychological distress, and a written disclosure intervention. *Journal of Trauma & Dissociation, 6*(3), 83–104.

Freyd, J. J., Klest, B., & DePrince, A. P. (2010). Avoiding awareness of betrayal: Comment on Lindblom and Gray (2009). *Applied Cognitive Psychology, 24*(1), 20–26.

Freyd, J. J., & Quina, K. (2000). Feminist ethics in the practice of science: The contested memory controversy as example. In M. Brabeck (Ed.), *Practicing ethics in feminist psychology* (pp. 101–124). Washington, DC: American Psychological Association.

Garry, M., & Polaschek, D. L. L. (2000). Imagination and memory. *Current Directions in Psychological Science, 9*, 6–10.

Geraerts, E. (2012). Cognitive underpinnings of recovered memories of childhood abuse. In R. F. Belli (Ed.), *True and false recovered memories: Toward a reconciliation of the debate* (pp. 175–191). *Vol. 58: Nebraska symposium on motivation*. New York: Springer.

Geraerts, E., Lindsay, D. S., Merckelbach, H., Jelicic, M., Raymaekers, L., Arnold, M. M., et al. (2009). Cognitive mechanisms underlying recovered-memory experiences of childhood sexual abuse. *Psychological Science, 20*(1), 92–98.

Geraerts, E., Schooler, J. W., Merckelbach, H., Jelicic, M., Hauer, B. J. A., & Ambadar, Z. (2007). The reality of recovered memories: Corroborating continuous and discontinuous memories of childhood sexual abuse. *Psychological Science, 18*, 564–567.

Germer, F. (1991, May 11). Ex-beauty queen's sister acknowledges father molestered her, too. *Rocky Mountain News*, p. 6.

Ghetti, S., Edelstein, R. S., Goodman, G. S., Cordòn, I. M., Quas, J. A., Alexander, K. W., et al. (2006). What can subjective forgetting tell us about memory for childhood trauma? *Memory & Cognition, 34*(5), 1011–1025.

Gill, E. (1988). *Treatment of adult survivors of childhood abuse*. Walnut Creek, CA: Launch Press.

Gold, S. N. (2000). *Not trauma alone: Therapy for child abuse survivors in family and social context*. Philadelphia: Brunner/Routledge.

Gold, S. N. (2004). The relevance of trauma to general clinical practice. *Psychotherapy, 41*(4), 363–373.

Gold, S. N., & Brown, L. S. (1997). Therapeutic responses to delayed recall: Beyond recovered memory. *Psychotherapy: Theory, Research, Practice, Training, 32*, 182–191.

Gold, S. M., Hughes, D. M., & Swingle, J. M. (1999). Degrees of memory of childhood sexual abuse among women survivors in therapy. *Journal of Family Violence, 14*(1), 35–46.

Goldsmith, R., Freyd, J.J., & DePrince, A.P. (in press). Betrayal trauma: Associations with psychological and physical symptoms in young adults. *Journal of Interpersonal Violence*.

Goodman, G. S., Ghetti, S., Quas, J. A., Edelstein, R. S., Alexander, K. W., Redlich, A. D., et al. (2003). A prospective study of memory for child sexual abuse: New findings relevant to the repressed-memory debate. *Psychological Science, 14*, 113–118.

Greenhoot, A. F., McCloskey, L., & Glisky, E. (2005). A longitudinal study of adolescents' recollections of family violence. *Applied Cognitive Psychology, 19*(6), 719–774.

Grassian, S., & Holtzen, D. (1996). Memory of sexual abuse by a parish priest. Paper presented at Trauma and Memory: An International Research Conference. Portsmouth, New Hampshire.

Hardt, J., & Rutter, M. (2004). Validity of adult retrospective reports of adverse childhood experiences: Review of the evidence. *Journal of Child Psychology and Psychiatry, 45*(2), 260–273.

Herman, J. (1981). *Father-daughter incest*. Cambridge, MA: Harvard University Press.

Herman, J. (1992). *Trauma and recovery*. New York: Basic Books.

Herman, S. (2005). Improving decision making in forensic child sexual abuse evaluations. *Law and Human Behavior, 29*(1), 87–120.

Herman, J. L., & Harvey, M. R. (1997). Adult memories of childhood trauma: A naturalistic clinical study. *Journal of Traumatic Stress, 10*(4), 557–571.

Herman, J. L., & Shatzow, E. (1987). Recovery and verification of memories of childhood sexual trauma. *Psychoanalytic Psychology, 4*(1), 1–14.

Hulette, A. C., Kaehler, L. A., & Freyd, J. J. (2011). Intergenerational associations between trauma and dissociation. *Journal of Family Violence, 26*, 217–225.

Janoff-Bulman, R. (1992). *Shattered assumptions: Toward a new psychology of trauma*. New York: Free Press.

Johnson, S. (1995). Past imperfect: 'Divided Memories' casts skeptical eye on repressed-memory movement. *Chicago Tribune*, p. C3.

Johnson, M. K. (2006). Memory and reality. *American Psychologist, 61*, 760–771.

Johnson, M. K., Foley, M. A., Suengas, A. G., & Raye, C. L. (1988). Phenomenal characteristics of memories for perceived and imagined autobiographical events. *Journal of Experimental Psychology. General, 177*, 371–376.

Johnson, M. K., Raye, C. L., Mitchell, K. J., & Ankudowich, E. (2012). The cognitive neuroscience of true and false memories. In R. F. Belli (Ed.), *True and false recovered memories: Toward a reconciliation of the debate* (pp. 15–52). *Vol. 58: Nebraska Symposium on Motivation.* New York: Springer.

Kaehler, L. A., & Freyd, J. J. (2009). Borderline personality characteristics: A betrayal trauma approach. *Psychological Trauma: Theory, Research, Practice, and Policy, 1,* 261–268.

Kaehler, L.A., & Freyd, J.J. (in press) Betrayal trauma and borderline personality characteristics: Gender differences. *Psychological Trauma: Theory, Research, Practice, and Policy.*

Kelley, L. (2009). *A comparison of life threat and betrayal as risk factors for posttraumatic stress disorder.* Doctoral Dissertation, Auburn University.

Koopman, C., Classen, C., & Spiegel, D. (1994). Predictors of posttraumatic stress symptoms among survivors of the Oakland/Berkeley, California firestorm. *The American Journal of Psychiatry, 151,* 888–894.

Koss, M. P. (1993). Detecting the scope of rape: A review of prevalence research methods. *Journal of Interpersonal Violence, 8,* 198–222.

Lane, S. M., & Zaragoza, S. (2007). A little elaboration goes a long way: The role of generation in eyewitness suggestibility. *Memory & Cognition, 35,* 1255–1266.

Lindbolm, K. M., & Gray, M. J. (2010). Relationship closeness and trauma narrative detail: A critical analysis of Betrayal Trauma Theory. *Applied Cognitive Psychology, 24,* 1–19.

Lindsay, D. S. (2009). Source monitoring. In H. L. Roediger, III (Ed.), *Cognitive psychology of memory.* Vol. 2 *of Learning and memory: A comprehensive reference,* 4 vols. (J. Byrne, Editor) (pp. 325–348). Oxford: Elsevier.

Loftus, E. F. (1975). Leading questions and the eyewitness report. *Cognitive Psychology, 7*(4), 560–572.

Loftus, E. F., Garry, M., & Feldman, J. (1994). Forgetting sexual trauma: What does it mean when 38% forget? *Journal of Consulting and Clinical Psychology, 62*(6), 1177–1181.

Loftus, E. F., Miller, D. G., & Burns, H. J. (1978). Semantic integration of verbal information into a visual memory. *Journal of Experimental Psychology: Human Learning and Memory, 4*(1), 19–31.

Loftus, E. F., & Pickrell, J. E. (1995). The formation of false memories. *Psychiatric Annals, 25,* 720–725.

Malacrida, C. (2006). Contested memories: efforts of the powerful to silence former inmates histories of life in an institution for 'mental defectives'. *Disability & Society, 21,* 397–410.

Mann, B. J., & Sanders, S. (1994). Child dissociation and the family context. *Journal of Abnormal Child Psychology: An official publication of the International Society for Research in Child and Adolescent Psychopathology, 22*(3), 373–388.

Marmar, C. R., Weiss, D. S., Schlenger, W. E., Fairbank, J. A., Jordan, B. K., Kulka, R. A., et al. (1994). Peritraumatic dissociation and posttraumatic stress in male Vietnam theater veterans. *The American Journal of Psychiatry, 151,* 902–907.

Mazzoni, G. A., Loftus, E. F., & Kirsch, E. (2001). Changing beliefs about implausible autobiographical events: A little plausibility goes a long way. *Journal of Experimental Psychology. Applied, 7,* 51–59.

Mazzoni, G., & Memon, A. (2003). Imagination can create false autobiographical memories. *Psychological Science, 14,* 186–188.

McNally, R. J. (2003). *Remembering trauma.* Cambridge, MA, US: Belknap Press/Harvard University Press.

McNally, R. J. (2012). Searching for repressed memory. In R. F. Belli, (Ed.), *True and false recovered memories: Toward a reconciliation of the debate* (pp. 121–147). *Vol. 58: Nebraska Symposium on Motivation.* New York: Springer.

McNally, R.J., Ristuccia, C.S., & Perlman, C.A. (2005). Forgetting of Trauma Cues in Adults Reporting Continuous or Recovered Memories of Childhood Sexual Abuse. *Psychological Science, 16*(4), 336–340.

Melchert, T. P. (1996). Childhood memory and a history of different forms of abuse. *Professional Psychology: Research and Practice, 27*(5), 438–446.

Melchert, T. P. (1999). Relations among childhood memory, a history of abuse, dissociation, and repression. *Journal of Interpersonal Violence, 14*(11), 1172–1192.

Melchert, T. P., & Parker, R. L. (1997). Different forms of childhood abuse and memory. *Child Abuse & Neglect, 21*(2), 125–135.

Miller, G. A. (1956). The magical number seven, plus or minus two: Some limits on our capacity for processing information. *Psychological Review, 63*(2), 81–97.

Miller, A. W., Coonrod, D. V., Brady, M. J., Moffitt, M. P., & Bay, R. C. (2004). Medical student training in domestic violence: A comparison of students entering residency training in 1995 and 2001. *Teaching and Learning in Medicine, 16*, 3–6.

Moulds, M. L., & Bryant, R. A. (2002). Directed forgetting in acute stress disorder. *Journal of Abnormal Psychology, 111*, 175–179.

Moulds, M. L., & Bryant, R. A. (2005). An investigation of retrieval inhibition in acute stress disorder. *Journal of Traumatic Stress, 18*, 233–236.

Nelson, K. (1993a). The psychological and social origins of autobiographical memory. *Psychological Science, 4*, 1–8.

Nelson, K. (1993b). Towards a theory of the development of autobiographical memory. In A. Collins, M. Conway, S. Gathercole, & P. Morris (Eds.), *Theories of memory* (pp. 185–283). Hillsdale, NJ: Erlbaum.

O'Rinn, S., Lishak, V., Muller, R.T., & Classen, C.C. (under review). Betrayal and its associations with memory disturbances among survivors of childhood sexual abuse.

Ogawa, J. R., Sroufe, L. A., Weinfield, N. S., Carlson, E. A., & Egeland, B. (1997). Development and the fragmented self: Longitudinal study of dissociative symptomatology in a nonclinical sample. *Development and Psychopathology, 9*(4), 855–879.

Olio, K. A., & Cornell, W. F. (1998). The facade of scientific documentation: A case study of Richard Ofshe's analysis of the Paul Ingram case. *Psychology, Public Policy, and Law, 4*(4), 1182–1197.

Pezdek, K. (1977). Cross-modality semantic integration of sentence and picture memory. *Journal of Experimental Psychology: Human Learning and Memory, 3*(5), 515–524.

Pezdek, K., & Blandón-Gitlin, I. (2008). Planting false memories for childhood sexual abuse only happens to emotionally disturbed people…not me and my friends. *Applied Cognitive Psychology, 23*, 162–169.

Pezdek, K., Blandón-Gitlin, I., & Gabbay, P. (2006a). Imagination and memory: Does imagining implausible events lead to false autobiographical memories? *Psychonomic Bulletin & Review, 13*, 764–769.

Pezdek, K., Blandón-Gitlin, I., Lam, S., Hart, R. E., & Schooler, J. (2006b). Is knowing believing?: The role of event plausibility and background knowledge in planting false beliefs about the personal past. *Memory & Cognition, 34*, 1628–1635.

Pezdek, K., Finger, K., & Hodge, D. (1997). Planting false childhood memories: The role of event plausibility. *Psychological Science, 8*, 437–441.

Pezdek, K., & Hodge, D. (1999). Planting false childhood memories in children: The role of event plausibility. *Child Development, 70*, 887–895.

Pezdek, K., & Roe, C. (1997). The suggestibility of children's memory for being touched: Planting, erasing, and changing memories. *Law and Human Behavior, 21*, 95–106.

Pezdek, K., & Taylor, J. (1999). Discriminating between accounts of true and false events. In D. F. Bjorklund (Ed.), *Research and theory in false-memory creation in children and adults* (pp. 69–91). Mahwah, NJ: Lawrence Erlbaum and Associates.

Piper, A., Jr. (1999). A skeptic considers, then responds to Cheit. *Ethics & Behavior, 9*(4), 277–293.

Plattner, B., Silvermann, M. A., Redlich, A. D., Carrion, V. G., Feucht, M., Friedrich, M. H., et al. (2003). Pathways to dissociation: Intrafamilial versus extrafamilial trauma in juvenile delinquents. *The Journal of Nervous and Mental Disease, 191*, 781–788.

Pope, K. S. (1997). Science as careful questioning: Are claims of a false memory syndrome based on evidence? *American Psychologist, 52*(9), 997–1006.

Pope, K. S., & Brown, L. S. (1996). *Recovered memories of abuse: Assessment, therapy, forensics.* Washington DC: American Psychological Association.

Putnam, F. W. (1997). *Dissociation in children and adolescents: A developmental perspective.* New York: Guilford Press.

Quina, K., & Brown, L. S. (Eds.). (2008). *Trauma and dissociation in incarcerated populations.* New York: Haworth Press.

Quina, K., & Carlson, N. (1989). *Rape, incest, and sexual harassment: A guide for helping survivors.* New York: Praeger, Inc.

Reichmann-Decker, A., DePrince, A. P., & McIntosh, D. N. (2009). Affective responsiveness, betrayal, and childhood abuse. *Journal of Trauma & Dissociation, 10*(3), 276–296.

Salter, A. C. (2003). *Predators: Pedophiles, rapists, and other sex offenders: Who they are, how they operate, and how we can protect ourselves and our children.* New York: Basic Books.

Scheflin, A. (1999). Ground lost: The false memory/recovered memory therapy debate. *UBM Medica Psychiatric Times, 16*(11), 1–6. Retrieved from http://www.psychiatrictimes.com/binary_content_servlet.

Schooler, J. W. (1994). Seeking the core: The issues and evidence surrounding recovered accounts of sexual trauma. *Consciousness and Cognition, 3,* 452–469.

Schooler, J. W., Ambadar, Z., & Bendiksen, M. A. (1997). A cognitive corroborative case study approach for investigating discovered memories of sexual abuse. In J.D. Read & D. S. Lindsay (Eds.), Recollections of trauma: *Scientific research and clinical practice*, 379–388. New York: Plenum.

Schultz, T. M., Passmore, J., & Yoder, C. Y. (2003). Emotional closeness with perpetrators and amnesia for child sexual abuse. *Journal of Child Sexual Abuse, 12,* 67–88.

Sears, R. R. (1936). Functional abnormalities of memory, with special reference to amnesia. *Psychological Bulletin, 33*(4), 229–274.

Shapiro, F. (2001). *Eye movement desensitization and reprocessing* (2nd ed.). New York: Guilford Press.

Sheiman, J. A. (1999). Sexual abuse history with and without self-report of memory loss: Differences in psychopathology, personality, and dissociation. In L. M. Williams & V. L. Banyard (Eds.), *Trauma & memory* (pp. 139–148). Thousand Oaks, CA: Sage.

Simeon, D. (2006, November). *Attention and memory processes in dissociative disorders.* Paper presented at the annual meeting of International Society for Traumatic Stress Studies, Hollywood, CA.

Sivers, H., Schooler, J., & Freyd, J. J. (2002). Recovered memories. In V. S. Ramachandran (Ed.), *Encyclopedia of the human brain* (Vol. 4, pp. 169–184). San Diego: Academic.

Sloutsky, V. M., & Fisher, A. V. (2004). When development and learning decrease memory: Evidence against category-based induction in children. *Psychological Science, 15*(8), 553–558.

Smith, D. W., Letourneau, E. J., Saunders, B. E., Kilpatrick, D. G., Resnick, H. S., & Best, C. L. (2000). Delay in disclosure of childhood rape: Results from a national survey. *Child Abuse & Neglect, 24,* 273–287.

Spiegel, D. & Cardeña, E. (1991). Disintegrated experience: The dissociative disorders revisited. *Journal of Abnormal Psychology, 100* (Special issue: Diagnoses, dimensions, and DSM-IV: The science of classification), 366–378.

Stoler, L. R. (2001) *Recovered and continuous memories of childhood sexual abuse: A quantitative and qualitative analysis.* (Doctoral Dissertation, University of Rhode Island.) *Dissertation Abstracts International,* 61(10-B), 5582.

Tang, S.S., & Freyd, J.J. (in press). Betrayal trauma and gender differences in posttraumatic stress. *Psychological Trauma: Theory, Research, Practice, and Policy.*

Terr, L. (1990). *Too scared to cry: Psychic trauma in childhood.* New York: Harper Collins.

Tessler, M. & Nelson, K. (1994). Making memories: The influence of joint encoding on later recall by young children. Consciousness and Cognition: *An International Journal, 3*(3-4), 307–326.

Turell, S. C., & Armsworth, M. W. (2003). A Log-linear analysis of variables associated with self-mutilation behaviors of women with histories of child sexual abuse. *Violence Against Women, 9*(4), 487–512.

Taylor S, Asmundson GJG, & Carleton RN. (2006). Simple versus complex PTSD: A cluster analytic investigation. *Journal of Anxiety Disorders, 20*(4), 459–472.

Ullman, S. E. (2007). Relationship to perpetrator, disclosure, social reactions, and PTSD symptoms in child sexual abuse survivors. *Journal of Child Sexual Abuse, 15*(1), 19–36.

Ursano, R. J., Fullerton, C. S., Epstein, R. S., Crowley, B., Vance, K., Kao, T., et al. (1999). Peritraumatic dissociation and posttraumatic stress disorder following motor vehicle accidents. *The American Journal of Psychiatry, 156*, 1808–1810.

Veldhuis, C. B., & Freyd, J. J. (1999). Groomed for silence, groomed for betrayal. In M. Rivera (Ed.), *Fragment by fragment: Feminist perspectives on memory and child sexual abuse* (pp. 253–282). Charlottetown, PEI Canada: Gynergy Books.

Veltman, D. J., de Ruiter, M. B., Rombouts, S. A. R. B., Lazeron, R. H. C., Barkhof, F., van Dyck, R., et al. (2005). Neurophysiological correlates of increased verbal working memory in high-dissociative participants: A functional MRI study. *Psychological Medicine, 35*, 175–185.

Wade, K. A., Garry, M., Read, J. D., & Lindsay, S. (2002). A picture is worth a thousand lies: Using false photographs to create false childhood memories. *Psychonomic Bulletin & Review, 9*, 597–603.

Waldfogel, S. (1948). The frequency and affective character of childhood memories. *Psychological Monographs, 62*, 1–39.

Wagenaar, W. (1996). My memory: A study of autobiographical memory over six years. *Cognitive Psychology, 18*(2), 225–252.

Whitmire, L., Harlow, L. L., Quina, K., & Morokoff, P. J. (1999). *Childhood trauma and HIV: Women at risk*. New York: Taylor & Francis.

Widom, C. S., & Morris, S. (1997). Accuracy of adult recollections of childhood victimization: Part 2: Childhood sexual abuse. *Psychological Assessment, 9*(1), 34–46.

Williams, L. M. (1994). Recall of childhood trauma: A prospective study of women's memories of child sexual abuse. *Journal of Consulting and Clinical Psychology, 62*, 1167–1176 (for additional analyses see Freyd, 1996).

Williams, L. M. (1995). Recovered memories of abuse in women with documented child sexual victimization histories. *Journal of Traumatic Stress, 8*, 649–674 (for additional analyses see Freyd, 1996).

Williams, L. M. (2000). History and analysis of delayed discovery statutes of limitation in adult survivor litigation. *Journal of Aggression, Maltreatment & Trauma, 3*(2), 49–71.

Wilsnack, S. C., Wonderlich, S. A., Kristjanson, A. F., Vogeltanz-Holm, N. D., & Wisnack, R. W. (2002). Self-reports of forgetting and remembering childhood sexual abuse in a nationally representative sample of US women. *Child Abuse & Neglect, 26*(2), 139–147.

Zaragoza, M. S., & Lane, S. M. (1994). Source misattributions and the suggestibility of eyewitness memory. *Journal of Experimental Psychology. Learning, Memory, and Cognition, 20*, 934–945.

Zierler, S., Feingold, L., Laufer, D., Velentgas, P., Kantrowitz-Gordon, I., & Mayer, K. (1991). Adult survivors of childhood sexual abuse and subsequent risk of HIV infection. *American Journal of Public Health, 81*(5), 572–575.

Zurbriggen, E. L., & Becker-Blease, K. (2003). Predicting memory for childhood sexual abuse: "Non-significant" findings with the potential for significant harm. *Journal of Child Sexual Abuse, 12*, 113–121.

Epilogue: Continuing Points of Contention in the Recovered Memory Debate

Robert F. Belli

Abstract Four contentious issues in the recovered memory debate are explored. Volume contributors offer differing perspectives on the generalizability of laboratory research, on the role of emotion in memory, on the prevalence of false recoveries, and on the motivations that underlie differences in opinion, especially with regard to whether the debate ought to be framed within a larger sociopolitical context. The recovered memory debate is argued to center on two ethical concerns that happen to be in conflict, equality among groups on one hand and due process protections on the other. Additional movement toward reconciliation is possible with a fair assessment of all available evidence, with a mutual understanding of differing perspectives, and with civil discourse.

Keywords Emotion and memory • False memories • Scientific debate • Sociopolitical context

The history of the recovered memory debate has led to a number of contentious issues, some of which there has been movement toward reconciliation (Belli, 2012, this volume), and others which continue to be in dispute. Based on the contributions to this volume, which present a comprehensive picture of the continuing views of notable scholars who continue to explore the nature of recovered experiences, I have settled on four contentious issues that seem most profound as barriers to a full reconciliation of the pertinent issues. None of these issues are new to the debate, although each has been impacted by the most recent relevant evidence.

One of these issues concerns the extent to which laboratory research can be generalized to the real world, and hence, the extent to which laboratory findings on false

R.F. Belli (✉)
University of Nebraska, Lincoln, NE, USA
e-mail: bbelli2@unl.edu

R.F. Belli (ed.), *True and False Recovered Memories: Toward a Reconciliation of the Debate*, Nebraska Symposium on Motivation, DOI 10.1007/978-1-4614-1195-6_8, © Springer Science+Business Media, LLC 2012

memories and motivated forgetting can be generalized to whether child sexual abuse (CSA) events can be falsely remembered and forgotten. A related issue concerns the impact of emotion on memory, and whether the emotional experience associated with CSA victimization at its inception and during its recovery leads to qualitatively different memory processing in comparison to events that are not as emotionally charged. A third issue, as noted in my volume introduction (Belli, 2012), pertains to the prevalence of false recoveries, with some stating that they are all too common-place whereas others assert that they have only rarely occurred. As a fourth issue, I will explore different views of the impact of the sociopolitical context on the debate and how the intensity of the debate can be traced to a conflict between social and political ideals.

The Generalizability of Laboratory Research

Much of what has been debated in the so-called memory wars and its aftermath is the appropriate interpretation of the relevance of laboratory based research in providing insight on the development of true or false recoveries in the real world. At the height of the debate, concern was raised on whether laboratory work in false memories was relevant to the potential generation of false memories of CSA. Freyd and Gleaves (1996), for example, argued against generalizing laboratory demonstrations of false memories in the Deese-Roediger-McDermott (DRM) paradigm (Roediger & McDermott, 1995). Freyd and Gleaves pointed to two reasons for a lack of relevance: (1) the units of analysis in the DRM (words) differ from those in the real world (events), and (2) because childhood sexual abuse is implausible, and the related lures in the DRM are plausible, the DRM does not capture the level of relatedness between true and false memories that exists in the real world. More recently, Pezdek and Lam (2007) reiterated the notion that the DRM lacks relevance, as do other types of false memory paradigms, because these paradigms do not lead to the creation of false memories of entire events (see also DePrince, Allard, Oh, & Freyd, 2004).

Research by Geraerts and colleagues (Geraerts, 2012, this volume; Geraerts et al., 2009) challenges views that the DRM is not relevant to the creation of false recoveries of CSA. Geraerts and colleagues have shown that those who recovered memories via suggestive therapy were most susceptible to producing false memories in a DRM task in comparison to other groups. Although Geraerts interprets these results as being consistent with the likelihood that some individuals have a heightened propensity to develop false memories in both the laboratory and the real world, DePrince et al. (2012, this volume) question this level of generalizability. Instead of an increased susceptibility to creating false memories of entire CSA events, DePrince et al. consider the DRM results of Geraerts et al. as pointing to a heightened susceptibility in misremembering details of events, and point to the possibility that the suggestive therapy participants overall had true whole event or gist recoveries but may have remembered the abuse details as more positive than they were.

It is not only the generalization of laboratory-based false memories that have been questioned. Garry and Loftus (2005) questioned the generalization of laboratory-based research on motivated forgetting (see Anderson & Huddleston, 2012, this volume) on the forgetting of CSA events. Indeed, Anderson and Huddleston are sensitive not to generalize too readily; they recognize that their laboratory work cannot replicate the complexity, emotional content, and personal relevance of real CSA. Yet, Anderson and Huddleston also express optimism as their work is based on a model in which unwanted memories can be suppressed in the presence of constant cues, mirroring the tenet of BTT (Freyd, 1996; see also DePrince et al., 2012, this volume) that incestuous abuse will likely have more forgetting in comparison to stranger abuse despite the constant opportunity for remembering the CSA in the former case due to being in continual presence of the perpetrator.

In dealing with questions about the generalizability of laboratory-based research, it must be emphasized that experimental psychology is founded on the principle that well controlled laboratory studies provide a theoretical understanding of the operation of fundamental cognitive processes, and that these theories based on fundamentals are generalizable to the real world (Banaji & Crowder, 1989; Gallo, 2010; Wade et al., 2007). As revealed by the contributions of Johnson, Raye, Mitchell, and Ankudowich, (2012, this volume) and Anderson and Huddleston (2012, this volume), an understanding of fundamental cognitive and neural processes explains the development of false memories and the inhibition of unwanted memories, respectively. Pertaining to the DRM task directly, Gallo (2010) observes that a theoretical understanding of the fundamental cognitive and neural processes that lead to false memory generation in the DRM will be able to shed insight on the observation that individuals who have developed false memories in the real world–such as remembering a past life (Meyersburg, Bogdan, Gallo, & McNally, 2009)—are also more susceptible to the DRM illusion. Similarly, seeking a more thorough theoretical understanding of the operation of fundamental processes is likely to be the best arbiter in determining whether one should draw distinctions between generating false memories to whole events in comparison to developing false memories for the details of events.

The Impact of Emotion on Memory

Controversy regarding the impact of emotion on memory cannot be better illustrated by the differing perspectives of the contributors regarding the ability to remember traumatic experiences. For McNally (2012, this volume), traumatic experiences are never forgotten, and hence, true recoveries exist precisely because the abuse events, when experienced, were not traumatic (see also McNally & Geraerts, 2009). Although Brewin (2012, this volume) accepts that some experiences of child sexual abuse may not be traumatic, he shares the views of DePrince et al. (2012, this volume) that victimization is often associated with high levels of negative emotion including fright, embarrassment, betrayal, a sense of powerlessness, and concern for one's well-being that are appropriately characterized as trauma. Whereas some of this difference in opinion can be accounted for by different meanings assigned to the term trauma—for McNally the term trauma is restricted to events that are life threatening whereas for Brewin and DePrince et al. their definition of trauma is broader—there are nevertheless clear distinctions in these points of view on how trauma impacts memory.

Brewin's model considers that experiences with trauma that often accompany CSA lead to severe psychological consequences that directly impact the nature of cognitive processing. Trauma induces a fragmentation of the self so that the abuse experiences are often dissociated from the usual working self that interacts with daily life. Although involuntary remembering of abuse events governed by internal or external cues have the potential of bringing abuse events to mind, the fragmentation of self may actively inhibit their awareness entirely, or mute the awareness so as to not threaten one's sense of well-being. Only when these traumatic experiences are able to become better integrated with the self that a full-blown recovery occurs, often characterized in a manner identical to the intrusive nature of PTSD flashbacks. In Brewin's model, trauma's impact is to promote structural abnormalities in the autobiographical knowledge base that promote extraordinary forgetting. In contrast to a special forgetting mechanism as proposed by Brewin, McNally considers that although CSA victims may not think about abusive events for many years, it is precisely because the abuse is not traumatic (in the sense of being life threatening) that it is open to the same level of lack of attention that would characterize other ordinary events that children experience which are confusing and unpleasant.

Experimental psychologists often prefer to explain all memory processes via an appeal to ordinary mechanisms as they are more parsimonious and introduce less skepticism than introducing special mechanisms (Lindsay, 1998). There is also historical precedent to a preference for ordinary processing, even when emotion is involved. At one time it was widely held that flashbulb memories that accompany emotionally provoking culturally-shared tragedies such as the assassination of John Kennedy or the space shuttle Challenger explosion were remarkably accurate for an extended period of time because of special encoding mechanisms that imprinted the events into memory (Brown & Kulik, 1977). More recently, Talarico and Rubin (2003; see also Neisser & Harsch, 1992) have shown that flashbulb memories suffer from the same errors of omission and commission as memories of ordinary events. What is remarkable about flashbulbs is that people believe in their accuracy, which can be traced to a heightened sense of vividness in the details of what is remembered (even when these details are wrong) as predicted by the Source Monitoring Framework (see Johnson et al., 2012, this volume, on the role of emotion in memory errors).

Of course, the example of flashbulb memories may not characterize all emotional experiences. But whenever there are differences between the manner in which emotional and nonemotional experiences are remembered and forgotten, the key question is whether emotion impacts memory in a qualitatively different way, as suggested by an appeal to special memory mechanisms, or in a merely quantitative way by exaggerating how ordinary nonemotional processes operate (e.g., by adding to the vividness of details). Complicating the picture is that conjectured processes that have often denoted special memory mechanisms, such as repression and dissociation, are also viewed as having parallels in ordinary cognitive processing (Brewin, 1997). The dissociation that Brewin (2012, this volume) implicates in contributing to the fragmented self in someone exposed to trauma is an exaggeration of the multiple selves that all people maintain and which will constrain what information from the structure of autobiographical knowledge is most accessible given whatever aspect of the working self is most activated at any point in time (Conway, 2005). What is unclear is whether this exaggeration is a qualitative change, or one that can be viewed as an extension of ordinary cognitive processes.

Research reviewed by Anderson and Huddleston (2012, this volume) on retrieval inhibition provides some insights. Although retrieval inhibition can occur without emotion, in comparisons between emotional and neutral stimuli, some studies reveal greater retrieval inhibition for the emotional items (e.g., Depue, Banich, & Curran, 2006). Because a quantitative explanation would be hard pressed to find an ordinary mechanism that would lead to increased forgetting for stimuli that are more vivid or distinctive, a special memory—or forgetting—mechanism is suggested. In finding retrieval inhibition for negative but not for positive stimuli, Lambert, Good, and Kirk (2010) considered their results as supporting a "repression hypothesis." However, as there are equivocal results in the research that has explored retrieval inhibition for emotional items (see Anderson & Huddleston), any conclusions regarding the potential presence of a special retrieval inhibition forgetting mechanism for negative items are premature.

The Prevalence of False Recoveries

Among the volume contributors, the contribution of DePrince et al. (2012, this volume) is the only one to explicitly challenge the notion that a substantive proportion of recovered memory experiences are false. They point to two issues. First, they consider that any application of suggestive techniques in therapy has been implemented by ill trained therapists and hence, the prevalence of the use of these techniques is quite low. Second, and especially in their assessment of the finding of Geraerts and colleagues (see Geraerts, 2012, this volume), they reason that there is no solid evidence that the use of suggestive techniques will lead to false memories of CSA. Their views are in direct contrast to Geraerts and also to Johnson et al. (2012, this volume) as these contributors consider that suggestive techniques have been used all too often, and that their use can lead to false recoveries.

A number of pieces of evidence point to suggestive therapeutic techniques as leading to false memories of CSA. During the late 1980s and early 1990s there were a number of publications in the professional literature (e.g., Claridge, 1992; Courtois, 1988, 1992; Dolan, 1991; Ellenson, 1985; McCann & Pearlman, 1990) and self-help books targeted to lay audiences (e.g., Bass & Davis, 1988; Blume, 1990; Engel, 1989; Fredrickson, 1992) that had advocated the use of memory recovery techniques. Anecdotes, including some from court cases, emerged during this time in which memories that were recovered with encouragement of therapy invited skepticism for a number of reasons. Some of these memories depicted events at very early ages—such as before the age of 1½ years—in which the abuse was alleged to have occurred, some portrayed an amnesia so dense that repeated brutalizations across decades and into young adulthood had been forgotten, and some involved countless perpetrators in conspiracy including satanic cults and infanticide that have never been documented (Ganaway, 1989; Loftus, 1993, 1997; Loftus & Ketchum, 1994; Ofshe & Watters, 1994; Wagenaar, 1996). Considerable experimental work has shown that false memories of holistic childhood events can be created in controlled laboratory conditions that mirror the kinds of memory recovery techniques that were being illustrated in the clinical literature and self-help books (e.g., Hyman, Husband, & Billings, 1995; Lindsay, Hagen, Read, Wade, & Garry, 2004; Mazzoni & Memon, 2003). In the latter half of the 1990s, trauma therapists, some of whom had once condoned the use of memory recovery techniques, noted a period of time in which "clinical excesses and errors" (Courtois, 1997, p. 342) had occurred, or acknowledged that a "minority of therapists have used questionable 'memory recovery' techniques" (Briere, 1997, p. 26), and hence put forward a set of guidelines designed to minimize the occurrence of false memories during trauma therapy (see especially Courtois, 1999; Lindsay & Briere, 1997).

Surveys of licensed therapy practitioners in North America have also revealed that a substantial minority have used suggestive techniques among clients who had been suspected of being victims of child sexual abuse (Legault & Laurence, 2007; Polusny & Follette, 1996; Poole, Lindsay, Memon, & Bull, 1995). Supporting the notion that using suggestive techniques leads to false memories, Legault and Laurence and Poole et al. did find modest correlations between the number of techniques used and rates of recovered memories of CSA during therapy. In terms of estimates of the prevalence of recovered memories in therapy, these surveys provide estimates of between 20% and 40% of clinicians who had at least one client recover a memory of CSA during the past year, and Legault and Laurence found that their respondents had reported a mean of 4.3% of clients with recovered memories during the past 2 years. In a survey of a U.S. national probability sample of women, Wilsnack, Wonderlich, Kristjanson, Volgentanz-Holm, and Wilsnack (2002) found that among respondents reporting a recovery experience of CSA, approximately 8% (unweighted) recovered their memory during the course of professional treatment (see also DePrince et al.), with the remainder having recovered spontaneously (recovery on one's own). Hence, at this point in time, the available surveys of clinicians and the general public do not provide a consistent picture of the extent to which memories are recovered in the context of therapy. Differences among surveys are likely a function of estimation errors including question wording, respondent characteristics, and considerable sampling error when few data points are available (see Groves, 1989, for a review of estimation errors in surveys). Further, although the surveys of practitioners indicate that suggestive memory recovery techniques are used surprisingly often, and that there is an association between their use and the occurrence of recoveries during therapy, these surveys provide no direct evidence of memory recovery techniques leading to false memories.

With regard to question wording, the survey of Wilsnack et al. (2002) is potentially problematic in not adequately accounting for persons who believe that they were victims of CSA, but who have no explicit memories for the abuse (see McNally, 2012, this volume, on uncovering research participants who fit this description). Such beliefs may be false. After screening respondents with a question on whether they had felt they had been a victim of CSA with a family member as a perpetrator, respondents in Wilsnack et al. were then asked to categorize their abuse, in a mutually exclusive fashion, as having always been remembered, or having been recovered on one's own or with the help of a professional (among other categories that none of the respondents had endorsed). It appears likely that any persons who had a belief that they were abused with no explicit memories would have endorsed the category indicative of a spontaneous recovery.

Within this context of uncertainty regarding the prevalence of false recoveries of CSA, several points are deserving of attention. First, even if the prevalence of false memories that result from suggestive therapy is very low, given the large numbers of persons in the population, the total number of persons with false memories would still be quite large (Lindsay, 1997). Second, the available evidence supports the conclusion that a considerable majority of persons who are victimized by CSA have some level of continuity in remembering their abuse, and hence, fully recovered memories of CSA events—whether true or false—constitute a minority of cases. The reasons for fully recovered memories being rarer than continuous memories may be a function of individual differences; only certain individuals may have the necessary cognitive control to forget abuse, or to be highly susceptible to suggestions, as indicated by Anderson and Huddleston (2012, this volume) and Geraerts (2012, this volume), respectively. Finally, as noted above, there is consensus, at least among the contributors to this volume, that any use of suggestive techniques in therapy is an inappropriate practice and that memory recovery should not be a goal of trauma therapy.

The Impact of the Sociopolitical Context on the Debate

As I had noted in my introduction to this volume (Belli, 2012), the recovered memory debate is a topic most apt for the Nebraska Symposium on Motivation not only because of the critical role of motivation in underlying the cognitive mechanisms responsible for both true and false recoveries, but also because the evidence and arguments that practitioners and scientists have offered to the debate are fueled by motivational and ethical concerns. DePrince et al. (2012, this volume) are very explicit about the motivations that guide their orientation. In contrasting privileged versus marginal voices, DePrince et al. portray the tragedy of CSA as a continuing vestige of a patriarchal culture in which dominance still largely resides among adult males. Victims of CSA, primarily but not always girls, have marginal voices to which perpetrators merely ask that we do nothing, that we keep the voices of their victims quiet. Extending the notion of the sociopolitical context as one in which certain groups are more privileged than others, DePrince et al. observe that scientific voices are also privileged ones, and that the authoritativeness that derives from these voices can either help to empower those voices in the margins, or can further discourage their being heard.

A controversial implication of DePrince et al.'s analysis regarding the sociopolitical context, and the role of scientific thought in either legitimizing or diminishing those victimized by CSA, is that those who have offered evidence and arguments in favor of false recoveries are engaging in practices that further the injustices that penetrate our culture. This implication is not new, and in the history of the recovered memory debate, advocates of the false recovery position have been sensitive to this critique and have offered their own perspectives regarding it. It must be emphasized that this implication cannot be effectively countered by the denunciation of CSA— indeed, the vast majority of those who have weighed in on the side of the false memory position do acknowledge CSA as being disturbingly common, tragic, and morally reprehensible—as what is implied is that advocating the likelihood of false memories is to provide an excuse for some to discredit reports of CSA more generally. Similarly, despite the recovered memory debate as not involving any attempt by researchers to question the fundamental accuracy of the reports of those who have continuously remembered being victimized by CSA, there continues to be concern that skepticism targeted to the veracity of any proportion of recovered memories can lead to some people to doubt the accuracy of continuously remembered abuse as well.

As one countering theme, Belli and Loftus (1994) argued that any skepticism that arises in the veracity of victims' reports has its source in the extraordinary and seemingly impossible abusive events that had been recovered with the assistance of therapy. Hence, the onus of diminishing the voices of those victimized by CSA is not on those who warned about the dangers of suggestive therapy, but on those who engaged in suggestive therapeutic techniques. Another common theme was to assert that both CSA and false recoveries of abuse were tragic; with regard to the latter, the tragedy resides in both the needless suffering among those who had falsely recovered and in the needless endangering of the health of family relationships (e.g., Belli & Loftus; Lindsay & Read, 1994; Yapko, 1994). And yet another countering approach has been for advocates of the false recovery position to emphasize that the debate is one involving the properties of memory. Loftus (1997), for example, has asserted that the debate is not one "about the reality or the horror of sexual abuse, incest, and violence against children," rather it is a "debate about memory" (p. 176).

Although each of these countering positions has merit, they do not directly address the very reasonable argument expressed by DePrince et al. that the sociopolitical context does impact psychological science in profound ways (see also Freyd & Quina, 2000; Pezdek & Lam, 2007). Foremost, it should be acknowledged that social and political concerns drive which observations in the real world are deserving of scientific attention in the pursuit to uncover fundamental psychological processes. As noted by Wade et al. (2007):

> ...Let us not forget that psychological scientists study false memories because we have looked in the real world and see what happens. Psychological science tries to understand behavior *out there* by bringing it into the laboratory, not the other way around. This reductionism is, of course, typical for other scientific disciplines as well. For example, it would be nonsensical to argue that the research molecular biologists carry out on HIV is irrelevant to AIDS in real patients (p. 26, emphasis in the original).

One of the real world concerns that have led to considerable scientific research into false memories has been to expose the dangers of eyewitness unreliability with the hope of stemming the injustice that follows from wrongful convictions (McMurtrie, 2007). In the context of the recovered memory debate, any false accusations of CSA are troubling in and of themselves. Yet, they become even more damaging when introduced as evidence into a criminal investigation or entered as evidence into a court of law. There can be no doubt that the recovered memory debate would not have become so heated if it weren't because criminal accusations were being made on the basis of events that had not been remembered for many years, and which were apparently stimulated in the context of therapy (Loftus, 1993; Read & Lindsay, 1994). One of the principal threats to realizing the ideals of a free society are the dangers of false criminal accusations, or even more dramatically, the power of the state to mistakenly confine (or execute) citizens who are innocent of any wrong doing.

With regard to the impact of the sociopolitical context on the recovered memory debate, its influence led to two sources of injustice coming into conflict, one that emphasized inequalities between genders and groups, and one that observed that safeguards to the ideals of a free society were being challenged by the yet unforeseen overreliance on the reliability of eyewitness memory. Although DePrince at al. are correct regarding the injustices that have existed, and continue to exist, within a culture that has been dominated by adult males, and how scientific investigation cannot escape from this culture, gender or group power differences are not the only source of injustice that pervades our society. Within the sociopolitical context, both CSA and wrongful criminal accusations (and convictions) go beyond individual tragedies. They are both social tragedies as the occurrence of either threatens social and political ideals, ideals that are worth defending in the name of justice.

The Current Status of the Debate

As illustrated by the contributions to this volume, since the height of the so-called memory wars there has been considerable research that has provided valuable information relevant to understanding recovery experiences. There is movement toward a reconciliation of points of view as seen by a consensus—at least among the volume contributors—that a substantive proportion of recovered memories of CSA are authentic representations of actual abuse. Although there is continuing disagreement on the prevalence of false recoveries, there is consensus that suggestive therapeutic techniques are dangerous in having the potential to promote false memories and that memory recovery should not be a goal of trauma therapy.

Yet, as also seen by the contributions to this volume, there are continuing points of contention that reflect many of the same arguments which have been made throughout the history of the debate. It also must be recognized that the call for civility and the need to move toward a middle ground are not new (see especially Lindsay & Briere, 1997). The reasons for resistance to a fuller reconciliation largely reside in social ideals that have conflicting perspectives regarding how the debate should be framed, what research questions should be pursued, and how research findings should be interpreted.

With regard to social ideals, one may be tempted to directly compare the blight of CSA against the prevalence of therapy-induced false recoveries as to which is more problematic. With this direct comparison, there is no doubt that CSA is a far more egregious problem; abuse has had a longer history and considerably more people have been affected by it (Lindsay & Read, 1994). Yet, such a comparison ignores the larger issues that are raised by those social ideals that encompass the debate. Both CSA and therapy-induced illusory memories are symptomatic of much broader social and political concerns, with the former, equality among groups, and with the latter, due process protections from false accusations. From the perspective of this broader sociopolitical context, one can see that issues of inequality and imperfections in due process are both ancient, and both have adversely affected countless persons.

Because the recovered memory debate is embroiled in frustrations that people are experiencing in realizing worthy social ideals that have happened to come into conflict, achieving a complete reconciliation will be difficult, but not impossible. Hopefully, continuing progress toward reconciliation will occur, but the future may also witness a retrenchment into more divisive positions. For reconciliation to continue to move forward, all must be able to provide a fair assessment of the available evidence, appreciate the reasons that underlie different points of view, and project a civility in tone.

References

Anderson, M. C., & Huddleston, E. (2012, this volume). Towards a cognitive and neurobiological model of motivated forgetting. In R. F. Belli (Ed.), *True and false recovered memories: Toward a reconciliation of the debate* (pp. 53–120). *Vol. 58: Nebraska Symposium on Motivation.* New York: Springer.

Banaji, M. R., & Crowder, R. G. (1989). The bankruptcy of everyday memory. *The American Psychologist, 44,* 1185–1193.

Bass, E., & Davis, L. (1988). *The courage to heal: A guide for women survivors of child sexual abuse.* New York: Harper & Rowe.

Belli, R. F., & Loftus, E. F. (1994). Recovered memories of childhood abuse: A source monitoring perspective. In S. J. Lynn & J. Rhue (Eds.), *Dissociation: Theory, clinical, and research perspectives* (pp. 415–433). New York: Guilford Press.

Belli, R. F. (2012, this volume). Introduction: In the aftermath of the so-called memory wars. In R. F. Belli (Ed.), *True and false recovered memories: Toward a reconciliation of the debate* (pp. 1–13). *Vol. 58: Nebraska Symposium on Motivation*. New York: Springer.

Blume, E. S. (1990). *Secret survivors: Uncovering incest and its aftereffects in women*. New York: Ballantine.

Brewin, C. R. (1997). Clinical and experimental approaches to understanding repression. In J. D. Read & D. S. Lindsay (Eds.), *Recollections of trauma: Scientific evidence and clinical practice* (pp. 145–163). New York: Plenum.

Brewin, C. R. (2012, this volume). A theoretical framework for understanding recovered memory experiences. In R. F. Belli (Ed.), *True and false recovered memories: Toward a reconciliation of the debate* (pp. 149–173). *Vol. 58: Nebraska Symposium on Motivation*. New York: Springer.

Briere, J. (1997). An integrated approach to treating adults abused as children, with specific reference to self-reported recovered memories. In J. D. Read & D. S. Lindsay (Eds.), *Recollections of trauma: Scientific evidence and clinical practice* (pp. 25–41). New York: Plenum.

Brown, R., & Kulik, J. (1977). Flashbulb memories. *Cognition, 5*, 73–99.

Claridge, K. (1992). Reconstructing memories of abuse: A theory-based approach. *Psychotherapy, 29*, 243–252.

Conway, M. A. (2005). Memory and the self. *Journal of Memory and Language, 53*(4), 594–628.

Courtois, C. A. (1988). *Healing the incest wound: Adult survivors in therapy*. New York: Norton.

Courtois, C. A. (1992). The memory retrieval process in incest survivor therapy. *Journal of Child Sexual Abuse, 1*, 15–31.

Courtois, C. A. (1997). Informed clinical practice and the standard of care. In J. D. Read & D. S. Lindsay (Eds.), *Recollections of trauma: Scientific evidence and clinical practice* (pp. 337–361). New York: Plenum.

Courtois, C. A. (1999). *Recollections of sexual abuse: Treatment principles and guidelines*. New York: Norton.

DePrince, A. P., Allard, C. B., Oh, H., & Freyd, J. J. (2004). What's in a name for memory errors? Implications and ethical issues arising from the use of the term "false memory" for errors in memory for details. *Ethics & Behavior, 14*, 201–233.

DePrince, A., Brown, L., Cheit, R., Freyd, J., Gold, S. N., Pezdek, K., & Quina, K. (2012, this volume). Motivated forgetting and misremembering: Perspectives from Betrayal Trauma Theory. In R. F. Belli (Ed.), *True and false recovered memories: Toward a reconciliation of the debate* (pp. 193–242). *Vol. 58: Nebraska Symposium on Motivation*. New York: Springer.

Depue, B. E., Banich, M. T., & Curran, T. (2006). Suppression of emotional and nonemotional content in memory: Effects of repetition on cognitive control. *Psychological Science, 17*, 441–447.

Dolan, Y. M. (1991). *Resolving sexual abuse*. New York: Norton.

Ellenson, G. S. (1985). Detecting a history of incest: A predictive syndrome. *The Journal of Contemporary Social Work, 9*, 525–532.

Engel, B. (1989). *The right to innocence: Healing the trauma of childhood sexual abuse*. New York: Ballantine.

Fredrickson, R. (1992). *Repressed memories: A journey to recovery from sexual abuse*. New York: Simon & Schuster.

Freyd, J. J. (1996). *Betrayal trauma: The logic of forgetting childhood abuse*. Cambridge, MA: Harvard University Press.

Freyd, J. J., & Gleaves, D. H. (1996). "Remembering" words not presented in lists: Relevance to the current recovered/false memory controversy. *Journal of Experimental Psychology. Learning, Memory, and Cognition, 22*, 811–813.

Freyd, J. J., & Quina, K. (2000). Feminist ethics in the practice of science: The contested memory controversy as an example. In M. Brabeck (Ed.), *Practicing feminist ethics in psychology* (pp. 100–124). Washington, DC: American Psychological Association.

Gallo, D. A. (2010). False memories and fantastic beliefs: 15 years of the DRM illusion. *Memory & Cognition, 38*, 833–848.

Ganaway, G. K. (1989). Narrative truth: Clarifying the role of exogenous trauma in the etiology of MPD and its variants. *Dissociation, 2*, 205–220.

Garry, M., & Loftus, E. F. (2005). I am Freud's brain. *The Skeptical Inquirer, 28*, 16–18.

Geraerts, E. (2012, this volume). Cognitive underpinnings of recovered memories of childhood abuse. In R. F. Belli (Ed.), *True and false recovered memories: Toward a reconciliation of the debate* (pp. 175–191). *Vol. 58: Nebraska Symposium on Motivation*. New York: Springer.

Geraerts, E., Lindsay, D. S., Merckelbach, H., Jelicic, M., Raymaekers, L., Arnold, M. M., et al. (2009). Cognitive mechanisms underlying recovered memory experiences of childhood sexual abuse. *Psychological Science, 20*, 92–98.

Groves, R. M. (1989). *Survey errors and survey costs*. New York: Wiley.

Hyman, I. E., Husband, T. H., & Billings, F. J. (1995). False memories of childhood experiences. *Applied Cognitive Psychology, 9*, 181–197.

Johnson, M. K., Raye, C. L., Mitchell, K. J., & Ankudowich, E. (2012, this volume). The cognitive neuroscience of true and false memories. In R. F. Belli (Ed.), *True and false recovered memories: Toward a reconciliation of the debate* (pp. 15–52). *Vol. 58: Nebraska Symposium on Motivation*. New York: Springer.

Lambert, A. J., Good, K. S., & Kirk, I. J. (2010). Testing the repression hypothesis: Effects of emotional valence on memory suppression in the think-no think task. *Consciousness and Cognition, 19*, 281–293.

Legault, E., & Laurence, J.-R. (2007). Recovered memories of childhood sexual abuse: Social worker, psychologist, and psychiatrist reports of beliefs, practices, and cases. *Australian Journal of Clinical and Experimental Hypnosis, 35*, 111–133.

Lindsay, D. S. (1997). Increasing sensitivity. In J. D. Read & D. S. Lindsay (Eds.), *Recollections of trauma: Scientific evidence and clinical practice* (pp. 1–16). New York: Plenum.

Lindsay, D. S. (1998). Depolarizing views on recovered memory experiences. In S. J. Lynn & K. M. McConkey (Eds.), *Truth in memory* (pp. 481–494). New York: Guilford.

Lindsay, D. S., & Briere, J. (1997). The controversy regarding recovered memories of childhood sexual abuse: Pitfalls, bridges, and future directions. *Journal of Interpersonal Violence, 12*, 631–647.

Lindsay, D. S., Hagen, L., Read, J. D., Wade, K. A., & Garry, M. (2004). True photographs and false memories. *Psychological Science, 15*, 149–154.

Lindsay, D. S., & Read, J. D. (1994). Psychotherapy and memories of childhood sexual abuse: A cognitive perspective. *Applied Cognitive Psychology, 8*, 281–338.

Loftus, E. F. (1993). The reality of repressed memories. *The American Psychologist, 48*, 518–537.

Loftus, E. F. (1997). Dispatch from the (un)civil memory wars. In J. D. Read & D. S. Lindsay (Eds.), *Recollections of trauma: Scientific evidence and clinical practice* (pp. 171–194). New York: Plenum.

Loftus, E. F., & Ketchum, K. (1994). *The myth of repressed memory*. New York: St. Martin's.

Mazzoni, G., & Memon, A. (2003). Imagination can create false autobiographical memories. *Psychological Science, 14*, 186–188.

McCann, I. L., & Pearlman, L. A. (1990). *Psychological trauma and the adult survivor: Theory, therapy, and transformation*. New York: Brunner/Mazel.

McMurtrie, J. (2007). Incorporating Elizabeth Loftus's research on memory into reforms to protect the innocent. In M. Garry & H. Hayne (Eds.), *Do justice and let the sky fall: Elizabeth F. Loftus and her contributions to science, law, and academic freedom* (pp. 171–191). Mahwah, NJ: Erlbaum.

McNally, R. J., & Geraerts, E. (2009). A new solution to the recovered memory debate. *Perspectives on Psychological Science, 4*, 126–134.

McNally, R. J. (2012, this volume). Searching for repressed memory. In R. F. Belli (Ed.), *True and false recovered memories: Toward a reconciliation of the debate* (pp. 121–147). *Vol. 58: Nebraska Symposium on Motivation*. New York: Springer.

Meyersburg, C. A., Bogdan, R., Gallo, D. A., & McNally, R. J. (2009). False memory propensity in people reporting recovered memories of past lives. *Journal of Abnormal Psychology, 118,* 399–404.

Neisser, U., & Harsch, N. (1992). Phantom flashbulbs: False recollections of hearing the news about Challenger. In E. Winograd & U. Neisser (Eds.), *Affect and accuracy in recall* (pp. 9–31). New York: Cambridge University Press.

Ofshe, R., & Watters, E. (1994). *Making monsters: False memories, psychotherapy, and sexual hysteria.* New York: Scribner.

Pezdek, K., & Lam, S. (2007). What research choices have cognitive psychologists used to study "False memory", and what are the implications of these choices? *Consciousness and Cognition, 16,* 2–17.

Polusny, M. A., & Follette, V. M. (1996). Remembering childhood sexual abuse: A national survey of psychologists' clinical practices, beliefs, and personal experiences. *Professional Psychology: Research and Practice, 27,* 41–52.

Poole, D. A., Lindsay, D. S., Memon, A., & Bull, R. (1995). Psychotherapy and recovered memories of childhood sexual abuse: U. S. and British practitioners' opinions, practices, and experiences. *Journal of Consulting and Clinical Psychology, 63,* 426–437.

Read, J. D., & Lindsay, D. S. (1994). Moving toward a middle ground on the 'false memory debate': Reply to commentaries on Lindsay and Read. *Applied Cognitive Psychology, 8,* 407–435.

Roediger, H. L., III, & McDermott, K. B. (1995). Creating false memories: Remembering words not presented in lists. *Journal of Experimental Psychology. Learning, Memory, and Cognition, 21,* 803–814.

Talarico, J. M., & Rubin, D. C. (2003). Confidence, not consistency, characterizes flashbulb memories. *Psychological Science, 14,* 455–461.

Wade, K. A., Sharman, S. J., Garry, M., Memon, A., Mazzoni, G., Merckelbach, H., et al. (2007). False claims about false memory research. *Consciousness and Cognition, 16,* 18–28.

Wagenaar, W. A. (1996). Autobiographical memory in court. In D. C. Rubin (Ed.), *Remembering our past: Studies in autobiographical memory* (pp. 180–196). New York: Cambridge University Press.

Wilsnack, S. C., Wonderlich, S. A., Kristjanson, A. F., Volgentanz-Holm, N. D., & Wilsnack, R. W. (2002). Self-reports of forgetting and remembering childhood sexual abuse in a nationally representative sample of US women. *Child Abuse & Neglect, 26,* 139–147.

Yapko, M. D. (1994). *Suggestions of abuse: True and false memories of childhood sexual trauma.* New York: Simon & Schuster.

Index